JEAN PIAGET

With the assistance of seven collaborators

The

Moral Judgment

of the Child

Translated by Marjorie Gabain

THE FREE PRESS

NEW YORK LONDON TORONTO SYDNEY SINGAPORE

Printed in the United States of America

FIRST FREE PRESS PAPERBACK EDITION 1965
by arrangement with Routledge & Kegan Paul, Ltd.

printing number
20

Contents

Foreword

READERS will find in this book no direct analysis of child morality as it is practised in home and school life or in children's societies. It is the moral judgment that we propose to investigate, not moral behaviour or sentiments. With this aim in view we questioned a large number of children from the Geneva and Neuchâtel schools and held conversations with them, similar to those we had had before on their conception of the world and of causality. The present volume contains the results of these conversations.

First we had to establish what was meant by respect for rules from the child's point of view. This is why we have begun with an analysis of the rules of a social game in the obligatory aspect which these possess for a *bona fide* player. From the rules of games we have passed to the specifically moral rules laid down by adults and we have tried to see what idea the child forms of these particular duties. Children's ideas on lying were selected as being a privileged example. Finally we have examined the notions that arose out of the relations in which the children stood to each other and we were thus led to discuss the idea of justice as our special theme.

Having reached this point, our results seemed to us sufficiently consistent to be compared to some of the hypotheses now in favour among sociologists and writers on the psy-

chology of morals. It is to this final task that we have devoted
our fourth chapter.

We are more conscious than anybody of the defects as of
the advantages of the method we have used. The great danger,
especially in matters of morality, is that of making the child
say whatever one wants him to say. There is no infallible
remedy for this; neither the good faith of the questioner nor
the precautionary methods which we have laid stress upon
elsewhere[1] are sufficient. The only safeguard lies in the collaboration of other investigators. If other psychologists take
up our questions from different view-points and put them to
children of differing social environment, it will be possible
sooner or later to separate the objective from the arbitrary
elements in the results which we bring forward in this work.
An analogous task has been undertaken in various countries
with regard to child logic and children's ideas on causality;
and while certain exaggerations of which we had been guilty
came to light in this way, the results up to date in no way
tend to discourage us in the use of the method we have
adopted.

The advantages of this method seem to us to be that it
makes evident what observation left to itself can only surmise.
During the last few years, for example, I have been engaged
in taking down the spontaneous remarks made by my two
little girls, to whom I have never set the questions examined
in *The Child's Conception of the World* or in *The Child's
Conception of Causality*. Now, broadly speaking, the tendencies to Realism, Animism, Artificialism and dynamic Causality, etc., come very clearly to light, but the meaning of
these children's most interesting "whys," as of many of their
chance remarks, would have almost completely eluded me if
I had not in the past questioned hundreds of children per-
sonally on the same subjects. A child's spontaneous remark
is, of course, more valuable than all the questioning in the
world. But in child psychology such a remark cannot be seen

[1] See *The Child's Conception of the World*, Kegan Paul, which in
the sequel will be designated by the letters *C.W.* My other books,
*Language and Thought in the Child, Judgment and Reasoning in
the Child*, and *The Child's Conception of Causality*, will be re-
ferred to by the initials *L.T., J.R.*, and *C.C.* respectively.

in its right perspective without the work of preparation constituted by those very interrogatories.

The present book on child morality is just such a preliminary piece of work. It is my sincere hope that it may supply a scaffolding which those living with children and observing their spontaneous reactions can use in erecting the actual edifice. In a sense, child morality throws light on adult morality. If we want to form men and women, nothing will fit us so well for the task as to study the laws that govern their formation.

The Moral Judgment of the Child

Chapter 1

The Rules of the Game[1]

CHILDREN'S GAMES constitute the most admirable social institutions. The game of marbles, for instance, as played by boys, contains an extremely complex system of rules, that is to say, a code of laws, a jurisprudence of its own. Only the psychologist, whose profession obliges him to become familiar with this instance of common law, and to get at the implicit morality underlying it, is in a position to estimate the extraordinary wealth of these rules by the difficulty he experiences in mastering their details.

If we wish to gain any understanding of child morality, it is obviously with the analysis of such facts as these that we must begin. All morality consists in a system of rules, and the essence of all morality is to be sought for in the respect which the individual acquires for these rules. The reflective analysis of Kant, the sociology of Durkheim, or the individualistic psychology of Bovet all meet on this point. The doctrines begin to diverge only from the moment that it has to be explained how the mind comes to respect these rules. For our part, it will be in the domain of child psychology that we shall undertake the analysis of this "how."

Now, most of the moral rules which the child learns to respect he receives from adults, which means that he receives

[1] With the collaboration of Mme. V. J. Piaget, MM M. Lambercier and L. Martinez.

them after they have been fully elaborated, and often elaborated, not in relation to him and as they are needed, but once and for all and through an uninterrupted succession of earlier adult generations.

In the case of the very simplest social games, on the contrary, we are in the presence of rules which have been elaborated by the children alone. It is of no moment whether these games strike us as "moral" or not in their contents. As psychologists we must ourselves adopt the point of view, not of the adult conscience, but of child morality. Now, the rules of the game of marbles are handed down, just like so-called moral realities, from one generation to another, and are preserved solely by the respect that is felt for them by individuals. The sole difference is that the relations in this case are only those that exist between children. The little boys who are beginning to play are gradually trained by the older ones in respect for the law; and in any case they aspire from their hearts to the virtue, supremely characteristic of human dignity, which consists in making a correct use of the customary practices of a game. As to the older ones, it is in their power to alter the rules. If this is not "morality," then where does morality begin? At least, it is respect for rules, and it appertains to an enquiry like ours to begin with the study of facts of this order. Of course the phenomena relating to the game of marbles are not among the most primitive. Before playing with his equals, the child is influenced by his parents. He is subjected from his cradle to a multiplicity of regulations, and even before language he becomes conscious of certain obligations. These circumstances even exercise, as we shall see, an undeniable influence upon the way in which the rules of games are elaborated. But in the case of play institutions, adult intervention is at any rate reduced to the minimum. We are therefore in the presence here of realities which, if not amongst the most elementary, should be classed nevertheless amongst the most spontaneous and the most instructive.

With regard to game rules there are two phenomena which it is particularly easy to study: first the *practice* of rules, *i.e.,* the way in which children of different ages effectively apply rules: second the *consciousness* of rules, *i.e.,* the idea which children of different ages form of the character of these game rules, whether of something obligatory and sacred or of something subject to their own choice, whether of heteronomy or autonomy.

It is the comparison of these two groups of data which constitutes the real aim of this chapter. For the relations which exist between the practice and the consciousness of rules are those which will best enable us to define the psychological nature of moral realities.

One word more. Before embarking upon an analysis of the practice or of the consciousness of rules, we must first give some account of the actual content of these rules. We must therefore establish the social data of the problem. But we shall confine ourselves only to what is indispensable. We have not attempted to establish the sociology of the game of marbles; this would have meant finding out how this game was played in the past and how it is now played in different parts of the world (it is actually played by Negro children). Even confining ourselves to French Switzerland, we believe it would need several years of research to discover all the local variants of the game and, above all, to outline the history of these variants throughout the last few generations. Such an enquiry, which might be useful to the sociologist, is superfluous for the psychologist. All the latter needs in order to study how rules are learned is a thorough knowledge of a given custom in actual use, just as in order to study child language, all he needs is to know a given dialect, however localized, without troubling to reconstruct all its semantic and phonetic changes in time and space. We shall therefore confine ourselves to a short analysis of the content of the game as it is played in Geneva and Neuchâtel, in the districts where we conducted our work.

§ 1. THE RULES OF THE GAME OF MARBLES

Three essential facts must be noted if we wish to analyse simultaneously the practice and the consciousness of rules.

The first is that among children of a given generation and in a given locality, however small, there is never one single way of playing marbles, there are quantities of ways. There is the "square game" with which we shall occupy ourselves more especially. A square is drawn on the ground and a number of marbles placed within it; the game consists in aiming at these from a distance and driving them out of the enclosure. There is the game of "courate" where two players aim at each other's marble in indefinite pursuit. There is the game of "troyat" from "trou" (=hole) or "creux" (=hollow), where the marbles are piled into a hole and have to be dislodged by means of a heavier marble, and so on. Every child is familiar with several games, a fact that may help according to his age to reinforce or to weaken his belief in the sacred character of rules.

In the second place, one and the same game, such as the Square game, admits of fairly important variations according to when and where it is played. As we had occasion to verify, the rules of the Square game are not the same in four of the communes of Neuchâtel [2] situated at 2-3 kilometres from each other. They are not the same in Geneva and in Neuchâtel. They differ, on certain points, from one district to another, from one school to another in the same town. In addition to this, as through our collaborators' kindness we were able to establish, variations occur from one generation to another. A student of twenty assured us that in his village the game is no longer played as it was "in his days." These variations according to time and place are important, because children are often aware of their existence. A child who has moved from one town, or merely from one school building to another will often explain to us that such and such a rule is in force in one place but not in the other. Very often, too, a child will tell us that his father played differently from him. Last of all, there is the boy of 14 who has given up playing because he is beginning to feel superior to the little ones, and who, according to his temperament, laughs or mourns over the fact that the customs of his generation are going by the board instead of being piously preserved by the rising generation.

Finally, and clearly as a result of the convergence of these local or historical currents, it will happen that one and the same game (like the Square game) played in the playground of one and the same school admits on certain points of sev-

[2] Neuchâtel, La Coudre, Hauterive and Saint-Blaise.

eral different rules. Children of 11 to 13 are familiar with these variants, and they generally agree before or during the gave to choose a given usage to the exclusion of others. These facts must therefore be borne in mind, for they undoubtedly condition the judgment which the child will make on the value of rules.

Having mentioned these points, we shall give a brief exposition of the rules of the Square game, which will serve as a prototype, and we shall begin by fixing the child's language so as to be able to understand the reports of the conversations which will be quoted later on. Besides, as is so often the case in child psychology, some aspects of this language are in themselves highly instructive.

A marble is called "un marbre" in Neuchâtel and "un cœillu" or "un mapis" in Geneva. There are marbles of different value. The cement marble has the place of honour. The "carron" which is smaller and made of the more brittle clay is of less value because it costs less. The marbles that are used for throwing[3] and are not placed inside the square are called according to their consistency "corna" (if in carnelian), "ago," or "agathe," "cassine" (glass ball with coloured veins), "plomb" (large marble containing lead), etc. Each is worth so many marbles or so many "carrons." To throw a marble is to "tirer" (shoot) and to touch another marble with one's own is to "tanner" (hit).

Then comes a set of terms of ritual *consecration*, that is, of expressions which the player uses in order to announce that he is going to perform such-and-such an operation and which thus consecrate it ritually as an accomplished fact. For, once these words have been uttered, the opponent is powerless against his partner's decision; whereas if he takes the initiative by means of the terms of ritual *interdiction*, which we shall examine in a moment, he will in this way prevent the operation which he fears. For example, in order to play first in circumstances when it is possible to do so, the child will say (at Neuchâtel) "prems"—obviously a corrup-

---

[3] The English technical equivalent is the generic term "shooter" which we shall use in the interrogatories given below. For the rest we have generally retained the French words as one cannot be sure that the English terms mean exactly the same. [Trans.]

tion of the word "premier" (first). If he wants to go back to
the line that all the players start from at their first turn and
which is called the "coche," [4] he simply says "coche." If he
wishes to advance or retreat to a distance twice as great, he
says "deux coches," or if to a distance of one, two, or three
hand-breadths he says "one (or two, or three) empans"
(spans). If he wishes to place himself in relation to the square
at a distance equal to that at which he finds himself at a given
moment, but in another direction (so as to avoid the probable
attacks of his opponent) he says "du mien" (mine), and if
he wishes to prevent his opponent from doing the same thing
he says "du tien" (yours). This applies to Neuchâtel. In
Geneva these displacements are expressed by the terms "faire
une entasse" or "entorse" (to make a twist). If you wish to
give up your turn and be "dead" until your opponent has
moved, you say "coup passé" (my turn passed).

As soon as these terms have been uttered in circumstances
which of course are carefully regulated by a whole juridical
system, the opponent has to submit. But if the opponent
wishes to anticipate these operations, it is sufficient for him
to pronounce the terms of ritual *interdiction,* which at Neuchâtel are simply the same terms but preceded by the prefix
"fan," from "défendu" (forbidden). For example, "fan-du-
mien," "fan-du-tien," "fan-coche," "fan-coup-passé," etc.
Some children, not having understood this prefix, which does
not, after all, correspond with anything in the speech they
hear around them, say "femme-du-tien," "femme-coche," etc.

Two more particularly suggestive terms of consecration
should be noted, which are current among the little Genevans:
"glaine" and "toumiké." When a player places a marble of
superior value in the square, thinking that he has put down
an ordinary marble (say an "ago" instead of a "cœillu") he
is naturally allowed, if he has noticed his mistake, to pick up
his "ago" and put an ordinary marble in its place. Only a
dishonest opponent would take advantage of his partner's
absent-mindedness and pocket this "ago" after having hit it.
The children we questioned on this point were unanimous in
pronouncing such procedure equivalent to stealing. But if, on

[4] English, pitch-line (sometimes). [Trans.]

the other hand, the opponent spots his partner's mistake in time and utters the word "toumiké" or (by doubling the last syllable) "toumikémik," then the absent-minded player no longer has the right to pick up his "ago"; he must leave it on the ground like a common-or-garden "cœillu," and if one of the players succeeds in hitting it, this player will be allowed in all fairness to take possession of it. This shows us a very interesting example of a word consecrating a mistake and by doing so changing a dishonest action into one that is legitimate and recognized as such by all. We have here for the first time an example of that formalism, which belongs to certain aspects of childish morality, and into whose nature we shall go more deeply in the sequel in connection with objective responsibility.

In the same way, the word "glaine" legitimatizes piracy in certain well-defined conditions. When one of the players has succeeded, either by luck or by skill, in winning all his partners' marbles, it is a point of honour similar to that which sociologists designate with the term "potlatch" that he should offer to play a fresh set and should himself place in the square the necessary marbles, so as to give his less fortunate playmates the chance of recovering a portion of their possessions. If he refuses, of course no law can force him to do this; he has won and there is the end of it. If, however, one of the players pronounces the word "glaine" then the whole gang falls upon the miser, throws him down, empties his pockets and shares the booty. This act of piracy which in normal times is profoundly contrary to morality (since the marbles collected by the winner constitute his lawfully acquired possession) is thus changed into a legitimate act and even into an act of retributive justice approved by the general conscience when the word "glaine" has been pronounced.[5]

At Neuchâtel we noticed neither "glaine" nor "toumiké," but, on the other hand, we found "cougac." When one of the

[5] This word "glaine" really has a wider sense. According to several children it entitles whoever pronounces it simply to pick up all the marbles that are on the ground when a discussion arises about them, or if a player forgets to take possession of what is his due. It is in this sense that the word is taken, for instance, in Philippe Monnier's, *Le Livre de Blaise* (3rd ed., p. 135).

players has won too much (therefore in the situation just described) his defeated partner can force him to offer to play another set by uttering the word "cougac" (probably derived from coup-gagné just as "prems" was from premier). If the winner wishes to evade the obligation laid upon him by the fateful word, he has only to anticipate the blow by saying "fan-cougac."

Our reason for emphasizing these linguistic peculiarities is only to show from the first the juridical complexity of game rules. It is obvious that these facts could be analysed more fundamentally from other points of view. One could, for example, work out the whole psychology of consecration and interdiction in connection with the child and, above all, the psychology of social games. But these questions are really outside our scope.[6] Let us therefore return to what is the essential point so far as we are concerned, namely, the rules themselves.

The Square game thus consists, in a word, in putting a few marbles in a square, and in taking possession of them by dislodging them with a special marble, bigger than the rest. But when it comes to details this simple schema contains an indefinite series of complications. Let us take them in order, so as to get some idea of their richness.

First of all, there is the "pose" or outlay. One of the players draws a square and then each places his "pose." If there are two players, each one puts down two, three, or four marbles. If there are three players, each put down two marbles. If there are four or more players, it is customary to put down only one marble each. The main thing is equality: each one puts down what the others do. But in order to reach equality the relative value of the marbles must be taken into account. For an ordinary marble, you must put down eight "carrons." A little "corna" is worth eight "marbres," sixteen "carrons," and so on. The values are carefully regulated and correspond roughly to the price paid at the shop round the corner. But alongside of financial operations proper, there are

[6] With regard to social games we are awaiting the publication of R. Cousinet's book which will incorporate all the valuable material which this author has been accumulating for so many years.

between children various exchanges in kind which appreciably alter current values.

Then the game begins. A certain distance is agreed upon where the "coche" is drawn; this is the line from which the players start. It is drawn parallel to and generally one or two metres away from one of the sides of the square, and from it each player will fire his first shot. (To "fire" is to throw one's shooter—"agathe" or "cornaline"—into the square.)

All, therefore, start from the coche. In some games you return to the coche at each fresh turn, but it is more usual after the first shot to play from the place that your marble has rolled to. Sometimes this rule is limited by saying that the marble must not be further removed from the square than the coche. Thus if your marble has rolled two metres away from the square in any direction whatsoever, you bring it back to a distance of 1m. 50 if this is the distance at which the coche itself stands.

But before the game begins you must settle who is to play first. For the first player has the advantage of "firing" into a square full of marbles, whereas those who follow are faced only with what is left after the gains of the preceding players. In order to know who is to begin, a series of well-known rites are put in action. Two children walk towards each other stepping heel to toe, and whichever steps on the other's toe has the right to begin. Or else rhymed formulæ or even syllables devoid of any meaning are recited in sacramental order. Each syllable corresponds to a player, and he on whom the last syllable falls is the lucky one. In addition to these customary usages there is a method of procedure peculiar to the game of marbles. Each boy throws his "shooter" in the direction of the coche or of a line specially traced for the purpose. Whoever comes nearest up to the line begins. The others follow in order of their nearness up to the line. The last to play is the boy who has gone beyond the coche, and if several have gone beyond it, the last to play will be the boy whose marble has gone furthest.

The order of the players having been settled in this way, the game begins. Each player in turn stands behind the coche and "fires" into the square. There are three ways of throwing one's marble: "Piquette" (Engl., "shooting") which consists in projecting the marble by a jerk of the thumb, the marble being placed against the thumb-nail and kept in place by the first finger; "Roulette" (Engl., "bowling") which consists simply in rolling your marble along the ground, and "Poussette" (Engl., "hunching") which consists in addition in carrying your hand along with it over a sufficient distance to correct the initial direction. Poussette is always banned and may in this connection be compared to the push stroke of a bad billiard player. At Neuchâtel it is customary to say "fan-poussette" or again "femme-poussette." In Geneva, the simpler expression "défendu de trainer" (dragging forbidden) is in use. Roulette ("bowling") is also generally banned ("fan-roulette") but is at times tolerated, in which case everyone will of course have the right to play in this way, and absolute equality before the law will even be agreed upon at the beginning of the game.

The players are therefore throwing in the manner that has been agreed upon. Suppose one of the marbles included in the square has been hit. If it has gone outside the square it becomes the property of the boy who has dislodged it. If it remains inside the enclosure it cannot be taken. If, finally, it remains on the line the case is judged by the partners: a marble which is half outside is regarded as out, not otherwise. Here, naturally, a whole lot of subsidiary rules will establish the procedure in disputed cases. There remains the case of the marble with which one shoots (the shooter, or taw, etc.) remaining in the square or failing to lie beyond one of the lines of the square by at least half of its diameter: its owner is "cuit" (dished), *i.e.*, he cannot play any more. If this marble is projected outside the square by that of another player, it becomes, like the others, the latter's property, except in the case of special conventions generally agreed upon at the beginning of the game. Finally, there are the possible complications arising from cases of rebounding marbles. A marble that bounces out of the square off another is sometimes not held to be won, and *a fortiori* in the case of a marble of value.[7] In other cases, everything that goes outside the enclo-

7 This is expressed by saying that the "revenette" does not count.

sure belongs to the player who has expelled it. The particular cases that arise in this way are settled in conformity with principles that are established either before or during the game by mutual agreement between all the participants.

Then comes the question of the number of "shots" to be allowed to each. The player who has succeeded in winning one or more marbles has the right to play again, and so on, for as long as he wins. But sometimes the following reservation is made: for the first round in each game every player plays once in turn, independently of gains or losses. Here again, therefore, it is a matter of previous arrangement.

In addition—and this is an essential rule—everyone has the right not only to "fire" at the marbles in the square, but also to "tanner" (hit) his neighbour's shooter, even outside the enclosure and indeed wherever it may happen to be in the course of the game. And of course the great difficulty is to shoot at the square without placing yourself within reach of your partners. This is why, when a shot would involve too many risks, you are allowed to say "coup-passé" and to remain where you are, provided, of course, that no one has foreseen this decision and said "fan-coup-passé." And this, really, is why you are allowed to change your position provided you place yourself at the same distance from the square as before, and provided you first say "du mien" (mine), unless, once again, your opponent has anticipated your move by saying "du tien" (yours).

Finally, a series of special rules deserves mention, the observance of which depends upon the particular town or school in question. The first player who says "place-pour-moi" (place for me) is not obliged to take up his position at one of the corners of the square. Any player who has succeeded in winning the equivalent of his "pose" (*i.e.*, two marbles if he has placed two in the square, and so on) can say "queue-de-pose" which will allow him to have the first shot from the coche in the next game, and so on.

The game, regulated in this way by an indefinite number of rules, is carried on until the square is empty. The boy who has pocketed the largest number of marbles has won.

§ 2. THE INTERROGATORY AND ITS GENERAL RESULTS

The rules that we have outlined above constitute a well-marked social reality, "independent of individuals" (in Durkheim's sense) and transmitted, like a language, from one generation to another. This set of customs is obviously more or less plastic. But individual innovations, just as in the case of language, succeed only when they meet a general need and when they are collectively sanctioned as being in conformity with the "spirit of the game." But while fully recognizing the interest attaching to this sociological aspect of the problem, it was from a different standpoint that we raised the questions which we are now going to study. We simply asked ourselves (1) how the individuals adapt themselves to these rules, *i.e.*, how they observe rules at each age and level of mental development; (2) how far they become conscious of rules, in other words, what types of obligation result (always according to the children's ages) from the increasing ascendancy exercised by rules.

The interrogatory is therefore easy to carry out. During the first part, it is sufficient to ask the children (we questioned about 20 boys ranging from 4 to 12-13) how one plays marbles. The experimenter speaks more or less as follows. "Here are some marbles." (The marbles are placed on a large baize-covered table beside a piece of chalk.) "You must show me how to play. When I was little I used to play a lot, but now I've quite forgotten how to. I'd like to play again. Let's play together. You'll teach me the rules and I'll play with you." The child then draws a square, takes half the marbles, puts down his "pose," and the game begins. It is important to bear in mind all possible contingencies of the game and to ask the child about each. This means that you must avoid making any sort of suggestions. All you need do is to appear completely ignorant, and even to make intentional mistakes so that the child may each time point out clearly what the rule is. Naturally, you must take the whole thing very seriously, all through the game. Then you ask who has won and why, and if everything is not quite clear, you begin a new set.

It is of paramount importance during this first half of the

interrogatory to play your part in a simple spirit and to let the child feel a certain superiority at the game (while not omitting to show by an occasional good shot that you are not a complete duffer). In this way the child is put at ease, and the information he gives as to how he plays is all the more conclusive. Many of our children became absorbed in the game to the extent of treating me completely as one of them. "You are dished!" cries Ben (10 years) when my marble stops inside the square.

In the case of the little ones, who find difficulty in formulating the rules which they observe in practice, the best way is to make them play in pairs. You begin by playing with one of them in the manner described above, and ask him to tell you all the rules he knows. Then you make the same request of the second boy (the first being no longer present), and finally you bring the two together and ask them to have a game. This control experiment is not needed for older children, except in doubtful cases.

Then comes the second part of the interrogatory, that, namely, which bears upon the consciousness of rules. You begin by asking the child if he could invent a new rule. He generally does this easily enough, but it is advisable to make sure that it really is a new rule and not one of the many existing variants of which this particular child may already have knowledge. "I want a rule that is only by you, a rule that you've made up yourself and that no one else knows— the rule of N—— (the child's name)." Once the new rule has been formulated, you ask the child whether it could give rise to a new game: "Would it be all right to play like that with your pals? Would they want to play that way? etc." The child either agrees to the suggestion or disputes it. If he agrees, you immediately ask him whether the new rule is a "fair" rule, a "real" rule, one "like the others," and try to get at the various motives that enter into the answers. If, on the other hand, the child disagrees with all this, you ask him whether the new rule, could not by being generalized become a real rule. "When you are a big boy, suppose you tell your new rule to a lot of children, then perhaps they'll all play that way and everyone will forget the old rules. Then which rule will be fairest—yours that everyone knows, or the old one that everyone has forgotten?" The formula can naturally be altered in accordance with the turn which the conversation is taking, but the main point is to find out whether one may legitimately alter rules and whether a rule is fair or just because it conforms to general usage (even newly introduced), or because it is endowed with an intrinsic and eternal value.

Having cleared up this point it will be easy enough to ask the two following questions. (1) Have people always played as they do to-day: "Did your daddy play this way when he was little, and your grand-dad, and children in the time of William Tell, Noah, and Adam and Eve, etc., did they all play the way you showed me, or differently?" (2) What is the origin of rules: Are they invented by children or laid down by parents and grown-ups in general?

Sometimes it is best to begin by these last two questions before asking whether rules can be changed; this avoids perseveration, or rather reverses its direction, and so facilitates the interpretation of the answers. All this part of the interrogatory, moreover, requires extremely delicate handling; suggestion is always ready to occur, and the danger of romancing is ever present. But it goes without saying that the main thing is simply to grasp the child's mental orientation. Does he believe in the mystical virtue of rules or in their finality? Does he subscribe to a heteronomy of divine law, or is he conscious of his own autonomy? This is the only question that interests us. The child has naturally got no ready-made beliefs on the origin and endurance of the rules of his games; the ideas which he invents then and there are only indices of his fundamental attitude, and this must be steadily borne in mind throughout the whole of the interrogatory.

The results which we obtained from this double interrogatory and which we shall examine in greater detail later on, are roughly the following.

From the point of view of the practice or application of rules four successive stages can be distinguished.

A first stage of a purely *motor* and *individual* character, during which the child handles the marbles at the dictation of his desires and motor habits. This leads to the formation of more or less ritualized schemas, but since play is still purely individual, one can only talk of motor rules and not of truly collective rules.

The second may be called *egocentric* for the following reasons. This stage begins at the moment when the child receives from outside the example of codified rules, that is to say, some time between the ages of two and five. But though the child imitates this example, he continues to play either by himself without bothering to find play-fellows, or with others, but without trying to win, and therefore without attempting to unify the different ways of playing. In other words, children of this stage, even when they are playing together, play each one "on his own" (everyone can win at once) and without regard for any codification of rules. This dual character, combining imitation of others with a purely individual use of the examples received, we have designated by the term Egocentrism.

A third stage appears between 7 and 8, which we shall call the stage of incipient *cooperation*. Each player now tries to win, and all, therefore, begin to concern themselves with the question of mutual control and of unification of the rules. But while a certain agreement may be reached in the course of one game, ideas about the rules in general are still rather vague. In other words, children of 7-8, who belong to the same class at school and are therefore constantly playing with each other, give, when they are questioned separately, disparate and often entirely contradictory accounts of the rules observed in playing marbles.

Finally, between the years of 11 and 12, appears a fourth stage, which is that of the *codification of rules*. Not only is every detail of procedure in the game fixed, but the actual code of rules to be observed is known to the whole society. There is remarkable concordance in the information given by children of 10-12 belonging to the same class at school, when they are questioned on the rules of the game and their possible variations.

These stages must of course be taken only for what they are worth. It is convenient for the purposes of exposition to divide the children up in age-classes or stages, but the facts present themselves as a continuum which cannot be cut up into sections. This continuum, moreover, is not linear in character, and its general direction can only be observed by schematizing the material and ignoring the minor oscillations which render it infinitely complicated in detail. So that ten children chosen at random will perhaps not give the impression of a steady advance which gradually emerges from the interrogatory put to the hundred odd subjects examined by us at Geneva and Neuchâtel.

If, now, we turn to the consciousness of rules we shall find a progression that is even more elusive in detail, but no less clearly marked if taken on a big scale. We may express this by saying that the progression runs through three stages, of which the second begins during the egocentric stage and ends towards the middle of the stage of cooperation (9-10), and of which the third covers the remainder of this co-operating stage and the whole of the stage marked by the codification of rules.

During the first stage rules are not yet coercive in character, either because they are purely motor, or else (at the beginning of the egocentric stage) because they are received, as it were, unconsciously, and as interesting examples rather than as obligatory realities.

During the second stage (apogee of egocentric and first half of cooperating stage) rules are regarded as sacred and untouchable, emanating from adults and lasting forever. Every suggested alteration strikes the child as a transgression.

Finally, during the third stage, a rule is looked upon as a law due to mutual consent, which you must respect if you want to be loyal but which it is permissible to alter on the condition of enlisting general opinion on your side.

The correlation between the three stages in the development of the consciousness of rules and the four stages relating to their practical observance is of course only a statistical correlation and therefore very crude. But broadly speaking the relation seems to us indisputable. The collective rule is at first something external to the individual and consequently sacred to him; then, as he gradually makes it his own, it comes to that extent to be felt as the free product of mutual agreement and an autonomous conscience. And with regard to practical use, it is only natural that a mystical respect for laws should be accompanied by a rudimentary knowledge and application of their contents, while a rational and well-founded respect is accompanied by an effective application of each rule in detail.

There would therefore seem to be two types of respect for rules corresponding to two types of social behaviour. This conclusion deserves to be closely examined, for if it holds good, it should be of the greatest value to the analysis of child morality. One can see at once all that it suggests in regard to the relation between child and adult. Take the insubordination of the child towards its parents and teachers, joined to its sincere respect for the commands it receives and its extraordinary mental docility. Could not this be due to that complex of attitudes which we can observe during the egocentric stage and which combines so paradoxically an unstable practice of the law with a mystical attitude towards it? And will not cooperation between adult and child, in so far as it can be realized and in so far as it is facilitated by co-operation between children themselves, supply the key to the interiorization of commands and to the autonomy of the moral consciousness? Let us therefore not be afraid of devoting a certain amount of time to the patient analysis of the rules of a game, for we are here in possession of a method infinitely more supple, and consequently more sure, than that of merely questioning children about little stories, a method which we shall be obliged to adopt in the latter part of this book.

§ 3. THE PRACTICE OF RULES. I. THE FIRST TWO STAGES

We need not dwell at any length upon the first stage, as it is not directly connected with our subject. At the same time, it is important that we should know whether the rules which come into being previous to any collaboration between children are of the same type as collective rules.

Let us give a handful of ten marbles to a child of three years and four months and take note of its reactions:

Jacqueline has the marbles in her hands and looks at them with curiosity (it is the first time she has seen any); then she lets them drop on to the carpet. After this she puts them in the hollow of an arm-chair. *"Aren't they animals?—*Oh, no.— *Are they balls?—*Yes." She puts them back on the carpet and lets them drop from a certain height. She sits on the carpet with her legs apart and throws the marbles a few inches in front of her. She then picks them up and puts them on the arm-chair and in the same hole as before. (The arm-chair is studded with buttons which create depressions in the material.) Then she collects the lot and lets them drop, first all together, then one by one. After this she replaces them in the arm-chair, first in the same place and then in the other holes. Then she piles them up in a pyramid: *"What are marbles?—What do you think?— . . ."* She puts them on the floor, then back on to the arm-chair, in the same holes.—We both go out on to the balcony: she lets the marbles drop from a height to make them bounce.

The following days, Jacqueline again places the marbles on the chairs and arm-chairs, or puts them into her little saucepan to cook dinner. Or else she simply repeats the behaviour described above.

Three points should be noted with regard to facts such as these. In the first place, the lack of continuity and direction in the sequence of behaviour. The child is undoubtedly trying first and foremost to understand the nature of marbles and to adapt its motor schemas to this novel reality. This is why it tries one experiment after another: throwing them, heaping them into pyramids or nests, letting them drop, making them bounce, etc. But once it has got over the first moments of astonishment, the game still remains incoherent, or rather still subject to the whim of the moment. On days when the child plays at cooking dinner, the marbles serve as food to be stewed in a pot. On days when it is interested in classifying and arranging, the marbles are put in heaps in the holes of arm-chairs, and so on. In the general manner in which the game is carried on there are therefore no rules.

The second thing to note is that there are certain regularities of detail, for it is remarkable how quickly certain particular acts in the child's behaviour become schematized and even ritualized. The act of collecting the marbles in the hollow of an arm-chair is at first simply an experiment, but it immediately becomes a motor schema bound up with the perception of the marbles. After a few days it is merely a rite, still performed with interest, but without any fresh effort of adaptation.

In the third place, it is important to note the symbolism[8] that immediately becomes grafted upon the child's motor schemas. These symbols are undoubtedly enacted in play rather than thought out, but they imply a certain amount of imagination: the marbles are food to be cooked, eggs in a nest, etc.

This being so, the rules of games might be thought to derive either from rites analogous to those we have just examined or from a symbolism that has become collective. Let us briefly examine the genesis and ultimate destiny of these modes of behaviour.

Genetically speaking, the explanation both of rites and of symbols would seem to lie in the conditions of preverbal motor intelligence. When it is presented with any new thing, a baby of 5 to 8 months will respond with a dual reaction; it will accommodate itself to the new object and it will assimilate the object to earlier motor schemas. Give the baby a marble, and it will explore its surface and consistency, but will at the same time use it as something to grasp, to suck, to rub against the sides of its cradle, and so on. This assimilation of every fresh object to already existing motor schemas may be conceived of as the starting point of ritual acts and symbols, at any rate from the moment that assimilation becomes stronger than actual accommodation itself. With regard to ritual acts, indeed, one is struck by the fact that from the age of about 8 to 10 months all the child's motor schemas, apart from moments of adaptation in the real sense, gives rise to a sort of functioning in the void, in which the child takes pleasure as in a game. Thus, after having contracted the habit of pressing her face against her parents' cheeks, crumpling up her nose and breathing deeply the while, Jacqueline began to perform this rite as a joke, crumpling up her nose and breathing deeply in advance, merely suggesting contact with another person's face, but without, as before, expressing any particular

8 We use the term "symbol" in the sense given to it in the linguistic school of Saussure, as the contrary of sign. A sign is arbitrary, a symbol is motivated. It is in this sense, too, that Freud speaks of symbolic thought.

affection by the act. Thus from being actual, and incorporated in an effective adaptation this schema has become ritualized and serves only as a game.[9] Or again, Jacqueline in her bath is engaged in rubbing her hair; she lets go of it to splash the water. Immediately, she repeats the movement, touching her hair and the water alternately, and during the next few days the schema has become ritualized to such an extent that she cannot strike the surface of the water without first outlining the movement of smoothing her hair.[10] In no way automatic, this rite is a game that amuses her by its very regularity. Anyone observing a baby of 10 to 12 months will notice a number of these rites which undoubtedly anticipate the rules of future games.

As for symbols, they appear towards the end of the first year and in consequence of the ritual acts. For the habit of repeating a given gesture ritually, gradually leads to the consciousness of "pretending." The ritual of going to bed, for instance (laying down one's head and arranging the corner of the pillow with the hundred and one complications which every baby invents), is sooner or later utilized "in the void," and the smile of the child as it shuts its eyes in carrying out this rite is enough to show that it is perfectly conscious of "pretending" to go to sleep. Here already we have a symbol, but a "played" symbol. Finally, when language and imagery come to be added to motor intelligence, the symbol becomes an object of thought. The child who pushes a box along saying "tuff-tuff" is assimilating in imagination the box's movement to that of a motor-car: the play symbol has definitely come into being.

This being so, can one seek among rites and symbols for the origin of the actual rules of games? Can the game of marbles, with its infinite complexity both with regard to the actual rules and to all that relates to the verbo-motor system of signs in use—can the game of marbles, then, be conceived simply as the result of an accumulation of individual rites and symbols? We do not think that it can. We believe that the individual rite and the individual symbol constitute the sub-

9 Age: 10 months.
10 Age: 12 months.

structure for the development of rules and collective signs, its necessary, but not its sufficient condition. There is something more in the collective rule than in the motor rule or the individual ritual, just as there is something more in the sign than in the symbol.

With regard to motor or ritualistic rules, there can be no doubt that they have something in common with rules in the ordinary sense, namely the consciousness of regularity. When we see the delight taken by a baby of 10 to 12 months or a child of 2-3 in reproducing a given behaviour in all its details, and the scrupulous attention with which it observes the right order in these operations, we cannot help recognizing the *Regelbewusstsein* of which Bühler speaks. But we must distinguish carefully between the behaviour into which there enters only the pleasure of regularity, and that into which there enters an element of obligation. It is this consciousness of obligation which seems to us, as to Durkheim[11] and Bovet,[12] to distinguish a rule in the true sense from mere regularity.

Now this element of obligation, or, to confine ourselves to the question of the practice of rules, this element of obedience intervenes as soon as there is a society, *i.e.*, a relation between at least two individuals. As soon as a ritual is imposed upon a child by adults or seniors for whom he has respect (Bovet), or as soon, we would add, as a ritual comes into being as the result of the collaboration of two children, it acquires in the subject's mind a new character which is precisely that of a rule. This character may vary according to the type of respect which predominates (respect for the senior or mutual respect) but in all cases there enters an element of submission which was not contained in the rite pure and simple.

In actual fact, of course, there is every degree of variety between the simple regularity discovered by the individual and the rule to which a whole social group submits itself. Thus during the egocentric stage we can observe a whole series of cases in which the child will use a rule as a mere

11 *L'Education Morale.*
12 "Les Conditions de l'Obligation de la Conscience", *Année Psychol.*, 1912.

rite, to be bent and modified at will, while at the same time he already tries to submit to the common laws. Just as the child very soon acquires the use of language and of the abstract and general concepts while retaining in his attitude to these much that still belongs to egocentric modes of thought and even to the methods peculiar to symbolic and play thought, so, under the rules that are impôsed upon him, he will for a long time contrive (in all good faith, needless to say) to maintain his own phantasy in the matter of personal decisions. But this factual continuity between ritual and rule does not exclude a qualitative difference between the two types of behaviour.

Let us not, however, anticipate what will be said in our analysis of the consciousness of rules, but return to the matter of ritual. The individual rite develops quite naturally, as we have just shown, into a more or less complex symbolism. Can this symbolism be regarded as the starting point of that system of obligatory verbo-motor signs which are connected with the rules of every collective game? As with the previous problem, we believe that the symbol is a necessary, but not a sufficient condition of the appearance of signs. The sign is general and abstract (arbitrary), the symbol is individual and motivated. If the sign is to follow upon the symbol, a group must therefore strip the individual's imagination of all its personal fantasy and then elaborate a common and obligatory imagery which will go hand in hand with the code of rules itself.

Here is an observation showing how far removed are individual rites and symbols from rules and signs, though moving towards these realities in so far as collaboration between children becomes established.

Jacqueline (after the observations given above) is playing with Jacques (2 years, 11 months and 15 days), who sees marbles for the first time. I. Jacques takes the marbles and lets them drop from a height one after another. After which he picks them up and goes away. II. Jacques arranges them on the ground, in a hollow and says, *"I'm making a little nest."* Jacqueline takes one and sticks it in the ground in imitation. III. Jacques also takes one, buries it and makes a mud-pie above it. He digs it up and begins over again. Then he takes 2 at a time which he buries. Then 3, 4, 5 and up to 6 at a time, increasing the number of marbles systematically each time by one. Jacqueline imitates him: she first puts one marble down and makes a mud-pie over it, then two or three at random and without adopting a fixed system of progression. IV. Jacques puts all the marbles on a pile, then he places an india-rubber ball beside them and says: *"That's the Mummy ball and the baby balls."* V. He piles them together again and covers them up with earth which he levels down. Jacqueline imitates him but with only one marble which she covers up without levelling the earth. She adds: *"It's lost,"* then digs it up and begins over again.

This example shows very clearly how all the elements of individual fantasy or symbolism remain uncommunicated; as soon as the game takes on an imaginative turn each child evokes its favourite images without paying any attention to anyone else's. It will also be observed how totally devoid of any general direction are the ritualized schemas successively tried. But as soon as there is reciprocal imitation (end of II and whole of III) we have the beginnings of a rule: each child tries to bury the marbles in the same way as the other, in a common order only more or less successfully adhered to. In bringing out this aspect, the observation leads us to the stage of egocentrism during which the child learns other peoples' rules but practises them in accordance with his own fantasy.

We shall conclude this analysis of the first stage by repeating that before games are played in common, no rules in the proper sense can come into existence. Regularities and ritualized schemas are already there, but these rites, being the work of the individual, cannot call forth that submission to something superior to the self which characterizes the appearance of any rule.

The second stage is the stage of *egocentrism*. In studying the practice of rules we shall make use of a notion which has served on earlier occasions in the descriptions we have given of the child's intellectual behaviour; and, in both cases, indeed, the phenomenon is of exactly the same order. Egocentrism appears to us as a form of behaviour intermediate between purely individual and socialized behaviour. Through imitation and language, as also through the whole content of adult thought which exercises pressure on the child's mind as soon as verbal intercourse has become possible, the child begins, in a sense, to be socialized from the end of its first year. But the very nature of the relations which the child sustains with the adults around him prevents this socialization for the moment from reaching that state of equilibrium which is propitious to the development of reason. We mean, of course, the state of cooperation, in which the individuals, regarding each other as equals, can exercise a mutual control and thus attain to objectivity. In other words, the very nature of the relation between child and adult places the child apart, so that his thought is isolated, and while he believes himself to be sharing the point of view of the world at large he is really still shut up in his own point of view. The social bond itself, by which the child is held, close as it may seem when viewed from outside, thus implies an unconscious intellectual egocentrism which is further promoted by the spontaneous egocentrism peculiar to all primitive mentality.

Similarly, with regard to the rules of games, it is easy to see, and greater authorities than ourselves[13] have already pointed out that the beginnings of children's games are characterized by long periods of egocentrism. The child is dominated on the one hand by a whole set of rules and examples that are imposed upon him from outside. But unable as he is, on the other hand, to place himself on a level of equality with regard to his seniors, he utilizes for his own ends, unaware even of his own isolation, all that he has succeeded in grasping of the social realities that surround him.

To confine ourselves to the game of marbles, the child of 3 to 5 years old will discover, according to what other children he may happen to come across, that in order to play this game one must trace a square, put the marbles inside it, try to expel the marbles from the square by hitting them with

[13] Stern in his *Psychology of Early Childhood* notes the identity of the stages we have established in children's conversations with those he has himself established with regard to play, pp. 177 and 332.

another marble, start from a line that has been drawn beforehand, and so on. But though he imitates what he observes,
and believes in perfect good faith that he is playing like the
others, the child thinks of nothing at first but of utilizing these
new acquisitions for himself. He plays in an individualistic
manner with material that is social. Such is egocentrism.

Let us analyse the facts of the case.

MAR (6) [14] seizes hold of the marbles we offer him, and
without bothering to make a square he heaps them up together and begins to hit the pile. He removes the marbles he
has displaced and puts them aside or replaces them immediately without any method. "Do you always play like that?—
In the street you make a square.—Well, you do the same as
they do in the street.—*I'm making a square, I am.*" (He
draws the square, places the marbles inside it and begins to
play again.) I play with him, imitating each of his movements.
"Who has won?—*We've both won.*—But who has won most?
. . ."—(Mar does not understand.)

BAUM (6½) begins by making a square and puts down
three marbles, adding: "*Sometimes you put 4, or 3, or 2.*—
Or 5?—*No, not 5, but sometimes 6 or 8.*—Who begins when
you play with the boys?—*Sometimes me, sometimes the other
one.*—Isn't there a dodge for knowing who is to begin?—
No.—Do you know what a coche is?—*Rather!*" But the
sequel shows that he knows nothing about the coche and
thinks of this word as designating another game. "And which
of us will begin?—*You.*—Why?—*I want to see how you do
it.*" We play for a while and I ask who has won: "*The one
who has hit a mib,*[15] *well, he has won.*—Well! who has won?—
I have, and then you." I then arrange things so as to take 4
while he takes 2: "Who has won?—*I have, and then you.*"
We begin again. He takes two, I none. "Who has won?—
I have.—And I?—*You've lost.*"

[14] The numbers in brackets give the child's age. The words of the
child are in italics, those of the examiner in Roman lettering.
Quotation marks indicate the beginning and end of a conversation
reported *verbatim*. All the subjects are boys unless the letter G
is added, indicating that the subject is a girl.
[15] English equivalent for "marbre." [Trans.]

LOEFF (6) often pretends to be playing with Mae, of whom we shall speak later. He knows neither how to make a square nor to draw a coche. He immediately begins to "fire" at the marbles assembled in a heap and plays without either stopping or paying any attention to us. "Have you won?— *I don't know. I think I have.*—Why?—*Yes, because I threw the mibs.*—and I?—*Yes, because you threw the mibs.*"

DESARZ (6): "Do you play often?—*Yes, rather!*—With whom?—*All by myself.*—Do you like playing alone best?— *You don't need two. You can play only one.*" He gathers the marbles together without a square and "fires" into the heap.

Let us now see how two children, who have grown accustomed to playing together, set about it when they are left alone. They are two boys of whom one (Mae) is a very representative example of the present stage, while the other (Wid) stands at the border line between the present stage and the next. The analyses of these cases will be all the more conclusive as the children in question are no mere beginners at the game.

MAE (6) and WID (7) declare that they are always playing together. Mae tells us that they both *"played again, yesterday."* I first examine Mae by himself. He piles his marbles in a corner without counting them and throws his shooter into the pile. He then places 4 marbles close together and puts a fifth on top (in a pyramid). Mae denies that a square is ever drawn. Then he corrects himself and affirms that he always does so: "How do you and Wid know which is to begin?— *One of the two throws his shooter and the other tries to hit it. If he hits it, he begins."* Mae then shows us what the game consists in: he throws his shooter without taking into account the distances or the manner of playing ("piquette"), and when he succeeds in driving a marble out of the square he immediately puts it back. Thus the game has no end. "Does it go on like that all the time?—*You take one away to make a change* (he takes a marble out of the square, but not the one that he has touched). *It'll only be finished when there's only one left* (he 'fires' again twice). *One more shot, and then you take one away.*" Then he affirms: *"every third shot you take one away."* He does so. Mae removes a marble every third shot independently of whether he has hit or missed, which is completely irregular and corresponds to nothing in the game as habitually played, or as we have seen it played in Neuchâtel or Geneva. It is therefore a rule which he has invented then and there but which he has the impression of remembering because it presents a vague analogy with what really happens when the player removes the marble he has just "hit" (touched). This game of Mae's is therefore a characteristic game of the second stage, an egocentric game in which "to win" does not mean getting the better of the others, but simply playing on one's own.

Wid, whom I now prepare to question and who has not assisted at Mae's interrogatory, begins by making a square. He places 4 marbles at the 4 corners and one in the middle (the same disposition as Mae's, which was probably a deformation of it). Wid does not know what to do to decide which is to begin, and declares that he understands nothing of the method which Mae had shewn me as being familiar to both of them (trying to hit one's partner's shooter). Wid then throws his shooter in the direction of the square, knocking out one marble which he puts in his pocket. Then I take my turn, but fail to touch anything. He plays again and wins all the marbles, one after the other, keeping them each time. He also declares that when you have knocked a marble out, you have the right to play another shot straight away. After having taken everything he says: *"I've won."* Wid therefore belongs to the third stage if this explanation is taken as a whole, but the sequel will show that he takes no notice of Mae's doings when they are playing together. Wid stands therefore at the boundary line which separates the stage of egocentrism from the stage of cooperation.

I then tell Mae to come into the room and the two children begin to play with each other. Mae draws a square and Wid disposes the marbles in accordance with his habitual schema. Mae begins (he plays "Roulette" whereas Wid most of the time plays "Piquette") and dislodges four marbles. *"I can play four times, now,"* adds Mae. This is contrary to all the rules, but Wid finds the statement quite natural. So one game succeeds another. But the marbles are placed in the square by one child or the other as the spirit moves them (according to the rules each must put his "pose") and the dislodged marbles are sometimes put straight back into the square, sometimes retained by the boy who has won them. Each plays from whatever place he chooses, unchecked by his partner, and each "fires" as many times as he likes (it thus often happens that Mae and Wid are playing at the same time).

I now send Wid out of the room and ask Mae to explain the game to us for a last time. Mae places 16 marbles in the middle of the square. "Why so many as that? *So as to win.—* How many do you put down at home with Wid?—*I put five, but when I'm alone, I put lots.*" Mae then begins to play and dislodges a marble which he puts on one side. I do the same. The game continues in this way, each playing one shot at a time without taking the dislodged marbles into account (which is contrary to what Mae was doing a moment ago). Mae then places five marbles in the square, like Wid. This time I arrange the five marbles as Mae himself had done at the beginning of the interrogatory (four close together and one on top) but Mae seems to have forgotten this way of doing things. In the end Mae plays by taking away a marble every three shots, as before, and says to us; *"It's so that it should stop."*

We have quoted the whole of this example in order to show how little two children from the same class at school, living in the same house, and accustomed to playing with each other, are able to understand each other at this age. Not only do they tell us of totally different rules (this still occurs throughout the third stage), but when they play together they do not watch each other and do not unify their respective rules even for the duration of one game. The fact of the matter is that neither is trying to get the better of the other: each is merely having a game on his own, trying to hit the marbles in the square, *i.e.*, trying to "win" from his point of view.

This shows the characteristics of the stage. The child plays for himself. His interest does not in any way consist in competing with his companions and in binding himself by common rules so as to see who will get the better of the others. His aims are different. They are indeed dual, and it is this mixed behaviour that really defines egocentrism. On the one hand, the child feels very strongly the desire to play like the other boys, and especially like those older than himself; he longs, that is to say, to feel himself a member of the very honorable fraternity of those who know how to play marbles correctly. But quickly persuading himself, on the other hand, that his playing is "right" (he can convince himself as easily on this point as in all his attempts to imitate adult behaviour) the child thinks only of utilizing these acquisitions for himself: his pleasure still consists in the mere development of skill, in carrying out the strokes he sets himself to play. It is, as in the previous stage, essentially a motor pleasure, not a social one. The true "socius" of the player who has reached this stage is not the flesh and blood partner but the ideal and abstract elder whom one inwardly strives to imitate and who sums up all the examples one has ever received.

It little matters, therefore, what one's companion is doing, since one is not trying to contend against him. It little matters what the details of the rules may be, since there is no real contact between the players. This is why the child, as soon as he can schematically copy the big boys' game, believes himself to be in possession of the whole truth. Each for himself, and all in communion with the "Elder": such might be the formula of egocentric play.

It is striking to note the affinity between this attitude of children of 4 to 6 in the game of marbles and the attitude of those same children in their conversations with each other. For alongside of the rare cases of true conversation where there is a genuine interchange of opinions or commands, one can observe in children between 2 and 6 a characteristic type of pseudo-conversation or "collective monologue," during which the children speak only for themselves, although they wish to be in the presence of interlocutors who will serve as a stimulus. Now here again, each feels himself to be in communion with the group because he is inwardly addressing the Adult who knows and understands everything, but here again, each is only concerned with himself, for lack of having dis-associated the "ego" from the "socius."

These features of the egocentric stage will not, however,

appear in their full light until we come to analyse the consciousness of rules which accompanies this type of conduct.

§ 4. THE PRACTICE OF RULES. II. THIRD AND FOURTH STAGES

Towards the age of 7-8 appears the desire for mutual understanding in the sphere of play (as also, indeed, in the conversations between children). This felt need for understanding is what defines the third stage. As a criterion of the appearance of this stage we shall take the moment when by "winning" the child refers to the fact of getting the better of the others, therefore of gaining more marbles than the others, and when he no longer says he has won when he has done no more than to knock a marble out of the square, regardless of what his partners have done. As a matter of fact, no child, even from among the older ones, ever attributes very great importance to the fact of knocking out a few more marbles than his opponents. Mere competition is therefore not what constitutes the affective motive-power of the game. In seeking to win the child is trying above all to contend with his partners *while observing common rules*. The specific pleasure of the game thus ceases to be muscular and egocentric, and becomes social. Henceforth, a game of marbles constitutes the equivalent in action of what takes place in discussion in words: a mutual evaluation of the competing powers which leads, thanks to the observation of common rules, to a conclusion that is accepted by all.

As to the difference between the third and fourth stages, it is only one of degree. The children of about 7 to 10 (third stage) do not yet know the rules in detail. They try to learn them owing to their increasing interest in the game played in common, but when different children of the same class at school are questioned on the subject the discrepancies are still considerable in the information obtained. It is only when they are at play that these same children succeed in understanding each other, either by copying the boy who seems to know most about it, or, more frequently, by omitting any usage that might be disputed. In this way they play a sort of simplified game. Children of the fourth stage, on the contrary, have thoroughly mastered their code and even take pleasure in juridical discussions, whether of principle or merely of procedure, which may at times arise out of the points in dispute.

Let us examine some examples of the third stage, and, in order to point more clearly to the differentiating characters of this stage, let us begin by setting side by side the answers of two little boys attending the same class at school and accustomed to playing together. (The children were naturally questioned separately in order to avoid any suggestion between them, but we afterwards compared their answers with one another.)

BEN (10) and NUS (11, backward, one year below the school standard) are both in the fourth year of the lower school and both play marbles a great deal. They agree in regarding the square as necessary. Nus declares that you always place 4 marbles in the square, either at the corners or else 3 in the center with one on top (in a pyramid). Ben, however, tells us that you place 2 to 10 marbles in the enclosure (not less than 2, not more than 10).

To know who is to begin you draw, according to Nus, a line called the "coche" and everyone tries to get near it: whoever gets nearest plays first, and whoever goes beyond it plays last. Ben, however, knows nothing about the coche: you begin *"as you like.*—Isn't there a dodge for knowing who is to play first?—*No.*—Don't you try with the coche?—*Yes, sometimes.*—What is the coche?— . . . (he cannot explain)." On the other hand, Ben affirms that you "fire" the first shot at a distance of 2 to 3 steps from the square. A single step is not enough, and *"four isn't any good either."* Nus is ignorant of this law and considers the distance to be a matter of convention.

With regard to the manner of "firing," Nus is equally tolerant. According to him you can play "piquette" or " roulette," but *"when you play piquette everyone must play the same. When one boy says that you must play roulette, everyone plays that way."* Nus prefers roulette because *"that is the best way"*: piquette is more difficult. Ben, however, regards piquette as obligatory in all cases. He is ignorant, moreover, of the term roulette and when we show him what it is he says: *"That is bowled piquette!* [Fr., Piquette roulée] *That's cheating!"*

According to Nus everyone must play from the coche, and all through the game. When, after having shot at the square you land anywhere, you must therefore come back to the coche to "fire" the next shot. Ben, on the contrary, who on this point represents the more general usage, is of opinion that only the first shot should be fired from the coche: after that *"you must play from where you are."*

Nus and Ben thus agree in stating that the marbles that have gone out of the square remain in the possession of the boy who dislodged them. This is the only point, this and the actual drawing of the square, on which the children give us results that are in agreement.

When we begin to play, I arrange to stay in the square (to leave my shooter inside the enclosure). *"You are dished* (Fr. cuit), cries Ben, delighted, *you can't play again until I get you out!"* Nus knows nothing of this rule. Again, when I play carelessly and let the shooter drop out of my hand, Ben exclaims *"Fan-coup"* to prevent me from saying "coup-passé" and having another shot. Nus is ignorant of this rule.

At one point Ben succeeds in hitting my shooter. He concludes from this that he can have another shot, just as though he had hit one of the marbles placed in the square. Nus, in the same circumstances does not draw the same conclusions (each must play in turn according to him) but deduces that he will be able to play the first shot in the next game.

In the same way, Ben thinks that everyone plays from the place the last shot has led him to and knows the rule that authorizes the player to change places, saying *"du mien"* or *"un empan,"* whereas Nus, who has certainly heard those words, does not know what they mean.

These two cases, chosen at random out of a class of 10-year-old pupils, show straight away what are the two differential features of the second stage. 1) There is a general will to discover the rules that are fixed and common to all players (cf. the way Nus explains to us that if one of the partners plays piquette *"everyone must play the same"*). 2) In spite of this there is considerable discrepancy in the children's information. Lest the reader should think the above examples exceptional here are, on the same point, the answers of another child from the same class:

Ross (11; I): *"First, every one puts two marbles on the square. You can make the square bigger when there are more playing."* Ross knows the method of the coche for knowing who is to begin. Like Nus, he allows both roulette and piquette. He also allows what is not only contrary to all established usages but also to the sense of the words, a way of playing which he calls "femme-poussette" which consists in carrying one's hand along with the marble as one throws it (push stroke in billiards). Now this is always forbidden, and the very word that Ross has deformed says so—"fan-poussette." According to Ross, you play from the place you have reached with the last shot, and when you have won a marble you have the right to another shot straight away. To change your place you must say "du mien." *"If a stone gets in our way, you say 'coup-passé' and have another shot. If it slips* [if the marble slips out of your hand] *you say 'laché'* (Engl. 'gone'). *If you don't say that, you can't have another turn. It's the rules!"* Ross here stands mid-way between Nus and Ben. Finally, Ross knows of a rather peculiar custom which is unknown to Nus and Ben. *"If you stay in the square you can be hit and then he picks up the marbles* [=If your shooter stays inside the square and is touched by your opponent's shooter, he is entitled to all the marbles in the square]. *He* (the opponent) *can have two shots* [to try and hit the shooter in question] *and if he misses the first he can take* [at the second shot] *the shooter from anywhere* [though of course only from the outside of the square] *and make the marbles go out* [=take them]." This rule has generally only been described to us by children of the fourth stage, but the rest of Ross' interrogatory is typically third stage.

Such then is the third stage. The child's chief interest is no longer psycho-motor, it is social. In other words, to dislodge a marble from a square by manual dexterity is no longer an aim in itself. The thing now is not only to fight the other boys but also and primarily to regulate the game with a whole set of systematic rules which will ensure the most complete reciprocity in the methods used. The game has therefore become social. We say "become" because it is only after this stage that any real cooperation exists between the players. Before this, each played for himself. Each sought, it is true, to imitate the play of older boys and of the initiated, but more for the satisfaction, still purely personal, of feeling himself to be a member of a mystical community whose sacred institutions are handed down by the elders out of the remote past, than from any real desire to cooperate with his playmates or with anyone else. If cooperation be regarded as more social than this mixture of egocentrism and respect for one's seniors which characterizes the beginnings of collective life among children, then we may say that it is from the third stage onwards that the game of marbles begins to be a truly social game.

As yet, however, this cooperation exists to a great extent only in intention. Being an honest man is not enough to make one to know the law. It is not even enough to enable us to solve all the problems that may arise in our concrete "moral experience." The child fares in the same way during the present stage, and succeeds, at best, in creating for himself a "provisional morality," putting off till a later date the task of setting up a code of laws and a system of jurisprudence. Nor do boys of 7 to 10 ever succeed in agreeing amongst themselves for longer than the duration of one and the same game; they are still incapable of legislating on all possible cases that may arise, for each still has a purely personal opinion about the rules of the game.

To use an apter comparison, we may say that the child of 7 to 10 plays as he reasons. We have already[16] tried to establish the fact that about the age of 7 or 8, precisely, that is to say, at the moment when our third stage appears, in the very poor districts where we conducted our work,[17] discus-

---

[16] *J.R.,* chap. IV.
[17] We take this opportunity of reminding the reader of what has not been sufficiently emphasized in our earlier books, viz. that most of our research has been carried out on children from the poorer parts of Geneva. In different surroundings the age averages would certainly have been different.

sion and reflection gain an increasing ascendency over unproved affirmation and intellectual egocentrism. Now, these new habits of thought lead to genuine deductions (as opposed to primitive "transductions") and to deductions in which the child grapples with a given fact of experience, either present or past. But something is still lacking if deduction is to be generalized and made completely rational: the child must be able to reason formally, *i.e.*, he must have a conscious realization of the rules of reasoning which will enable him to apply them to any case whatsoever, including purely hypothetical cases (mere assumptions). In the same way, a child who, with regard to the rules of games, has reached the third stage, will achieve momentary coordinations of a collective order (a well ordered game may be compared on this point to a good discussion), but feels no interest as yet in the actual legislation of the game, in the discussions of principle which alone will give him complete mastery of the game in all its strictness. (From this point of view the juridico-moral discussions of the fourth stage may be compared to formal reasoning in general.)

It is, on an average, towards the age of 11 or 12 that these interests develop. In order to understand what is the practice of rules among children of this fourth stage let us question separately several children from the same class at school, and we shall see how subtle are their answers, and how well they agree with one another.

RIT (12), GROS (13) and VUA (13) often play marbles. We questioned them each separately and took steps to prevent them from communicating to each other during our absence the contents of our interrogatory.

With regard to the square, the "pose," the manner of throwing, and generally speaking all the rules we have already examined, these three children are naturally in full agreement with each other. To know who is to play first, Rit, who has lived in two neighbouring villages before coming to town, tells us that various customs are in usage. You draw a line, the coche, and whoever gets nearest to it plays first. If you go beyond the line, either, according to some, it does not matter, or else *"there is another game: when you go beyond the line, you play last."* Gros and Vua know only of this custom, the only one that is really put into practice by the boys of the neighbourhood.

But there are complications about which the younger boys left us in the dark. *"Whoever,* according to Gros, *says 'queue' plays second. It's easier because he doesn't get 'hit'* [=if a player's shooter lands near the square, it is exposed to hits from the other players]." In the same way, Vua tells us that *"whoever says 'queue de deux' plays last."* And he adds the following rule, also recognized by Gros: *"When you are all at the same distance from the coche whoever cries 'egaux-queque' plays second"* (the problem is therefore to play sufficiently soon still to find marbles in the square, but not first, for fear of being hit).

On the other hand, Gros tells us: *"Whoever takes out two* [two of the marbles placed inside the square, *i.e.,* the equivalent of the player's 'pose'] *can say 'queue-de-pose.' In that way he can play second from the coche in the next game."* And Vua: *"When there are two outside* [when two marbles have been knocked out of the square] *you can dare to say 'queue-de-pose,' and you can play second from the coche again in the second game."* Rit gives us the same information.

This is not all. According to Rit, *"if you say 'deux-coups-de-coche' you can have two shots from the line. If you say 'deux-coups-d'empan' you play the second shot from where you are. You can only say that when the other* [=the opponent] *has made up his pose* [=has won back as many marbles as he had originally deposited in the square]." This rule is observed in the same way by the other two children.

In addition, there is a whole set of rules, unknown to the younger boys, which bear upon the position of the marbles in the square. According to Gros *"the first boy who says 'place-pour-moi'* [Eng., place-for-me] *does not have to place himself at one of the corners of the square,"* and *"the one who has said 'places-des-marbres'* (Engl., place for the marbles) *can put them down as he likes, in a 'troyat'* (all in a heap) *or at the four corners."* Vua is of the same opinion and adds: *"If you say 'place-pour-toi-pour-tout-le-jeu'* (Engl., your-place-for-the-whole-game) *the other chap* [=the opponent] *must stay at the same place."* Rit, who knows both these rules, adds the further detail that *"you can't say 'place-pour-moi" if you have already said 'place-pour-toi.' "* This gives some idea of the complications of procedure!

Our three legal experts also point the measures of clemency in use for the protection of the weak. According to Vua *"if you knock out three at one shot and there's only one left* [one marble in the square] *the other chap* [the opponent] *has the right to play from half-way* [half-way between the coche and the square] *because the first boy has made more than his 'pose.' "* Also: *"the boy who has been beaten is allowed to begin."* According to Gros, *"if there is one marble left at the end, the boy who has won, instead of taking it, can give it to the other chap."* And again, *"When there's one boy who has won too much, the others say 'coujac,' and he is bound to play another game."*

The number of shots at the disposal of each player also gives rise to a whole series of regulations on which the three boys lay stress, as before, in full agreement with each other. For the sake of brevity we refer the reader on this point to the general rules outlined in Section I.

There is only one point on which we saw our subjects differ. Rit who, it will be remembered, has known the game in three different districts, tells us that the boy whose shooter stays inside the square may generally come out of it. He added, it is true, that in some games the player in such a plight is "dished" (Fr., *brulé*), but this rule does not seem to him obligatory. Vua and Gros, on the contrary, are of opinion that in all cases *"when you stay inside the square you are dished."* We think we may confuse Vua by saying: "Rit didn't say that!—*The fact is,* answers Vua, *that sometimes people play differently. Then you ask each other what you want to do.*—And if you can't agree?—*We scrap for a bit and then we fix things up."*

These answers show what the fourth stage is. Interest seems to have shifted its ground since the last stage. Not only do these children seek to cooperate, to "fix things up," as Vua puts it, rather than to play for themselves alone, but also —and this undoubtedly is something new—they seem to take a peculiar pleasure in anticipating all possible cases and in codifying them. Considering that the square game is only one of the five or ten varieties of the game of marbles, it is almost alarming in face of the complexity of rules and procedure in the square game, to think of what a child of twelve has to store away in his memory. These rules, with their overlapping and their exceptions, are at least as complex as the current rules of spelling. It is somewhat humiliating, in this connection, to see how heavily traditional education sets about the task of making spelling enter into brains that assimilate with such ease the mnemonic contents of the game of marbles. But then, memory is dependent upon activity, and a real activity presupposes interest.

Throughout this fourth stage, then, the dominating interest seems to be interest in the rules themselves. For mere cooperation would not require such subtleties as those attending the disposition of the marbles in the square ("place-pour-moi," "place-des-marbres," "place-pour-toi-pour-tout-le-jeu," etc.). The fact that the child enjoys complicating things at will proves that what he is after is rules for their own sake. We have described elsewhere[18] the extraordinary behavior of eight boys of 10 to 11 who, in order to throw snow-balls at each other, began by wasting a good quarter-of-an-hour in electing a president, fixing the rules of voting, then in dividing themselves into two camps, in deciding upon the distances of the shots, and finally in foreseeing what would be the sanctions to be applied in cases of infringement of these laws. Many other facts analogous to this could be culled from studies that have been made on children's societies.

In conclusion, the acquisition and practice of the rules of a game follow very simple and very natural laws, the stages of which may be defined as follows: 1) Simple individual regularity. 2) Imitation of seniors with egocentrism. 3) Cooperation. 4) Interest in rules for their own sake. Let us now see whether the consciousness of rules describes in its evolution an equally uncomplicated curve.

§ 5. Consciousness of Rules. I. The First Two Stages

As all our results have shown, consciousness of rules cannot be isolated from the moral life of the child as a whole.

[18] *J.R.*, p. 96.

We might, at the most, study the practical applications of rules without bothering about obedience in general, *i.e.,* about the child's whole social and moral behaviour. But as soon as we try, as in the present case, to analyse a child's feelings and thoughts about rules, we shall find that he assimilates them unconsciously along with the commands to which he is subjected taken as a whole. This comes out particularly clearly in the case of the little ones, for whom the constraint exercised by older children evokes adult authority itself in an attenuated form.

Thus the great difficulty here, even more than with the practice of rules, is to establish the exact significance of the primitive facts. Do the simple individual regularities that precede the rules imposed by a group of players give rise to the consciousness of rules, or do they not? And if they do, is this consciousness directly influenced by the commands of adults? This very delicate point must be settled before we can embark upon the analysis of the more transparent data furnished by the interrogatory of older children. With regard to consciousness of rules, we shall designate as the first stage that which corresponds to the purely individualistic stage studied above. During this stage the child, as we noted, plays at marbles in its own way, seeking merely to satisfy its motor interests or its symbolic fantasy. Only, it very soon contracts habits which constitute individual rules of a sort. This phenomenon, far from being unique, is the counterpart of that sort of ritualization of behaviour which can be observed in any baby before it can speak or have experienced any specifically moral adult pressure. Not only does every act of adaptation extend beyond its content of intellectual effort into a ritual kept up for its own sake, but the baby will often invent such rituals for its own pleasure; hence the primitive reactions of very young children in the presence of marbles.

But in order to know to what consciousness of rules these individual schemas correspond it should be remembered that from its tenderest years everything conspires to impress upon the baby the notion of regularity. Certain physical events (alternation of day and night, sameness of scenery during walks, etc.) are repeated with sufficient accuracy to produce an awareness of "law," or at any rate to favour the appearance of motor schemas of prevision. The parents, moreover, impose upon the baby a certain number of moral obligations, the source of further regularities (meals, bed-time, cleanliness, etc.) which are completely (and to the child indissociably) connected with the external regularities. From its earliest months the child is therefore bathed in an atmosphere of rules, so that the task of discerning what comes from itself in the rites that it respects and what results from the pressure of things or the constraint of the social environment is one of extreme difficulty. In the content of each ritual act it is certainly possible to know what has been invented by the child, what discovered in nature, and what imposed by the adult. But in the consciousness of rules, taken as a formal structure, these differentiations are non-existent from the point of view of the subject himself.[19]

An analysis of the rites practised by older children, however, will allow us to introduce a fundamental distinction at this point. On the one hand, certain forms of behaviour are, as it were, ritualized by the child himself (*e.g.*, not to walk on the lines that separate the paving stones from the kerb of the pavement). Now, so long as no other factor intervenes, these motor rules never give rise to the feeling of obligation proper. (This is true even of the example we selected intentionally just now—that of a simple game which only becomes obligatory when it becomes connected later on with a pact, *i.e.*, with a social operation, for the pact with oneself is undoubtedly a derivative of the pact with others.) On the other hand, certain rules—it matters not whether they were previously invented by the child, imitated, or received from outside—are at a given moment sanctioned by the environment, *i.e.*, approved of or enjoined. Only in such a case as this are rules accompanied by a feeling of obligation. Now, although it is always difficult to know to what extent an obligatory rule covers up in the mind of a child of one or two years a motor ritual, it is at any rate obvious that the two things are psy-

[19] *e.g.* Heat burns (physical law), it is forbidden to touch the fire (moral law) and the child playing about in the kitchen will amuse himself by touching every piece of furniture except the stove (individual ritual). How can the subject's mind distinguish at first between these three types of regularity?

chologically distinct. And this distinction should be borne in mind when we come to the study of the rules of the game.

The reader will recognize in the way in which we have stated the problem the striking thesis of M. Bovet on the genesis of the feeling of moral obligation in man's conscience: the feeling of obligation only appears when the child accepts a command emanating from someone whom he respects. All the material analysed in the present work, beginning with the facts relating to consciousness of the rules of the game, confirm this thesis, which is parallel rather than contradictory to Durkheim's doctrine of the social genesis of respect and morality. The only change we wish to effect in Bovet's theory is to extend it and to introduce alongside of the unilateral respect of the younger child for the grown-up, the mutual respect that is entertained among equals. Consequently, a collective rule will appear to us as much the product of the reciprocal approbation of two individuals as of the authority of one individual over another.

What then does consciousness of rules amount to during our first stage? In so far as the child has never seen anyone else play, we can allow that it is engaged here upon purely personal and individual ritual acts. The child, enjoying as it does any form of repetition, gives itself schemas of action, but there is nothing in this that implies an obligatory rule. At the same time, and this is where the analysis becomes so difficult, it is obvious that by the time a child can speak, even if it has never seen marbles before, it is already permeated with rules and regulations due to the environment, and this in the most varied spheres. It knows that some things are allowed and others forbidden. Even in the most modern form of training one cannot avoid imposing certain obligations with regard to sleeping, eating, and even in connection with certain details of no apparent importance (not to touch a pile of plates, daddy's desk, etc., etc.). It is therefore quite possible that when the child comes across marbles for the first time, it is already convinced that certain rules apply to these new objects. And this is why the origins of consciousness of rules even in so restricted a field as that of the game of marbles are conditioned by the child's moral life as a whole.

This becomes clear in the second stage, the most interesting for our thesis. This second stage sets in from the moment when the child, either through imitation or as the result of verbal exchange, begins to want to play in conformity with certain rules received from outside. What idea does he form of these rules? This is the point that we must now try to establish.

We made use of three groups of questions for the purpose of analysing the consciousness of rules in this second stage. Can rules be changed? Have rules always been the same as they are to-day? How did rules begin? Obviously the first of these questions is the best. It is the least verbal of the three. Instead of making the child think about a problem that has never occurred to him (as do the other two), it confronts the subject with a new fact, a rule invented by himself, and it is relatively easy to note the child's resulting reactions, however clumsy he may be in formulating them. The other two questions, on the contrary, incur all the objections that can be made against questioning pure and simple—the possibility of suggestion, of perseveration, etc. We are of opinion, nevertheless, that these questions have their use, if only as indices of the respect felt for rules and as complementary to the first.

Now, as soon as the second stage begins, i.e., from the moment that the child begins to imitate the rules of others, no matter how egocentric in practice his play may be, he regards the rules of the game as sacred and untouchable; he refuses to alter these rules and claims that any modification, even if accepted by general opinion, would be wrong.

Actually, it is not until about the age of 6 that this attitude appears quite clearly and explicitly. Children of 4-5 seem, therefore, to form an exception and to take rules rather casually, a feature which, if judged purely externally, recalls the liberalism of older children. In reality, we believe that this analogy is superficial, and that little children, even when they seem not to be so, are always conservative in the matter of rules. If they accept innovations that are proposed to them, it is because they do not realize that there was any innovation.

Let us begin by one of the more difficult cases, the difficulty being all the greater because the child is very young and consequently very much inclined to romance.

FAL (5) is at the second stage with regard to the practice of rules. "Long ago when people were beginning to build the town of Neuchâtel, did little children play at marbles the way you showed me?—*Yes.*—Always that way?—*Yes.*—How did you get to know the rules?—*When I was quite little my brother showed me. My Daddy showed my brother.*—And how did your daddy know?—*My Daddy just knew. No one told him.*—How did he know?—*No one showed him!*" "Am I older than your Daddy?—*No, you're young. My Daddy had been born when we came to Neuchâtel. My Daddy was born before me.*—Tell me some people older than your daddy.—*My grand-dad.*—Did he play marbles?—*Yes.*—Then he played before your daddy?—*Yes, but not with rules!* [said with great conviction].—What do you mean by rules?— . . . [Fal does not know this word, which he has just heard from our lips for the first time. But he realizes that it means an essential property of the game of marbles; that is why he asserts so emphatically that his grand-dad did not play with rules so as to show how superior his daddy is to everyone else in the world.]—Was it a long time ago when people played for the first time?—*Oh, yes.*—How did they find out how to play?—*Well, they took some marbles, and then they made a square, and then they put the marbles inside it . . . etc.* [he enumerates the rules that he knows].—Was it little children who found out or grown-up gentlemen?—*Grown-up gentlemen.*—Tell me who was born first, your daddy or your grand-dad?—*My Daddy was born before my grand-dad.*—Who invented the game of marbles?—*My Daddy did.*—Who is the oldest person in Neuchâtel?—*I dunno.*—Who do you think? —*God.*—Did people know how to play marbles before your daddy?—*Other gentlemen played* [before? at the same time?]. —In the same way as your daddy?—*Yes.*—How did they know how to?—*They made it up.*—Where is God?—*In the sky.*—Is he older than your daddy?—*Not so old.*" "Could one find a new way of playing?—*I can't play any other way.* —Try . . . [Fal does not move]. Couldn't you put them like this [we place the marbles in a circle without a square]?— *Oh, yes.*—Would it be fair?—*Oh, yes.*—As fair as the square? —*Yes.*—Did your daddy use to play that way or not?—*Oh, yes.*—Could one play still other ways?—*Oh, yes.*" We then arrange the marbles in the shape of a T, we put them on a matchbox, etc. Fal says he has never seen this done before, but that it is all quite fair and that you can change things as much as you like. Only his daddy knows all this!

Fal is typical of the cases we were discussing above. He is ready to change all the established rules. A circle, a T., anything will do just as well as the square. It looks, at first, as though Fal were not near those older children who, as we shall see, no longer believe in the sacred character of rules and adopt any convention so long as it is received by all. But in reality this is not the case. However great a romancer Fal may be, the text of which we have quoted the greater part seems to show that he has a great respect for rules. He attributes them to his father, which amounts to saying that he regards them as endowed with divine right. Fal's curious ideas about his father's age are worth noting in this connection; his daddy was born before his grand-dad, and is older than God! These remarks, which fully coincide with those collected by M. Bovet,[20] would seem to indicate that in attributing the rules to his father, Fal makes them more or less contemporaneous with what is for him the beginning of the world. Characteristic, too, is the manner in which the child conceives this invention of rules on the part of his father: this gentleman thought of them without having been told or shown anything, but other gentlemen may equally have thought of the same thing. This is not, in our opinion, mere psittacism. One should be careful, of course, not to read into these remarks more logic than they contain: they simply mean that rules are sacred and unchangeable because they partake of paternal authority. But this affective postulate can be translated into a sort of infantile theory of invention, and of the eternity of essences. To the child who attaches no precise meaning to the terms "before" and "after" and who measures time in terms of his immediate or deeper feelings, to invent means almost the same thing as to discover an eternal and pre-existing reality in oneself. Or to put it more simply, the child cannot differentiate as we do between the activity which con-

[20] P. Bovet, *The Child's Religion*, London, 1930.

sists in inventing something new and that which consists in remembering the past. (Hence the mixture of romancing and exact reproduction which characterizes his stories or his memory.) For the child, as for Plato, intellectual creation merges into reminiscence.[21] What, then, is the meaning of Fal's tolerance with regard to the new laws we suggested to him? Simply this, that confident of the unlimited wealth of rules in the game of marbles, he imagines, as soon as he is in possession of a new rule, that he has merely rediscovered a rule that was already in existence.

In order to understand the attitude of the children of the early part of the second stage—they all answer more or less like Fal—we must remember that up till the age of 6-7 the child has great difficulty in knowing what comes from himself and what from others in his own fund of knowledge. This comes primarily from his difficulty in retrospection (see *J. R.*, Chap. IV, § 1), and secondly from the lack of organization in memory itself. In this way the child is led to think that he has always known something which in fact he has only just learned. We have often had the experience of telling a child something which immediately afterwards he will imagine himself to have known for months. This indifference to distinctions of before and after, old and new, explains the inability of which we spoke just now to differentiate between invention and reminiscence. The child very often feels that what he makes up, even on the spur of the moment, expresses, in some way, an eternal truth. This being so, one cannot say that very young children have no respect for rules because they allow these to be changed; innovations are not real innovations to them.

Added to this there is a curious attitude which appears throughout the whole of the egocentric stage, and which may be compared to the mental states characteristic of inspiration. The child more or less pleases himself in his application of the rules. At the same time, Fal and others like him will allow any sort of change in the established usage. And yet they one and all insist upon the point that rules have always been the

---

[21] Cf. *C.W.*, p. 52, the case of Kauf (8; 8): this child believes that the stories she tells were written in her brain by God. *"Before I was born, he put them there."*

same as they are at present, and that they are due to adult authority, particularly the authority of the father. Is this contradictory? It is so only in appearance. If we call to mind the peculiar mentality of children of this age, for whom society is not so much a successful cooperation between equals as a feeling of continuous communion between the ego and the Word of the Elder or Adult, then the contradiction ceases. Just as the mystic can no longer dissociate his own wishes from the will of his God, so the little child cannot differentiate between the impulses of his personal fancy and the rules imposed on him from above.

Let us now pass on to the typical cases of this stage, *i.e.*, to children who out of respect to rules are hostile to any innovation whatsoever.

We must begin by quoting a child of 5½ years, LEH, whose reaction was among the most spontaneous that we had occasion to note. Leh was telling us about the rules of the game before we had questioned him about consciousness of rules. He had just begun to speak and was showing us how to play from the coche (which was about the only thing in the game that he knew) when the following dialogue took place. We asked Leh quite simply if everyone played from the coche or whether one could not (as is actually done) put the older ones at the coche and let the little ones play closer up. *"No, answered Leh, that wouldn't be fair.—Why not?—Because God would make the little boy's shot not reach the marbles and the big boy's shot would reach them."* In other words, divine justice is opposed to any change in the rules of marbles, and if one player, even a very young one were favored in any way, God Himself would prevent him from reaching the square.

PHA (5½): "Do people always play like that?—*Yes, always like that.*—Why?—*'Cos you couldn't play any other way.*—Couldn't you play like this [we arrange the marbles in a circle, then in a triangle]?—*Yes, but the others wouldn't want to.*—Why?—*'Cos squares is better.*—Why better?— . . ." We are less successful, however, with regard to the origins of the game: "Did your daddy play at marbles before you were born?—*No, never, because I wasn't there yet!*—But he was a child like you before you were born.—*I was there already when he was like me. He was bigger."* "When did people begin to play marbles?—*When the others began, I began too."* It would be impossible to outdo Pha in placing oneself at the centre of the universe, in time as well as in space! And yet Pha feels very strongly that rules stand above him: they cannot be changed.

GEO (6) tells us that the game of marbles began with *"people, with the Gentlemen of the Commune* [the Town Council whom he has probably heard mentioned in connection with road-mending and the police].—How was that?— *It came into the gentlemen's heads and they made some marbles.*—How did they know how to play?—*In their head. They taught people. Daddies show little boys how to.*—Can one play differently from how you showed me? Can you change the game?—*I think you can, but I don't know how* [Geo is alluding here to the variants already in existence].— Anyhow?—*No there are no games you play anyhow.*—Why? —*Because God didn't teach them* [the Town Council].—Try and change the game.—[Geo then invents an arrangement which he regards as quite new and which consists in making a big square with three rows of three marbles in each].—Is that one fair, like the other one?—*No, because there are only three lines of three.*—Could people always play that way and stop playing the old way?—*Yes, M'sieu.*—How did you find this game?—*In my head.*—Can we say, then, that the other games don't count and this is the one people must take?— *Yes, M'sieur. There's others too that the Gentlemen of the Commune know.*—Do they know this one that you have made up?—*Yes* [!].—But it was you who found it out. Did you find that game in your head?—*Yes.*—How?—*All of a sudden. God told it to me.*—You know, I have spoken to the gentlemen of the Commune, and I don't think they know your new game.—*Oh!* [Geo is very much taken aback].— But I know some children who don't know how to play yet. Which game shall I teach them, yours, or the other one?— *The one of the Gentlemen of the Commune.*—Why?—*Because it is prettier."* "Later on when you are a big man and have got moustaches perhaps there won't be many children left who play the game of the Gentlemen of the Commune. But there may be lots of boys who play at your game. Then which game will be fairest, yours, which will be played most, or the game of the Gentlemen of the Commune, which will be nearly forgotten?—*The game of the Gentlemen of the Commune.*"

The case of Geo comes as a beautiful confirmation of what we said in connection with Fal, viz., that for little children inventing a game comes to the same thing as finding in one's head a game that has already been anticipated and classified by the most competent authorities. Geo attributes the game he has invented to divine inspiration, and supposes it to be already known to the "Gentlemen of the Commune." As soon as we undeceive him he undervalues his own invention and refuses to regard it as right even if ratified by general usage.

MAR (6), whose behaviour in the practice of rules we have already examined in § 3, declares that in the time of his daddy and of Jesus, people played as they do now. He refuses to invent a new game. *"I've never invented games."* We then suggest a new game which consists of putting marbles on a box and making them fall off by hitting the box: "Can one play like this?—*Yes* [He does so, and seems to enjoy it].—Could this game ever become a fair game?—*No, because it's not the same.*" Another attempt calls forth the same reaction.

STOR (7) tells us that children played at marbles before Noah's ark: "How did they play?—*Like we played.*—How did it begin?—*They bought some marbles.*—But how did they learn?—*His daddy taught them.*" Stor invents a new game in the shape of a triangle. He admits that his friends would be glad to play at it, *"but not all of them. Not the big ones, the quite big ones.*—Why?—*Because it isn't a game for the big ones.*—Is it as fair a game as the one you showed me?—*No.* —Why?—*Because it isn't a square.*—And if everyone played that way, even the big ones, would it be fair?—*No.*—Why not?—*Because it isn't a square.*"

With regard to the practical application of rules all these children therefore belong to the stage of egocentrism. The result is clearly paradoxical. Here are children playing more or less as they choose; they are influenced, it is true, by a few examples that have been set before them and observe

roughly the general schema of the game; but they do so without troubling to obey in detail the rules they know or could
know with a little attention, and without attributing the least
importance to the most serious infringements of which they
may be guilty. Besides all this, each child plays for himself,
he pays no attention to his neighbour, does not seek to control
him and is not controlled by him, does not even try to beat
him—"to win" simply means to succeed in hitting the marbles
one has aimed at. And yet these same children harbour an almost mystical respect for rules: rules are eternal, due to the
authority of parents, of the Gentlemen of the Commune, and
even of an almighty God. It is forbidden to change them, and
even if the whole of general opinion supported such a change,
general opinion would be in the wrong: the unanimous consent of all the children would be powerless against the truth
of Tradition. As to any apparent changes, these are only
complementary additions to the initial Revelation: thus Geo
(the most primitive of the above cases, and therefore nearest
to those represented by Fal and so confirming what we said
about the latter) believes the rule invented by him to be
directly due to a divine inspiration analogous to the inspiration of which the Gentlemen of the Commune were the first
recipients.

In reality, however, this paradox is general in child behavior and constitutes, as we shall show towards the end of
the book, the most significant feature of the morality belonging to the egocentric stage. Childish egocentrism, far from
being asocial, always goes hand in hand with adult constraint. It is presocial only in relation to cooperation. In all
spheres, two types of social relations must be distinguished:
constraint and cooperation. The first implies an element of
unilateral respect, of authority and prestige; the second is
simply the intercourse between two individuals on an equal
footing. Now egocentrism is contradictory only to cooperation, for the latter alone is really able to socialize the individual. Constraint, on the other hand, is always the ally of
childish egocentrism. Indeed it is because the child cannot
establish a genuinely mutual contact with the adult that he
remains shut up in his own ego. The child is, on the one
hand, too apt to have the illusion of agreement where actually

he is only following his own fantasy; the adult, on the other, takes advantage of his situation instead of seeking equality. With regard to moral rules, the child submits more or less completely in intention to the rules laid down for him, but these, remaining, as it were, external to the subject's conscience, do not really transform his conduct. This is why the child looks upon rules as sacred though he does not really put them into practice.

As far as the game of marbles is concerned, there is therefore no contradiction between the egocentric practice of games and the mystical respect entertained for rules. This respect is the mark of a mentality fashioned, not by free cooperation between equals, but by adult constraint. When the child imitates the rules practised by his older companions he feels that he is submitting to an unalterable law, due, therefore, to his parents themselves. Thus the pressure exercised by older on younger children is assimilated here, as so often, to adult pressure. This action of the older children is still constraint, for cooperation can only arise between equals. Nor does the submission of the younger children to the rules of the older ones lead to any sort of cooperation in action; it simply produces a sort of mysticism, a diffused feeling of collective participation, which, as in the case of many mystics, fits in perfectly well with egocentrism. For we shall see eventually that cooperation between equals not only brings about a gradual change in the child's practical attitude, but that it also does away with the mystical feeling towards authority.

In the meantime let us examine the subjects of the final period of the present stage. We found only three stages with reward to consciousness of rules, whereas there seemed to be four with regard to the practice of the game. In other words, the cooperation that sets in from the age of 7-8 is not sufficient at first to repress the mystical attitude tŏ authority, and the last part of the present stage (in the consciousness of rules) really coincides with the first half of the cooperative stage (in the practice of the game).

BEN (10 yrs.), whose answers we have given with regard to the practice of rules (third stage) is still at the second stage from the point of view that is occupying us just now: "Can one invent new rules?—*Some boys do, so as to win more marbles, but it doesn't always come off. One chap* [quite recently, in his class] *thought of saying 'Deux Empans'* (two spans) *so as to get nearer* [actually this is a rule already known to the older boys]. *It didn't come off.*—And with the little ones?—*Yes, it came off all right with them.*—Invent a rule.—*I couldn't invent one straight away like that.*—Yes you could. I can see that you are cleverer than you make yourself out to be.—*Well, let's say that you're not caught when you are in the square.*—Good. Would that come off with the others?—*Oh, yes, they'd like to do that.*—Then people could play that way?—*Oh, no, because it would be cheating.*—But all your pals would like to, wouldn't they?—*Yes, they all would.*—Then why would it be cheating?—*Because I invented it: it isn't a rule! It's a wrong rule because it's outside of the rules. A fair rule is one that is in the game.*—How does one know if it is fair?—*The good players know it.*—And suppose the good players wanted to play with your rule?—*It wouldn't work. Besides they would say it was cheating.*—And if they all said that the rule was right, would it work?—*Oh, yes, it would. . . . But it's a wrong rule!*—But if they all said it was right how would anyone know that it was wrong?—*Because when you are in the square it's like a garden with a fence, you're shut in* [so that if the shooter stays inside the square, you are 'dished'].—And suppose we draw a square like this [we draw a square with a break in one of the sides like a fence broken by a door]?—*Some boys do that. But it isn't fair. It's just for fun for passing the time.*—Why?—*Because the square ought to be closed.*—But if some boys do it, is it fair or not?—*It's both fair and not fair.*—Why is it fair?— *It is fair for waiting* [for fun].—And why is it not fair?— *Because the square ought to be closed.*—When you are big, suppose everyone plays that way, will it be right or not?— *It will be right then because there will be new children who will learn the rule.*—And for you?—*It will be wrong.*—And what will it be 'really and truly'?—*It will really be wrong.*" Later on, however, Ben admits that his father and grandfather played differently from him, and that rules can therefore be changed by children. But this does not prevent him from sticking to the view that rules contain an intrinsic truth which is independent of usage.

Borderline cases like these are particularly interesting. Ben stands midway between the second and third stages. On the one hand, he has already learned, thanks to cooperation, the existence of possible variations in the use of rules, and he knows, therefore, that the actual rules are recent and have been made by children. But on the other hand, he believes in the absolute and intrinsic truth of rules. Does cooperation, then, impose upon this child a mystical attitude to law similar to the respect felt by little children for the commands given them by adults? Or is Ben's respect for the rules of the game inherited from the constraint that has not yet been eliminated by cooperation? The sequel will show that the latter interpretation is the right one. Older children cease to believe in the intrinsic value of rules, and they do so in the exact measure that they learn to put them into practice. Ben's attitude should therefore be regarded as a survival of the features due to constraint.

Generally speaking, it is a perfectly normal thing that in its beginnings cooperation—on the plane of action—should not immediately abolish the mental states created—on the plane of thought—by the complexus: egocentricity and constraint. Thought always lags behind action and cooperation has to be practised for a very long time before its consequences can be brought fully to light by reflective thought. This is a fresh example of the law of *prise de conscience* or conscious realization formulated by Claparède[22] and of the time-lag[23] or "shifting" which we have observed in so many other spheres (see *J. R.*, Chap. V, § 2 and *C. C.*, 2nd part). A phenomenon such as this is, moreover, well fitted to simplify the problem of egocentrism in general since it explains

[22] This term (Claparède's *prise de conscience*) simply means "coming into consciousness," and has nothing to do with intellectual formulation. [*Trans.*].

[23] This is the term that has been selected by the author for the French *décalage*, a somewhat more complex notion which in previous volumes, cf. *L.T.*, p. 208, ff., has been rendered as a process of "shifting." [*Trans.*].

why intellectual egocentrism is so much more stubborn than egocentrism in action.

§ 6. Consciousness of Rules. II. Third Stage

After the age of 10 on the average, *i.e.*, from the second half of the cooperative stage and during the whole of the stage when the rules are codified, consciousness of rules undergoes a complete transformation. Autonomy follows upon heteronomy: the rule of a game appears to the child no longer as an external law, sacred in so far as it has been laid down by adults; but as the outcome of a free decision and worthy of respect in the measure that it has enlisted mutual consent.

This change can be seen by three concordant symptoms. In the first place, the child allows a change in the rules so long as it enlists the votes of all. Anything is possible, so long as, and to the extent that you undertake to respect the new decisions. Thus democracy follows on theocracy and gerontocracy: there are no more crimes of opinion, but only breaches in procedure. All opinions are tolerated so long as their protagonists urge their acceptance by legal methods. Of course some opinions are more reasonable than others. Among the new rules that may be proposed, there are innovations worthy of acceptance because they will add to the interest of the game (pleasure in risks, art for art's sake, etc.). And there are new rules that are worthless because they give precedence to easy winning as against work and skill. But the child counts on the agreement among the players to eliminate these immoral innovations. He no longer relies, as do the littles ones, upon an all-wise tradition. He no longer thinks that everything has been arranged for the best in the past and that the only way of avoiding trouble is by religiously respecting the established order. He believes in the value of experiment in so far as it is sanctioned by collective opinion.

In the second place, the child ceases *ipso facto* to look upon rules as eternal and as having been handed down unchanged from one generation to another. Thirdly and finally, his ideas on the origin of the rules and of the game do not differ from ours: originally, marbles must simply have been rounded pebbles which children threw about to amuse themselves, and rules, far from having been imposed as such by adults, must have become gradually fixed on the initiative of the children themselves.

Here are examples:

Ross (11) belongs to the third stage in regard to the practise of rules. He claims that he often invents new rules with his playmates: *"We make them [up] sometimes. We go up to 200. We play about and then hit each other, and then he says to me: 'If you go up to 100 I'll give you a marble.'* Is this new rule fair like the old ones, or not?—*Perhaps it isn't quite fair, because it isn't very hard to take four marbles that way!*—If everyone does it, will it be a real rule, or not?—*If they do it often, it will become a real rule.*—Did your father play the way you showed me, or differently?—*Oh, I don't know. It may have been a different game. It changes. It still changes quite often.*—Have people been playing for long?—*At least fifty years.*—Did people play marbles in the days of the 'Old Swiss'?—*Oh, I don't think so.*—How did it begin?—*Some boys took some motor balls* (ball bearings) *and then they played. And after that there were marbles in shops.*—Why are there rules in the game of marbles?—*So as not to be always quarrelling you must have rules, and then play properly.*—How did these rules begin?—*Some boys came to an agreement amongst themselves and made them.*—Could you invent a new rule?—*Perhaps . . .* [he thinks] *you put three marbles together and you drop another from above on to the middle one.*—Could one play that way?—*Oh, yes.*—Is that a fair rule like the others?—*The chaps might say it wasn't very fair because it's luck. To be a good rule, it has to be skill.*—But if everyone played that way, would it be a fair rule or not?—*Oh, yes, you could play just as well with that rule as with the others."*

MALB (12) belongs to the fourth stage in the practice of rules: "Does everyone play the way you showed me?—*Yes.* —And did they play like that long ago?—*No.*—Why not?—*They used different words.*—And how about the rules?—*They didn't use them either, because my father told me he didn't play that way.*—But long ago did people play with the same rules?—*Not quite the same.*—How about the rule not hitting for one?—*I think that must have come later.*—Did they play marbles when your grandfather was little?—*Yes.* —Like they do now?—*Oh, no, different kinds of games.*— And at the time of the battle of Morat?—*No, I don't think they played then.*—How do you think the game of marbles began?—*At first, children looked for round pebbles.*—And the rules?—*I expect they played from the coche. Later on, boys wanted to play differently and they invented other rules.* —And how did the coche begin?—*I expect they had fun hitting the pebbles. And then they invented the coche.*—Could one change the rules?—*Yes.*—Could you?—*Yes, I could make up another game. We were playing at home one evening and we found out a new one* [he shows it to us].—Are these new rules as fair as the others?—*Yes.*—Which is the fairest, the game you showed me first or the one you invented?—*Both the same.*—If you show this new game to the little ones what will they do?—*Perhaps they will play at it.*— And if they forget the square game and only play this one, which will be the true game, the new one that will be better known, or the old one?—*The best known one will be the fairest."*

GROS (13 yrs. at the fourth stage in the practice of the rules) has shown us the rules as we saw above. "Did your father play that way when he was little?—*No, they had other rules. They didn't play with a square.*—And did the other boys of your father's time play with a square?—*There must have been one who knew, since we know it now.*—And how did that one know about the square?—*They thought they would see if it was nicer than the other game.*—How old was the boy who invented the square?—*I expect thirteen* [his own age].—Did the children of the Swiss who lived at the time of the battle of Morat play at marbles?—*They may have played with a hole, and then later on with a square.*—And in the time of David de Purry [a periwigged gentleman whose statue on one of the public squares of Neuchâtel is known to all]?—*I expect they had a bit of a lark too!*—Have rules changed since the square was invented?—*There may have been little changes.*—And do the rules still change?—*No. You always play the same way.*—Are you allowed to change the rules at all?—*Oh, yes. Some want to, and some don't. If the boys play that way* (changing something) *you have to play like they do.*—Do you think you could invent a new rule?—*Oh, yes . . .* [he thinks]; *you could play with your feet.*—Would it be fair?—*I don't know. It's just my idea.*—And if you showed it to the others would it work?—*It would work all right. Some other boys would want to try. Some wouldn't, by Jove! They would stick to the old rules. They'd think they'd have less of a chance with this new game.*—And if everyone played your way?—*Then it would be a rule like the others.*—Which is the fairest now, yours or the old one?—*The old one.*—Why?—*Because they can't cheat.* (Note this excellent justification of rules: the old rule is better than the innovation, not yet sanctioned by usage, because only the old rule has the force of a law and can thus prevent cheating.) And if nearly everyone played with their feet, then which would be fairest?—*If nearly everyone played with their feet, then that would be the fairest.*"—Finally we ask Gros, "Suppose there are two games, an easy one where you win often, and a difficult one where you win seldom, which would you like best?—*The most difficult. You end by winning that way.*"

VUA (13), whose answers about the practice of rules we have already examined (4th stage) tells us that his father and his grandfather played differently from him. "In the days of the 'Three Swiss' did boys play at marbles?—*No. They had to work at home. They played other games.*—Did they play marbles in the days of the battle of Morat?—*Perhaps, after the war.*—Who invented this game?—*Some kids. They saw their parents playing at bowls, and they thought they might do the same thing.*—Could other rules be invented?—*Yes* [he shows us one he has invented and which he calls 'the line' because the marbles are arranged in a row and not in a square].—Which is the real game, yours or the square?—*The square, because it is the one that is always used.*—Which do you like best, an easy game or a difficult one?—*The more difficult, because it is more interesting. The 'Troyat'* (a game that consists in heaping the balls into piles) *is not quite the real game. Some boys invented it. They wanted to win all the marbles.*" On this point Vua seems to be answering like a child of the preceding stage who will invoke the "real game" that conforms to tradition as against contemporary innovations. But Vua seems to us rather to be contrasting a demagogic procedure (the "Troyat," which by allowing too great a part to chance gives rise to illicit and immoral gains) with practices that are in keeping with the spirit of the game, whether they are ancient, like the square, or recent like his own game. The proof of this would seem to lie in the following remarks relating to his own playing: "Is the game you invented as fair as the square, or less fair?—*It is just as fair because the marbles are far apart* (therefore the game is difficult).—If in a few years' time everyone played your line game and only one or two boys played the square game, which would be the fairest, the line or the square?—*The line would be fairest.*"

BLAS (12, 4th stage in the practice of rules) thinks that the game of marbles must have begun round about 1500 at the time of the Reformation. *"Children invented the game. They made little balls with earth and water and then they amused themselves by rolling them about. They found it was rather fun making them hit, and then they had the idea of inventing a game, and they said that when you hit anyone else's marble with your own you could have the marble you hit. After that I expect they invented the square, so that you should have to make the marbles go out of the square. They invented the line, so that all the marbles should be at the same distance. They only invented it later. When cement was discovered, marbles were made like they are to-day. The marbles of earth weren't strong enough, so the children asked the manufacturers to make some in cement."* We ask Blas to make up a new rule, and this is what he thinks of. First there must be a competition, and whoever makes his marbles go furthest can play first. But the rule seems *"bad because you'd have to run too far back to fetch the marbles."* He then thinks of another which consists in playing in two squares one inside the other. "Would everyone want to play that way?—*Those who invented it would.*—Later on, if your game is played just as much as the square, which will be the fairest?—*Both the same."*

The psychological and educational interest of all this stands out very clearly. We are now definitely in the presence of a social reality that has rational and moral organization and is yet peculiar to childhood. Also we can actually put our finger upon the conjunction of cooperation and autonomy, which follows upon the conjunction of egocentrism and constraint.

Up to the present, rules have been imposed upon the younger children by the older ones. As such they had been assimilated by the former to the commands given by adults. They therefore appeared to the child as sacred and untouchable, the guarantee of their truth being precisely this immutability. Actually this conformity, like all conformity, remained external to the individual. In appearance docile, in his own eyes submissive and constantly imbued as it were with the spirit of the Elders or the Gods, the child could in actual fact achieve little more than a simulation of sociality, to say nothing of morality. External constraint does not destroy egocentrism. It covers and conceals when it does not actually strengthen it.

But from henceforward a rule is conceived as the free pronouncement of the actual individual minds themselves. It is no longer external and coercive: it can be modified and adapted to the tendencies of the group. It constitutes no revealed truth whose sacred character derives from its divine origin and historical permanence; it is something that is built up progressively and autonomously. But does this not make it cease to be a real rule? Is it perhaps not a mark of decadence rather than of progress in relation to the earlier stage? That is the problem. The facts, however, seem definitely to authorize the opposite conclusion: it is from the moment that it replaces the rule of constraint that the rule of cooperation becomes an effective moral law.

In the first place, one is struck by the synchronism between the appearance of this new type of consciousness of rules and a genuine observation of the rules. This third stage of rule consciousness appears towards the age of 10-11. And it is at this same age that the simple cooperation characteristic of the third stage in the practice of rules begins to be complicated by a desire for codification and complete application of the law. The two phenomena are therefore related to each other.

But is it the consciousness of autonomy that leads to the practical respect for the law, or does this respect for the law lead to the feeling of autonomy? These are simply two aspects of the same reality: when a rule ceases to be external to children and depends only on their free collective will, it becomes incorporated in the mind of each, and individual obedience is henceforth purely spontaneous. True, the difficulty reappears each time that the child, while still remaining faithful to a rule that favours him, is tempted to slur over some article of the law or some point of procedure that favours his opponent. But the peculiar function of cooperation is to lead the child to the practice of reciprocity, hence of moral universality and generosity in his relations with his playmates.

This last point introduces us to yet another sign of the bond between autonomy and true respect for the law. By modifying rules, *i.e.*, by becoming a sovereign and legislator in the democracy which towards the age of 10-11 follows upon the earlier gerontocracy, the child takes cognizance of the *raison d'être* of laws. A rule becomes the necessary condition for agreement. *"So as not to be always quarrelling,"* says Ross, *"you must have rules and then play properly* [=stick to them]." The fairest rule, Gros maintains, is that which unites the opinion of the players, *"because* [then] *they can't cheat."*

Thirdly, what shows most clearly that the autonomy achieved during this stage leads more surely to respect for rules than the heteronomy of the preceding stage is the truly political and democratic way in which children of 12-13 distinguish lawless whims from constitutional innovation. Everything is allowed, every individual proposition is, by rights, worthy of attention. There are no more breaches of opinion, in the sense that to desire to change the laws is no longer to sin against them. Only—and each of our subjects was perfectly clear on this point—no one has the right to introduce an innovation except by legal channels, *i.e.*, by previously persuading the other players and by submitting in advance to the verdict of the majority. There may therefore be breaches but they are of procedure only: procedure alone is obligatory, opinions can always be subjected to discussion.

Thus Gros tells us that if a change is proposed *"Some want to and some don't. If boys play that way* [allow an alteration] *you have to play like they do."* As Vua said in connection with the practice of rules (§ 4) *"sometimes people play differently. Then you ask each other what you want to do. . . . We scrap for a bit and then we fix things up."*

In short, law now emanates from the sovereign people and no longer from the tradition laid down by the Elders. And correlatively with this change, the respective values attaching to custom and the rights of reason come to be practically reversed.

In the past, custom had always prevailed over rights. Only, as in all cases where a human being is enslaved to a custom that is not part of his inner life, the child regarded this Custom imposed by his elders as a sort of Decalogue revealed by divine beings (*i.e.*, adults, including God, who is, according to Fal, the oldest gentleman in Neuchâtel after his own father). With the result that, in the eyes of a little child, no alteration of usage will dispense the individual from remaining faithful to the eternal law. Even if people forget the square game, says Ben, and adopt another, this new game *"will really be wrong."* The child therefore distinguishes between a rule that is true in itself and mere custom, present or future. And yet he is all the time enslaved to custom and not to any juridico-moral reason or reality distinct from this custom and superior to it. Nor indeed is this way of thinking very different from that of many conservative adults who delude themselves into thinking that they are assisting the triumph of eternal reason over present fashion, when they are really the slaves of past custom at the expense of the permanent laws of rational cooperation.

But from now on, by the mere fact of tying himself down to certain rules of discussion and collaboration, and thus cooperating with his neighbours in full reciprocity (without any false respect for tradition nor for the will of any one individual) the child will be enabled to dissociate custom from the rational ideal. For it is of the essence of cooperation as opposed to social constraint that, side by side with the body of provisional opinion which exists in fact, it also allows for an ideal of what is right functionally implied in the very mechanism of discussion and reciprocity. The constraint of tradition imposes opinions or customs, and there is an end of it. Co-operation imposes nothing except the actual methods of intellectual or moral interchange (Baldwin's[24] synnomic as op-posed to his syndoxic). Consequently we must distinguish alongside of the actual agreement that exists between minds, an ideal agreement defined by the more and more intensive application of the processes of mental interchange.[25] As far as our children are concerned, this simply means that in addi-tion to the rules agreed upon in a given group and at a given moment (constituted morality or rights in the sense in which M. Lalande speaks of "raison constituée")[26] the child has in mind a sort of ideal or spirit of the game which cannot be formulated in terms of rules (constitutive morality or rights in the sense of "raison constituante"). For if there is to be any reciprocity between players in the application of estab-lished rules or in the elaboration of new rules, everything must be eliminated that would compromise this reciprocity (inequalities due to chance, excessive individual differences in skill or muscular power, etc.). Thus usages are gradually purified in virtue of an ideal that is superior to custom since it arises from the very functioning of cooperation.

This is why, when innovations are proposed to the child, he regards them as fair or unfair not only according as they are likely or not to rally the majority of players in their favour, but also according as they are in keeping with that spirit of the game itself, which is nothing more or less than the spirit of reciprocity. Ross tells us, for instance, concern-ing his own proposition, *"Perhaps it isn't quite fair, because it isn't very hard to take four marbles that way,"* and again, *"The chaps might say it wasn't very fair because it's luck. To be a good rule, it has to be skill."* The Troyat, Vua in-forms us, is less fair than the square (though equally wide-spread and equally well known to former generations), because it was invented *"to win all the marbles."* In this way,

[24] J. M. Baldwin, *Genetic Theory of Reality.*
[25] See our article, "Logique génétique et sociologie," *Revue Philo-sophique,* 1928.
[26] Lalande, A., "Raison constituante et raison constituée," *Revue des Cours et des Conférence.*

Vua draws a distinction between demagogy and a sane democracy. In the same way, Gros and Vua prefer difficult games because they are more "interesting": cleverness and skill now matter more than winning. Art for art's sake is far more disinterested than playing for gain.

In a word, as soon as we have cooperation, the rational notions of the just and the unjust become regulative of custom, because they are implied in the actual functioning of social life among equals—a point which will be developed in the third chapter of this book. During the preceding stages, on the contrary, custom overbore the issue of right, precisely in so far as it was deified and remained external to the minds of individuals.

Let us now see what sort of philosophy of history the child will adopt in consequence of having discovered democracy. It is very interesting, in this connection, to note the following synchronism. The moment a child decides that rules can be changed, he ceases to believe in their endless past and in their adult origin. In other words, he regards rules as having constantly changed and as having been invented and modified by children themselves. External events may of course play a certain part in bringing this about. Sooner or later, for example, the child may learn from his father that the game was different for previous generations. But so unmistakable is the correlation (on the average, of course) between the appearance of this new type of consciousness of rules and the disappearance of the belief in the adult origin of the game that the connection must be founded on reality. Is it, then, the loss of belief in the divine or adult origin of rules that allows the child to think of innovations, or is it the consciousness of autonomy that dispels the myth of revelation?

Only someone completely ignorant of the character of childish beliefs could imagine that a change in the child's ideas about the origin of rules could be of a nature to exercise so profound an influence on his social conduct. On the contrary, here as in so many cases, belief merely reflects behaviour. There can be no doubt that children very rarely reflect upon the original institution of the game of marbles. There are even strong reasons for assuming that as far as the children we examined are concerned such a problem never even entered their heads until the day when a psychologist had the ridiculous idea of asking them how marbles were played in the days of the Old Swiss and of the Old Testament. Even if the question of the origin of rules did pass through the minds of some of these children during the spontaneous interrogatories that so often deal with rules in general (*L. T.*, Chap. V, §§ 5 and 10) the answer which the child would give himself would probably be found without very much reflection. In most cases the questions we asked were entirely new to the subject, and the answers were dictated by the feelings which the game had aroused in them in varying intensity. Thus, when the little ones tell us that rules have an adult origin and have never changed, one should beware of taking this as the expression of a systematic belief; all they mean is that the laws of the game must be left alone. And when, conversely, the older ones tell us that rules have varied and were invented by children, this belief is perhaps more thought out since it is held by more developed subjects, but it is still only valuable as an indication: the child simply means that he is free to make the law.

We may well ask ourselves, then, whether it is legitimate to question the child about such verbal beliefs, since these beliefs do not correspond to thought properly so called, and since the child's true thought lies much deeper, somewhere below the level of formulation. But in our opinion these beliefs have their interest because the same phenomena reappear in adult mental life and because the psychological facts lead by a series of intermediate steps to metaphysical systems themselves. What Pareto,[27] basing his relatively simple conclusions on such a wealth of erudition, has called "derivations" are really present in germ in our children's remarks about the origin of games. These remarks have no intellectual value, but they contain a very resistant, affective and social element— the "residuum" to quote Pareto again. To the residuum peculiar to the conforming attitude of the little ones correspond the derivations "divine or adult origin" and "permanence in

[27] *Traité de Sociologie générale.*

history." To the residuum peculiar to the more democratic attitude of the older children correspond the derivations "natural (childish) origin" and "progress."

One more fundamental question must still be discussed. How is it that democratic practice is so developed in the games of marbles played by boys of 11 to 13, whereas it is still so unfamiliar to the adult in many spheres of life? Of course it is easier to agree upon some subjects than on others, and feeling will not run so high on the subject of the rules of the "Square" as in an argument about the laws of property or the legitimacy of war. But apart from these questions (and after all, is it so obvious that social questions are more important to us than are the rules of a game to the child of 12?) there are others of greater psychological and sociological interest. For it must not be forgotten that the game of marbles is dropped towards the age of 14-15 at the latest. With regard to this game, therefore, children of 11-13 have no seniors. The following circumstance is important. Since they no longer have to endure the pressure of play-mates who impose their views by virtue of their prestige, the children whose reactions we have been studying are clearly able to become conscious of their autonomy much sooner than if the game of marbles lasted till the age of 18. In the same way, most of the phenomena which characterize adult societies would be quite other than they are if the average length of human life were appreciably different from what it is. Sociologists have tended to overlook this fact, though Auguste Comte pointed out that the pressure of one generation upon the other was the most important phenomenon of social life.

We shall have occasion to see, moreover, that towards the age of 11 the consciousness of autonomy appears in a large number of different spheres. Whether this is the repercussion of collective games on the whole moral life of the child is a question which will be taken up later.

§ 7. A GIRLS' GAME: "ÎLET CACHANT"

Before drawing any general conclusion from the facts set out above, it may be useful to see whether they are peculiar to the game of marbles as played by boys or whether similar examples cannot be found in different fields. For this purpose we studied, with the same method, but questioning only girls, a much simpler game than the game of marbles.

The most superficial observation is sufficient to show that in the main the legal sense is far less developed in little girls than in boys. We did not succeed in finding a single collective game played by girls in which there were as many rules and, above all, as fine and consistent an organization and codification of these rules as in the game of marbles examined above. A significant example in this connection is the game of "Marelle" (Engl., Hop-scotch) (also called "la Semaine" or "le Ciel") which consists in hopping on one leg and kicking a stone through various sections drawn on the ground representing the days of the week or anything else one likes. The few rules embodied in this game (not to put the other foot down, to make the pebble go into the right square with one kick, not to let the pebble stop on a boundary line, permission to rest in a special section called Heaven, etc.) show well enough how possible it would have been to complicate the game by constructing new rules on these initial data. Instead of which girls, though they are very fond of this game and play it much oftener than boys, have applied all their ingenuity in inventing new figures. For the game of Marelle exists in a multitude of forms; the sections drawn in chalk on the pavement succeed one another in a straight line, in parallel lines, in the shape of a spiral, a circle, an oval, of the pipe of a stove, etc. But each game in itself is very simple and never presents the splendid codification and complicated jurisprudence of the game of marbles. As to the game of marbles itself, the few little girls who take any interest in it seem more concerned with achieving dexterity at the game than with the legal structure of this social institution.

As the extremely polymorphous nature of the game of Marelle made any interrogatory on rule consciousness difficult, we decided to study a very simple game containing a minimum of rules and to try and find out up to what point girls look upon rules as obligatory. In this case, as in those already dealt with, what interests us of course is to see what types of obligation appear at different ages and whether the youngest children are those who are most hostile to any alteration in the social heritage. As the game is simple and only girls are questioned, the conditions before us are as different as possible from the boys' game of marbles. Such analogies as do eventually appear will therefore be all the more valuable.

The game of "îlet cachant" is one of the most primitive forms of the game of hide-and-seek. The little girl who is îlet (the derivation of the word seems to be "il est," as the expressions "îlet courant," "îlet cachant," etc., seem to suggest) remains at a spot called the "tauche" (= the place one touches) while the others hide. Once the signal has been given the girl who is "îlet" begins to look for the others who try to reach the "tauche" before being caught. Whoever is caught is "îlet" for the next game. The first to play "îlet" is selected according to the well-known ritual formula, "Une boule—deux boules—trois boules—roulent!" etc. The little girls call this "plunging." "The last to plunge is îlet."

The game being so simple, we shall not waste time by describing the stages during which it is learnt and the rules are put into practice. It will be sufficient to distinguish two stages—one before the age of 7 and one which extends from 6-7 years to 11-12.

During the first of these stages, which here again we can designate as the stage of *egocentrism*, the children take great pleasure in imitating the ordered doings of their elders, but in practice know nothing of their *raison d'être;* each plays essentially for himself, just for the fun of running about or hiding, and above all, so as to do the same as the others.

JACQUELINE (5; 7) is initiated into the game of "îlet" by an older friend (10 yrs.) who has immense prestige in her eyes, and she plays with this friend and with a few children of 8 to 12. As long as the game lasts (about three-quarters of an hour) she runs and hides with apparently the greatest enjoyment but without understanding the point of the "tauche." As soon as one of the children runs towards "home" crying *I've touched it,"* Jacqueline also runs to touch it ritually but without any relation to the other's conduct. She is quite happy playing her own little game on the fringe of the real game.

The following days she behaves in the same way. Several days later she plays for half an hour, alone with the friend who has initiated her. This is what she does: 1) she still does not understand why you touch or hit the "tauche" but goes on touching it as soon as her playmate does (which is quite senseless, since the other child touches home to escape from her); 2) while she is waiting for her playmate to hide, she cheats in all good faith (she looks round on the sly, pretending to cover her face with her hands, she askes me for information who am simply an onlooker, etc.); 3) she enjoys losing quite as much as winning, her sole aim being to do the same as her older friend, though all the time she is running and hiding and shouting entirely on her own.

The analogy strikes one at once between this and the behaviour of contemporary marble players: imitation of seniors mixed with egocentric play, no competition, no mutual control in the matter of rules. The child knows that there are rules and respects their external manifestation: thus Jacqueline insists upon touching the "home" ritually, because she feels that this is an obligatory rite in the serious performance of the game of "îlet." But this is far more participation in the life of the older children than an effort to cooperate with them. As for the application of rules, it allows for any amount of individual caprice (there is not even any consciousness of cheating) since the aim of the game is not yet social in the sense of ordered competition.

But after the age of 6-7 in the average the child changes in his attitude and begins to observe rules. What matters to him now is not so much to do what the older ones are doing, though still acting entirely for himself, as beating his partners by doing exactly the same thing as they. Hence the appearance of mutual control in the application of the law, together with an effective respect for obligations (not to cheat when one is "he," etc.). We shall call this the stage of *cooperation.*

The next point to settle is, what are the feelings which the little girls entertain towards rules? When we suggest some modification in the accepted usages, shall we meet with an opposition that increases as the child grows older, or shall we find that girls, like boys, gradually subordinate rules to mutual agreement and abandon the absolutely binding element in tradition?

The facts give unmistakable answer, though they point to a slight difference from what we observed in boys. Where the analogy is complete is that girls also begin by regarding the law as untouchable and innovations as illegitimate, and admit later on that rules become endowed with the force of law in so far as they are ratified by the collective will. On the other hand—and this rather complicated our interrogatory, in relation to what we know about boys—this change of orientation takes place on the average towards the age of 8, that is to say, it almost completely coincides with the inception of the cooperating stage. This early tolerance is clearly connected with the somewhat loosely knit character of the game of "îlet-cachant."

Roughly speaking, we can distinguish three stages. The first is contemporaneous with the beginnings of the game itself, with the first half, that is, of the egocentric stage. At this stage, the child seems ready to change all the rules and to show no inner respect for tradition and the example of its seniors. But, as we saw in the case of the game of marbles, this is so only in appearance, and the child accepts proposed modifications in so far as it believes them to correspond with earlier decrees. Thus Jacqueline touches the "home" in so far as she sees this rite practised by others, but if anyone neglects to carry out this duty, she is in no way scandalized, deeming that this too is among the things that "are done." There is no need to go over this period again, which in any case is a short one and very difficult to analyse for lack of any consistency in the children's answers.

During a second stage, extending on the average up to the end of the seventh year, the little girls we questioned showed themselves to be firmly attached to the prevailing usage. Also, like boys, they think that rules are of adult and quasi-divine origin.

MOL (6½): "Are there things you must do and things you

mustn't do in this game?—*Yes. The things you must do are the rules of the game.*—Could you invent a new rule?— . . . —Supposing you said that the third who plunged was 'he'?—*Yes.*—Would it be all right to play that way or not?—*It'd be all right.*—Is it a fair rule like the others?—*Less fair.*—Why? —*Because the last one has to be 'he.'*—And if everyone played that way, would it become a fair rule?—*No.*—Why?— *Because the game isn't like that.*—How did the rules begin?— . . . —How do you know how to play?—*I learn'd the first time. I didn't know how. We played with a little girl who told us.*—And how did the little girl know?—*She learn'd.*—And did your Mummy play when she was little?—*Yes. The school-teacher taught her.*—But how did it begin?—*People learn'd with the school-teacher.*—Who made up the rules, grown-ups or children?—*Grown-ups.*—And if a child invents a new rule, is that all right?—*No it isn't.*—Why not?—*Because they don't know how to.*"

AGE (7 yrs.) admits that the third child to be caught could be regarded as "he," but she refuses to recognize this new rule as fair. "Is it a real rule?—*Yes.*—Is it fair?—*No. Because that is not the way you play.*" (The conversation is resumed after break.) "Would that new rule be all right?—*No, because the first one who is caught has to be 'he.'*—Why?—*Because otherwise it wouldn't be fair.*—But if everyone played like that?—*It wouldn't do because the third mustn't be 'he'.*"

BON (7 yrs.) admits that her companions would be pleased with such an innovation, but this would be *"not fair.*—Why? —*Because it upsets the whole game, because it's wrong.*"

ROS (8½) invents a new rule: *"You might say that only one goes and hides and then the others would go and look for her.*—Would that be all right for playing?—*Yes.*—Is this new way fairer than the other way or less fair?—*Less fair.*— Why?—*Because you don't play with that one.*—But if everyone played that way?—*Then it would be just a little bit fair.* —Why a little bit?—*Because, after all, it is a little the same way.*—But it isn't quite fair?—*No.*—Why?— . . . —And if everyone agreed to play that way would it be the same, or would it not?—*It would be all right* (reluctantly).—Which is best, always to play the same way or to change?—*To change* (still reluctantly).—Why?—*Because that game is truer.*—

Which one?—*Not the one I made up.*—Then is it best to change it or to leave it as it is?—*Best to leave it.*" The game of "îlet cachant" has been invented by "*a Gentleman.*" "Has it been changed since then, or is it the same as when it was invented?—*Yes, it hasn't been changed.*—But if people want to, they can change it?—*Yes.*—Can children?—*Yes.*—If they invent something will it be more fair or less fair?—*Less fair.* —Why?—*Because it isn't the real game.*—What is the real game?—*The one the gentleman invented.*—Why?—*Because that is the one you always play.*"

Lil (8; 10): "How did the game begin the very first time of all?—*I think a lady invented it.*—Do you think the game has changed since then?—*People may have changed it.*—Who changed it, grown-ups or children?—*Grown-ups.*—But do you think children can change it?—*Yes, they can.*—Could you, for instance, if you wanted to?—*Oh, if I wanted to, yes.*— Would it do or would it not do?—*It would do just as well.*— Would your friends be pleased?—*They'd be just as pleased.* —Would it be as fair or less fair?—*Less fair.*—Fair in what way?—*I think the lady who invented it invented it better.*— Why?—*Because grown-ups are cleverer, because they have been at school longer than children.*"

These examples show that girls of this stage, while perhaps not quite so keen on conformity as boys, show a sufficient feeling for tradition to ensure respect for rules. We even come across the divine right of mothers to lay down the laws of "îlet cachant." Buc tells us at 6 years old that *"God taught them."*

But at the age of 8 a good half of the girls we questioned have changed their attitude and declare that the new rule is as good as the old, provided it is practicable and, above all, provided it rallies all the votes. It is on this point that the girls, more tolerant and more easily reconciled to innovations, struck us as being slightly different from the boys.

Bag (10; 4) is asked to judge a new rule suggested by one of her companions and which consists in not *"struggling"* when you are caught. "Is it just as fair or less fair?—*Just as fair.*—Is it a real rule or not?—*A real rule.*—What is a real rule?—*It's something you play at really and truly.*—But no one has played yet with the rule invented by your friend; is it real all the same, or not?—*It is real.*—Would it work?—*Yes.*—Would your friends be pleased or not?—*Not pleased, because they'd never want to be 'he'* (in that way).—And if they agreed about it, would it be fair or not?—*Yes.*"

CHO (9 yrs.): "Is this rule as real as the others?—*No.*—Why?—*Because you never play that way.*—Would it be all right to play that way?—*Yes.*—Would your friends like it?—*Yes.*—Is this new rule more fair or less fair than the other?—*Both the same.*—Which is the most real?—*Both the same.*—How did rules begin?—*Somebody invented them.*—Who?—*A child . . . There were some kids who were playing and the others did the same thing.*—Were the rules those children made fair?—*Yes.*—When is a rule fair?—*When it's all right for playing.*—When is it real?—*When it's all right for playing.*"

These reactions, which are characteristic of what we found in girls, are thus both like and unlike those of boys. They are alike in so far as cooperation between the players brings about the gradual diminution of rule mysticism: the rule is no longer an imperative coming from an adult and accepted without discussion, it is a means of agreement resulting from cooperation itself. But girls are less explicit about this agreement and this is our reason for suspecting them of being less concerned with legal elaborations. A rule is good so long as the game repays it.

Little girls are therefore extremely tolerant, and it never occurs to them to introduce a *distinguo* and to codify the possible cases or even the very conditions of agreement.

Is this difference due to the somewhat loosely-knit character of the game of "îlet cachant" or to the actual mentality of little girls? Both these suppositions probably amount to the same thing, since we noticed that all girls' games are marked by this polymorphism and tolerance. The question, moreover, does not interest us here, and it is not this contrast which we propose to study. All that needs to be emphasized from the point of view of the psychology of rules is that, in spite of these differences in the structure of the game and, apparently, in the players' mentality, we find the same process at work as in the evolution of the game of marble: first a mystical respect for the law, which is conceived as untouchable and of transcendental origin, then a cooperation that liberates the individuals from their practical egocentrism and introduces a new and more immanent conception of rules.

§ 8. CONCLUSIONS: I. MOTOR RULES AND THE TWO KINDS OF RESPECT

In order to pursue our analysis with any profit we shall have to draw from the material that has been presented above certain conclusions which will serve as guiding hypotheses in the chapters that are to follow. In other words, we shall try to find in the various stages we have examined certain evolutionary processes which are likely to reappear in our future enquiries.

Two prefatory questions confront us. The first has to do with differences of structure and differences of degree. Rules evolve as the child grows older; neither the practice nor the consciousness of rules is the same at six as it is at twelve. Is the difference one of nature or of degree? After having done our utmost to show that child thought differs from adult thought not only in degree but in its very nature, we confess that we no longer know precisely what is meant by these terms. From the methodological point of view their meaning is, of course, perfectly clear; they tell us to beware of facile analogies and to look for the less obvious differences before pointing to resemblances that will stand out of themselves. But how does the matter stand from the theoretical point of view? Psychologically, as M. Bergson has well shown, every difference of degree or quantity is also a difference of quality. Conversely, it is difficult to think of a difference in kind without the presence of at least some functional continuity, so that between two successive structures a succession of intermediate degrees could be found. For instance, after having tried to describe the child's mentality as distinct from the adult's we have found ourselves obliged to include it in our descriptions of the adult mind in so far as the adult still remains a child. This happens particularly in the case of moral psychology, since certain features of child morality always appear to be closely connected with a situation that from the first predominates in childhood (egocentrism, resulting from the inequality between the child and the adult surrounding which presses upon him) but which may recur in adult life, especially in the strictly conformist and gerontocratic societies designated as primitive. Conversely, in certain circumstances where he experiments in new types of conduct by cooperating with his equals, the child is already an adult. There is an adult in every child and a child in every adult. The difference in nature reduces itself to this. There exist in the child certain attitudes and beliefs which intellectual development will more and more tend to eliminate: there are others which will acquire more and more importance. The latter are not simply derived from the former but are partly antagonistic to them. The two sets of phenomena are to be met both in the child and in the adult, but one set predominates in the one, the other in the other. It is, we may say, simply a question of the proportions in which they are mixed; so long as we remember that every difference of proportion is also a difference of general quality, for the spirit is one and undivided.

Between the various types of rules which we shall give there will therefore be at once continuity and qualitative difference: continuity of function and difference of structure. This renders arbitrary any attempt to cut mental reality up into stages. The matter is further complicated by the "Law of conscious realization" and the resulting time-lag. The appearance of a new type of rule on the practical plane does not necessarily mean that this rule will come into the subject's consciousness, for each mental operation has to be relearnt on the different planes of action and of thought. There are therefore no inclusive stages which define the whole of a subject's mental life at a given point of his evolution; the stages should be thought of as the successive phases of regular processes recurring like a rhythm on the superposed planes of behavior and of consciousness. A given individual may, for example, have reached the stage of autonomy with regard to a certain group of rules, while his consciousness of these rules, together with the practice of certain more subtle rules, will still be coloured with heteronomy.[28] We cannot therefore speak of global or inclusive stages characterized as such by autonomy or heteronomy, but only of phases of heteronomy or autonomy which define a process that is repeated for each new set of rules or for each new plane of thought or reflection.

A second prefatory question faces us: that of society and the individual. We have sought to contrast the child and the civilized adult on the ground of their respective social attitudes. The baby (at the stage of motor intelligence) is asocial, the egocentric child is subject to external constrait but has little capacity for cooperation, the civilized adult of to-day presents the essential character of cooperation between differentiated personalities who regard each other as equals. There are therefore three types of behavior: motor behaviour, egocentric behaviour (with external constraint), and cooperation. And to these three types of social behaviour there correspond three types of rules: motor rules, rules due to unilateral respect, and rules due to mutual respect. But here again, one must beware of laying down the law: for things are motor, individual and social all at once. As we shall have occasion to show, rules of cooperation are in some respects the outcome of the rules of coercion and of the motor rules. On the other hand, coercion is applied during the first days of an infant's life, and the earliest social relations contain the germs of cooperation. Here again, it is not so much a question of these successive features themselves as of the proportions in which they are present. Moreover, the way in which conscious realization and the time-lag from one level to another come into play is a further bar to our arranging these phenomena in a strict sequence, as though they made a single appearance and then disappeared from the scene once and for all.

With these reservations in mind, let us then try to outline the processes which govern the evolution of the idea of rules. And if language and discursive thought which, according to

[28] A child of 10 will, for example, show signs of autonomy in his application of the rules of the game of marbles, but will give proof of heteronomy in the extent to which he is conscious of these rules and in his application of rules relating to lying and justice.

a famous metaphor, are necessarily cinematographic in character, tend to lay too much emphasis on discontinuity, let it be understood once and for all, that any over-sharp discontinuities are analytical devices and not objective results.

To continue, our enquiry into the nature of games would seem to reveal the existence of three types of rules, and the problem before us will be to determine the exact relations between them. There is the *motor rule*, due to preverbal motor intelligence and relatively independent of any social contact; the *coercive rule* due to unilateral respect; and the *rational rule* due to mutual respect. Let us examine these three rules in succession.

The motor rule. In its beginnings the motor rule merges into habit. During the first few months of an infant's life, its manner of taking the breast, of laying its head on the pillow, etc., becomes crystallized into imperative habits. This is why education must begin in the cradle. To accustom the infant to get out of its own difficulties or to calm it by rocking it may be to lay the foundations of a good or of a bad disposition. But not every habit will give rise to the knowledge of a rule. The habit must first be frustrated, and the ensuing conflict must lead to an active search for the habitual. Above all, the particular succession must be perceived as regular, *i.e.*, there must be judgment or consciousness of regularity (*Regelbewusstsein*). The motor rule is therefore the result of a feeling of repetition which arises out of ritualization of schemas of motor adaptation. The primitive rules of the game of marbles (throwing the marbles, heaping them, burying them, etc.) which we observed towards the age of 2-3 are nothing else. The behaviour in question starts from a desire for a form of exercise which takes account of the particular object that is being handled. The child begins by incorporating the marbles into one or the other of the schemas of assimilation already known to him, such as making a nest, hiding under earth, etc. Then he adapts these schemas to the nature of the object by preventing the marbles from rolling away by putting them in a hole, by throwing them, etc. This mixture of assimilation to earlier schemas and adaptation to the actual conditions of the situation is what defines motor intelligence. But—and this is where rules come into existence—as soon as a balance is established between adaptation and assimilation, the course of conduct adopted becomes crystallized and ritualized. New schemas are even established which the child looks for and retains with care, as though they were obligatory or charged with efficacy.

But is this early behaviour accompanied by consciousness of obligation or by a feeling of the necessity of the rule? We do not think so. Without the feeling of regularity which goes to the formation of any intelligence and already so clearly characterizes motor intelligence, the consciousness of obligation would no doubt never make its appearance. But there is more in this consciousness of obligation than a mere perception of regularity, there is a feeling of respect and authority which, as Durkheim and Bovet have clearly shown, could not come from the individual alone. One might even be tempted to say that rules only begin when this consciousness of obligation, *i.e.*, when the social element has made its appearance. But the material we have collected all goes to show that this obligatory and sacred character only marks an episode in the evolution of rules. After being unilateral, respect becomes mutual. In this way, the rule becomes rational, *i.e.*, it appears as the fruit of a mutual engagement. And what is this rational rule but the primitive motor rule freed from individual caprice and submitted to the control of reciprocity?

Let us therefore turn to the influence of inter-individual relations in the constitution of rules. In the first place, we repeat, the social element is to be found everywhere. From the hour of its birth certain regularities of conduct are imposed upon the infant by the adult, and, as we have shown elsewhere (*C.W.* and *C.C.*), every regularity observed in nature, every "law" appears to the child for a long time as both physical and moral. Even in connection with the pre-verbal stage, characterized as it is by the motor rule in all its purity, people have spoken of child "sociology." Thus Mme Ch. Bühler, in her interesting studies on the first year, has very accurately noted how much more interested a baby is in people than in things. Two considerations, however, forbid us to regard these facts as playing a very important part in the development of motor rules. In the first place, a baby, as Mme Bühler has acutely noted, is more interested in adults than in its contemporaries. Now, surely this shows either that an interest in what is big, powerful, and mysterious (to say nothing of the interest in food and physical comfort bound up with the person of the parents) still outweighs any social interest, or—what perhaps comes to the same thing—that inter-individual relations based on admiration and unilateral respect are stronger than relations based on cooperation. In either case, a baby of 10-12 months, which elaborates all sorts of ritual acts connected with the objects it handles, may be influenced indirectly by its feelings for the adult, but neither the baby nor anyone observing it could distinguish these influences from the rest of what constitutes its universe. But the same child at about two, once he is able to speak or to understand what is said to him, will be acutely conscious of the rules that are imposed upon him (sitting down to meals or going to bed when he would like to go on playing) and will distinguish them perfectly well from the motor rules or rituals which he has himself established in the course of his games. It is the increasing constraint exercised upon the child by those around him that we regard as the intervention of the social factor.

In the case of play rules, the discontinuity between this process and the purely motor processes is obvious. On a given occasion, the child meets with others, older than himself, who play marbles according to a code. Immediately he feels that he *ought* to play in the same way himself; immediately he assimilates the rules adopted in this way to the totality of commands which control his way of living. In other words, he immediately places the example of children older than himself on the same plane as the hundred and one other customs and obligations imposed by adults. This is not an explicit process of reasoning. The child of three or four is saturated with adult rules. His universe is dominated by the idea that things are as they ought to be, that everyone's actions conform to laws that are both physical and moral, in a word, that there is a Universal Order. The revelation of the rules of the game, of "the real game" as played by his seniors is immediately incorporated into this universe. A rule imitated in this way is felt from the first as something obligatory and sacred.

Only, the main result of our enquiry, and one which will receive repeated confirmation in the latter part of this book, is that the social factor is not just one thing. If there is relative discontinuity between the early motor activity and adult intervention, the discontinuity is no less marked between the unilateral respect which accompanies this intervention and the mutual respect which gradually comes into being later on. Once again, let there be no misunderstanding: the qualities in question are not more important than the proportions in which they are mixed. Between the unilateral respect of the little child who receives a command without even the possibility of disagreement and the mutual respect of two adolescents who exchange their points of view there is room for any number of intermediate stages. Constraint is never unadulterated, nor, therefore, is respect ever purely unilateral: the most submissive child has the feeling that he can, or could, argue that a mutual sympathy surrounds relationships that are most heavily charged with authority. And conversely, cooperation is never absolutely pure: in any discussion between equals, one of the disputants can always exert pressure on the other by making overt or hidden appeals to custom and authority. Cooperation, indeed, seems rather to be the limiting term, the ideal equilibrium to which all relations of constraint tend. As the child grows up, his relations with adults approximate to equality, and as communities develop, their group ideas leave more room for free discussion between individuals. Nevertheless, every time the proportion of constraint and cooperation is changed, mental states and conduct are marked by a correspondingly fresh quality, so that, however artificial the analysis may seem, it is necessary to distinguish these two processes as leading to different results.

Let us begin with *unilateral respect* and the *coercive rule* to which it leads. The outstanding fact here, and what differentiates this type of respect from its successor, is the close connection which we have noted between respect due to the constraint of older children or adults and the egocentric behaviour of the child between 3 and 7. Let us therefore examine this point afresh in order to establish its general significance.

The facts are, it will be remembered, as follows. On the

one hand, the child knows that there are rules, the "real rules," and that they must be obeyed because they are obligatory and sacred; but on the other hand, although the child vaguely takes note of the general scheme of these rules (making a square, aiming at the square, etc.) he still plays more or less as he did during the previous stage, *i.e.*, he plays more or less for himself, regardless of his partners, and takes more pleasure in his own movements than in the observance of the rules themselves, thus confusing his own wishes with universality.

The right interpretation of these facts calls for very close scrutiny, so easy is it to fall into mistakes in dealing with the problem of the socialization of the child. In the first place, let us remind the reader that the behaviour of children of 3 to 7 with regard to the game of marbles is comparable on all points to the behavior of children of the same age in regard to their conversations or to their social and intellectual life in general. But the egocentrism common to all these types of behaviour admits of at least two interpretations. Some people think—and in all our previous works we have claimed to be of their number—that egocentrism is presocial in the sense that it marks a transition between the individual and the social, between the motor and quasi-solipsistic stage of the baby and the stage of cooperation proper. However closely connected with unilateral respect egocentrism may be, this mixture of coercion and subjectivity which characterizes the stage lasting from 2 to 7 years does seem to us less social than cooperation (which is the one determining factor in the formation of the rational elements in ethics and in logic). Other thinkers, on the contrary, consider egocentric behaviour to be in no way presocial—the social element remaining identical with itself throughout all the various stages—but take it to be, as it were, parasocial behaviour, analogous to what occurs in the adult when private feeling obscures his objectivity or when he is left out of a conversation from which he is precluded by his incompetence or stupidity.[29] Thinkers belonging to this second group can see no essential

[29] See Blondel, "Le Langage et la Pensée chez l'enfant d'après un livre récent." *Revue Hist. Phil. Rel.* (Strasburg), Vol. IV (1924), p. 474 *et seq.*

difference between cooperation and coercion; hence their view that the social factor is a permanent element throughout the whole course of mental development.

The data with which the present discussion is concerned would seem to be of a nature to remove these ambiguities. Egocentrism is both presocial, in view of the eventual cooperation, and parasocial, or simply social, in relation to the constraint of which it constitutes the most direct effect.

To understand this we need only analyse the relations of the younger to the older children. Every observer has noted that the younger the child, the less sense he has of his own ego. From the intellectual point of view, he does not distinguish between external and internal, subjective and objective. From the point of view of action, he yields to every suggestion, and if he does oppose to other people's wills a certain negativism which has been called "the spirit of contradiction"[30] this only points to his real defencelessness against his surroundings. A strong personality can maintain itself without the help of this particular weapon. The adult and the older child have complete power over him. They impose their opinions and their wishes, and the child accepts them without knowing that he does so. Only—and this is the other side of the picture—as the child does not dissociate his ego from the environment, whether physical or social, he mixes into all his thoughts and all his actions, ideas and practices that are due to the intervention of his ego and which, just because he fails to recognize them as subjective, exercise a check upon his complete socialization. From the intellectual point of view, he mingles his own fantasies with accepted opinions, whence arise pseudo lies (or sincere lies), syncretism, and all the features of child thought. From the point of view of action, he interprets in his own fashion the examples he has adopted, whence the egocentric form of play we were examining above. The only way of avoiding these individual refractions would lie in true cooperation, such that both child and senior would each make allowance for his own individuality and for the realities that were held in common.

[30] See Mme Reynier, "L'Esprit de contradiction chez l'enfant," *La Nouvelle Education,* V. 1926, pp. 45-52.

But this presupposes minds that know themselves and can take up their positions in relation to each other. It therefore presupposes intellectual equality and reciprocity, both of them factors that are not brought about by unilateral respect as such.

Egocentrism in so far as it means confusion of the ego and the external world, and egocentrism in so far as it means lack of cooperation, constitute one and the same phenomenon. So long as the child does not dissociate his ego from the suggestions coming from the physical and from the social world, he cannot cooperate, for in order to cooperate one must be conscious of one's ego and situate it in relation to thought in general. And in order to become conscious of one's ego, it is necessary to liberate oneself from the thought and will of others. The coercion exercised by the adult or the older child is therefore inseparable from the unconscious egocentrism of the very young child.

If, now, we turn to children's societies below the age of 8, we shall constantly meet with phenomena of this order. No setting seems so favourable to the contagion and even the constraint of the older ones than these early societies; not a gesture of the little ones but has been, as it were, commanded or suggested to them. We have not here any autonomous individuals, any conscious minds that impose themselves in virtue of an inner law to which they themselves are subject. And yet there is far less unity, far less real cooperation than in a society of 12-year-olds. Egocentrism and imitation are one,[31] and the same applies later on to autonomy and cooperation. It is therefore no mere chance that nearly all little children assimilate the rules learned in these surroundings to the moral rules imposed by adults and by the parents themselves.

It is perhaps possible to go further and to connect egocentrism with the belief in the divine origin of institutions. Childish egocentrism is in its essence an inability to differentiate between the ego and the social environment. Now the result of this non-differentiation is that the mind is unwittingly dominated by its own tendencies, in so far as these are not

[31] See *L.T.*, p. 41.

diminished or rendered conscious by cooperation. But at the same time, all the opinions and commands that are adopted appear to be endowed with a transcendental origin. We have already (§ 5) drawn attention to the very significant difficulty experienced by very young children in distinguishing between what they have invented themselves and what has been imposed upon them from outside. The mind's content is felt both as very familiar and as superpersonal, permanent and in a sense revealed. Nothing is more characteristic of childhood memories than this complex sensation of gaining access to one's most intimate possessions and at the same time of being dominated by something greater than oneself which seems like a source of inspiration. There is little mysticism without an element of transcendence, and, conversely, there is no transcendence without a certain degree of egocentrism. It may be that the genesis of these experiences is to be sought in the unique situation of the very young child in relation to adults. The theory of the filial origin of the religious sense seems to us singularly convincing in this connection.

To return, however, to our analysis of the game of marbles, it is a highly significant fact that it is the younger and not the older children who believe in the adult origin of rules, although they are incapable of really putting them into practice. The belief here is analogous to that prevalent in conformist communities, whose laws and customs are always attributed to some transcendental will. And the explanation is always the same. So long as a practice is not submitted to conscious, autonomous elaboration and remains, as it were, external to the individual, this externality is symbolized as transcendence. Now in the case of the child, exteriority and egocentrism go hand in hand in so far as egocentrism is preserved by the constraint exercised from outside. If, therefore, the children of the earlier stages were those who showed the maximum respect for rules together with the most pronounced belief in their transcendental origin, this was not due to any fortuitous resemblance. The two features coexisted in virtue of an inner logic which is the logic of unilateral respect.

Let us now deal with *mutual respect* and *rational rules*. There is, in our opinion, the same relation between mutual respect and autonomy as between unilateral respect and egocentrism, provided the essential qualification be added, that mutual respect far more than unilateral respect, joins forces with the rationality already incipient in the motor stage, and therefore extends beyond the phase that is marked by the intervention of constraint and egocentrism.

We have, in connection with the actual facts examined, pointed to the obvious correlation between cooperation and the consciousness of autonomy. From the moment that children really begin to submit to rules and to apply them in a spirit of genuine cooperation, they acquire a new conception of these rules. Rules become something that can be changed if it is agreed that they should be, for the truth of a rule does not rest on tradition but on mutual agreement and reciprocity. How are these facts to be interpreted? In order to understand them, all we have to do is to take as our starting-point the functional equation uniting constraint and egocentrism and to take the first term of the equation through the successive values which link up constraint and cooperation. At the outset of this genetic progression, the child has no idea of his own ego; external constraint works upon him and he distorts its influence in terms of his subjectivity, but he does not distinguish the part played by his subjectivity from that played by the environmental pressure. Rules therefore seem to him external and of transcendental origin, although he actually fails to put them into practice. Now, in so far as constraint is replaced by cooperation, the child dissociates his ego from the thought of other people. For as the child grows up, the prestige of older children diminishes, he can discuss matters more and more as an equal and has increasing opportunities (beyond the scope of suggestion, obedience, or negativism) of freely contrasting his point of view with that of others. Henceforward, he will not only discover the boundaries that separate his self from the other person, but will learn to understand the other person and be understood by him. So that cooperation is really a factor in the creation of personality, if by personality we mean, not the unconscious self of childish egocentrism, nor the anarchical self of egoism in general, but the self that takes up its stand on the norms of reciprocity and objective discussion, and knows how to submit to these in order to make itself respected. Personality is thus the opposite of the ego[32] and this explains why the mutual respect felt by two personalities for each other is genuine respect and not to be confused with the mutual consent of two individual "selves" capable of joining forces for evil as well as for good. Cooperation being the source of personality, rules cease, in accordance with the same principle, to be external. They become both the constitutive factors of personality and its fruit, in accordance with the circular process so frequently emplified in the course of mental development. In this way autonomy succeeds heteronomy.

This analysis will have shown how new in quality are the results of mutual respect as compared with those that arose out of unilateral respect. And yet the former is the outcome of the latter. Mutual respect is, in a sense, the state of equilibrium towards which unilateral respect is tending when differences between child and adult, younger and older are becoming effaced; just as cooperation is the form of equilibrium to which constraint is tending in the same circumstances. In spite of this continuity in the facts it is necessary, nevertheless, to distinguish between the two kinds of respect, for their products differ as greatly as do autonomy and egocentrism.

It can even be maintained that mutual respect and cooperation are never completely realized. They are not only limiting terms, but ideals of equilibrium. Everywhere and always the quota of generally accepted rules and opinions weighs, however lightly, on the individual spirit, and it is only in theory that the child of 12-14 can submit all rules to a critical examination. Even the most rational of adults does not subject to his "moral experience" more than an infinitesimal proportion of the rules that hedge him round. Anxious though he was to escape from his "provisional morality," Descartes retained it to the end of his days.

But we are not concerned with the question as to whether cooperation is ever completely realized or whether it remains only a theoretical ideal. Psychologically, the same rule is a

[32] See Ramon Fernandez, *De la Personnalité,* Au Sans Pareil (Paris), 1928

completely different reality for the child of 7 who regards it as sacred and untouchable and for the child of 12 who, without interfering with it, regards it as valid only after it has been mutually agreed upon. The great difference between constraint and cooperation or between unilateral respect and mutual respect, is that the first imposes beliefs or rules that are ready made and to be accepted *en bloc,* while the second only suggests a method—a method of verification and reciprocal control in the intellectual field, of justification and discussion in the domain of morals. It matters little whether this method be applied immediately to all the rules imposed by the environment or only to one aspect of behaviour: once it has come into existence it has the right to be applied to everything.

This fundamental difference between constraint and cooperation (the one laying down ready-made rules, the other giving a method for the elaboration of rules) will supply us straight away with an answer to an objection which is bound to crop up in the course of our analysis of the products of mutual respect. Supposing, it will be said, that mutual respect does constitute the essential factor in the behaviour of children of 12-13 and over, how can we attribute to it a genuinely moral effect? It is easy enough to see that mutual consent is sufficient to explain the establishment of rules of the game, since the child is urged to play both by interest and by pleasure. But when we come to actual moral rules (not to lie, not to steal, etc.), why is it that mutual respect does not make the children come to some agreement on the subject of what adults consider to be wrong? Take a band of young ruffians whose collective activity consists in thieving and in playing practical jokes on honest folk; is not the mutual consent subsisting between its members comparable, psychologically, to the mutual respect that holds between marble players? Now, apart from the fact that there is honour among thieves, this difficulty can easily be disposed of. In the first place, a distinction should, as we have seen, be drawn between mutual consent in general and mutual respect. There may be mutual consent in vice, since nothing will prevent the anarchical tendencies of one individual from converging with those of another individual. Whereas the word "respect" implies (at least as regards mutual respect) admiration for a personality precisely in so far as this personality subjects itself to rules. Mutual respect would therefore seem to be possible only within what the individuals themselves regard as morality.

Moreover, as soon as cooperation comes into being (in the moral as well as in the intellectual field) one must distinguish between the method and its results, or, as a contemporary logician has so cogently put it, between "constitutive reason" (practical or theoretical) and "constituted reason." There are two kinds of rules, those that are constitutive and render possible the exercise of cooperation, and those that are constituted and are the result of this very exercise. We have already been led to make this distinction in connection with the rules of a game. The rules of the Square, of the Coche, etc., which are observed by children of 11-13 are "constituted" rules, due to mutual consent and capable of being altered by general opinion. The precedence given to justice as opposed to chance, on the other hand, of effort over easy gain are "constitutive" rules, for without this "spirit of the game" no cooperation would be possible. In the same way, so-called moral rules can, generally speaking, be divided into constituted rules dependent upon mutual consent, and constitutive rules or functional principles which render cooperation and reciprocity possible. But how can these constitutive rules be regarded as themselves the outcome of mutual respect since they are necessary to the latter's formation? The difficulty here is purely formal. Between mutual respect and the rules which condition it there exists a circular relation analogous to that which holds between organ and function. Since cooperation is a method, it is hard to see how it could come into being except by its own exercise. No amount of constraint could determine its emergence. If mutual respect does derive from unilateral respect, it does so by opposition.

We are faced, then, with three types of rules: the motor rule, the coercive rule founded on unilateral respect, and the rational rule (constituted or constitutive) due to mutual respect. We have outlined above the relation in which the last two types stand to each other. We have examined elsewhere how the first two succeed one another. It remains for us to show what are the relations of the rational rule to the motor rule.

Generally speaking, one can say that motor intelligence contains the germs of completed reason. But it gives promise of more than reason pure and simple. From the moral as from the intellectual point of view, the child is born neither good nor bad, but master of his destiny. Now, if there is intelligence in the schemas of motor adaptation, there is also the element of play. The intentionality peculiar to motor activity is not a search for truth but the pursuit of a result, whether objective or subjective; and to succeed is not to discover a truth.

The motor rule is therefore a sort of experimental legality or rational regularity, and at the same time a play ritual. It will take one or other of these two forms according to circumstances. Now, at the moment when language and imagination are added to movement, egocentrism directs the child's activity towards subjective satisfaction, while, at the same time, adult pressure imposes on his mind a system of realities which at first remains opaque and external. Constraint and egocentrism therefore interpose between motor intelligence and reason a complexus of realities which seem to interrupt the continuity of evolution. It is at this point that the motor rule is followed by the coercive rule, a crystallized social product which shows the sharpest contrast with the fragile tentative products of the initial motor intelligence, though, as we have seen, egocentric play continues in a sense the early gropings of the motor stage.

But as the element of constraint is gradually eliminated by cooperation, and the ego is dominated by the personality, the rational rule so constituted recaptures the advantages of the motor rule. The play of 11-year-old children is in some ways closer to the motor accommodation of the one-year-old child in all its richness and truly experimental qualities than to the play of 7-year-olds. The boy of eleven plans his strokes like a geometrician and an artist in movement, just as the baby acts as a mechanician in handling objects and as an experimenter in inventing its rules. At the age of 6 or 7, on the contrary, the child is apt to neglect this element of invention, and to confine himself to imitation and the preservation of rites. But the immense superiority of the eleven-year-old player over the one-year-old, a superiority perhaps acquired by passing through the intermediate stage, is that his motor creations are no longer at the mercy of individual fantasy. The eleven-year-old has re-discovered the schema of experimental legality and rational regularity practised by the baby. But the motor rule found by the baby tends constantly to degenerate into play ritual, whereas the eleven-year-old invents nothing without the collaboration of his equals. He is free to create, but on condition of submitting to the norms of reciprocity. The motor being and the social being are one. Harmony is achieved by the union of reason and nature, whereas moral constraint and unilateral respect oppose supernature to nature and mysticism to rational experiment.

The discussion of the game of marbles seems to have led us into rather deep waters. But in the eyes of children the history of the game of marbles has quite as much importance as the history of religion or of forms of government. It is a history, moreover, that is magnificently spontaneous; and it was therefore perhaps not entirely useless to seek to throw light on the child's judgment of moral value by a preliminary study of the social behaviour of children amongst themselves.

§ 9. CONCLUSIONS: II. RESPECT FOR THE GROUP OR RESPECT FOR PERSONS. SEARCH FOR A GUIDING HYPOTHESIS

Before pursuing our analysis any further, it will be well to consider the results we have so far obtained in the light of the two principal hypotheses that have been brought forward concerning the psychological nature of respect and moral laws. If we refuse to accept Kant's view of respect as inexplicable from the point of view of experience,[33] only two solutions remain. Either respect is directed to the group and results from the pressure exercised by the group upon the individual or else it is directed to individuals and is the outcome of the relations of individuals amongst themselves. The first of these theses is upheld by Durkheim, the second by M. Bovet. The moment has not yet come for us to discuss

[33] Kant, *Metaphysics of Ethics,* pp. 9-10 and 104-113.

these doctrines for their own sake, but at the same time we must, without anticipating our final critical examination, develop a working hypothesis that will take account of all possible points of view. This is all the more indispensable since the discrepancy between results obtained by these authors is chiefly due, as will be shown later on, to differences of method. Now, a method is just what we are looking for at present in order to enable us to pass from the study of the rules of games to the analysis of moral realities imposed upon the child by the adult. It is only from the point of view of the right method to adopt that we shall here shortly touch upon the vexed question of the individual and society.

One way of attacking the problem is to analyse and explain the rules objectively, taking account of their connection with social groups defined by their morphology. This is the method which Durkheim used, and no one would think of denying his contribution to the subject of the evolution of moral realities. The mere fact of individuals living in groups is sufficient to give rise to new features of obligation and regularity in their lives. The pressure of the group upon the individual would thus explain the appearance of this *sui generis* feeling which we call respect and which is the source of all religion and morality. For the group could not impose itself upon the individual without surrounding itself with a halo of sanctity and without arousing in the individual the feeling of moral obligation. A rule is therefore nothing but the condition for the existence of a social group; and if to the individual conscience rules seem to be charged with obligation, this is because communal life alters the very structure of consciousness by inculcating into it the feeling of respect.

It is a striking fact, in this connection, that even such ephemeral groupings as those formed by children's societies or created primarily for the purpose of play have their rules and that these rules command the respect of individual minds. It is also curious to note how stable these rules remain in their main features and in their spirit throughout successive generations, and to what degree of elaboration and stylization they attain.

But, as we have shown above, rules, although their content continues to be the same, do not remain identical throughout the child's social development from the point of view of the kind of respect connected with them.

For very young children, a rule is a sacred reality because it is traditional; for the older ones it depends upon mutual agreement. Heteronomy and autonomy are the two poles of this evolution. Does Durkheim's method enable us to explain these facts?

No one has felt more deeply than Durkheim nor submitted to a more searching analysis the development and disappearance of obligatory conformity. In societies of a segmented type conformity is at its maximum: each social unit is a closed system, all the individuals are identical with each other except in the matter of age, and tradition leans with its full weight on the spirit of each. But as a society increases in size and density the barriers between its clans are broken down, local conformities are wiped out as a result of this fusion, and individuals can escape from their own people's supervision. And above all, the division of labour which comes as the necessary result of this increasing density differentiates the individuals from one another psychologically and gives rise to individualism and to the formation of personalities in the true sense. Individual heteronomy and autonomy would thus seem to be in direct correlation with the morphology and the functioning of the group as a whole.

Now, does this analysis apply to our children's societies? In many respects, undoubtedly, it does. There is certainly a resemblance between segmented or mechanical solidarity and the societies formed by children of 5 to 8. As in the organized clan so in these groups, temporarily formed and isolated in relation to each other, the individual does not count. Social life and individual life are one. Suggestion and imitation are all-powerful. All individuals are alike except for differences of prestige and age. The traditional rule is coercive and conformity is demanded of all.

As to the gradual disappearance of conformity as the child grows older, this too we could explain by some of the factors defined by Durkheim. To the increasing size and density of social groups and to the ensuing liberation of the individual we can compare the fact that our children, as they grow older, take part in an ever-increasing number of local traditions.

The marble player of 10 or 12 will discover, for example, that there are other usages in existence besides those to which he is accustomed; he will make friends with children from other schools who will free him from his narrow conformity, and in this way a fusion will take place between clans which up till then had been more or less isolated. At the same time, the growing child detaches himself more and more from his family circle, and since at first he assimilates games to the duties laid down for him by adults, the more he escapes from family conformity, the greater change will his consciousness of rules undergo.

If, however, we are able to compare all these facts to the growth of societies in size and density, we can do so only from the point of view of the gradual diminution of the supervision exercised over individuals. In other words, the outstanding fact in the evolution of game rules is that the child is less and less dominated by the "older ones." There is little or no progressive division of labour among children; such differentiations as arise are psychological and not economic or political. If, therefore, children's societies do, in a sense, develop from the segmented to the more highly organized type, and if there is a correlative evolution from conformity to individualistic cooperation, or from heteronomy to autonomy, this process, though we may describe it in the objective terms of sociology, must be attributed first and foremost to the morphology and activity of the various age classes of the population.

In other words, the main factor in the obligatory conformity of very young children is nothing but respect for age —respect for older children, and, above all, respect for adults. And if, at a given moment, cooperation takes the place of constraint, or autonomy that of conformity, it is because the child, as he grows older, becomes progressively free from adult supervision. This came out very clearly in the game of marbles. Children of 11 to 13 have no others above them in this game, since it is one that is only played in the lower school. But apart from this, the boy begins at this age to feel himself more and more on the same level as adolescents and to free himself inwardly from adult constraint. As a result, his moral consciousness undergoes the alterations we have outlined above. There can be no doubt that this phenomenon is peculiar to our civilization and therefore falls under the Durkheimian scheme. In our societies the child of 13 escapes from the family circle and comes in contact with an ever-increasing number of social circles which widen his mental outlook. Whereas in so-called primitive communities, adolescence is the age of initiation, therefore of the strongest moral constraint, and the individual, as he grows older, becomes more and more dependent. But keeping in mind only our societies of children, we see that cooperation constitutes the most deep-lying social phenomenon, and that which has the surest psychological foundations. As soon as the individual escapes from the domination of age, he tends towards cooperation as the normal form of social equilibrium.

In short, if, putting other considerations aside for the moment, we seek only to find a working hypothesis, the methodological difficulty of Durkheimism seems to be the following with regard to the different kinds of respect. Durkheim argues as though differences from one age or from one generation to another were of no account. He assumes homogeneous individuals and tries to find out what repercussion different modes of grouping would have upon their minds. All that he gets at in this way is profoundly true, but it is incomplete. We have only to make the impossible supposition of a society where everyone would be of the same age, of a society formed by a single generation indefinitely prolonged, to realize the immense significance attaching to age relations and especially to the relations between adults and children. Would such a society ever have known anything of obligatory conformity? Would it be acquainted with religion or at any rate with the religions that taught transcendence? Would unilateral respect with all its repercussions upon the moral consciousness be observed in such a group as this? We only wish to ask these questions. Whichever way they are answered, there can be no doubt that cooperation and social constraint deserve to be far more sharply contrasted than they usually are, the latter being perhaps nothing more than the pressure of one generation upon the other, whereas the former constitutes the deepest and most important social relation that can go to the development of the norms of reason.

This influence exercised by age brings us to the second possible view of the psychology of rules, we mean that held by M. Bovet. Theoretically, and in his method, M. Bovet recognizes only individuals. Only, instead of becoming involved, as others have been in a barren discussion on the limits of what is social and what is individual, M. Bovet admits that respect, the feeling of obligation, and the making of rules presuppose the interaction of at least two individuals. On this point his method is parallel to Durkheim's and in no way opposed to it. For the real conflict lies between those who want to explain the moral consciousness by means of purely individual processes (habit, biological adaptation, etc.) and those who admit the necessity for an inter-individual factor. Once grant that two individuals at least must be taken into account if a moral reality is to develop, then it matters not whether you describe the facts objectively, as Durkheim did, or at least tried to do, or whether you describe them in terms of consciousness.[34] How, asks M. Bovet, does the sense of duty appear? Two conditions, he says, are necessary, and their conjunction sufficient. 1) The individual must receive a command from another individual; the obligatory rule is therefore psychologically different from the individual habit or from what we have called the motor rule. 2) The individual receiving the command must accept it, *i.e.*, must respect the person from whom it came. M. Bovet differs on this point from Kant, since he regards respect as a feeling directed to persons and not to the rule as such. It is not the obligatory character of the rule laid down by an individual that makes us respect this individual, it is the respect we feel for the individual that makes us regard as obligatory the rule that he lays down. The appearance of the sense of duty in a child thus admits of the simplest explanation, namely that he receives commands from older children (in play) and from adults (in life), and that he respects older children and parents.

It will be seen that our results completely confirm this view of the matter. Before the intervention of adults or of older

[34] See R. Lacombe's conclusive remarks, *La Méthode sociologique de Durkheim*. Also d' Essertier, *Psychologie et Sociologie*, Paris, Alcan, and many other contributions to the subject.

children there are in the child's conduct certain rules that we have called motor rules. But they are not imperative, they do not constitute duties but only spontaneous regularities of behaviour. From the moment, however, that the child has received from his parents a system of commands, rules and, in general, the world order itself seem to him to be morally necessary. In this way, as soon as the little child encounters the example of older children at marbles, he accepts these suggestions and regards the new rules discovered in this way as sacred and obligatory.

But the problem which faces us and which M. Bovet has himself clearly formulated and discussed is how this morality of duty will allow for the appearance of the morality of goodness.

The problem is two-fold. In the first place, the primitive consciousness of duty is essentially heteronomous, since duty is nothing more than the acceptance of commands received from without. How then, asks M. Bovet, will the child come to distinguish a "good" from a "bad" respect, and, after having accepted without distinction everything that was laid down for him by his environment, how will he learn to make his choice and to establish a hierarchy of values? In language which exactly recalls that in which Durkheim describes the effect of increasing social density on the minds of the individuals, M. Bovet points here to the effect of conflicting influences and even of contradictory commands: the child pulled in several directions at once is forced to appeal to his reason in order to bring unity into the moral material. Already we have autonomy, but since reason does not create new duties and can only choose from among the orders received, this autonomy is still only relative. In the second place, alongside of the sense of duty we must, according to M. Bovet, distinguish a sense of goodness, a consciousness of something attractive and not merely obligatory, a consciousness that is fully autonomous. In contrast to Durkheim who, while he fully recognized this dualism of duty and good nevertheless tried to trace them both to the same efficient cause, viz., pressure of the group, M. Bovet leaves the question open, and does so intentionally.

It is at this point, so it seems to us, that the part played by mutual respect comes in. Without going outside M. Bovet's fertile hypothesis, according to which all the moral sentiments are rooted in the respect felt by individuals for each other, we can, nevertheless, distinguish different types of respect. It seems to us an undeniable fact that in the course of the child's mental development, unilateral respect or the respect felt by the small for the great plays an essential part: it is what makes the child accept all the commands transmitted to him by his parents and is thus the great factor of continuity between different generations. But it seems to us no less undeniable, both in view of the results we have so far obtained and of the facts we shall examine in the rest of the book, that as the child grows in years the nature of his respect changes. In so far as individuals decide questions on an equal footing—no matter whether subjectively or objectively—the pressure they exercise upon each other becomes collateral. And the interventions of reason, so rightly noted by M. Bovet, for the purpose of explaining the autonomy now acquired by morality, are precisely the outcome of this progressive cooperation. Our earlier studies led us to the conclusion that the norms of reason, and in particular the important norm of reciprocity, the source of the logic of relations, can only develop in and through cooperation. Whether cooperation is an effect or a cause of reason, or both, reason requires cooperation in so far as being rational consists in "situating oneself" so as to submit the individual to the universal. Mutual respect therefore appears to us as the necessary condition of autonomy under its double aspect, intellectual and moral. From the intellectual point of view, it frees the child from the opinions that have been imposed upon him while it favours inner consistency and reciprocal control. From the moral point of view, it replaces the norms of authority by that norm immanent in action and in consciousness themselves, the norm of reciprocity in sympathy.

In short, whether one takes up the point of view of Durkheim or of M. Bovet, it is necessary, in order to grasp the situation, to take account of two groups of social and moral facts—constraint and unilateral respect on the one hand, cooperation and mutual respect on the other. Such is the guiding hypothesis which will serve us in the sequel and which will lead us in examining the moral judgments of children to dissociate from one another two systems of totally different origin. Whether we describe the facts in the terms of social morphology or from the point of view of consciousness (and the two languages are, we repeat, parallel and not contradictory) it is impossible to reduce the effects of cooperation to those of constraint and unilateral respect.

Chapter 2

Adult Constraint and Moral Realism[1]

WE HAVE HAD occasion to see during our analysis of the rules of a game that the child begins by regarding these rules not only as obligatory, but also as inviolable and requiring to be kept to literally. We also showed that this attitude was the result of the constraint exercised by the older children on the younger and of the pressure of adults themselves, rules being thus identified with duties properly so called.

It is this problem of unilateral or one-sided respect, or of the effects of moral constraint, that we shall now approach through a more direct study of the child's conception of his duties and of moral values in general. But the subject is vast; and we shall try to limit the range of enquiry as much as possible. We shall therefore confine ourselves to an aspect of the question which has perhaps received less attention than others—the moral judgment itself. We were able before to observe concurrently external and internal facts, to analyse both practice and consciousness of rules. But now, in view of the enormously greater technical difficulties which attend the study of the relations between children and adults, we shall have to limit ourselves to the consciousness of rules, and even to the most crystallized and least living part of this

[1] In collaboration with M. N. Maso.

consciousness—we mean what may be called the theoretical moral judgment as opposed to that which occurs in actual experience. But we are able to confine ourselves to this special problem because numerous works have already told us all about the child's practice of moral rules and the conflicts that take place in his mind. A particularly large amount of work has been done, for example, on the subject of lying. Research of this kind is therefore the equivalent to the descriptions we have given of the practice of rules in the sphere of play, and it is therefore quite natural that we should confine ourselves to the study of children's judgments on such matters, judgments about lying, about truthfulness, etc.

In thus comparing the moral judgments of the child with what we know of his behaviour in the corresponding spheres of action, we shall endeavour to show that, as we were led to conclude in the case of game rules, the earliest forms assumed by a child's sense of duty are essentially heteronomous forms. We shall return, in this connection, to our hypotheses concerning the relations of heteronomy and egocentrism. Heteronomy, as we saw, was in no way sufficient to produce a mental change, and constraint and egocentrism were good bedfellows. This is more or less the same result as we shall find in studying the effects of adult constraint. Finally, we saw that cooperation was necessary for the conquest of moral autonomy. Now, such a hypothesis can be proved only by a close analysis of the way in which moral rules are at a given moment assimilated and freely adopted by the child.

In this chapter we shall study primarily the effects of moral constraint, though we shall also establish some of the landmarks for the outline of cooperation which will be given later on. Now, moral constraint is closely akin to intellectual constraint, and the strictly literal character which the child tends to ascribe to rules received from without bears, as we shall see, a close resemblance to the attitudes he adopts with regard to language and the intellectual realities imposed upon him by the adult. We can make use of this analogy to fix our nomenclature and shall speak of *moral realism* to designate on the plane of judgments of value what corresponds to "nominal realism" and even verbalism or conceptual realism on the plane of theoretical reasoning. Not only this, but just as realism in general (in the sense in which we have used the word in our previous books, see *C.W.*, first part) results both from a confusion between subjective and objective (hence from egocentrism) and from the intellectual constraint of the adult, so also does moral realism result from the intersection of these two kinds of causes.

We shall therefore call moral realism the tendency which the child has to regard duty and the value attaching to it as self-subsistent and independent of the mind, as imposing itself regardless of the circumstances in which the individual may find himself.

Moral realism thus possesses at least three features. In the first place, duty, as viewed by moral realism, is essentially heteronomous. Any act that shows obedience to a rule or even to an adult, regardless of what he may command, is good; any act that does not conform to rules is bad. A rule is therefore not in any way something elaborated, or even judged and interpreted by the mind; it is given as such, ready made and external to the mind. It is also conceived of as revealed by the adult and imposed by him. The good, therefore, is rigidly defined by obedience.

In the second place, moral realism demands that the letter rather than the spirit of the law shall be observed. This feature derives from the first. Yet it would be possible to imagine an ethic of heteronomy based on the spirit of the rules and not on their most hard and fast contents. Such an attitude would already have ceased to be realist; it would tend towards rationality and inwardness. But at the very outset of the moral evolution of the child, adult constraint produces, on the contrary, a sort of literal realism of which we shall see many examples later on.

In the third place, moral realism induces an objective conception of responsibility. We can even use this as a criterion of realism, for such an attitude towards responsibility is easier to detect than the two that precede it. For since he takes rules literally and thinks of good only in terms of obedience, the child will at first evaluate acts not in accordance with the motive that has prompted them but in terms of their exact conformity with established rules. Hence this objective responsibility of which we shall see the clearest manifestations in the moral judgment of the child.

§ 1. THE METHOD

Before proceeding to the analysis of the facts, it will be as well to discuss in a few words the method we propose to adopt. The only good method in the study of moral facts is surely to observe as closely as possible the greatest possible number of individuals. Difficult children, whom parents and teachers send or ought to send up for psycho-therapeutic treatment, supply the richest material for analysis. In addition to this, education in the home constantly gives rise to the most perplexing problems. Now, the removal of these problems cannot always, unfortunately for the children, depend solely upon the "common sense" of the parents, and the educational technique necessary for their solution is, in some respects, the best instrument of analysis at the disposal of the psychologist. We shall therefore do our utmost in the sequel to give as valid only such results as do not contradict observation in family life.

Only, here again, as in the case of intellectual notions, while pure observation is the only sure method, it allows for the acquisition of no more than a small number of fragmentary facts. And we therefore consider that it must be completed by questioning children at school. We shall speak of these interrogatories now, whilst we may have to postpone until a later date the publication of the observations we have been able to make on our own children. If, however, questioning in the intellectual field is relatively easy, in spite of the many difficulties of method which it raises, in the moral sphere it can only be, as it were, about reality once removed. You can make a child reason about a problem of physics or logic. That brings you into contact, not indeed with spontaneous thought, but at least with thought in action. But you cannot make a child act in a laboratory in order to dissect his moral conduct. A moral problem presented to the child is far further removed from his moral practice than is an intellectual problem from his logical practice. It is only in the domain of games—if there—that the methods of the laboratory will enable us to analyse a reality in the making. As to the moral rules which the child receives from the adult, no direct investigation is to be thought of by interrogation. Let us therefore make the best of it and try to examine, not the act, but simply the judgment of moral value. In other words, let us analyse, not the child's actual decisions nor even his memory of his actions, but the way he evaluates a given piece of conduct.

Here, moreover, a fresh difficulty raises its head. We shall not be able to make the child realize concretely the types of behaviour that we submit to him for judgment, as we could in handing him a game of marbles or a mechanism of any sort. We shall only be able to describe them by means of a story, obviously a very indirect method. To ask a child to say what he thinks about actions that are merely told to him —can this have the least connection with child morality? On the one hand, it may be that what the child thinks about morality has no precise connection with what he does and feels in his concrete experience. Thus the interrogatory of children of 5 to 7 about marbles revealed the strangest discrepancy between actual practice of the rules and reflection about them. On the other hand, it may also be that what the child actually understands of the stories suggested to him bears no relation to what he would think if he were to witness these scenes himself.

We must not attempt to solve these difficulties of method by means of any *a priori* considerations. We wish only to draw attention to them and to the theoretical interest of the problems which they raise. For we are faced with purely general questions on the relations that hold between verbal judgment and the practical application of thought, whether intellectual or moral. It is quite true that research on intelligence is easier than on morality; but this holds only of the functioning of thought, not of its content. When, in order to get at this content, one is obliged, as we have been in the past, to question the child about his own beliefs, the problem is the same. The question may therefore be formulated as follows. Does verbal thought, *i.e.*, thought that works upon ideas evoked by language and not upon objects perceived in the course of action, does verbal thought consist in the conscious realization[2] (allowing of course for various systematic distortions) of truly spontaneous thought, or does it sustain with the latter no relations whatever? Be the answer what it may, this question is one of fundamental importance in human psychology. Is man merely a maker of phrases that have no relation to his real actions, or is the need to formulate part of his very being? The question strikes deep, and to solve it we must, amongst other things, study it in the child. In the child as in ourselves there is a layer of purely verbal thought superposed, as it were, over his active thought. It is not only during the interrogatories that he invents stories. He is telling them to himself all the time, and it is relatively easy to prove that the stories invented in psychological experiments are roughly analogous to those that arise spontaneously. (We were able to show, for example, that the results obtained by questioning the child on the various aspects of his conception of the world corresponded in the main with what was revealed by direct observation and by the analysis of "whys" in particular.) But the problem remains. In what relation does the verbal thought of the child stand to his active and concrete thought?

The problem is of special interest in the sphere of morality, and the difficulties of the method we are going to use must be subjected to systematic scrutiny. The object of this scrutiny will not be the justification or condemnation of our method (any method that leads to constant results is interesting, and only the meaning of the results is a matter for discussion) but to help towards a more definite statement of the problem of "moral theories."

To begin with the adult. There are, on the one hand, authors who deem it indispensable for the mind to codify its norms, or at any rate to reflect upon the nature of moral action. Such people therefore accept, with or without discussion, this postulate of an existing relation between moral reflection and moral practice—saying either that the latter springs from the former, or that reflection is the conscious realization of action or action coming into consciousness. There are, on the other hand, individuals whose personal con-

[2] See footnote on p. 64.

duct, incidentally, may be beyond criticism, but who do not believe in "morality." Kant and Durkheim are typical representatives of the first tendency, Pareto is the most typical of living authors of the second.[3] According to him, only actions exist, some of which are logical, others non-logical, *i.e.*, instinctive, or coloured with affectivity. Added to this and on a completely different plane there is a sort of rambling chatter, whose function is to reinforce action but whose contents may be devoid of any intelligible meaning. This chatter—multiform and arbitrary "derivations" founded on the affective residues of non-logical actions—this chatter is what constitutes our ethical theories!

The point, then, that we have to settle is whether the things that children say to us constitute, as compared to their real conduct, a conscious realization or a "derivation," reflection (in the etymological sense of the word) or psittacism. . . . We do not claim to have solved the problem completely. Only direct observation can settle it. But to enable us to give the casting vote to observation, we shall first have to find out what are the child's verbal ideas on morality. And this is why we consider our researches to be useful, whatever may be their ultimate result. Moreover, the study of rules which we undertook in the last chapter has already supplied us with the most precious indication. Broadly speaking, we found there to be in this domain a certain correspondence (not simple but yet quite definable) between children's judgments about rules and their practice of these same rules. Let us therefore carry our analysis of the problem a stage further.

What, in the first place, are the relations between judgment of value and the moral act itself? Here is a child who declares it to be perfectly legitimate to tell his father about his brother's misdeeds. Another child answers that even if the father asks, it is "horrid" [4] (Fr., *vilain*) to tell tales: it is

---

[3] *Traité de Sociologie Générale*, 2 Vol., Payot.
[4] While in most of the interrogatories we have translated *vilain* by "naughty," the reader should note that the English word has an exclusively authoritative ring which the French has not. Children can only be naughty in reference to grown-ups. Indeed, the word is so powerful a weapon in the hands of adult constraint in

better to "spin a yarn" (Fr. *dire des blagues*) than to let a brother be punished. The problem is to know whether in practice these two children would really have considered valid the two courses of action which they recommend verbally.

We must be on our guard here against a certain ambiguity. Some experimenters have tried to measure the moral value of a child by testing of his moral judgment. Mlle Descoeudres, for example, holds the view that a child who pronounces correctly on the values of actions he is told about, is, on the whole, better than one whose moral judgment is less acute.[5] This may be, but it is also conceivable that intelligence alone might suffice to sharpen the child's evaluation of conduct without necessarily inclining him to do good actions. In this case an intelligent scamp would perhaps give better answers than a slow-witted but really good-hearted little boy. Besides, how is the psychologist to classify the moral worth of children even by the ordinary common-sense standards? Such a classification, possible in extreme cases, would run the risk of inaccuracy in normal cases, which are precisely those where we want to know whether testing moral judgment will help us to know the child.

But apart from this question, which does not really interest us here, it may well be asked whether the judgment of value given by the child during an interrogatory is the same as he would give in practice, independently of the actual decision which he would take. A given child, for example, will tell us during the interrogation that the lie *a* is worse than the lie *b*. Now, whether he tells lies himself or not, whether, that is, he is or is not what he calls "good," we take the liberty to wonder whether, in action, he will still consider lie *a* worse than lie *b*. What we are after is not how the child puts his moral creed into practice (we saw in connection with the game of marbles that a mystical respect for rules can go hand in hand with a purely egocentric applica-

---

this country that its use in any verbal experiments made on English children would probably give appreciably different results from those based on the word *vilain*. [Trans.]

[5] A. Descoeudres, "Sur le Jugement moral," *L' Intermédiaire des Educateurs,* II, p. 54 (1914).

tion of them) but how he judges of good and evil in the performance of his own actions. It is from this point of view only that we set ourselves the problem of discovering whether the judgments of value given in the interrogatories do or do not correspond to the genuine evaluations of moral thought.

Now, it may be that there is correlation between verbal or theoretical judgment and the concrete evaluations that operate in action (independently of whether these evaluations are followed up by real decisions). We have often noted that in the intellectual field the child's verbal thinking consists of a progressive coming into consciousness, or conscious realization of schemas that have been built up by action. In such cases verbal thought simply lags behind concrete thought, since the former has to reconstruct symbolically and on a new plane operations that have already taken place on the preceding level. Old difficulties, which have been overcome on the plane of action will therefore reappear or merely survive on the verbal plane. There is a time-lag between the concrete phases and the verbal phases of one and the same process. It may therefore very well be that in the moral sphere there is simply a time-lag between the child's concrete evaluations and his theoretical judgment of value, the latter being an adequate and progressive conscious realization of the former. We shall meet with children who, for example, take no account of intentions in appraising actions on the verbal plane (objective responsibility), but who, when asked for personal experiences, show that they take full account of the intentions that come into play. It may be that in such cases the theoretical simply lags behind the practical moral judgment and shows in an adequate manner a stage that has been superseded on the plane of action.

But there may also be no connection whatever between the two. On this view, the child's moral theories would be mere chatter, unrelated to his concrete evaluations. Further —and the eventuality is still more important in the moral than in the intellectual sphere— it may be for the benefit of the adult rather than for his own use that the child gives his answers. Let there be no mistake on this point: it is quite certain that in the great majority of cases the child is perfectly sincere during the experiment. Only, he is quite likely to think that what is expected of him is a moral lecture rather that an original reflection. We have talked with children of 10, for example, who defended the moral value of "telling tales," but who made a *volte face* as soon as they saw we were not convinced. Thus their real thought was masked and hidden even from their own eyes by the momentary desire to pronounce moral precepts pleasing to the adult. True, only the older ones reacted in this way. But does not this show that the little ones do not dissociate their own thought from what they hear constantly being said by their parents and teachers? Is it not the case that the verbal thought of the child up to 10-11 is simply a repetition or a distortion of adult thought, bearing no relation to the real moral evaluations which the child practises in his own life?

To settle this point we can turn to what we learned in our enquiry into the game of marbles. On the one hand, we were able to see how the children put the rules into practice and how they evaluated their duties as players in the midst of the game itself. On the other hand, we succeeded in collecting on the subject of these same rules certain moral theories obviously made up on the spot and therefore grounded on purely theoretical moral judgments. Now there was, we repeat, between the action and the theory of the child a correspondence that was, if not simple, at least definable. To the egocentric practice of rules which goes hand in hand with a feeling of respect for elder or adult, there corresponds a theoretical judgment which turns a rule into something mystical and transcendental. In this first case, theoretical judgment does not correspond to action itself but to the judgments that accompany action. But this is quite natural, since egocentrism is unconscious, and only the respect to which the child believes that he is submitting himself is conscious. To the rational practice of rules, which goes hand in hand with mutual respect, there corresponds a theoretical judgment which attributes to rules a purely autonomous character. Thus in the sphere of play at least, theoretical judgment corresponds to practical judgment. This does not mean that theoretical judgment interprets the child's real action but that in the main it corresponds to the judgments pronounced by the child in the course of his action. We can at the most admit that verbal judgment lags behind effective judgment: the idea of autonomy appears in the child about a year later than cooperative behaviour and the practical consciousness of autonomy.

With regard to the domains we are now approaching (lying, justice, etc.) we may therefore advance the hypothesis that the verbal and theoretical judgment of the child corresponds, broadly speaking, with the concrete and practical judgments which the child may have made on the occasion of his own actions during the years preceding the interrogatory. There can be no doubt that verbal thought lags behind active thought, but it does not seem to us to be unrelated to the past stages of active thought. The future will show whether this hypothesis is too bold. In any case, verbal thought, whether moral or intellectual, deserves the closest study. Nor is it peculiar to the child. In the adult, as the work of Pareto sufficiently shows, it plays a considerable part in the mechanism of social life.

Finally, allowance must be made for the fact that the verbal evaluations made by our children are not of actions of which they have been authors or witnesses, but of stories which are told to them. The child's evaluation will therefore be, as it were, verbal to the second degree. The psychologist Fernald [6] has tried to obviate this disadvantage by the following device. He tells the children several stories and then simply asks them to classify them. Mlle Descoeudres, applying this method, submits, for example, five lies to children, who are then required to classify them in order of gravity. This, roughly, is also the procedure that we shall follow, though we shall of course not deny ourselves the right, once the classification has been made, to converse freely with the children so as to get at the reasons for their evaluations.

But the greatest caution must be exercised in order to avoid needless complications. For instance, it does not seem to us possible to tell the children more than two stories at a time. If the subject is confronted with a series, the classifi-

[6] Fernald, *American Journal of Insanity,* April 1912.

cation will call for an intellectual effort that has nothing to do with moral evaluation: he will forget three stories out of five, and will compare any two at random, which gives results of no particular interest. Further, after using the usual stories, we soon realized that their style placed them far beyond the child's complete comprehension. In psychology one must speak to children in their own language, otherwise the experiment resolves itself into a trial of intelligence or of verbal understanding.

But even when we have taken all these precautions, one problem still remains: if the child had witnessed the scenes we describe to him, would he judge them in the same manner? We think not. In real life the child is in the presence, not of isolated acts, but of personalities that attract or repel him as a global whole. He grasps people's intentions by direct intuition and cannot therefore abstract from them. He allows, more or less justly, for aggravating and attenuating circumstances. This is why the stories told by the children themselves often give rise to different evaluations from those suggested by the experimenter's stories. Only, we repeat it, it may simply be the case that the evaluations obtained from the stories that were told to them lag in time behind the direct evaluations of daily life.

In conclusion, the results of our method do not seem to us devoid of interest. For they are relatively constant and, above all, they evolve with a certain regularity according to age. All that we have said before about the criteria of good clinical interrogatories (*C.W.*, Introd.) applies here. And, in addition, it is our belief that in everyday life, as in the course of the interrogatory, the child must often be faced not only with concrete actions but also with accounts and verbal appraisals of actions. It is therefore important to know what is his attitude in such circumstances. In short, here as always, the way of really tackling the problem is not to accept and record the results of the experiment, but to know how to place them in regard to the child's real life taken as a whole. And this cannot be done at the outset of our enquiry into this most difficult field of research.

§ 2. OBJECTIVE RESPONSIBILITY. I. CLUMSINESS AND STEALING

We noted, in connection with the rules of a game, that the child seems to go through a stage when rules constitute an obligatory and untouchable reality. We must now see how far this moral realism goes, and in particular whether adult constraint, which is probably its cause, is sufficient to give rise to the phenomenon of objective responsibility. For all that we have been saying about the difficulties of interpretation in the study of the moral judgments of children need not put a stop to our enquiry in this matter. It is immaterial whether the objective responsibility of which we are about to give examples is connected with the whole of the child's life or only with the most external and verbal aspects of his moral thought. The problem still remains as to where this responsibility comes from and why it develops.

The questions put to the children on this point are those whose results we shall study first, but they were actually the last that we thought of. We began, by way of introduction, with the problem of judgments relating to telling lies. In making this analysis, of which we shall speak in the following sections, we immediately noticed that the younger children often measured the gravity of a lie not in terms of the motives which dictated it, but in terms of the falseness of its statements. It was in order to verify the existence and the generality of this tendency to objective responsibility that we devised the following questions.

The first set of questions deals with the consequences of clumsiness. Clumsiness plays, however unjustly, an enormously important part in a child's life, as he comes into conflict with his adult surrounding. At every moment, the child arouses the anger of those around him by breaking, soiling, or spoiling some object or other. Most of the time such anger is unjustifiable, but the child is naturally led to attach a meaning to it. On other occasions, his clumsiness is more or less due to carelessness or disobedience, and an idea of some mysterious and immanent justice comes to be grafted on to the emotions experienced at the time. We therefore tried to make the children compare the stories of two kinds of clumsiness, one, entirely fortuitous or even the result of a well-intentioned act, but involving considerable material damage, the other, negligible as regards the damage done but happening as the result of an ill-intentioned act.

Here are the stories:

I. A. A little boy who is called John is in his room. He is called to dinner. He goes into the dining room. But behind the door there was a chair, and on the chair there was a tray with fifteen cups on it. John couldn't have known that there was all this behind the door. He goes in, the door knocks against the tray, bang go the fifteen cups and they all get broken!

B. Once there was a little boy whose name was Henry. One day when his mother was out he tried to get some jam out of the cupboard. He climbed up on to a chair and stretched out his arm. But the jam was too high up and he couldn't reach it and have any. But while he was trying to get it he knocked over a cup. The cup fell down and broke.

II. A. There was a little boy called Julian. His father had gone out and Julian thought it would be fun to play with his father's ink-pot. First he played with the pen, and then he made a little blot on the table cloth.

B. A little boy who was called Augustus once noticed that his father's ink-pot was empty. One day that his father was away he thought of filling the ink-pot so as to help his father, and so that he should find it full when he came home. But while he was opening the ink-bottle he made a big blot on the table cloth.

III. A. There was once a little girl who was called Marie. She wanted to give her mother a nice surprise, and cut out a piece of sewing for her. But she didn't know how to use the scissors properly and cut a big hole in her dress.

B. A little girl called Margaret went and took her mother's scissors one day that her mother was out. She played with them for a bit. Then as she didn't know how to use them properly she made a little hole in her dress.

When we have analysed the answers obtained by means of these pairs of stories, we shall study two problems relating to stealing. As our aim is for the moment to find out whether the child pays more attention to motive or to material results, we have confined ourselves to the comparison of selfishly motivated acts of stealing with those that are well-intentioned.

IV. A. Alfred meets a little friend of his who is very poor. This friend tells him that he has had no dinner that day because there was nothing to eat in his home. Then Alfred goes into a baker's shop, and as he has no money, he waits till the baker's back is turned and steals a roll. Then he runs out and gives the roll to his friend.

B. Henriette goes into a shop. She sees a pretty piece of ribbon on a table and thinks to herself that it would look very nice on her dress. So while the shop lady's back is turned (while the shop lady is not looking), she steals the ribbon and runs away at once.

V. A. Albertine had a little friend who kept a bird in a cage. Albertine thought the bird was very unhappy, and she was always asking her friend to let him out. But the friend wouldn't. So one day when her friend wasn't there, Albertine went and stole the bird. She let it fly away and hid the cage in the attic so that the bird should never be shut up in it again.

B. Juliet stole some sweeties from her mother one day that her mother was not there, and she hid and ate them up.

About each of these pairs of stories we ask two questions: 1) Are these children equally guilty (or as the young Genevese say "la même chose vilain" [7])? 2) Which of the two is the naughtiest, and why? It goes without saying that each of these questions is the occasion for a conversation more or less elaborate according to the child's reaction. It is also as well to make the subjects repeat the stories before questioning them. The way the child reproduces the story is enough to show whether he has understood it.

We obtained the following result. Up to the age of 10, two types of answer exist side by side. In one type actions are evaluated in terms of the material result and independently

[7] See footnote, p. 115.

of motives; according to the other type of answer motives alone are what counts. It may even happen that one and the same child judges sometimes one way, sometimes the other. Besides, some stories point more definitely to objective responsibility than others. In detail, therefore, the material cannot be said to embody stages properly so called. Broadly speaking, however, it cannot be denied that the notion of objective responsibility diminishes as the child grows older. We did not come across a single definite case of it after the age of 10. In addition, by placing the answers obtained under 10 into two groups defined respectively by objective and by subjective responsibility (reckoning by answers given to each story and not by children, since each child is apt to vary from one story to another) we obtained 7 as the average age for objective responsibility, and 9 as the average age for subjective responsibility. Now, we were unable to question children under 6 with any profit because of the intellectual difficulties of comparison. The average of 7 years therefore represents the youngest of the children. If the two attitudes simply represented individual types or types of family education, the two age averages ought to coincide. But since this is not so, there must be some degree of development present. We can at least venture to submit that even if the objective and the subjective conceptions of responsibility are not, properly speaking, features of two successive stages, they do at least define two distinct processes, one of which on the average precedes the other in the moral development of the child, although the two partially synchronize.

Having made this point clear, let us now turn to the facts, beginning with the stories about clumsiness. Here are typical answers showing a purely objective notion of responsibility.

I. STORIES OF THE BROKEN CUPS

GEO (6): "Have you understood these stories?—*Yes.*— What did the first boy do?—*He broke eleven cups.*—And the second one?—*He broke a cup by moving roughly.*—Why did the first one break the cups?—*Because the door knocked them.*—And the second?—*He was clumsy. When he was getting the jam the cup fell down.*—Is one of the boys naughtier than the other?—*The first is because he knocked over twelve cups.*—If you were the daddy, which one would you punish most?—*The one who broke twelve cups.*—Why did he break them?—*The door shut too hard and knocked them. He didn't do it on purpose.*—And why did the other boy break a cup?—*He wanted to get the jam. He moved too far. The cup got broken.*—Why did he want to get the jam? —*Because he was all alone. Because his mother wasn't there.* —Have you got a brother?—*No, a little sister.*—Well, if it was you who had broken the twelve cups when you went into the room and your little sister who had broken one cup while she was trying to get the jam, which of you would be punished most severely?—*Me, because I broke more than one cup."*

Schma (6): "Have you understood the stories? Let's hear you tell them.—*A little child was called in to dinner. There were fifteen plates on a tray. He didn't know. He opens the door and he breaks the fifteen plates.*—That's very good. And now the second story?—*There was a child. And then this child wanted to go and get some jam. He gets on to a chair, his arm catches on to a cup, and it gets broken.*—Are those children both naughty, or is one not so naughty as the other?—*Both just as naughty.* Would you punish them the same?—*No. The one who broke fifteen plates.*—And would you punish the other one more, or less?—*The first broke lots of things, the other one fewer.*—How would you punish them?—*The one who broke the fifteen cups: two slaps. The other one, one slap."*

Const (7) G.: "Tell me those two stories.—*There was a chair in the dining room with cups on it. A boy opens the door, and all the cups are broken.*—And now the other story? —*A little boys wants to take some jam. He tried to take hold of a cup and it broke.*—If you were their mother, which one would you punish most severely?—*The one who broke the cups.*—Is he the naughtiest?—*Yes.*—Why did he break them? —*Because he wanted to get into the room.*—And the other? —*Because he wanted to take the jam.*—Let's pretend that you are the mummy. You have two little girls. One of them breaks fifteen cups as she is coming into the dining room, the other breaks one cup as she is trying to get some jam while you are not there. Which of them would you punish most severely?—*The one who broke the fifteen cups."* But Const who is so decided about our stories goes on to tell us some personal reminiscences in which it is obviously subjective responsibility that is at work. "Have you ever broken anything?—*A cup.*—How?—*I wanted to wipe it, and I let it drop.*—What else have you broken?—*Another time, a plate.* —How?—*I took it to play with.*—Which was the naughtiest thing to do?—*The plate, because I oughtn't to have taken it.* —And how about the cup?—*That was less naughty because I wanted to wipe it.*—Which were you punished most for, for the cup or for the plate?—*For the plate.* Listen, I am going to tell you two more stories. A little girl was wiping the cups. She was putting them away, wiping them with the cloth, and she broke five cups. Another little girl is playing with some plates. She breaks a plate. Which of them is the naughtiest? —*The one who broke the five cups."* This shows that in the case of her own personal recollections (where, incidentally, the number of objects broken does not come in) subjective responsibility alone is taken into account. As soon as we go back to the stories, even basing them on the child's recollections, objective responsibility reappears in all its purity!

II. THE STORIES OF THE INK-STAINS

CONST (7) G., whose answers we have just been examining repeats correctly the story of the blot of ink: *"A little boy sees that his father's ink-pot is empty. He takes the ink-bottle, but he is clumsy and makes a big blot.*—And the other one?—*There was a boy who was always touching things. He takes the ink and makes a little blot.*—Are they both equally naughty or not?—*No.*—Which is the most naughty?—*The one who made the big blot.*—Why?—*Because it was big.*—Why did he make a big blot?—*To be helpful.*—And why did the other one make a little blot?—*Because he was always touching things. He made a little blot.* —Then which of them is the naughtiest?—*The one who made a big blot."*

GEO (6) also understands the stories and knows that the two children's intentions were quite different. But he regards as the naughtiest *"the one who made the big blot.*—Why?— *Because that blot is bigger than the other one."*

III. THE STORY OF THE HOLES

GEO (6) is equally successful in understanding these two stories. *"The first wanted to help her mother and she made a big hole in her frock. The other one was playing and made a little hole.*—Is one of these little girls naughtier than the others?—*The one who wanted to help her mother a little is the naughtiest because she made a big hole. She got scolded."*

CONST (7) G. repeats the stories as follows: *"A little girl wanted to make a handkerchief for her mother. She was clumsy, and made a big hole in her frock.*—And the other one?—*There was a little girl who was always touching things. She took some scissors to play and made a little hole in her frock.*—Which of them is naughtiest?—*The one who made the big hole.*—Why did she make this hole?—*She wanted to give her mother a surprise.*—That's right. And the other one? —*She took the scissors because she was always touching things and made a little hole.*—That's right. Then which of the little girls was nicest?—. . . (hesitation).—Say what you think.—*The one who made the little hole is the nicest.*—If you were the mother you would have seen everything they did. Which would you have punished most?—*The one who made a big hole.*—And which one would you have punished least?—*The one who made the little hole.*—And what would the one who made the big hole say when you punished her most?—*She would say, I wanted to give a surprise.*—And the other one?—*She was playing.*—Which one ought to be punished most?—*The one who made the big hole.*—Let's pretend that it was you who made the big hole so as to give your mother a surprise. Your sister is playing and makes the little hole. Which ought to be punished most?—*Me.*—Are you quite sure, or not quite sure?—*Quite sure.*—Have you ever made holes?—*Never.*—Is what I am asking you quite easy?—*Yes.*—Are you quite sure you meant what you said? —*Yes."*

These answers reveal the strength of the resistance offered to the counter-suggestions we attempted to make, and they also show what store the children set by material results, in spite of the fact that they have perfectly well understood the story and consequently the intentions of its characters, and what little account they take of the intentions which have indirectly caused these material happenings.

Such facts as these taken by themselves of course prove nothing. Before speaking about objective responsibility, we must ask ourselves whether the child does not draw a distinction analogous to that which the adult makes in the case of ethics and of certain legal punishments. One can without any loss of honour be run in for having broken police regulations. One can be the object of a legal sentence devoid of any penal element (cf. Durkheim's restitutive and retributive punishment). In the same way, then, when a child pronounces a little girl to be "naughty" because she has made a big hole in her dress, although he knows that her intentions were not only innocent but admirable, does he not simply mean that she has damaged her parents materially and therefore deserves a purely legal punishment devoid of any moral significance?

The question arises in the same form in connection with stealing, as we shall see presently. But with regard to lying, since all question of material damage can be disregarded, we shall endeavour to prove that the child's judgments really do imply objective responsibility. An analogous conclusion may therefore be formulated concerning the present examples. Here preoccupation about material damage certainly outweighs any question of obedience or disobedience to rules. But this is a form of objective responsibility only in so far as the child fails to distinguish the element of civic responsibility, as it were, from the penal element. Now, on the verbal plane where we have taken up our stand it seems to us that this differentiation is one that hardly enters into the subject's mind. Responsibility is thus still held to be objective, even from the moral point of view.

Before carrying our analysis any further and in order to place the previous attitudes in their true perspective, let us examine the answers that contradict those which we have just dealt with and which relate to the same pairs of stories:

I. STORY OF THE BROKEN CUPS

Here, to begin with, is a rather exceptional case of a 6-year-old child. (Most of the children of 6 gave us answers which corresponded to the type of objective responsibility.)

SCHMA (6½, G., forward intellectually and looking more like a girl of 8) begins by telling us that the two boys of the story are *"equally naughty,"* and that they must be punished *"Both just the same."* "Well, I think one of them is naughtier than the other. Which one do you think?—*Both the same.* —Have you never broken anything?—*No, I never have. My brother has.*—What did he break?—*A cup and a pail.*— How?—*He wanted to fish. He broke half my pail, and then afterwards he broke it again on purpose to annoy me.*—Did he also break a cup?—*He had wiped it and was putting it on the edge of the table and it fell.*—What day was he naughtiest, the day he broke the pail or the day he broke the cup? —*The pail.*—Why?—*He broke my pail on purpose.*—And the cup?—*He didn't do that on purpose. He put it right on the edge and it broke.*—And in the stories I told you, which boy is naughtiest, the one who broke the fifteen cups or the one who broke one cup?—*The one who wanted to take the jam because he wanted to eat it."* Thus by appealing to her personal memories one sees that Schma can be led to judge according to subjective responsibility.

MOL (7): "Which is naughtiest?—*The second, the one who wanted to take the jam-pot, because he wanted to take something without asking.*—Did he catch it?—*No.*— Was he the naughtiest all the same?—*Yes.*—And the first?— *It wasn't his fault. He didn't do it on purpose."*

CORM (9): *"Well, the one who broke them as he was coming isn't naughty, 'cos he didn't know there was any cups. The other one wanted to take the jam and caught his arm on a cup.*—Which one is the naughtiest?—*The one who wanted to take the jam.*—How many cups did he break?— *One.*—And the other boy?—*Fifteen.*—Which one would you punish most?—*The boy who wanted to take the jam. He knew, he did it on purpose."*

GROS (9): "What did the first one do?—*He broke fifteen cups as he was opening a door.*—And the second one?— *He broke one cup as he was taking some jam.*—Which of these two silly things was naughtiest, do you think?—*The one where he tried to take hold of a cup was* [the silliest] *because the other boy didn't see* [that there were some cups behind the door]. *He saw what he was doing.*—How many

did he break?—*One cup.*—And the other one?—*Fifteen.*—
Then which one would you punish most?—*The one who
broke one cup.*—Why?—*He did it on purpose. If he hadn't
taken the jam, it wouldn't have happened.*"

Nuss (10): The naughtiest is "*the one who wanted to take
the jam.*—Does it make any difference the other one having
broken more cups?—*No, because the one who broke fifteen
cups didn't do it on purpose.*"

II. STORY OF THE INK-STAINS

Sci (6): "What did the first one do?—*He wanted to please
his daddy. He saw that the ink-pot was empty and thought
he would fill it. He made a big spot on his suit.*—And the
second one?—*He wanted to play with his daddy's ink, and
he made a little spot.*—Which is the naughtiest?—*The one
who played with the ink pot. He was playing with it. The
other wanted to be kind.*—Did the one who wanted to be
kind make a big spot or a little one?—*He made a big spot,
the other boy made a little one.*—Does it not matter the first
one having made a big spot?—*All the same, the other wanted
more to do something wrong. The one who made a little spot
wanted to do something more wrong than the other.*"

Gros (9): "*The one who wanted to be helpful, even if
the stain is bigger, mustn't be punished.*"

Nuss (10). The naughtiest is "*the one who made the little
stain, because the other one wanted to help.*"

III. THE STORY OF THE HOLES

Sci (6) repeats the stories as follows: "*The first one
wanted to give her mother a surprise. She pricked herself
and made a big hole in her frock. The second one liked
touching everything. She took the scissors and made a little
hole in her dress.*—Which one is naughtiest?—*The one who
wanted to take the scissors. She made a little hole in her
frock. She is the naughtiest.*—Which one would you punish
most, the one who made a little hole, or the other one?—
*Not the one who made a big hole; she wanted to give her
mother a surprise.*"

Corm (9). The naughtiest is "*the second. She oughtn't to
have taken the scissors to play with. The first one didn't do
it on purpose. You can't say that she was naughty.*"

These answers show what fine shades even some of the

youngest children we questioned could distinguish and how well able they were to take intentions into account. The hypothesis may therefore be advanced that evaluations based on material damage alone are the result of adult constraint refracted through childish respect far rather than a spontaneous manifestation of the child mind. Generally speaking, adults deal very harshly with clumsiness. In so far as parents fail to grasp the situation and lose their tempers in proportion to the amount of damage done, in so far will the child begin by adopting this way of looking at things and apply literally the rules thus imposed, even if they were only implicit. And in so far as the parents are just, and, above all, in so far as the growing child sets up his own feelings as against the adult's reactions, objective responsibility will diminish in importance.

With regard to stealing we also found two groups of answers, and here again, while both objective and subjective responsibility are to be found at all ages between 6 and 10, it is the latter that predominates as the child develops.

Here are examples of objective responsibility:

IV. THE STORY OF THE ROLL AND OF THE RIBBON

SCI (6) who showed signs of a subjective conception of responsibility in regard to clumsiness, changes his attitude here. He repeats the stories as follows: *"A boy was with his friend. He stole a roll and gave it to his friend. A little girl wanted a ribbon, and put it round her frock to look pretty. —Is one of them naughtier than the other?—Yes. . . . No. They're just the same.—*Why did the first one steal the roll? *—Because his friend liked it.—*Why did the little girl steal the ribbon?*—Because she was longing for it.—*Which one would you punish most?*—The boy who stole the roll and gave it to his brother instead of keeping it for himself.—* Was it naughty to give it?*—No. He was kind. He gave it to his brother.—*Must one of them be punished more than the other?*—Yes. The little boy stole the roll to give to his brother. He must be punished more. Rolls cost more."*

SCHMA (6) repeats the stories as follows: *"There was a boy. As his friend had had no dinner, he took a roll and put in his pocket and gave it to his friend. A little girl went into a shop. She saw a ribbon. She says, it would be nice to put on my dress, she says. She took it.*—Is one of these children naughtier than the other?—*The boy is, because he took a roll. It's bigger.*—Ought they to be punished?—*Yes. Four slaps for the first.*—And the girl?—*Two slaps.*—Why did he take the roll?—*Because his friend had had no dinner.*—And the other child?—*To make herself pretty."*

GEO (6): "Which of them is the naughtiest?—*The one with the roll, because the roll is bigger than the ribbon."* And yet Geo is like the other children perfectly well aware of the motives involved.

V. THE STORY OF THE CAGE AND OF THE SWEETS

DESA (6): *"The little girl had a friend who had a cage and a bird. She thought this was too unkind. So she took the cage and let the bird out.*—And the other one?—*A little girl stole a sweet and ate it.*—Are they both equally naughty or is one of them naughtier than the other?—*The one who stole the cage is naughtiest.*—Why?—*Because she stole the cage.*— And the other one?—*She stole a sweet.*—Is that one more or less naughty than the first?—*Less. The sweet is smaller than the cage.*—If you were the daddy, which one would you punish most?—*The one who stole the cage.*—Why did she steal it?—*Because the bird was unhappy.*—And why did the other one steal the sweet?—*To eat it."*

These cases of objective responsibility are thus all three of 6-year-olds. We found none above 7 years in the case of this kind of story. Here are some definite cases of subjective responsibiilty found in connection with the same stories. They are nearly all children of 9 and 10. The types are therefore better dissociated with regard to age than in the case of the stories about clumsiness.

IV. STORY OF THE ROLL AND THE RIBBON

CORM (9) tells the two stories correctly. "What do you think about it?—*Well, the little boy oughtn't to have stolen. He oughtn't to have stolen it, but to have paid for it. And the other one, she oughtn't to have stolen the ribbon either.*— Which of them is the naughtiest?—*The little girl took the ribbon for herself. The little boy took the roll too, but to give it to his friend who had had no dinner.*—If you were the school teacher, which one would you punish most?— *The little girl."*

Nuss (10): "Which one is the naughtiest?—*The little girl is because she took it for herself."*

V. STORY OF THE CAGE AND THE SWEETS

Sci (6): "Which one is naughtiest?—*The one who steals the sweet. The first one took the cage so as to set the little bird free."*

Corm (9), G.: *"It was good of the little girl who wanted to set the little bird free. The other one oughtn't to have eaten the sweet."*

Gros (9): *"The one who stole the sweet, that was naughtier.*—Why?—*Because the other let the little bird go free again."*

Thus these answers present us with two distinct moral attitudes—one that judges actions according to their material consequences, and one that only take intentions into account. These two attitudes may co-exist at the same age and even in the same child, but broadly speaking, they do not synchronize. Objective responsibility diminishes on the average as the child grows older, and subjective responsibility gains correlatively in importance. We have therefore two processes partially overlapping, but of which the second gradually succeeds in dominating the first.

What explanation can we give of these facts? The objective conception of responsibility arises, without any doubt, as a result of the constraint exercised by the adult. But the exact meaning of this constraint has still to be established, because in cases of theft and clumsiness it is exercised in a rather different form from what appears in cases of lying. For in some of the cases we have been examining it is quite certain that adults, or some adults, apply their own sanctions, whether "diffused" (blame) or "organized" (punishment), in conformity with the rules of objective responsibility. The average housewife (most of the children we examined came from very poor districts) will be more angry over fifteen cups than over one, and independently, up to a point, of the offender's intentions. Broadly speaking, then, one may say that it is not only the externality of the adult command in relation to the child's mind that produces the effects we are discussing, it is the example of the adult himself. In cases of lying, on the other hand, we shall find that it is almost entirely in spite of the adult's intention that objective responsibility imposes itself upon the child's mind.

Restricted though the question under discussion may appear, it has a very distinct interest. When the adult allows himself to evaluate acts of clumsiness and pilfering in terms of their material result, there can be no doubt that in most people's eyes he is unjust. On the other hand, those parents who try to give their children a moral education based on intention, achieve very early results as is shown by current observation and the few examples of subjective responsibility we were able to note at 6 or 7. How is it, then, that in most of the cases under 9-10 years the child accepts so completely the criterion of objective responsibility and even outdoes the average adult on this point? The child is much more of an objectivist, so to speak, than the least intelligent parent. Also, most parents draw a distinction which the children precisely neglect to make: they scold, that is, according to the extent of the material damage caused by the clumsy act, but they do not regard the act itself exactly as a moral fault. The child on the contrary seems, as we have noted before, not to differentiate the legal or, as it were, the purely police aspect from the moral aspect of the question. It is "naughtier" to make a big spot on your coat than a small one, and this in spite of the fact that the child knows perfectly well that the intentions involved may have been good. To commit certain acts is therefore, in a sense, wrong in itself, independently of the psychological context. With regard to stealing, which is unanimously held up to children as a grave moral offence, this phenomenon appears even more clearly. Nearly all the children under 9-10, while paying full tribute to the thief's intentions, consider the theft of the roll and the cage a more culpable act both from a police and from a moral point of view than that of the ribbon or the sweet. Now, we can understand anyone condemning a theft regardless of the object pursued, but it is rather curious to see little children adopting an exclusively material criterion when they are asked to compare two such dissimilar acts as are described in our stories.

The problem involved in all this is the following. What is the origin of this initial predominance of judgments of objective responsibility, surpassing in scope and intensity what may have been done or said to the children by adults? Only one answer seems to us to be possible. The rules imposed by the adult, whether verbally (not to steal, not to handle breakable objects carelessly, etc.) or materially (anger, punishments) constitute categorical obligations for the child, before his mind has properly assimilated them, and no matter whether he puts them into practice or not. They thus acquire the value of ritual necessities, and the forbidden things take on the significance of taboos. Moral realism would thus seem to be the fruit of constraint and of the primitive forms of unilateral respect. Is this an inevitable product or an accidental result? This is the point we shall try to settle in connection with lying.

But before going too far in our generalizations, let us remember that the child's answers are given in answer to stories that are told to him and do not arise out of really experienced facts. As in the case of method we may therefore ask ourselves whether these verbal evaluations do or do not correspond with the child's real thoughts. These evaluations certainly change as the child grows older, and they also seem to be the result of some systematic influence. But are they a mere derivative, a verbal and therefore ineffectual deduction from the words spoken by adults, or do they correspond with a genuine attitude, moulded by unilateral respect and conditioning the child's behaviour before they inspire his sayings?

As we noticed in certain cases, the child pays far more attention to intentions where his own memories are concerned than when he is being questioned about one or other of our little stories. Such a fact as this surely shows us that if the child's objectivist attitude (unmistakable enough in his theoretical thought) corresponds to anything in his concrete and active thought, there must have been a time-lag taking place between one of these manifestations and the other, for the theoretical attitude is certainly a late-comer as compared to the practical. But the problem goes deeper than this, and the question may be raised whether at any moment in the immediate experiences of his moral life, or at any rate in those connected with clumsiness and lying, the child has ever been dominated by the notion of objective responsibility.

Immediate observation—the only judge in the matter—is sufficiently explicit on this point. It is very easy to notice —especially in very young children, under 6-7 years of age— how frequently the sense of guilt on the occasion of clumsiness is proportional to the extent of the material disaster instead of remaining subordinate to the intentions in question. I have often noticed in the case of my own children, who have never been blamed for involuntary clumsiness, how difficult it was to take away from them all sense of responsibility when they chanced to break an article or soil some linen. Which of us cannot recall the accusing character which such a minor accident would take on as soon as it had happened, rising, with all the suddenness of a shock and overwhelming us with a sense of guilt that was the more burning, the more unexpected and the more irreparable the disaster. To be sure, all sorts of factors come into play (the sense of "immanent" justice, affective associations with previous carelessness, fear of punishment, etc.). But how could the material damage be felt as a fault if the child were not applying in a literal and realistic manner a whole set of rules, implicit and explicit, for which he feels respect?

We can therefore put forward the hypothesis that judgments of objective responsibility occurring in the course of our interrogatory were based upon a residue left by experiences that had really been lived through. Although new material may since have enriched the child's moral consciousness and enabled him to discern the nature of subjective responsibilty, these earlier experiences are sufficient, it would seem, to constitute a permanent foundation of moral realism which reappears on each fresh occasion. Now, since thought in the child always lags behind action, it is quite natural that the solution of theoretical problems such as we mad~ use of should be formed by means of the older and more habitual schemas rather than the more subtle and less robust schemas that are in process of formation. Thus an adult who may be in the midst of reviewing all his values and experiencing feelings of which the novelty surprises him, will, if he is suddenly faced with the necessity of solving someone else's problems, very probably appeal to moral principles which he has discarded for himself. For example, he will, if he is not given time to reflect, judge his neighbour's actions with a severity which would be incomprehensible in view of his present deeper tendencies, but which effectively corresponds to his previous system of values. In the same way, our children may perfectly well take account of intentions in appraising their own conduct, and yet confine themselves to considerations of the material consequences of actions in the case of the characters involved in our stories, who are indifferent to them.

How, then, does subjective responsibility appear and develop within the limited domain we are analysing at present? There is no doubt that by adopting a certain technique with their children, parents can succeed in making them attach more importance to intentions than to rules conceived as a system of ritual interdictions. Only the question is, whether this technique does not involve perpetually taking care not to impose on their children any duties properly so called, and placing mutual sympathy above everything else? It is when the child is accustomed to act from the point of view of those around him, when he tries to please rather than to obey, that he will judge in terms of intentions. So that taking intentions into account presupposes cooperation and mutual respect. Only those who have children of their own know how difficult it is to put this into practice. Such is the prestige of parents in the eyes of the very young child, that even if they lay down nothing in the form of general duties, their wishes act as law and thus give rise automatically to moral realism (independently, of course, of the manner in which the child eventually carries out these desires). In order to remove all traces of moral realism, one must place oneself on the child's own level, and give him a feeling of equality by laying stress on one's own obligations and one's own deficiencies. In the sphere of clumsiness and of untidiness in general (putting away toys, personal cleanliness, etc.), in short in all the multifarious obligations that are so secondary for moral theory but so all-important in daily life (perhaps nine-tenths of the commands given to children relate to these material questions) it is quite easy to draw attention to one's own needs, one's own difficulties, even one's own blunders, and to point out their consequences, thus creating an atmosphere of mutual help and understanding. In this way the child will find himself in the presence, not of a system of commands requiring ritualistic and external obedience, but of a system of social relations such that everyone does his best to obey the same obligations, and does so out of mutual respect. The passage from obedience to cooperation thus marks a progress analogous to that of which we saw the effects in the evolution of the game of marbles: only in the final stage does the morality of intention triumph over the morality of objective responsibility.

When parents do not trouble about such considerations as these, when they issue contradictory commands and are inconsistent in the punishments they inflict, then, obviously, it is not because of moral constraint but in spite of and as a reaction against it that the concern with intentions develops in the child. Here is a child, who, in his desire to please, happens to break something and is snubbed for his pains, or who in general sees his actions judged otherwise than he judges them himself. It is obvious that after more or less brief periods of submission, during which he accepts every verdict, even those that are wrong, he will begin to feel the injustice of it all. Such situations can lead to revolt. But if, on the contrary, the child finds in his brothers and sisters or in his playmates a form of society which develops his desire for cooperation and mutual sympathy, then a new type of morality will be created in him, a morality of reciprocity and not of obedience. This is the true morality of intention and of subjective responsibility.

In short, whether parents succeed in embodying it in family life or whether it takes root in spite of and in opposition to them, it is always cooperation that gives intention precedence over literalism, just as it was unilateral respect that inevitably provoked moral realism. Actually, of course, there are innumerable intermediate stages between these two attitudes of obedience and collaboration, but it is useful for the purposes of analysis to emphasize the real opposition that exists between them.

§ 3. OBJECTIVE RESPONSIBILITY. II. LYING

In dealing with the judgments children make about lies we are penetrating a step further into the secret of childish evaluations. For there can be no doubt that lies present to the child's mind a far graver and more pressing problem than do clumsiness or even such exceptional actions as stealing. This is due to the fact that the tendency to tell lies is a natural tendency, so spontaneous and universal that we can take it as an essential part of the child's egocentric thought. In the child, therefore, the problem of lies is the clash of the egocentric attitude with the moral constraint of the adult. And this circumstance will enable us to pursue on this point the analysis we outlined in connection with the early stages of the practice and the consciousness of rules in a game.

The nature and diversity of childish lies are well known, thanks chiefly to the fine work done by W. Stern[8] and to the many other books which it inspired. Nor do we intend to pursue this line of enquiry. Our aim will be to undertake the analysis of the child's consciousness of lies, or, more precisely, of the manner in which the child judges and evaluates lying. We know why children lie. We know the educational difficulties which the question raises. The case is therefore exceptionally favourable to the study of moral judgment in the child. If we can see in the course of an interrogatory how children think about lies and how they evaluate them, it will be relatively easy for us to decide whether the answers they give correspond with what we know from other sources of the practice of lying and truthfulness.

From the first, childish evaluations appeared to us to be dominated by the notions of intentionality and objective responsibility, and it is around this problem that we have grouped our examinations. Our interrogatory bore mainly upon the three following points: definition of a lie, responsibility as a function of the lie's content, responsibility as a function of its material consequences. In addition to this we made a study of two points which will be dealt with in Section 4: may children lie to one another? and, why should one not lie?

[8] W. and C. Stern, *Erinnerung, Aussage und Lüge*, 3rd. ed., 1922.

The first question (definition of a lie) connects quite naturally with the problem of objective responsibility and moral realism. For what we have to find out is whether the child has understood that to tell a lie is wittingly and intentionally to betray the truth. Now even this preliminary question provoked the most suggestive answers and revealed the strength of realistic tendencies in the child.

The most primitive and, at the same time, from our present point of view, the most characteristic definition we were able to find was a purely realistic one: a lie is "a naughty word." Thus the child, while perfectly well acquainted with a lie when he meets one, identifies it completely with the oaths or indecent expressions which one is forbidden to use. Here are examples:

WEB (6): "What is a lie?—*It's when you say naughty things you oughtn't to say.*—What does 'naughty things' mean?—*Saying naughty words.*—Tell me a naughty word. Do you know any?—*Charogne* (Engl. lit., carrion). [This word is often used in Switzerland as an oath or a term of abuse and many people do not know its real meaning.]—Is that a lie?—*Yes.*—Why is it a lie?—*Because it is a naughty word.*—When I say 'Fool!' is that a lie?—*Yes.*—A boy once broke a cup, but he said he didn't do it. Was this a lie?—*Yes.*—Why?—*Because he had done it.*—You see this gentleman? [a student]. I say he is thirty-nine. Are you thirty-nine? [The student answers, 'No, only thirty-six.'] [To Web] Is it a lie to say he is thirty-nine when he is only thirty-six?—*Yes, it's a lie.*—Why?—*Because he's thirty-six.*—Is it a naughty lie, or not?—*Not naughty.*—Why?—*Because it is not a naughty word.*—Is saying that $2 + 2 = 5$ a lie, or not?—*Yes.*—Naughty, or not naughty?—*Not naughty.*—Why?—*Because it is not a naughty word.*"

LUD (6): "Do you know what a lie is?—*It's when you say naughty words.*—Tell me a naughty word that is a lie.—. . . —[Lud hesitates]—Fire away.—*M . . .* (Cambronne's word).—Is it a lie?—*Yes.*—Why?—*Because it is a naughty word.*—I'm going to tell you a story. A boy once broke a cup, and then he said he hadn't done it. Was that a lie?—*Yes.*—Why?—*Because he said he hadn't done it.*—Is it a naughty word?—*Yes.*—Why?—*Because it was he had broken the cup."*

Nus (6): "What is a lie?—*It's when you say naughty words.*—Do you know any naughty words?—*Yes.*—Tell me one.—*Charogne.*—Is it a lie?—*Yes.*—Why?—*Because you mustn't say naughty words.*—When I say 'Fool!' is it a lie?—*Yes."* Nus also allows that the story of the broken cup involves a lie.

Rad (6): *"A lie is words you mustn't say, naughty words."*

Tul (6). Same answers. "If I say 'fool' to someone, is it a lie?—*Yes.*—Why?—*Because it is a naughty word.*—And if he really is a fool is it a lie, or not?—*Yes.*—Why?—*Because it is a naughty word."*

Here finally is a child who hesitates between this definition and the right one.

Rib (7): "Do you know what a lie is?—*It's when you lie.* —What is lying?—*It's saying naughty words.*—When do people tell lies?—*When you say something that isn't true.*— Is a lie the same thing as a naughty word?—*No, it's not the same thing.*—Why not?—*They're not like each other.*—Why did you tell me that a lie is a naughty word?—*I thought it was the same thing."*

This definition of a lie, of which we found many examples among the younger children, though it is by no means general and does not characterize a definite stage, is of great interest in fixing the children's initial attitude to lies. For nothing, after all, is more completely external to the moral consciousness, nothing is more like an unmotivated taboo than an interdiction with regard to language. Why is one word perfectly proper, while another arouses everyone's indignation? The child doesn't know in the least. He submits to the linguistic constraint and accepts this mystery without question. But this surely is the very type of those obligations which remain foreign to his practical understanding. How then does he come to identify lies with "naughty words"?

It should be noted in the first place that no mere verbal confusion is here at work. The child who defines a lie as being a "naughty word" knows perfectly well that lying consists in not speaking the truth. He is not, therefore, mistaking one thing for another, he is simply identifying them one with another by what seems to us a quaint extension of the word "lie." Moreover, the relative frequency of this definition and the fact that this part of the interrogatory always came before the others would seem to indicate that this is no case of verbal suggestion due to the child's environment or to the interrogatory itself. There seems therefore to be only one explanation: to tell a lie is to commit a moral fault by means of language. And using naughty words also constitutes a fault committed by means of language. So that for the little child, who really feels no inner obstacle to the practice of lying, and who at six years old still lies more or less as he romances or as he plays, the two types of conduct are on the same plane. When he pronounces certain sentences that do not conform with the truth (and which his parents regard as genuine lies) he is astonished to find that they provoke the indignation of those around him and that he is reproached with them as with a fault. When he brings in certain expressive words from the street, the same thing happens. He concludes that there are things one may say and things one may not say, and he calls the latter "lies" whether they are indecent words or statements that do not conform with fact.

This identification of oaths and lies seems therefore to show how completely external to the child's own mind the interdiction of lying still remains in the early stages. This hypothesis agrees, moreover, with all that we know about the mind of the child under 7-8. Thus it will help us to see how perfectly natural are the "objectivistic" or realistic evaluations which we shall find the younger children giving later about the stories they are asked to compare.

A more advanced definition of lies which remains the usual one until fairly late (between 6 and 10 on the average) consists simply in saying, "A lie is something that isn't true." But the mere words here must not deceive us, and we must get at the implicit notions which they conceal. We have seen elsewhere (*J. R.*) how difficult it is for the child to give an adequate definition of the notions he uses owing to his inability to realize them consciously. In order, therefore, to know the meaning of the definition we have just given we must ascertain whether the child confuses lying with every kind of inaccuracy (especially with mistakes), or whether he implicitly considers a lie to have been told only when someone intentionally betrays the truth. In order to settle this point it will be sufficient to present to the child a certain number of stories, asking him each time whether a lie has been told or not (and why), whether there has been a mistake or not (and why), and whether there may not have been simultaneously a lie and a mistake.

The interrogatory shows that children of 5 to 7, while perfectly aware of the shade of difference between an intentional act and an involuntary mistake, do not tend to stress this distinction at all, and often, on the contrary, group both facts under the same name of "a lie."

Here are examples of this type of definition, which therefore constitutes the second type, if we regard as a first type that which identifies lies and naughty words:

CLAI (6): "Do you know what a lie is?—*It's when you say what isn't true.*—Is '2 + 2 = 5' a lie?—*Yes, it's a lie.*—Why?—*Because it isn't right.*—Did the boy who said that '2 + 2 = 5' know it wasn't right or did he make a mistake?—*He made a mistake.*—Then if he made a mistake, did he tell a lie or not?—*Yes, he told a lie.*—A naughty one?—*Not very.*—You see this gentleman [a student]?—*Yes.*—How old do you think he is?—*Thirty.*—I would say 28. [The student then says he is 36.]—Have we both told a lie?—*Yes, both lies.*—Naughty ones?—*Not so very naughty.*—Which is the naughtiest, yours or mine, or are they both the same?—*Yours is the naughtiest, because the difference is biggest.* [Cf. moral realism.]—Is it a lie, or did we just make a mistake?—*We made a mistake.*—Is it a lie all the same, or not?—*Yes, it's a lie.*"

WEB (6) already examined in connection with "naughty words" answers towards the end of the interrogatory like the last child: "Is making mistakes the same thing as telling lies?—*Not the same thing.*—I'm going to tell you a story. Once there was a boy who didn't know where the Rue des Acacias was (the street where Web lives). A gentleman asked him where it was. The boy answered 'I think it's over there, but I'm not sure.' And it wasn't over there! Did he make a mistake, or did he tell a lie?—*It was a lie.*—Did he make a mistake or not make a mistake?—*He made a mistake.* —Then it wasn't a lie?—*He made a mistake and it was a lie.*" This last answer should be especially noted for it shows how for some children the two notions overlap.

MAB (6): "What is a lie?—*When you talk nonsense.*— You tell me about something that is a lie.—*A boy once said he was a little angel, and it wasn't true.*—Why did he say that?—*For a joke.*—Are we allowed to tell lies?—*No.*—Why not?—*Because it's a sin and God doesn't want us to sin.*— A boy told me that $2 + 2 = 5$. Is it true?—*No, it makes 4.*— Was it a lie or did he make a mistake?—*He made a mistake.* —Is making a mistake the same as telling a lie or different?— *The same.*—Look at me. I'm 30. A boy told me I was 60. Was it a lie or did he make a mistake?—*It was a lie.*—Why? —*Because what he said was a sin.*" "Which is naughtiest, to make a mistake or to tell a lie?—*Both the same.*"

CHAP (7): "What is a lie?—*What isn't true, what they say that they haven't done.*—Guess how old I am.—*Twenty.* —No, I'm thirty. Was it a lie what you told me?—*I didn't do it on purpose.*—I know. But is it a lie all the same, or not?—*Yes, it is all the same, because I didn't say how old you really were.*—Is it a lie?—*Yes, because I didn't speak the truth.*—Ought you to be punished?—*No.*—Was it naughty or not naughty?—*Not so very naughty.*—Why?—*Because I spoke the truth afterwards!*"

These observations yield two conclusions. The first is that in practice the children can more or less distinguish between an intentional act and an involuntary error. The idea of intention (not just the intentional act but the idea of the intentional act, which is not the same thing) appears roughly at the same time as the first "whys," that is, at about the age of three. Nevertheless, during the next few years the child does not distinguish between intentional actions and others as clearly as we do. The proof of this is that his thinking is finalistic, animistic and artificialistic to a degree that the average adult does not suspect, and this is so precisely because he fails to dissociate involuntary, unconscious and mechanical movements from conscious psychological action (see *C.W.*). There was therefore some reason to doubt whether a child of 6-7 could really distinguish an involuntary error from an intentional lie. The answers we have just recorded seem to show that the distinction is, at the best, in process of formation.

Only—and this is our second conclusion—these realities are still not dissociated on the plane of moral reflection. Mistakes, although they are distinguished from lies proper, are still conceived as constituting lies. More precisely, a lie is defined in a purely objective manner, as an affirmation that does not conform with fact, and even if the child can recognize two types of statement—those which are, and those which are not intentionally false, he subsumes them both kinds under the category of "lies." This identification is analogous to that examined above between lies and "naughty words." But in this particular case the identification is probably helped by the child's lingering inability to dissociate between the ideas of an intentional act and of an involuntary act. For it may very well be that these ideas remain undifferentiated on the plane of reflection longer than they do on the plane of practice. This would supply us with one more example of that time-lag between action and thought of which we have already spoken. In support of this view it should be noted that the identification of mistakes and lies disappears towards the age of 8, *i.e.*, at the same time as the bulk of the phenomena of animism, artificialism, etc., *i.e.*, at the same time as the other signs of inability to dissociate the idea of the intentional from the idea of the involuntary.

Whether these interpretations are right or not, it is obvious that both the answers we have been discussing and the first type of definitions reveal in the child a tendency to consider lies in a purely realistic manner and independently of the intentions involved. This will be amply confirmed by the remainder of our analysis.

Let us now turn to the third type of definitions, or correct definitions of lies: any statement that is intentionally false is a lie. Not till about the age of 10-11 do we find this definition in an explicit form. But among the children who begin by saying "A lie is something that isn't true" the majority are actually thinking of deceit, that is to say of the intentional deed. Here are examples, beginning with such cases of implicitly correct definitions.

ZER (6), G.: "What is a lie?— . . . —Do you know this word?—*Yes.*—What does a lie mean?— . . . —A boy knocked over a chair and then he said he hadn't done it. Was it a lie?—*Yes.*—Why?—*Because he had done it.*—I say you are called Helen, is it true?—*No, I'm called Madeleine.* —Is it a lie?—*No.*—Why?— . . . —A little boy told me that $2 + 2 = 5$. Is it a lie, or did he make a mistake.—*He made a mistake.*—Is it a lie all the same?—*No, he made a mistake.*"

GAR (6): "What is a lie?—*It's disobeying.*—If you don't go into the garden when you've been asked to go, is it a lie? *No, M'sieu.*—Then what is a lie?—*When you do something wrong and then you don't tell.*—If a boy breaks a cup and then says it was the cat, is it a lie?—*Yes, M'sieu.*—A boy told me that $2 + 2 = 5$. Is that a lie?—*It's not a lie.*—Then what did he do?—*He wasn't paying attention.*"

BEC (7): "What is a lie?—*When you say something and then afterwards it isn't true.*—A child doesn't know the names of the streets (in Geneva). A gentleman asks him where the Rue de Carouge is, and the child tells him wrong. Is that a lie, or has he made a mistake?—*He didn't tell a lie.*—Why not?—*Because he made a mistake* [Cf. the 'because'].—Why did he make a mistake?—*Because when you make a mistake it's that you don't know, but a lie you know, but you say it isn't true* [= you don't say what you know]."

KE (7): "What is a lie?—*When you don't say things right.* —Is $2 + 2 = 5$ a lie?—*No, that's not one.*—Why did the boy who said it was tell me so?—*Perhaps he made a mistake.* —What is making a mistake?—*When you don't say things right.*—Is making a mistake the same thing as telling a lie?— *No.*—What is the difference?—*Making a mistake is when you don't say things right; a lie is true, only you don't say it* [= you know the truth but do not say it]. And a joke (*Fr.* une blague)?—*It's when you say something for a lark.*"

PUI (8). A lie is "*when you say what is not true.*—But

when Pui guesses our age wrong he says it is not a lie. Why?
—*Because I didn't know.*"

Here are some good explicit explanations.

LAU (8): "*A boy who tells a lie knows what he is doing,
but he doesn't want to say it. The other one* [who makes a
mistake] *does not know.*"

ARL (10): "*When you lie you're doing it on purpose,
when you make a mistake, you don't know.*"

KEI (10): "*A lie is when you deceive someone else. To
make a mistake is when you make a mistake* [deceive your-
self] (Fr. quand on se trompe)."

This preliminary analysis of the definitions brings out the
initial difficulty experienced by the child under 8 in understanding the true nature of a lie. Naturally inclined as he is
to think about himself rather than about others, the child
does not see the full significance of deceit. He lies as he
romances, so that the obligation not to lie, imposed upon
him by adult constraint, appears from the first in its most
external form: a lie is what does not agree with the truth
independently of the subject's intentions.

Let us now turn to the second and third parts of our interrogatory, that is, to the evaluation of the stories in terms of
the content and of the consequences of the lies. In order to
solve these questions we made use as before of stories to be
compared, and before examining the answers we obtained,
we must begin by discussing the significance of these stories.

The question of the evaluation of lies from the point of
view of their content is the problem of responsibility. Responsibility is here evaluated either as a function of the aim of the
lie (subjective) or as a function of its degree of falseness
(objective). The difficulty is therefore to find stories in which
the lie leads to no material result and is not accompanied by
any material circumstance whatsoever. For experience showed
us that any lie told in connection with an act of clumsiness
or of something analogous (breaking a cup and saying it was
the cat, losing the scissors and denying having done so, etc.)
is invariably considered worse than a lie that is not con-

comitant with action of this sort. The child cannot, in such cases, dissociate the lie from the accompanying act and therefore judges it in terms of the consequences of the act. These features will reappear later and will confirm what we hinted at in the last section. But for the moment they do not concern us. It is the lie itself in its actual content that we want the child to evaluate.

After much groping and hesitation we selected the three following pairs of stories. Each pair contains a lie or mere inaccuracy devoid of any evil intention but marking a glaring departure from fact, and a lie of quite probable content, but told with the manifest intention to deceive.

I. A.[9] "A little boy [or a little girl] goes for a walk in the street and meets a big dog who frightens him very much. So then he goes home and tells his mother he has seen a dog that was as big as a cow."

B. "A child comes home from school and tells his mother that the teacher had given him good marks, but it was not true; the teacher had given him no marks at all, either good or bad.[10] Then his mother was very pleased and rewarded him."

II. A. "A boy was playing in his room. His mother called and asked him to run a message for her. But he didn't feel like going out so he told his mother his feet were hurting. But it wasn't true; his feet were not hurting him in the least."

B. "A boy wanted very much to go for a ride in a car, but no one ever asked him. One day he saw a lovely motor car in the street and would have loved to be inside it. So when he got home he told them that the gentleman in the car had stopped and had taken him for a little drive. But it was not true; he had made it all up."

III. A. "A boy couldn't draw very well but he would have liked very much to be able to draw. One day he was looking at a very lovely drawing that another boy had done, and said: 'I did that drawing.'"

[9] Mlle Descoeudres (*loc. cit.*) is responsible for this story.
[10] The child must not be said to have had a bad mark, otherwise the subject will regard him as *ipso facto* "naughtier" independently of the superimposed lie.

B. "A boy was playing with the scissors one day when his mother was out and he lost them. When his mother came in he said that he hadn't seen them and hadn't touched them."

Here, finally, are the stories we used for the analysis of the children's evaluation in terms of the material results of the lies.

IV. A. "A child who didn't know the names of streets very well was not quite sure where the Rue de Carouge was [a street near the school where we were working]. One day a gentleman stopped him in the street and asked him where the Rue de Carouge was. So the boy answered, 'I think it is there.' But it was not there. The gentleman completely lost his way and could not find the house he was looking for."
B. "A boy knows the names of the streets quite well. One day a gentleman asks him where the Rue de Carouge is. But the boy wanted to play him a trick and said, it is there, and showed him the wrong street. But the gentleman didn't get lost, and managed to find his way again."
V. We also made use of several stories in which the lie is accompanied by clumsiness (breakages, stains, etc.).

We tell the children the stories, two at a time. Before questioning the subject it is best to make him tell the stories from memory so as to make sure that he has understood them and especially that he has grasped the intentions that come into play. This is done by asking the child after each story: "Why did the boy say that?" In general our subjects understood at once that story I. A involved a simple exaggeration due to fear, stories II B. and III. A mere inventions due to desire, etc., whereas stories I. B. and III. B related to genuine acts of deceit due to the desire for sweets, to laziness or the fear of a deserved punishment. Then having made sure that the child has understood, you ask him to compare the two stories and to say which of the two lies or of the two boys in question was "the naughtiest" and why.

The results obtained by means of this technique were definite and suggestive. In the matter of clumsiness and theft the child, it will be remembered, seemed to judge of actions from their most external aspect (their results) before taking any account of the intentions in play. The analysis of the evaluations relating to lies not only confirms this conclusion but allows us to go beyond it and to say that even apart from all consideration of the material consequences of actions the child's mind remaïns set in the direction of objective responsibility.

For our stories I to III reduce the part played by material circumstances to the minimum; so that when the child answers he will not be thinking of the actions about which the lie was told, but of the lie itself and of the liar's intentions. Now, what struck us was the fact that a large number of the younger children whom we questioned evaluated the lies, not according to the intentions of the liar, but according to the greater or lesser likelihood of the lying statement. In point of fact, judging by the first two types of definition which we have just been studying, we had every reason to expect that the more a statement departed from truth, the more it would seem to the child to be a lie. And this in fact is what we now see to be the case. But the extraordinary thing is that the judgment of value itself, *i.e.*, the fact of evaluating the lies or liars as "naughty" or "not naughty" should obey the same principle.

And yet this is what happens on the verbal and abstract plane on which our interrogatories are unfortunately placed.

Here are examples concerning our first three pairs of stories.

I. STORY OF THE DOG AND THE COW AND OF THE CHILD WHO PRETENDED TO HAVE GOOD MARKS

FEL (6) repeats the two stories correctly: "Which of these two children is naughtiest?—*The little girl who said she saw a dog as big as a cow.*—Why is she the naughtiest?—*Because it could never happen.*—Did her mother believe her?—*No because they never are* [dogs as big as cows)].—Why did she say that?—*To exaggerate.*—And why did the other one tell a lie?—*Because she wanted to make people believe that she had a good report.*—Did her mother believe her?—*Yes.*—Which would you punish most if you were the mother?—

*The one with the dog because she told the worst lies and was
the naughtiest."*

BUG (6): "Which is the naughtiest?—*The one with the
cow.*—Why is he the naughtiest?—*Because it isn't true.*—
And the one of the good marks?—*He is less naughty.*—Why?
—*Because his mother would have believed, because she
believed the lie.* [This is not a slip. We have met with many
cases of children 6-7 who, like Fel and Bug, measure the
naughtiness of a lie by the degree of its incredibility to adults.
Consequently the lie about the good marks is not so bad
because the mother will be easily taken in by it!]—And why
did the other child tell the lie about the cow?—*Because he
was telling his mother a lie.*—Which would you punish most?
—*The one who said he saw a dog as big as a cow."*

MAE (6): "Which of the two is the worst lie?—*The dog
who was as big as a cow.*—And if you had to punish those
children, which would you punish most?—*The one who said
he saw a dog as big as a cow.*—Why did the other one say
that the teacher had given him good marks?—*Because he had
been naughty and didn't dare say so."*

KE (7): "Which was the worst lie?—*The one who said
he saw a dog as big as a cow.*—Why is it the worst?—
Because there's no such thing (Fr. *Parce que ça n'existe pas*).
[Note this formula which expresses very well the point of
view of objective responsibility in the case of lies.]—Which
of the two children should be punished most?—*The one who
saw a dog as big as a cow.*—Why?—*Because it isn't true.
It's not nice.*—Why is it not nice?—*Because it isn't true.*—
Why did the other one say that his teacher had given him
good marks?—*So that his mother should buy him something.*
Why did the other one say he had seen a dog as big as a
cow?—*Just like that. Because he wanted to say something
like that* [to boast of having seen something wonderful].—
Why did he say something like that?—*Because he saw a cow,
perhaps. He didn't see properly."* Ke therefore understands
the two children's respective intentions perfectly well; but
he sticks none the less to his objective evaluation of their
responsibility.

ROC (7): "What do you think of these two lies? Are they
just the same, or is one worse than the other?—*One is worse*

than the other.—Which?—The one who saw a dog as big as a cow.—Why?—No one ever saw dogs as big as cows.—If you were the mother, which would you punish most?—*The one who told the lie about the cow."*

BURD (7): " *'The naughtiest' is the one who saw a dog as big as a cow. It is naughtier because his mother knew* [that it was false or impossible], *whereas the other one, the mother didn't know. If you say something that mother doesn't know, it is less naughty because his mother might believe. If the mother knows it isn't true, then it's a bigger lie."* It would be impossible to express more clearly the idea that the moral gravity of a lie is to be measured solely by the improbability of the lying statement: what mother believes is not naughty whereas the immediately obvious lie is naughty!

DRIV (7): "Which of these two boys is the naughtiest?— *The one who said he saw a dog as big as a cow.*—Is that naughtier?—*He is the naughtiest because he told the biggest lie.*—Why is it the biggest lie?—*Because he said a much bigger one than in the other story.*—Why?—*Because it couldn't have happened."*

SAV (7) says that the naughtiest is the lie about the dog *"because it couldn't be.*—And the one about the teacher?— *Yes, that could be, but it's not true.*—Which of these two children would you punish most?—*The one of the dog.*— Why?—*Because it couldn't happen.*—Did the mother believe the lie about the dog?—*No.*—And would the mother have believed the lie about the teacher?—*Perhaps.*—When is it naughtiest, when the mother believes the lie, or when she can't believe it?—*When you can't believe it."*

TROT (7): "Which one should be punished most?—*The one who saw a dog as big as a cow.*—Why is he the naughtiest?—*Because a dog is never as big as a cow.*—Did the mother believe it?—*No, she didn't believe it.*—And did the mother believe the lie about the teacher?—*Yes, sometimes you are good, sometimes you are not.*—Which of the two children would you punish most?—*The one with the dog.*— Why?—*Because it doesn't exist* [a dog as big as a cow] *and because at school sometimes you get punished, sometimes you don't."* [The second lie is therefore more plausible and consequently less naughty.]

Boh (9): "Which is the naughtiest?—*Both the same.*— If you were the father, which would you punish most?—*The one who said he saw a dog as big as a cow.*—Why?—*Because it couldn't be.*"

II. Lies of the child who complains of his feet so as not to go a message and of the child who boasts of having been in a motor car

Wid (6): "Which is the naughtiest?—*The one of the car.* —Why?—*It's a bigger lie than the other.*—Why?—*He tells more of a lie than the other.*" Note this quantitative expression [meaning that what he says is falser than] which brings out the point of view of objective responsibility.

Roc (7): "Which is naughtiest?—*The one of the car.*— Why?—*Because you can't take little girls for drives in cars.*"

Pie (7). The story of the sore feet "*is a lie.*—Why?— *Because he wanted to stay in.*—And the story of the motor car?—*That's a lie too.*—Why?—*Because he wanted to say that.*—Why did he want to say that?—*Because he wanted to take them in* (Fr. *faire le malin*).—Which was the naughtiest?—*The one of the car.*—Why?—*Because it was a bigger lie.*—Why?—*Because it was a longer sentence. It is bigger. It's naughtier.*—Why?—*Because he told his mother lots of things. Not just one sentence, but a long one* [= a complicated story].—If you had to punish them which would you punish most?—*The one of the car.*" This shows Pie's purely quantitative conception of the matter: the longer the story, the worse the lie!

Burd (7; 10): "Which is the naughtiest?—*The one with the car.*—Why?—*Because the mother knew he couldn't have gone in such a short time* [= go for a drive during his short absence]."

Driv (7; 6): "Which of the two boys was the naughtiest? —*The one who said he went in the car.*—Why?—*It was the biggest lie.*—Why do you think it was the biggest lie?—*Because he said he had been in a car and it was not true.*— And the other one who said his feet hurt, was that just as naughty or less naughty?—*Less naughty.*—Why?—*Because he said his feet hurt him.*—And was it true?—*No, M'sieu.*— Then why do you think it was a less naughty lie? . . . Why did he go and say his feet hurt him?—*So as not to go* [the messages].—And why did the other one go and say he had been for a drive?—*To make his mother believe he had.*— Which is the naughtiest?—*The one who said he had been in a car.*"

III. STORIES OF THE DRAWING AND OF THE SCISSORS

DEPR (8): "Which was the naughtiest?—*The one who said he had done the drawing.*—Why is he the naughtiest?— *Because everyone thought it wasn't him, and he said it was him.*—Why did he say that?—*So that everyone should think it was him.*—And the boy with the scissors, why did he tell a lie?—*So that his mother should not punish him.*—If you had to punish these children, which would you punish most? —*The one who said he had done the drawings.*—Why would you punish him most?—*Because he told a worse lie.*"

GREM (8; 10): "Which is the naughtiest?—*The one who said he had done the drawing.*—Why?—*Because he couldn't draw, and he said it was him.*—Why did he tell this lie?— *To boast.*—And why did the other one lie?—*He thought he would rather play than go and fetch the scissors.*—Which one would you punish most?—*The one who said he had done the drawing.*"

PIT (9): "Which is the naughtiest?—*The one with the drawing because he didn't know how to draw and he said he had done it.*—Why did he say that?—*Because he wanted to say it was him, just as though the others didn't know that he couldn't draw.*—And why did the other one tell a lie?— *He wanted to put the blame on someone else.*—Then which one would you punish most?—*The one with the drawing.*"

The general principle underlying these answers is clear. The more unlikely the lie, the more its contents mark a departure from reality, the worse it is. The lie about the dog that was as big as a cow is particularly naughty (*vilain*)[11] "Because it never could be," "Because there's no such thing," because "No one ever saw dogs as big as cows," because "It's a bigger lie." And, above all, the essential point is that it is a lie because "you can't believe it." Mother will see straight away that it is false and the lie will be exposed in

[11] The term *vilain* is that used more particularly by Genevan children to mean "wicked" or "immoral."

the presence of all. But there is nothing unusual about having
good marks at school. It is quite likely to happen, and
parents will readily believe it. It is therefore only a little lie,
all the more innocent because a mother is taken in by it. In
the same way, the lie about the motor car is bad because
"you can't take little girls for drives in cars" and "because it
is a longer sentence," therefore a story of some importance;
whereas to complain falsely of sore feet so as not to have
to run messages is "almost nothing for the mother" in so
far as she is taken in by it. Finally, to boast of being able to
draw a picture when you can't draw at all is all the worse
because of the fact that every one is able to verify the un-
likelihood of the statement.

We are therefore in the presence of judgments of objective
responsibility in an unadulterated state, or at any rate in a
much simpler form than those whose contents we analysed
in connection with clumsiness and stealing. In those cases it
was always a question whether the child was not fascinated
by the material aspect of the action, by the purely physical
damage done to the adults; whereas in the present cases the
material element is reduced to its minimum. We have on
the other hand lies whose intention is manifestly interested,
lies that really "deceive," as the child himself admits. On the
other hand we have simply romancing, jokes (*"blagues"*) or
exaggeration, as the child himself realizes. And yet the subjects we have quoted ignore the liars' intention, and, basing
themselves only on the degree of likelihood of the lie, judge
it from the most external and objectivistic standpoint.

There can therefore be no question of explaining these
facts by any inability on the children's part to understand
the stories. As can be quite clearly recognized, all the subjects
whose answers we have quoted understood the intentions
that entered into the matter. It is not from lack of psychological penetration that they evaluated lies according to the
criterion of objective responsibility; it is because intention
does not seem to them to count from the point of view of
morality itself.

But we must hasten to add that even on the plane of verbal
reflection, where our interrogatories take place, the notion of
objective responsibility is not held in all its purity by any

one child. It is always mixed with subjective responsibility. A given child, who pays no attention to the intentions involved in the story of the dog, will, on the contrary, judge the stories of the drawing and the scissors in accordance with the psychological context, and so on. There can therefore be no question of two real stages. All we can say is that objective responsibility is a phenomenon frequently to be found among the younger children but subsequently diminishing in importance.

Psychological statistics are notoriously open to suspicion, but the following little calculation may be of value in this connection as showing how objective responsibility changes with age. Taking as our unit not each separate child—since one and the same child may give answers according to both types of responsibility—taking as our unit, then, the answer given by each child in connection with each story, and dividing those units according to the two types of responsibility, objective and subjective, we find that the average age for the objective type is 7 while for the subjective it is 10. As these statistics deal only with children from 6 to 12 it will be seen that, broadly speaking, objective responsibility disappears in favour of subjective responsibility as the child advances in age.

And now, in order to get at the real significance of the preceding answers, let us by means of the same pairs of stories examine the reactions of children whose minds are directed towards the idea of subjective responsibility.

I. STORIES OF THE DOG AND OF THE GOOD MARKS

DUR (7): "Which is the naughtiest?—*Both the same.*— Exactly the same?—*One is a little naughtier.*—Which?—*The one who said the teacher had said he was very good.*—Why did he say that?—*So that they should give him something.*— And the other one?— . . . . —If you were the father, which would you punish most?—*The one of the teacher.*—Why?— *Because he is the naughtiest.*"

LOUR (8): "Which is the naughtiest?—*The one who told about the teacher.*—Why is he naughtiest?—*Because a dog like that doesn't exist and because it is naughtier to tell a lie.* [Thus Lour reverses the argumentation used by the previous subjects, and from the fact that a dog is never as big as a cow he concludes that to exaggerate in this way is not to lie.] —Why did the one with the teacher tell a lie?—*So that his mother should reward him.*—And the other one?—*For a joke* (Fr. *blague*).—Which would you punish most?—*The one who said what the teacher hadn't said."*

CHRA (8): The one who said he had seen a dog as big as a cow is less naughty *"because it was as a joke. The one of the teacher is naughtier because he had said it so that his mother should not scold him."*

DEP (8; 9): "Which is the naughtiest?—*The lie about the teacher.*—Why?—*Because the story about the dog is nothing, but the story about the teacher made the mother angry.*— Why did the first boy say he had seen a dog as big as a cow? —*Just for swank* (Fr. *Pour faire le petit crâneur*).—And the other one?—*So that his mother should not punish him.*— Which of these two children would you punish most?—*The one with the teacher.*—Why?—*Because absolutely the opposite* [of the truth]. *The one about the dog the little boy told his mother and father for a lark* (Fr. *une farce*).—Why did he tell it?—*Perhaps because it was a little calf."*

PIT (9; 3): The naughtiest is the one of the teacher *"because he said he had been very good so that his mother should give him some pennies or some chocolate.*—And why did the other one say he had seen a dog as big as a cow?— *Because he thought a cow was a dog and because his brain wasn't working properly."*

DELE (9): "*The naughtiest is the one of the teacher.*— Why is he naughtier than the other?—*Because the other one, it wasn't possible.*—Why did he say it was?—*Because the dog was very big.*—And why did the other one say that the teacher had given him a good mark?—*So that his mother should pet him."*

ARL (10): The naughtiest is the one *"who deceived his mother by saying that the teacher was pleased.*—Why is he the naughtiest?—*Because the mother knows quite well that there aren't any dogs as big as cows. But she believed the child who said the teacher was pleased.*—Why did the child say the dog was as big as the cow?—*To make them believe it. As a joke.*—And why did the other one say that the

teacher was pleased?—*Because he had done his work badly.*
—Was that a joke?—*No, it is a lie.*—Is a lie the same thing
as a joke?—*A lie is worse because it is bigger."*

KEI (10): "Which is the naughtier?—*The lie about the
teacher.*—Why?—*Because he deceived his mother.*—But so
did the other.—*But he* [the one of the teacher] *had said
something the teacher hadn't said.*—The other one too had
said something that wasn't true. [Our counter-suggestions,
no matter how insistent, are ineffectual.]—*He had told a
great big lie. The teacher hadn't said he was good.*—Why is
it naughtier than the lie about the dog?—*Because you can
see better that it* [the lie about the dog] *is not true. You
can't tell with the lie about the teacher.*—Why did he say he
had seen a dog as big as a cow?—*To make them believe he
had seen something marvellous."*

ROS (11): The lie about the teacher *"is a bigger lie because
it was a bad thing to do."*

II. STORIES OF THE MOTOR AND THE SORE FEET

SAV (7½): "Which is the naughtiest?—*The one with the
sore feet, I think.*—Why did he say that?—*So as not to go
out.*—And the other one?—*To take them in* [as a joke]."

FER (8): The naughtiest is the one who pretends his feet
hurt *"because he didn't want to go out and because he disobeyed his mother."*

LOURD (8) begins by saying that the naughtiest is the one
of the car. Then he adds spontaneously: *"I'm wrong. I would
punish the one who wouldn't go out.*—And what did the
other one do?—*That was for a joke."*

SCI (9; 7): "Which is the naughiest?—*The one with the
feet that hurt.*—Why?—*Because it wasn't true.*—Why did he
say that?—*So as not to go out.*—And the other one?—*To
make them believe that he had been in a car once.*—Which is
the naughtiest?—*The one with the bad feet."*

III. STORIES OF THE DRAWING AND OF THE SCISSORS

FER (8): "Which is the naughtiest?—*The first* [drawing].
He said it to swank. And the second one [scissors] *so as not
to be scolded.*—Quite right. Which is the naughtiest?—*The
second."*

LOURD (8): "Which is the naughtiest?—*The one of the
scissors, because he said that so as to keep them.*—And the

other?—*He said it so that people should praise him.*—Which would you punish most?—*The one of the scissors.*—Why not the other one?—*Because the boys in his class know quite well how he draws.*" Lourd therefore thinks that the more obvious a lie is, the less it matters—the converse of what was maintained by the votaries of objective responsibility.

DELA (9): The naughtiest is the one of the scissors. "Why did he say that?—*So that his mother shouldn't scold him.*—And why did the other boy say that he had done the drawing?—*To make the boys think that he could draw well.*"

What strikes one about these answers is that the very arguments used by the partisans of objective responsibility reappear but in support of the opposite thesis. The previous set of subjects regarded the lie about the dog and the cow as serious because it was unlikely, and the proof brought forward by the child was that the mother "didn't believe it" and "saw at once that it was a lie." The present subjects, on the contrary, regard the same circumstances as indicating that the lie is not serious: if you see straight away that a statement is false, it means that the person who makes it is not trying to deceive you but is exaggerating or making a mistake. Thus Arl does not consider that the story about the dog is a lie, since the mother knows that there are no dogs as big as cows. The less a lie appears to be one, the worse it is, which is the direct opposite of the view held by the younger children.

Let us now turn to the last point which we have to examine, namely objective responsibility as a function of the material consequences of the lie. In using stories invented for the preceding experiments we found that the child more or less consistently regarded a lie as all the more serious if it accompanied actions that had regrettable (material) results. Thus consequences outweigh intentions, as was the case in connection with clumsiness and stealing. For example:

QUEL (7): "A little boy upset an ink-pot on the table. When his father came back the boy told him it wasn't he who knocked over the ink-pot. He told him it was the cat!

Was it a lie?—*Yes.*—Naughty or not naughty?—*Naughty.*—
Why?—*Because it made a big stain."*

DUB (8): "Two children bought some eggs for their
mother. But they played on their way home and broke the
eggs. The first child broke twelve eggs, the other child, one.
When they got home they told their mother that a big dog
had jumped at them and broken the eggs. Was that telling
lies?—*Yes.*—Were both the lies equally naughty?—*No. One
was worse than the other.*—Which?—*The first, because he
broke more.*—But I am not talking about the first child, I
mean the first lie. What was the first lie?—*He said it was the
dog.*—And the second.—*He also said it was the dog.*—Then
are both lies equally naughty?—*No, the first is because the
boy broke most eggs."*

In other words, when a material action is too closely attached to the lie, the child has a certain difficulty in dissociat-
ing the lie in so far as it is psychological action from the
actual results of the concomitant external act. The only
interest of these examples is that they bring out this lack of
dissociation. It would be very difficult to carry the analysis
of children's evaluations any further by means of stories of
this kind because the data in question are not two, but three
in number: the lie, the concomitant act and the results of
the act. We therefore abandoned this type of question.

Instead, we tried to solve the problem systematically by
presenting to the children a pair of stories, one of which
contained a clearly intentional piece of deceit having no
appreciable physical consequences, the other a simple mistake,
but leading to harmful results. These are stories IVA and IVB
given at the beginning of this section: 1) A boy purposely
shows a gentleman the wrong way, but the gentleman does
not get lost. 2) A boy shows a gentleman the wrong way by
mistake and the gentleman gets lost. The result of the interrogatory is that here, as in the case of clumsiness and stealing,
some children think about the material consequences and
evaluate the lie from this point of view only; others think
only of the intention. The average age of the first is 7, that
of the second is 9. Thus we have here two distinct attitudes,
one of which seems to be more evolved than the other, but

examples of both are to be met with at any age between 6 and 12.

Here are examples of objective responsibility.

THE (6): "Which of the two is the naughtiest?—*The one who didn't know where the Rue de Carouge was.*—Why is he the naughtiest?—*The gentleman got lost.* Did the other one know where it was?—*Yes.*—Why didn't he say? *For a lark* (Fr. *pour rigoler*)."

VAL (7) repeats the stories quite correctly. "Which is the naughtiest?—*The one who got lost* [who made the gentleman lose his way].—Did he know the way, this boy, or did he not know it well?—*Not well.*—Which is the naughtiest, the one who didn't know the way and the gentleman got lost, or the one who knew, but didn't tell the gentleman, and the gentleman didn't get lost after all?—*The one who got lost.*"

FER (8): "Which is the naughtiest?—*The first, because he made the gentleman lose his way. With the second boy the gentleman didn't get lost.*"

CAR (8): The naughtiest is *"the one who made the gentleman lose his way, and the less naughty boy is the one who didn't make the gentleman lose his way.*—If you had to punish them, which would you punish most?—*The one who didn't know where it was. He made a mistake.*—But didn't the other one deceive the gentleman?—*Yes, but the gentleman didn't get lost.*—And if the gentleman had got lost?—*They would have both been equally naughty.*"

Here are examples of the other attitude beginning with an intermediate case.

CHAP (7½): "Is one of the boys naughtier than the other?—*No, they're both the same.*—Will the gentlemen be angry?—*Yes, one more than the other.*—Which?—*The one who didn't find his way.*—And if the gentlemen were to find the two boys again, what would happen?—*One of the gentlemen would scold the boy* [more than the other].—Which gentleman?—*The one who didn't find his way.*—Would he be right?—*No, he wouldn't be right, because the boy didn't know the way.*"

DUR (7): "Are they both the same, or is one naughtier

than the other?—*One is naughtier than the other.*—Which?
—*The one who did it for a lark.*—Did the gentleman get
lost, or not?—*He didn't get lost.*—And the other one, when
the boy made a mistake?—*He did get lost.*—Which boy
would you punish most?—*The one who did it for a lark.*"

CLAI (7): "Which is the naughtiest?—*The one who knew
where the street was* [therefore who practised deceit] *and
afterwards the gentleman didn't get lost.*"

QUEM (8½): "Which is the naughtiest?—*The one who
knew but didn't say where it was.*—Did the gentleman lose
his way?—*No, the gentleman didn't lose his way because he
asked another gentleman.*—And what did the gentleman in
the other story do?—*He lost his way.*"

LOURD (8; 3): The naughtiest *"was the lie of the boy who
knew it wasn't there. The other boy spoke without knowing
what he was saying.*—Should they be punished?—*The boy
who said it wrong was the one who ought to have said it
when he knew.*"

KEI (10): The naughtiest is the one *"who did it on purpose. The first one deceived somebody, but he didn't know
it.*"

These answers confirm our findings in connection with
clumsiness and stealing. The younger children are inclined
to ignore the intention and to think only of the actual result
of the action. The older ones, on the contrary, pay much
more attention to motives. Very interesting in this connection
is the answer given by Chap (7½ yrs.), who knows that
grown-ups too are apt to fix on the mere consequences of
the act, but who thinks, nevertheless, that the grown-up is
wrong and that the intention counts for more than the
material deed.

All these data would therefore seem to converge on one
point. The problem we must now discuss is how the child
ever gets beyond this moral realism and comes to judge of
conduct by intentions. At this point a more profound analysis
of the previous results and a few additional questions on the
reasons adduced for not lying will put us on the right lines.

§ 4. LYING AND THE TWO KINDS OF RESPECT

Why is it that during these early years lies seem to give rise to so paradoxical a realism in morality, a realism testifying to so faint a conception of what constitutes the real gravity of deceit? How, starting from objective responsibility, will the child ever attain to a psychological evaluation of lying? These two questions are closely bound up with each other.

The matter can be explained quite simply if we compare our present data with the far more certain results obtained by observing the development of the rules of games. For on this last point we were able to establish the existence of two distinct processes in the evolution of children's moral judgments. On the one hand, there was the constraint of the adult or older child which, far from putting an end to egocentric thought or behaviour, easily combined with it and led to a purely external and realistic conception of rules without effective influence on the practice of these rules. On the other hand, there was cooperation, which appeared to us to dislodge both egocentric practice and the mystical attitude to constraint, and led both to a successful application of rules and to a wider and more interiorized understanding of what they meant. The following reflections therefore suggest themselves in connection with lies. In the first place, moral realism is the result of the meeting of egocentrism and constraint. The child, owing to his unconscious egocentrism, tends spontaneously to alter the truth in accordance with his desires and to neglect the value of veracity. The rule that one must not lie, imposed by adult authority, will therefore seem all the more sacred in his eyes and will demand all the more "objective" an interpretation just because it does not in fact correspond with any felt inner need on his part. Hence, moral realism and objective responsibility, which stand for an inadequate practical application of the rule. In the second place, in so far as habits of cooperation will have convinced the child of the necessity of not lying, rules will become comprehensible, will become interiorized, and will no longer give rise to any judgments but those of subjective responsibility.

We shall examine these two points in succession. In the case of the first we shall simply point to the consequences of our preceding remarks, while in that of the second we shall analyse certain fresh material contained in the reasons given by children for and against lying.

Everyone knows, thanks to the fine work done by Stern and his followers, that until the age of 7-8 the child finds systematic difficulty in sticking to the truth. Without actually lying for the sake of lying, *i.e.*, without attempting to deceive anyone, and without even being definitely conscious of what he is doing, he distorts reality in accordance with his desires and his romancing. To him a proposition has value less as a statement than as a wish, and the stories, testimony and explanations given by a child should be regarded as the expression of his feelings rather than of beliefs that may be true or false. As Stern has said, there are such things as apparent or *pseudo-lies* ("Pseudo = oder Scheinlüge"). Since then, children's lies have been studied from every point of view, and everywhere the spontaneity of pseudo-lies before the age of 7-8 has found confirmation.

What has perhaps been less generally understood is that this feature of child psychology is of an intellectual as well as of a moral order, and that it is connected with the laws of child-thought in general and with the phenomenon of intellectual egocentrism in particular. For the need to speak the truth and even to seek it for oneself is only conceivable in so far as the individual thinks and acts as one of a society, and not of any society (for it is just the constraining relations between superior and inferior that often drive the latter to prevarication) but of a society founded on reciprocity and mutual respect, and therefore on cooperation.

For what, after all, is the spontaneous mental attitude of the individual? Even before the appearance of language, on the motor plane which we mentioned in connection with game rules, we find that although the child's activity is constantly being conditioned by an even closer adaptation to the things around him, it tends nevertheless to utilize these things for the sake of exercising some organic faculty or for the satisfaction of some psychobiological tendency. In this way things, external objects, are assimilated to more or less ordered motor schemas, and this continuous assimilation of objects the child's own activity is the starting point of play. Not only this, but when to pure movement are added language and imagination, the assimilation is strengthened, and wherever the mind feels no actual need for accommodating itself to reality, its natural tendency will be to distort the objects that surround it in accordance with its desires or its fantasy, in short to use them for its satisfaction. Such is the intellectual egocentrism that characterizes the earliest forms of child-thought.

It is to these circumstances that we must ascribe that striking feature of the child's first beliefs of being immediate and not controlled (of being, as Pierre Janet says, merely assertive and not "reflective"). Every thought that enters the head of a child of 2-3 does so from the first in the form of a belief and not in the form of a hypothesis to be verified. Hence the very young child's almost systematic romancing as a sort of game which the child plays with himself as well as with others and to which one cannot yet give the name of pseudo-lie, so close is the connection between primitive romancing and assertive belief. Hence, finally, the pseudo-lie which is a sort of romancing used for other people, and serving to pull the child out of any strait due to circumstances, from which he deems it perfectly natural to extricate himself by inventing a story. Just as, from the intellectual point of view the child will elude a difficult question by means of an improvised myth to which he will give momentary credence, so from the moral point of view, an embarrassing situation will give rise to a pseudo-lie. Nor does this involve anything more than an application of the general laws of primitive child thought, which is always directed towards its own satisfaction rather than to objective truth. It is as his own mind comes into contact with others that truth will begin to acquire value in the child's eyes and will consequently become a moral demand that can be made upon him. As long as the child remains egocentric, truth as such will fail to interest him and he will see no harm in transposing facts in accordance with his desires.

Thus we see that the child is almost led to tell lies—or what seem to us as lies from our point of view—by the very structure of his spontaneous thought. Given this situation, what will be the result of the laws laid down by adults about truthfulness? On the occasion of the first very obvious lies, or of those connected with some offence or other and told therefore with the object of averting punishment or scolding, the parents point out to the child that he has just done something very wrong and thus inculcate in him the respect for truth. We agree with M. Bovet in allowing that commands of this kind, laid down for the child by persons for whom he feels respect and often on the occasion of particularly strong affective situations, are sufficient to arouse in the child's mind obligations of conscience, *i.e.*, the feeling of certain definite duties such as that of not telling lies again. Moreover, as we saw in the game of marbles, a rule may be felt as sacred and obligatory without, for that matter, being properly applied. One may even say that in certain cases the more defective the application of a rule the more the rule will be felt as obligatory, given the continual conflicts (and consequently the feelings of guilt) which these infractions of the rule must lead to. Be that as it may, we can say that up till the age of 7-8, the child tends spontaneously to alter the truth, that this seems to him perfectly natural and completely harmless, but that he considers it a duty towards the adult not to lie, and recognizes that a lie is a "naughty" action. Moral realism and objective responsibility are the inevitable outcome of so paradoxical a situation.

Two groups of causes conspire, it is true, to bring about this result. The first group is of a general order and will be dealt with at the conclusion of this chapter: the child is a realist in every domain of thought, and it is therefore natural that in the moral sphere he should lay more stress on the external, tangible element than on the hidden motive. The second group of causes is peculiar to the situation we have been describing. It is obvious that if the desire for truthfulness does not correspond to something very fundamental in the child's nature, the adult's command, in spite of the nimbus that surrounds it, will always remain external, "stuck on" as it were, to a mind whose structure is of a different order. For the spirit of such a command could only be understood by experience. One must have felt a real desire to exchange thoughts with others in order to discover all that a lie can involve. And this interchange of thoughts is from the first not possible between adults and children, because the initial inequality is too great and the child tries to imitate the adult and at the same time to protect himself against him rather than really to exchange thoughts with him. The situation we have described is thus almost the necessary outcome of unilateral respect. The spirit of the command having failed to be assimilated, the letter alone remains. Hence the phenomena we have been observing. The child thinks of a lie as "what isn't true," independently of the subject's intentions. He even goes so far as to compare lies to those linguistic taboos, "naughty words." As for the judgment of responsibility, the further a lie is removed from reality, the more serious is the offence. Objective responsibility is thus the inevitable result of unilateral respect in its earliest stage.

Let us now turn to the second problem we set ourselves and let us ask how the child is going to acquire a real understanding of lying and become capable of judging of subjective responsibility. It follows quite naturally from what we have said that the passage from unilateral respect to mutual respect is what liberates the child from his moral realism. But before carrying the discussion any further, let us pause to examine certain facts that are very interesting in this connection.

For if what we have said is true, then two questions are forced upon us. The first is: what are the child's ideas about the moral utility of not lying? The next is: from what moment and in what conditions does the child consider it a moral fault to lie to his equals? And we shall see that the answers given to these two kinds of question go to show that in mutual respect and cooperation is to be found the real factor that brings about a progressive understanding of the law of truthfulness.

Let us first try to see why people should not tell lies. The reason most universally invoked and that which comes first chronologically is that you mustn't tell lies because "you get punished." Here are some examples:

ZAMB (6): "Why must we not tell lies?—*Because God punishes them.*—And if God didn't punish them?—*Then we could tell them.*"

ROC (7): "What happens when you tell lies?—*You get punished.*—And if you didn't get punished, would it be naughty to tell them?—*No.*—I'm going to tell you two stories. There were two kiddies and they broke a cup each. The first one says it wasn't him. His mother believes him and doesn't punish him. The second one also says that it wasn't him. But his mother doesn't believe him and punishes him. Are both lies that they told equally naughty?—*No.*—Which is the naughtiest?—*The one who was punished.*"

BURD (7) tells us, in connection with the stories of the dog and the school teacher, as we saw in the preceding paragraph, that the lie of which the mother knows that it is untrue is the worst. Then he adds spontaneously the following curious explanation: *"What she knows is the worst.*—Why? —*Because when she knows then she can scold at once. When she doesn't know she can't scold at once. The child doesn't know why he is being scolded. He doesn't remember any more.*—But when is a child naughtiest, when he is scolded at once or when he is not scolded at once?—*He is naughtier when he is scolded at once.*"

DELE (9): "Why is it naughty?—*Because you get punished.*—If telling lies wasn't punished would it be naughty? —*Oh, no!*"

The following observation recently made at the *Maison des Petits* by Mlle Lafendel is worth recording: A little girl of 6 had just told a lie. Mlle L. asked her if that was right. The answer was: *"It doesn't matter, my mummy can't see!"*

Note how closely observed is the situation as described by Burd. But what an extraordinary morality ordinary education produces—the child is all the naughtier for being scolded straight away! These children, in short, look upon lying as naughty because it is punished, and if it were not punished no guilt would attach to it. This is objective responsibility in its purest form. These facts, moreover, should not be interpreted as even a relative amorality. The child does not mean that it is enough to escape censure to be innocent. What these subjects think is simply that the punishment is the criterion of the gravity of the lie. Lies are forbidden, though one does not quite know why. The proof is that you get punished for it. If it were not punished, it would not be "naughty." What these answers mean, then, is that a lie is a fault in so far as it is forbidden by God or adults. This is heteronomy in its most naïve form and it confirms our interpretation of realism in its beginnings.

Here are some slightly more advanced answers. A lie is a fault in itself, and would remain so even if it were not punished.

DUR (7): "Are we allowed to tell lies?—*No. It's naughty.* —Why?—*Because we get punished.*—If we could tell them without being punished, would it be naughty or not naughty? —*Naughty.*—Supposing it was in a country where there were only children and where no one would know if we told lies, would it still be naughty to tell them or not?—*It would be naughty.*"

GIR (9): "Why is it naughty?—*Because we get punished.* —If you didn't know you had told a lie, would it be naughty too?—*It would be naughty, but less naughty* [we have here an interesting residue of the last type of answer].—Why would it be naughty?—*Because it is a lie all the same.*"

AUF (9): "If lies were not punished, would they still be wrong?—*They would still be wrong for the boy who said them.*"

ARL (10): "If lies were not punished, would they be naughty or not?—*Of course they would be naughty.*"

At a certain stage, then, rules become obligatory independently of punishments, that is to say, independently of the controlling power whence they emanate. This is the phenomenon to which P. Bovet has drawn attention. Commands, which are at first closely bound up with the person who imposes them, are later on elaborated by the child's reason and through this become universal. It is a process of the same order as that described by P. Janet in connection with his "rational" stage. The laws of conduct, like those of reflective thought, end by being placed above the actual context in which they are experienced, and thus become universal and absolute.

But even though they are generalized in this way, rules are none the less heteronomous. The child, it is true, takes the particular command that has been given him and raises it to the level of a universal law. This rational process of extension is probably already due to cooperation. But the rule may nevertheless persist in the form of an imperative that is external to the child's own conscience. We shall now see how this state of things is left behind at a given moment, thanks to the growing understanding of the child himself.

In point of fact, the older children of 10-12 generally invoke against lying reasons which amount to this: that truthfulness is necessary to reciprocity and mutual agreement. Among the alleged motives there will be found, it is true, a whole set of phrases inspired by adult talk: "We mustn't tell lies because it's of no use" (Arl, 10). "We must speak the truth . . . our conscience tells us to" (Hoff, 11). But along with these commendable but too often meaningless formulae we can observe a reaction which seems to be, if not altogether spontaneous at any rate founded on experience. The reaction in question implies that truthfulness is necessary because deceiving others destroys mutual trust. One is struck by the fact, in this connection, that while the younger children had regarded a lie as all the worse for being unbelievable, the older ones, on the contrary, condemn a lie in so far as it succeeds.

Here are some fresh examples of the attitude of the younger children on this point, which, incidentally, we had occasion to notice more than once during the preceding paragraph.

BUG (6): The lie about the dog is worse than the one about the good marks *"because his mother would have believed"* the latter.

ROC (7): Lies are *"not nice.—Why not?—Because sometimes you believe them and sometimes you don't.—Which* are worse, those you believe or those you don't believe?— *Those you don't believe.*—Two children both say they have sore feet so that they won't be sent messages. One is believed, the other not. Which one is naughtiest?—*The one you didn't believe.*—Why?—*Because you can make a mistake by looking* [=because in the case of the child who was believed, appearances might have let you think that he had a sore foot: the lie was probable and therefore less bad than that which had appearances too much against it]."

SAV (7): "When is a lie worse, when people believe it or when they don't believe it?—*When you can't believe in it.*"

The older children, on the contrary, hold that a lie is bad precisely in so far as it achieves its aim and succeeds in deceiving the other person. Those, therefore, who have really grasped the anti-social character of lying no longer say that we mustn't lie "because we get punished," but because to do so is contrary to reciprocity and to mutual respect.

DIN (8, forward): "Why must we not lie?—*Because if everyone lied no one would know where they were.*"

AUF (9): "Why is it naughty to tell a lie?—*Because mother believes it.*"—Exactly the opposite criterion from that used by the little ones.

LOC (10): "Why is it naughty to tell a lie?—*Because you can't trust people any more.*"

KEI (10): The lie about the school teacher is worse than the lie about the dog, because "*the one about the teacher you couldn't know* [that it was a lie]."

It would seem, then, that the evolution of the answers with age marks a definite progress in the direction of reciprocity. Unilateral respect, the source of the absolute command, taken literally, yields the place to mutual respect, the source of moral understanding. We can, indeed, distinguish three stages in this progress. In the first stage, a lie is wrong because it is an object of punishment; if the punishment were removed, it would be allowed. Then a lie becomes something that is wrong in itself and would remain so even if the punishment were removed. Finally, a lie is wrong because it is in conflict with mutual trust and affection. Thus the consciousness of lying gradually becomes interiorized and the hypothesis may be hazarded that it does so under the influence of cooperation. If we attribute the advance to the child's intelligence alone, which is constantly improving his understanding of what he originally took in a purely realistic sense, we are only shifting the question. For how does psychological intelligence advance with age if not by means of increased cooperation? Cooperation, of course, presupposes intelligence, but this circular relation is perfectly natural: Intelligence animates cooperation and yet needs this social instrument for its own formation.

If our hypothesis is correct, then we ought now to find—and this is the second question we have to examine—that lies between children, which are at first held to be legitimate, end by being proscribed from among the relations they hold with each other. And this indeed does prove to be the case.

Here, to begin with, are some answers given by the younger children, who hold that lies between children are allowed.

FEL (6): "Is it just the same to tell lies to grown-ups and to children?—*No.*—Which is naughtiest?—*To grown-ups.*—Why?—*Because they know it isn't true.* [Note the spontaneous reappearance of the realistic criterion: the more a lie shows, the worse it is.]—And how about children?—*It's allowed because they are smaller.*"

BLI (6): "*To a grown-up it's not the same thing as to children.*—Which is naughtiest?—*To grown-ups.*"

IRI (7): "And may you tell lies to other kiddies or not?—*Yes, M'sieu.*—Is it naughty or not?—*It's a little bit naughty too.*—Is it worse to grown-ups, or to other kiddies, or are they both the same?—*It's not so naughty to children*—Why? —*Because they are not big.*"

DRUS (7): "*It's naughtier to a grown-up. They are bigger than children, and little children can say naughty words to each other* [cf. the definition of a lie!]."

CARN (8): You can tell lies to children but not to grown-ups "*because a gentleman is worth more than a child.*"

EM (8; 5): "*A child doesn't know if it is true. A grown-up knows, so it's naughtier!*" Cf. the realistic criterion rising spontaneously in a child who has never been questioned by us before.

PI (9; 3): "*It's naughtier to a grown-up because they are older.*"

ER (9; 8): *"It doesn't matter to a child. You can tell him lies. But you mustn't to a grown-up."*

Almost all the older children, on the contrary, though they maintain that it is wrong to deceive adults, think that it is as bad or even worse to deceive one's comrades. You can say things for a joke, but a serious lie is as reprehensible between children as towards an adult.

Here are examples.

BOH (7; 10): "Can one tell children lies, or is that just as bad as telling them to grown-ups?—*They are both the same thing."*

DI (8; 6): *"It's just as bad to a child, because a child can't tell if you're lying or not, and he's not pleased."* The argument is exactly the opposite of Em's.

AUD (9½): *"It is worse to a child, because a child is smaller."*

DEN (11 yrs.): *"It's worse to a child because he'll believe it."*

COTT (12; 8): *"You get into more of a row with a grown-up, but they're just as bad as each other."*

CAL (12 yrs.): *"Sometimes you almost have to tell lies to a grown-up, but it's rotten to do it to another fellow."*

These answers[12] show how much the progress of solidarity between the children helps them to understand the true nature of lies. Compare, for example, Em's answers with those given by Di. To Em, who is dominated by authority, a lie is wrong in so far as it shows, but to Di, who has learned comradeship, a lie is wrong in so far as it deceives.

In conclusion, we can solve as follows the two questions we set ourselves above. If the younger children present all the features of an almost systematic moral realism, leading in certain cases to the predominance of objective over subjective responsibility, this is because of the *sui generis* relations holding between adult constraint and childish egocentrism. The child's unilateral respect for the adult obliges him to accept the latter's commands, even when these are not

[12] See statistics, p. 309.

such as can be put immediately into practice. Hence the externality of rules and the literal character of the moral judgments to which they give rise. If, conversely, the child's development is such as to interiorize these commands and to make his own the notion of subjective responsibility, this is because cooperation and mutual respect are giving him an increasingly vivid understanding of psychological and moral realities. Thus truthfulness gradually ceases to be a duty imposed by heteronomy and becomes an object envisaged as good by an autonomous personal conscience.

In short, the study of rules imposed upon the child by the adult broadly confirms what we learnt from the study of rules which younger children receive from older ones. However closely connected mutual and unilateral respect may be in the general continuity of mental phenomena, the two processes lead nevertheless to consequences that are qualitatively different.

§ 5. CONCLUSION: MORAL REALISM

We must now try to find what place our results occupy in the moral life of the child taken as a whole by restoring things to the right perspective which has inevitably suffered distortion through the method of interrogation.

Two distinct levels of activity are to be distinguished in moral thought. First, there is effective moral thought, "moral experience" which is built up gradually in action as the subject comes in contact with reality and meets with shocks and opposition. It is that which leads him to form such moral judgments as will guide him in each particular case as it comes his way and enable him to evaluate other people's actions when these concern him more or less directly. And there is also theoretical or verbal moral thought, bound to the former by all kinds of links, but as far removed from it as is reflective thought from immediate action. This verbal morality appears whenever the child is called upon to judge other people's actions that do not interest him directly or to give voice to general principles regarding his own conduct independently of his actual deeds.

The analysis we were able to make of the judgments on responsibility deals only with the child's theoretical moral thought, and is in no way concerned with his practical and concrete moral thought (differing in this from our enquiry on the rules of a game where we were able to keep both aspects of the question simultaneously in view). Now with regard to this verbal plane our results were fairly consistent. Though we could not point to any stages properly so called, which followed one another in a necessary order, we were able to define processes whose final terms were quite distinct from one another. These processes might mingle and overlap more or less in the life of each child, but they marked nevertheless the broad divisions of moral development. We saw, for example, that the child's theoretical morality could be subject either to the principles arising from unilateral respect (morality of heteronomy and objective responsibility) or to those based on mutual respect (morality of inwardness and subjective responsibility).

But the problem before us now and already touched upon in the methodological remarks at the opening of the present chapter is this. What do these results correspond to in the child's effective thought on morality? Two solutions are possible. It may be that verbal thought is a progressive conscious realization of concrete thought. In that case the moral realism we met with and studied would correspond to a moral realism effectively at work in action, a realism that would no doubt already have been left behind by the time the children talked about it theoretically, but a realism which would none the less give rise to spontaneous reactions expressed in concrete acts. But it may also be that this verbal morality, whose manifestations we have observed, corresponds to nothing at all in the child's effective thought. The children would therefore never have manifested any moral realism in their concrete decisions and judgments. Meeting in their lives with lies analogous to those of the dog as big as the cow or of the boy who pretended to have had good marks in order to be rewarded, they would never have hesitated to regard the second as worse than the first. And, in this case, verbal reflection alone would be sufficient to engender a form of pure psittacism bearing no relation to past or present action.

First let us remove a possible ambiguity. This second solution is not equivalent to saying that the interrogatory is the cause of the whole trouble. In life, the child is constantly finding himself in situations analogous to those described in the interrogatory. He hears his friends' misdeeds discussed, he has the chance of judging them from hearsay, and phenomena similar to those we have observed may very well occur in a perfectly spontaneous manner. In the same way, the results concerning animism or artificialism which we obtained earlier (see *C.W.*) correspond to remarks that can frequently be heard from the lips of children. But this is only shifting the problem a stage further off, and we still have to ask concerning these spontaneous verbal reflections: do they or do they not constitute the coming into consciousness of some effective form of thinking?

As a matter of fact, it is our belief that even for the child, theoretic moral reflection does constitute a progressive conscious realization of moral activity properly so-called. Consequently, we think that the results set out above correspond in a certain measure to real moral facts. But the relations between thought and action are very far from being as simple as is commonly supposed, and it will therefore be necessary to stress somewhat the point under discussion in order to grasp our results in their true perspective.

In the first place, as Claparède has shown so well, ideas or notions enter into consciousness in inverse order to that in which they actually arise: what comes first in the order of conscious realization (*prise de conscience*). So that if on the verbal plane moral realism seems to be a primitive fact, it does not follow that it is such on the plane of action itself. The notion of good which, generally speaking, appears later than the notion of pure duty, particularly in the case of the child, is perhaps the final conscious realization of something that is the primary condition of the moral life—the need for reciprocal affection. And since moral realism is, on the contrary, the result of constraint exercised by the adult on the child, it may perhaps be a secondary growth in comparison to the simple aspiration after good, while still remaining the first notion to be consciously realized when the child begins to reflect upon morality and to attempt formulation.

In the second place, to realize consciously is not simply

to throw into light ideas that have already been fully worked out. Conscious realization is a reconstruction and consequently a new and original construction superimposed upon the constructions already formed by action. As such, therefore, it comes on the scene later than action proper. Hence the time-lag noted by Stern, and which we have found in every sphere of child thought.[13] If, then, the moral realism we have noted between 6 and 8 on the average (we would not detect it under 6 because the youngest children could not sufficiently understand the stories used), if, then, this moral realism corresponds to something present in the moral activity itself, it is not during those years that we must seek for this something, but at a very much earlier period. For objective responsibility can perfectly well have been discarded long ago on the level of action and yet subsist on the level of theoretical thought. Besides, we saw examples of children who judged the stories we told them in accordance with the principles of objective responsibility, but who at the same time gave us personal reminiscences evaluated in complete conformity with the criterion of subjective responsibility. This being so, can we find during the first years of moral development instances of realism and objective responsibility that correspond to the phenomena which we observed on the verbal plane? We believe that we can.

In the first place it should be noted that, however averse one may be in education to the use of any constraint, even moral, it is not possible completely to avoid giving the child commands that are incomprehensible to it. In such cases— which are almost the rule in the traditional form of education based on authority—the mere fact of accepting the command almost invariably provokes the appearance of moral realism. Here are a few examples observed on one of the author's own children, on a child, therefore, whose parents have done all they could to avoid objective responsibility. The following observations will thus hold *a fortiori* for children in whose immediate *entourage* no special attention is devoted to this complex problem of moral autonomy and heteronomy.

[13] See *Bull. Soc. Française et Philos.*, 1928, pp. 97 *et seq.*, especially p. 105.

Jacqueline has never been punished in the strict sense of the term. At the worst, when she makes a scene, we leave her alone for a little while and tell her we shall come back when she can talk quietly again. She has never been given duties as such, nor have we ever demanded from her that sort of passive obedience without discussion which in the eyes of so many parents constitutes the highest virtue. We have always tried to make her understand the "why" of orders instead of laying down "categorical" rules. Above all, we have always put things to her in the light of cooperation: "to help mummy," to "please her parents," to "show her sister," etc. —are for her reasons for carrying out orders that cannot be understood in themselves. As to rules that are unintelligible to very little children, such as the rule of truthfulness, she has never even heard mention of them.

But in ordinary life it is impossible to avoid certain injunctions of which the purport does not immediately seem to have any sense from the child's point of view. Such are going to bed and having meals at given hours, not spoiling things, not touching the things on daddy's table, etc. Now, these commandments, received and applied before being really understood, naturally give rise to a whole ethic of heteronomy with a feeling of pure obligation, with remorse in case of violation of the law, etc.

For example, one evening I find Jacqueline, aged 2; 6 (15),[14] in bed, spoiling a towel by pulling out the threads one by one. Her mother has already often told her that it is a pity to do that, that it makes holes, that you can't mend the holes, etc. So I say to J.: "Oh, but mummy will be sad." J. answers calmly and even with an ill-concealed smile: *Yes. It makes holes. You can't mend"* . . . etc. I continue my lecture, but she obviously is not going to take me seriously. Still hiding her amusement with difficulty, she suddenly says to me *"Laugh!"* in so comic a tone, that in order to keep a straight face I quickly change the subject. J., very conscious of her powers of seduction, then says to me *"My little darling Daddy,"* and the incident ends. The next morning, however, J. wakes up full of it. Her first words refer to what had hap-

[14] 2; 6 (15)=2 years, 6 months and 15 days.

pened the night before. She thinks about the towel and asks her mother whether she isn't sad. So in spite of the first reaction showing such charming disrepect, my words had told and the command had brought about the usual consequences.

The evening of the same day, J. begins to pull the threads out of the towel again. Her mother repeats that it is a pity. J. listens attentively but says nothing. A moment later she is calling out and cries till someone comes to her: she simply wanted to see her parents again and make sure that they bore her no grudge.

We have here an example of a command bringing about, with or without apparent respect, a well-marked feeling of duty and of wrong. Now it seems obvious to us that such feelings are set up before the child has any clear consciousness of moral intention, or at any rate before it can distinguish between what is "done on purpose" (an action carried out knowingly and in voluntary defiance of the command) and what is "not done on purpose." A child of two and a half spoiling a bath towel has obviously no intention of doing harm. It is simply making an experiment in physics. Even if you ask it to stop, it may forget the command and begin again, or remember the rule too late to resist the first impulse. We would therefore not class J.'s conduct as described above among the acts of disobedience (which are by definition conscious) nor *a fortiori* among those committed with the intention of doing harm. And yet the sense of guilt is clearly present. It was not till after she was three years old that we noted in J. any reactions implying the notion that something "not done on purpose" could not be reckoned a fault. For instance, I say to her: "You know you're disturbing me just a little." Answer: *"I didn't think"* (in other words, "I didn't do it on purpose").[15] After the age of 4 months J., it is true, uses expressions like *"but it's your fault."* But these apply

[15] It is interesting to note that the moment when the idea of intention appears in the moral language of the child coincides more or less with the age of the first "whys." Indeed, as we have tried to show elsewhere (*L.T.*, chap. V), that the first "whys" correspond precisely to a need for motivation which results from the conscious realization of the intentionality of actions.

only to the material results and not to the intention. And it is just at this age, from the time when speech begins up to about three, that it is easiest to observe moral realism and objective responsibility in their pure and spontaneous state.

Let us turn, therefore, to obvious cases of objective responsibility. In the earliest stages of life cleanliness is a constant occasion for judgments of responsibility. Now it goes without saying that in such a domain the element of intentionality is almost entirely absent from the children's actions. Even the most orthodox Freudians cannot deny that in the vast majority of cases the child of one or two that cannot control its bodily functions when it is asleep or at play has simply not acquired the necessary physical control. Cases of intentional or even "unconscious" resistance to the rules of cleanliness are very rare at this age. Now, in spite of the purely automatic character of the reactions in question, parents are bound to ask their children to be careful. When accidents occur it is only natural that they should express their disappointment. In short, however delicately one may put the matter, there have to be commands and therefore duties. Now the curious thing is that the sense of guilt is proportional, not to the incidental negligence (as when the child forgets to "ask," etc.), but to the physical acts themselves.

For example, J. at 1; 11 (28) has been put to bed and given medicine of whose effects she has been informed. In spite of her mother's precautions, specially designed to avoid any reaction of shame or guilt, J. is greatly upset when the medicine works. Her face assumes an expression of distress, her eyes fill with tears, her mouth droops, and she is obviously experiencing the same feelings as if the thing had happened in normal circumstances through her own negligence.

But it must not be thought that this special domain is the only one propitious to the spontaneous development of objective responsibility. Any rule involving a material application admits of the same deviations. Another good example is that concerning food and the rules connected with it.

For some time J. has had a very small appetite, with the result that during this period of her life the essential rules of her universe were those appertaining to food. The World-Order decreed that one should take a cup of cocoa at four o'clock, a good bowlful of vegetables in the middle of the day, a few little drops (of hydrochloric acid) in water just before lunch, etc. Now once these orders had been accepted, right and wrong were defined by the conformity or non-conformity of actions in relation to them, and this independently of all possible intentions or circumstances. For example, one day J. at 2; 10 (7) is not very well and her mother feels that probably the usual plate of vegetables will be too much for her. Sure enough, after one or two mouthfuls J. shows signs of weariness. But she insists upon finishing her helping, because it is the rule. It is no good letting her off, she perseveres in her view, though she is not enjoying her food. Every time she is given a spoonful she cannot swallow it, but when the bowl is taken away she asks for it back, as though it were a sin not to empty it. Finally it is taken away and we try to reassure her by telling her that it is not her fault, that some days people are less hungry than others, etc. In spite of all these precautions taken by her mother, J. then begins to cry. Even when she has been comforted she still shows signs of remorse, promises to go to sleep, etc.

Another example. At the age of 2; 10 (23). J. is taking her hydrochloric acid as usual. But too many drops have been put in the glass, and J. is told that she need not drink it all. Sure enough, after taking a draught or two she complains that it prickles; she looks disgusted and even feels sick. All the same she wants to drink it all up. Her mother repeats that it is not necessary and lifts her down from her chair. J. bursts into tears as though she had done wrong. She comes back to the glass and insists upon drinking it up.

These last two examples seem to demonstrate how strong and spontaneous is the child's evaluation of objective responsibility. It is even staggering to find that in a little girl who has never known what authority is and whose parents make a point of cultivating autonomy of conscience in their children, the orders received should lead to so stubborn a moral realism. A rule emanating from the parents brings about a sense of duty against which the later attenuations of the parents themselves are for the moment powerless. It is true that in the three cases we have just quoted (cleanliness and rules about food) pride may play a certain part. The child will not admit defeat. But this very pride presupposes a realistic consciousness of rules. If the child did not consider it a sort of moral lapse in itself not to finish up her glass of medicine, her bowl of vegetables, or her cup of cocoa, she would not feel humiliated at being let off these obligations.[16]

A third group of examples relating to clumsiness must also be given. This will bring us back to the facts we have studied in the course of this chapter, since what we sought to analyse was precisely how the child evaluates the acts of clumsiness that he hears about in the set stories. Now, during the early years, a child will often regard his own clumsiness from a purely objective point of view, even to his own detriment.

J., at about 2 years old, is playing with a shell I have lent her. The shell is very fragile and breaks the first time it is dropped. J. is dismayed, and I have the greatest difficulty in persuading her that it is not her fault.

We need not dwell upon this example. It is a commonplace among children, and everyone will have had occasion to observe something like it. On this point too it is not until later that the child will differentiate involuntary clumsiness (pure accident) from clumsiness due to negligence or carelessness. In the early stages, it is only the result that counts.

In short, it is our belief that during the first years, the inevitable constraint of the adult—even if, as in the case of J., it is reduced to the minimum—necessarily brings about a certain moral realism which will be more or less marked according to the nature of the home and to the combined characters of parents and child. The moral realism which

16 We may add, in order to reassure the reader, that Jacqueline is by no means continually haunted by the commands which she respects.

later on we observe on the verbal plane would thus be the indirect result of these early phenomena.

But between the spontaneous moral realism of the early years and the theoretical moral realism which we analysed before, there is an intermediate link that must not be disregarded—we mean the judgment made by the child, not about his own actions, but about the conduct of his equals. As far as he himself is concerned he succeeds fairly soon (at about 3-4, when the first "whys" and the interest in motivation begin) in differentiating intentional faults from involuntary breaches of the moral code. And soon after this he learns to excuse himself by the plea of "not on purpose." But when it comes to the deeds of those around him, things appear in a very different light. Generally speaking, it is not going too far to say that the child—like ourselves—is more severe with others than with himself. The reason for this is quite simple. The conduct of other people appears in its outward shape long before we can understand the intentions behind it; so that we are apt immediately to compare this outward shape with the established rule and to judge the action by this essentially objective criterion. It is only by a continuous effort of generosity and sympathy that we can resist such a tendency and try to understand other people's reactions in terms of their intentions. It is obvious that the child is capable very early of such intropathy. But it is also obvious that during this phase where respect for rules still outweighs cooperation (the stage we have called "egocentric" in the game of marbles and in which rules are at once mystically accepted and egocentrically practised) it is also obvious, we repeat, that to judge psychologically will require a greater effort in the case of other people's actions than in that of our own. To put it differently, moral realism will last longer with regard to the evaluation of other people's conduct than with regard to that of one's own. And the facts, indeed, seem to bear this out.

Here from amongst many others is an observation which one of our students, Mme Weissfeller, has been kind enough to communicate to us. Parallels to it could be found in any child.

I. MAD (4 yrs.) says to her mother: *"You know, Mummy, I've wiped the dishes."* Ja (2½ yrs.) adds: *"Me too."* Mad: *"No, that's not true.—Yes.—No, you didn't wipe the dishes. So it's naughty to say that."* Mother: "Perhaps Ja is making a mistake and thinks she has wiped them." Mad: *"No, no, she didn't wipe them. It's not nice of her to say that. It was only me."*

II. Ja: *"You're all over spots, you are.*—Mad: *No. It's not true, it's not true.—It is true.*—Mad (furiously): *It's not true. That's nonsense. . . . Mummy, Ja is talking nonsense!"*

III. Ja, without meaning to, hurts Mad. Mad cries: *"Mummy, Ja is horrid. She hit me.*—But she didn't do it on purpose, she didn't want to hurt you.—*Yes she did, she did it on purpose. She hit me very hard. She hurt me very much."*

In dealing with the evaluation of the conduct of others we have approached the slightly artificial situation in which the child considers actions that are not directly observed but are described by means of a story. If moral realism lasts longer with regard to judgments made about others than in the purely individual domain, it goes without saying that its reign will be even further prolonged when it comes to the purely verbal examples contained in our stories. But here a third phenomenon comes in to complicate matters.

For the child's moral realism is certainly far more systematic on the plane of theory than on that of action, so that we would seem to be dealing here with something in the nature of a new and different phenomenon. The fact is that the conscious realization implied in all theoretical reflection does not merely repeat after a greater or lesser interval, what has effectively taken place in practical actions. There are, over and above the delays, distortions inherent in the very mechanism of reflection. For as soon as on immediate action there follows, or is superposed, a thought that is detached from reality and set free by the power of words or imagination, the mind is thrown out of focus, a whole set of illusions of perspective prevails, and especially the unconscious illusion of egocentrism. Thus it is that in the intellectual sphere, the child who tries to reason will be up against a series of difficulties which were conquered long ago by practical intelligence. Similarly, in the moral sphere when he simply has stories told to him, he will be led to make judgments devoid of pity and lacking in psychological insight, testifying therefore to a more or less systematic moral realism, whereas in real life he would undoubtedly sympathize with those whom from afar he regards as the greatest sinners.

We see, therefore, how the spontaneous moral realism of the early years, while it dwindles progressively with regard to the subject's own conduct, may very well develop elsewhere, first in the evaluation of other people's actions, and finally in reflection concerning purely theoretical cases involved in stories, in histories, and in social myths in general. If we were dealing with so-called primitive societies, we should have to add that these final products of moral realism, once they are consolidated by the social constraint of the group as a whole (in contrast to the elementary constraint of adults over children) are capable of reacting upon the actual minds of individuals by a repercussion that will be readily understood. But as we are speaking only of the child we may confine ourselves to the conclusion that moral realism does correspond to something effective and spontaneous in child thought. This result, moreover, is in complete agreement with what we found in the case of the game of marbles. Every rule, whether it be imposed upon the younger by the older child, or upon the child by the adult, begins by remaining external to the mind before it comes to be really interiorized. During this purely external phase, the most rigorous moral realism may very well go hand in hand with what seems to be the laxest and most egocentric practice.

Having cleared up this point let us now try to solve the problem of the nature of moral realism taken dynamically and reduced to the true proportions indicated by the preceding discussion. In other words, let us not any longer regard the results of our interrogatories as self-contained, but rather as the final and indirect outcome of a primitive and far more diffused tendency. It is this spontaneous moral realism—of which the children's theoretical talk is only the reflection—which we must now examine so as to establish its origin and conditions.

Moral realism seems to us to be due to the conjunction of two series of causes—those peculiar to the spontaneous thought of the child (childish "realism"), and those belonging to the constraint exercised by the adult. But this conjunction, far from being accidental, seems to us to be characteristic of the most general processes of child psychology as they occur in the intellectual as well as in the moral domain. For the fundamental fact of human psychology is that society, instead of remaining almost entirely inside the individual organism as in the case of animals prompted by their instincts, becomes crystallized almost entirely outside the individuals. In other words, social rules, as Durkheim has so powerfully shown, whether they be linguistic, moral, religious, or legal, etc., cannot be constituted transmitted, or preserved by means of an internal biological heredity, but only through the external pressure exercised by individuals upon each other. To put it in yet another way. As Bovet has demonstrated in the field of morals, rules do not appear in the mind of the child as innate facts, but as facts that are transmitted to him by his seniors, and to which from his tenderest years he has to conform by means of a *sui generis* form of adaptation. This, of course, does not prevent some rules from containing more than others an element of rationality, thus corresponding to the deepest functional constants of human nature. But whether they be rational or simply a matter of usage and consensus of opinion, rules imposed on the childish mind by adult constraint do begin by presenting a more or less uniform character of exteriority and sheer authority. So that instead of passing smoothly from an early individualism (the "social" element of the first months is only biologically social, so to speak, inside the individual, and therefore individualistic) to a state of progressive cooperation, the child is from his first year onwards in the grip of a coercive education which goes straight on and ends by producing what Claparède[17] has so happily called a veritable "short-circuit."

As a result of this we have three processes to consider: the spontaneous and unconscious egocentrism belonging to the individual as such, adult constraint, and cooperation.

[17] Claparède, *Experimental Education and Child Psychology.*

But—and this is the essential point—the spontaneous ego-centrism of the child, and the constraint of the adult, far from being each other's antitheses on all points, so far agree in certain domains as to give rise to paradoxical and singularly stable compromises. For cooperation alone can shake the child out of its initial state of unconscious egocentrism; whereas constraint acts quite differently and strengthens egocentric features (at any rate on certain points) until such time as cooperation delivers the child both from egocentrism and from the results of this constraint. We shall attempt to verify these statements with regard to moral realism, after which we shall compare this phenomenon with the precisely parallel processes that present themselves in the domain of child intelligence.

The first group of factors that tend to explain moral realism is therefore based on one of the most spontaneous features of child thought—realism in general. For the child is a realist, and this means that in almost every domain he tends to consider as external, to "reify" as Sully put it, the contents of his mind. And he has a systematic propensity for the reification of the contents of consciousness that are shared by all minds, whence his tendency to materialize and project into the universe the realities of social life.

Without going as far back as Baldwin's "projective" stage which is defined precisely by complete realism or the indissociation between what is subjective and what is objective, we could cite in support of our contention a large number of phenomena contemporary with moral realism itself.

It is particularly necessary to remember at this point the definite attitude taken up by children with regard to the products or the instruments of thought (see *C.W.*, Sect. I.). Dreams, for example, even when the child already knows that they are deceptive as to their contents, are, till about 7-8, systematically considered as an objective reality, as a sort of ethereal, rarefied picture floating in the air and fixed before our eyes. Names (comparable to moral rules in that they are transmitted and imposed by the adult surrounding) constitute an aspect of the objects themselves: each object has a name, co-substantial with its own nature, having always existed and been localized in the object. Finally, thought itself, instead of consisting in an internal activity, is conceived as a sort of material power in direct communication with the external universe.

In the domain of drawing, M. Luquet has given an admirable analysis of the phenomenon known as "intellectual realism." The child draws things as he knows them to be, not as he sees them. Of course such a habit is primarily a proof of the existence and extent of that rationalism that belongs to all thought and which alone can adequately account for the nature of perception. To perceive is to construct intellectually, and if the child draws things as he conceives them, it is certainly because he cannot perceive them without conceiving them. But to give up gradually the spurious absolutes situated away and apart from the context of relations that has been built up during experience itself is the work of a superior kind of rationality. When the child comes to draw things as he sees them, it will be precisely because he has given up taking isolated objects in and for themselves and has begun to construct real systems of relations which take account of the true perspective in which things are connected. Thus "intellectual realism," though it is the forerunner of authentic rationalism, also implies a deviation which consists in isolating too soon and therefore in "reifying" the early products of rational construction. It is therefore still "realism" in our sense of the term, that is to say, it is an illegitimate exteriorization of intellectual processes, an illegitimate fixation of each moment of the constructive movement.

Being therefore a realist in every domain, it is not surprising that the child should from the first "realize" and even "reify" the moral laws which he obeys. It is forbidden to lie, to steal, to spoil things, etc.—all, so many laws which will be conceived as existing in themselves, independently of the mind, and in consequence independently of individual circumstances and of intentions. For this is the place to recall the fundamental fact that, just because of the general realism of his spontaneous thought, the child, up to the age of about 7-8, always regards the notion of law as simultaneously moral and physical. Indeed, we have tried to show (*C.W.* and *C.C.*) that until the age of 7-8 there does not exist for the child a single purely mechanical law of nature. If clouds move swiftly when the wind is blowing, this is not only because of a necessary connection between the movement of the wind and that of the clouds; it is also and primarily because the clouds "must" hurry along to bring us rain, or night, etc. If the moon shines only by night and the sun only by day, it is not merely because of the material arrangements ensuring this regularity; it is primarily because the sun "is not allowed" to walk about at night, because the heavenly bodies are not masters of their destiny but are subject like all living beings to rules binding upon their wills. If boats remain afloat on the water while stones sink to the bottom, this does not happen merely for reasons relating to their weight; it is because things have to be so in virtue of the World-Order. In short, the universe is permeated with moral rules; physical regularity is not dissociated from moral obligation and social rule. Not that the last two are to be deemed more important than the first. Far from it. There is simply non-differentiation between the two ideas. The idea of physical regularity is as primitive as that of psychical or moral regularity, but neither is conceived independently of the other. It is only natural, therefore, that the moral rule should retain something physical about it. Like names, it is a part of things, a characteristic feature, and even a necessary condition of the universe. What, then, do intentions matter? The problem of responsibility is simply to know whether a law has been respected or violated. Just as if we trip, independently of any carelessness, we fall on to the ground in virtue of the law of gravity, so tampering with the truth, even unwittingly, will be called a lie and incur punishment. If the fault remains unnoticed, things themselves will take charge of punishing us (see following Chapter, § 3).

In short, moral realism seems to us from this point of view to be a natural and spontaneous product of child thought. For it is not nearly so natural as one would think for primitive thought to take intentions into account. The child is far more interested in the result than in the motivation of his own actions. It is cooperation which leads to the primacy of intentionality, by forcing the individual to be constantly occupied with the point of view of other people so as to compare it with his own. Indeed, one is struck to see how unconscious of itself and how little inclined to introspection is the egocentric thought of very young children (*J.R.*, Chap. IV., § 1 and 2). It may be objected to this that primitive thought seems, on the contrary, to be directed to a sort of universal intentionalism: childish animism consists in attributing intentions to all things, so also do the "whys," artificialism leads to the notion that nothing exists without a motive, etc. But this does not in any way contradict our thesis. For to attribute stereotyped intentions to every event is one thing, and to subordinate actions to the intentions that inspired them is another. The intentionalism that characterizes animism, artificialism, and the "whys" before 6-7 comes from a confusion between the psychical and the physical, whereas the priority of intentions over external rules implies an increasingly delicate differentiation between what is spiritual and what is material.

But these considerations are not sufficient to account for the phenomena we have observed, and we must now turn our attention to the second aspect of moral realism. For moral realism is also the product of adult constraint. Nor is there, as we have already pointed out, anything mysterious in this double origin. The adult is part of the child's universe, and the conduct and commands of the adult thus constitute the most important element in this World-Order which is the source of childish realism.

But there is more to it than this. It looks as though, in many ways, the adult did everything in his power to encourage the child to persevere in its specific tendencies, and to do so precisely in so far as these tendencies stand in the way of social development. Whereas, given sufficient liberty of action, the child will spontaneously emerge from his egocentrism and tend with his whole being towards cooperation, the adult most of the time acts in such a way as to strengthen egocentrism in its double aspect, intellectual and moral. Two things must be distinguished here, differing considerably in theoretical importance but of equal moment practically—the externality of adult commands and the lack of psychological insight in the average adult.

In the first place, moral commands almost inevitably remain external to the child—at any rate during the first years. Most parents burden their children with a number of duties of which the reason must long remain incomprehensible, such as not to tell lies of any kind, etc. Even in the most modern education, the child is forced to adopt a whole set of habits relative to food and cleanliness of which he cannot immediately grasp the why and the wherefore. All these rules are naturally placed by the child on the same plane as actual physical phenomena. One must eat after going for a walk, go to bed at night, have a bath before going to bed, etc., exactly as the sun shines by day and the moon by night, or as pebbles sink while boats remain afloat. All these things are and must be so; they are as the World-Order decrees that they should be, and there must be a reason for it all. But none of it is felt from within as an impulse of sympathy or of pity is felt. So that from the first we have a morality of external rules and a morality of reciprocity—or rather of the elements which will later on be utilized by moral reciprocity—and so long as these two moralities do not unite, the first will almost inevitably lead to a certain amount of realism.

But in the second place, and this unfortunately is no less important a consideration, the majority of parents are poor psychologists and give their children the most questionable of moral trainings. It is perhaps in this domain that one realizes most keenly how immoral it can be to believe too much in morality, and how much more precious is a little humanity than all the rules in the world. Thus the adult leads the child to the notion of objective responsibility, and consolidates in consequence a tendency that is already natural to the spontaneous mentality of little children.

It would be difficult, to be sure, to embark upon an objective enquiry in such matters. But if systematic investigation is lacking we have some precious sources of information which often enable us to plumb greater depths than are ever revealed by a mere accumulation of incomplete observations. Literature is at hand, moreover, to supplement scientific psychology. Edmund Gosse's autobiographic study, *Father and Son,* not to mention the many novels that revive almost unaltered the memories of childhood, tells us more than many a learned treatise on the subject. The individual examination of youthful delinquents or of "difficult" children is equally illuminating. Finally, it is impossible to psycho-analyse an adolescent or an adult without discovering that the subject's spontaneous anamnesia (always so full of interest) is crowded with the most definite memories relating to the mistakes which his parents made in bringing him up.

But although such methods alone will put exceptionally illuminating cases within our reach, it might perhaps be possible to set afoot an enquiry into the mentality of the "average parent" and to accumulate observations made in certain homogeneous and comparable situations, such for example as those in trains, especially on Sunday evenings after a day's outing. How can one fail to be struck on such occasions by the psychological inanity of what goes on: the efforts which the parents make to catch their children in wrong-doing instead of anticipating catastrophes and preventing the child by some little artifice or other from taking up a line of conduct which his pride is sure to make him stick to; the multiplicity of orders that are given (the "average parent" is like an unintelligent government that is content to accumulate laws in spite of the contradictions and the ever-increasing mental confusion which this accumulation leads to); the pleasure taken in inflicting punishments; the pleasure taken in using authority, and the sort of sadism which one sees so often in perfectly respectable folk, whose motto is that "the child's will must be broken," or that he must be "made to feel a stronger will than his."

Such a form of education leads to that perpetual state of tension which is the appanage of so many families, and which the parents responsible for it attribute, needless to say, to the inborn wickedness of the child and to original sin. But frequent and legitimate in many respects as is the child's revolt against such methods, he is nevertheless inwardly defeated in the majority of cases. Unable to distinguish precisely between what is good in his parents and what is open to criticism, incapable, owing to the "ambivalence" of his feelings towards them, of criticizing his parents objectively, the child ends in moments of attachment by inwardly admitting their right to the authority they wield over him. Even when grown up, he will be unable, except in very rare cases, to break loose from the affective schemas acquired in this way, and will be as stupid with his own children as his parents were with him.

It is clearly by this constraint exercised by one generation upon the other that we must seek to explain the rise and persistence of moral realism. Moral realism, rooted as it is in the whole of the child's spontaneous realism, is thus consolidated and stylized in a hundred ways by adult constraint. Such a meeting of the products of adult pressure with those of child mentality is no accident; it is not the exception but the rule in child psychology. And this can be only too easily explained, since it is through the age-long action, groping its way down the centuries, of the generations one upon the other that the essential elements of common morality and pedagogy have been formed by a mutual adaptation of the two mentalities thus confronted.

In order to show how natural is this double aspect of moral realism, let us compare it to a phenomenon which is its exact counterpart from the intellectual point of view —verbal realism, or verbalism, which results from the union between the spontaneous linguistic syncretism of the child and the verbal constraint of the adult.

One of the most striking features of the egocentric mentality from the intellectual point of view is syncretism, that is to say, perception, conception and reasoning by general ("global")[18] and unanalysed schemas. This phenomenon has been described by Decroly and by Claparède in the domain of perception, and it reappears in every aspect of child thought—explanation, understanding, reasoning, etc. (see *L.T.*, Chap. IX.). We found it to be particularly prevalent in the domain of verbal understanding. A sentence, a story, a proverb will give the child the impression that he has completely understood it as soon as he has succeeded in constructing out of it a sort of general inclusive schema, or "global" meaning, even when individual words or groups of

[18] In *L.T.* (1st Ed.) we translated the word *global* by "general" as the use of "global" had not yet been incorporated into current psychological terminology. It means, of course, the opposite of "analysed." [Trans.]

words are still quite incomprehensible to him. Such an attitude is closely bound up with egocentrism. For it is discussion and mutual criticism that urge us to analyse things; left to ourselves we are quickly satisfied with a "global," and consequently, a subjective explanation. Now "global" syncretism quite naturally leads the child to verbalism. Since every word obtains its meaning as a function of these syncretic schemas, words end by acquiring a substance of their own independently of reality. What, now, are the effects of adult constraint with regard to this verbalism? Does it progressively diminish this product of egocentrism or does it consolidate it? In so far as the adult can cooperate with the child, that is to say, can discuss things on an equal footing and collaborate with him in finding things out, it goes without saying that his influence will lead to analysis. But in so far as his words are spoken with authority, in so far, especially, as verbal instruction outweighs experiment in common, it is obvious that the adult will consolidate childish verbalism. Unfortunately it is the second alternative that is most often realized in the teaching given in schools and even in the home. The prestige of the spoken word triumphs over any amount of active experiment and free discussion. Schools have been held responsible for the verbalism of children. This is not quite correct, as verbalism arises out of certain spontaneous tendencies in the child. But the school, instead of creating an atmosphere favourable to the diminution of these tendencies, does base its teaching upon them and consolidate them by making use of them.

All this will have served to show the parallelism between moral and intellectual facts in the domain of realism. Moral realism and verbalism are therefore the two clearest manifestations of the way in which adult constraint combines with childish egocentrism.

GENERAL CONCLUSION

The results obtained in the course of our study of moral realism confirm those of our analysis of the game of marbles. There seem to exist in the child two separate moralities, of which, incidentally, the consequences can also be discerned in adult morality. These two moralities are due to formative processes which, broadly speaking, follow on one another without, however, constituting definite stages. It is possible, moreover, to note the existence of an intermediate phase. The first of these processes is the moral constraint of the adult, a constraint which leads to heteronomy and consequently to moral realism. The second is cooperation which leads to autonomy. Between the two can be discerned a phase during which rules and commands are interiorized and generalized.

Moral constraint is characterized by unilateral respect. Now, as M. Bovet has clearly shown, this respect is the source of moral obligation and of the sense of duty: every command coming from a respected person is the starting-point of an obligatory rule. This has been abundantly confirmed by our enquiry. The obligation to speak the truth, not to steal, etc., are all so many duties which the child feels very deeply, although they do not emanate from his own mind. They are commands coming from the adult and accepted by the child. Originally, therefore, this morality of duty is essentially heteronomous. Right is to obey the will of the adult. Wrong is to have a will of one's own. There is no room in such an ethic for what moralists have called "the good" in contrast to "the right" or pure duty, since the good is a more spontaneous ideal and one that attracts rather than coerces mind. The relations between parents and children are certainly not only those of constraint. There is a spontaneous mutual affection, which from the first prompts the child to acts of generosity, and even of self-sacrifice, to very touching demonstrations which are in no way prescribed. And here no doubt is the starting point for that morality of good which we shall see developing alongside of the morality of right or duty, and which in some persons completely replaces it. The good is a product of cooperation. But the relation of moral constraint which begets duty can of itself lead to nothing but heteronomy. In its extreme forms it leads to moral realism.

Then comes an intermediate stage, which M. Bovet has noted with great subtlety[19]; the child no longer merely obeys

[19] See also Baldwin's *Social and Ethical Interpretations in Mental Development.*

the commands given him by the adult but obeys the rule itself, generalized and applied in an original way. We have observed this phenomenon in connection with lying. At a given moment the child thinks that lies are bad in themselves and that even if they were not punished, one ought not to lie. Here, undoubtedly, is a manifestation of intelligence working on moral rules as on all other data by generalizing them and differentiating between them. But the autonomy towards which we are moving is still only half present: there is always a rule that is imposed from outside and does not appear as the necessary product of the mind itself.

How does the child ever attain to autonomy proper? We see the first signs of it when he discovers that truthfulness is necessary to the relations of sympathy and mutual respect. Reciprocity seems in this connection to be the determining factor of autonomy. For moral autonomy appears when the mind regards as necessary an ideal that is independent of all external pressure. Now, apart from our relations to other people, there can be no moral necessity. The individual as such knows only anomy and not autonomy. Conversely, any relation with other persons, in which unilateral respect takes place, leads to heteronomy. Autonomy therefore appears only with reciprocity, when mutual respect is strong enough to make the individual feel from within the desire to treat others as he himself would wish to be treated.

And this is the subject we shall try to analyse in the course of the next chapter.

Chapter 3

Cooperation and the Development of the Idea of Justice

OUR STUDY OF the rules of a game led us to the conclusion that there exist two types of respect, and consequently two moralities—a morality of constraint or of heteronomy, and a morality of cooperation or of autonomy. We became familiar in the course of the last chapter with certain aspects of the first. The second, which will occupy us now, is unfortunately much more difficult to study; for while the first can be formulated in rules and thus lends itself to interrogation, the second must be sought chiefly among the more intimate impulses of the mind or in social attitudes that do not easily admit of definition in conversations held with the children. We have established its juridical aspect, so to speak, in studying the social play of children between 10 and 12. We must now go further, and penetrate into the child's actual consciousness. And this is where things begin to be complicated.

But if the affective aspect of cooperation and reciprocity eludes interrogation, there is one notion, probably the most rational of all moral notions, which seems to be the direct result of cooperation and of which the analysis can be at-

[1] With the collaboration of Mlles M. Rambert, N. Baechler, and A. M. Feldweg.

197

tempted without encountering too much difficulty—we mean the notion of justice. It will therefore be on this point that most of our efforts will be directed.

The conclusion which we shall finally reach is that the sense of justice, though naturally capable of being reinforced by the precepts and the practical example of the adult, is largely independent of these influences, and requires nothing more for its development than the mutual respect and solidarity which holds among children themselves. It is often at the expense of the adult and not because of him that the notions of just and unjust find their way into the youthful mind. In contrast to a given rule, which from the first has been imposed upon the child from outside and which for many years he has failed to understand, such as the rule of not telling lies, the rule of justice is a sort of immanent condition of social relationships or a law governing their equilibrium. And as the solidarity between children grows we shall find this notion of justice gradually emerging in almost complete autonomy.

It was these considerations which prompted us to introduce into this chapter the study of a question which is not directly connected with the notion of justice—that of the solidarity between children and the conflicts into which this solidarity enters with adult authority in cases of "tale-telling." This analysis will enable us to determine at what age solidarity begins to be efficacious. And we shall find that it is precisely after this age that the equalitarian notion of justice begins to assert itself with sufficient strength to overcome the authority of the adult.

Finally, to this study of the notion of justice must be joined, needless to say, at least a summary analysis of children's ideas about punishments. Distributive justice, which is defined by equality, has always been connected in the general mind with retributive justice, which is defined by due proportion between acts and punishments. Although the second aspect of the notion of justice is less closely connected with the problem of cooperation it must also, of course, be submitted to examination. Indeed, we shall deal with it first so as to leave our subsequent analysis untrammelled by considerations of this particular aspect of the question.

The plan we shall follow is then as follows. We shall begin by studying the problem of punishments, then that of collective responsibility and of so-called "immanent" justice (in which the punishment is supposed to emanate from things themselves). After which, by way of transition, we shall examine the conflict between retributive justice and distributive justice. Having reached this point, we shall proceed to the analysis of the relations between distributive justice and authority (also between childish solidarity and authority), then to the study of justice between children, and we shall wind up with a general discussion of the relations between justice and cooperation.

§ 1. THE PROBLEM OF PUNISHMENTS AND RETRIBUTIVE JUSTICE

There are in existence two distinct ideas of justice. We say that an award is unjust when it penalizes the innocent, rewards the guilty, or when, in general, it fails to be meted out in exact proportion to the merit or guilt in question. On the other hand, we say that a division is unjust when it favours some at the expense of others. In this second acceptation of the term, the idea of justice implies only the idea of equality. In the first acceptation of the term, the notion of justice is inseparable from that of reward and punishment, and is defined by the correlation between acts and their retribution.

It seems to us more profitable to begin with the first of these two ways of thinking because it is the one we can relate most directly to adult constraint and to the problems examined in the last chapter. It is also very probably the more primitive of the two conceptions of justice, if by primitive is meant, not so much what is early in point of time but what is most overlaid with elements that will be eliminated in the course of mental development. For there exists in certain notions about retribution a factor of transcendence and obedience which a more autonomous form of morality tends to eliminate. In any case, the problem is to determine whether these two notions develop *pari passu* or whether the second does not tend to predominate over the first.

But in any interrogation of children on punishments we are, of course, up against considerable technical difficulties, because on such a subject the child is far more likely to offer the questioner the usual little family lecture than to show him his real feelings on the question—feelings which he but rarely has occasion to put into words, and which, perhaps, do not altogether admit of formulation. We therefore adopted a more oblique method of approach.

In order to find out up to what point children regarded punishments as just, we decided to split up the difficulty. In the first place, one can, without throwing any doubt upon the notion of retribution itself, suggest different types of punishment to the child and then ask him which is the most fair. In this way it is possible to contrast with expiatory punishment—the only true punishment in the eyes of those who believe in the primacy of retributive justice[2]—a punishment by reciprocity which is simply derived from the idea of equality. It goes without saying that the child's reaction to such problems as these will be highly instructive from the point of view of the evolution of the retributive idea. In the second place, and once this point has been gained, it will be possible to try and find out whether the child regards punishment as just and as efficacious by making him compare (in pairs) stories where the children are punished and stories where the parents are content to reproach their children and explain to them the consequences of their actions. The subject is then asked to say which of these children will be most likely to commit the forbidden deed again, those who have or those who have not been the object of punishment.

Once these points have been cleared up—but not till then —it will be possible, in talking to the child, to enlarge a little upon the subject and thus lead him on to general questions such as what punishments are for, whether there is any reason for retribution, and so on. This discussion, which would be purely verbal if it came at the beginning, can be main-

[2] See how Durkheim (*Education Morale,* pp. 188-192) revives and rejuvenates the doctrine of expiation in support of his doctrine of penality.

tained on the concrete plane in so far as it draws upon the judgments which the child has just pronounced concerning the stories he has been told.

Very briefly, the result we shall be led to is the following. Two types of reaction are to be found with regard to punishment. Some think that punishment is just and necessary; the sterner it is, the juster, and it is efficacious in the sense that the child who has been duly chastized will in the future do his duty better than others. Others do not regard expiation as a moral necessity; among possible punishments those only are just that entail putting things right, a restoration of the *status quo ante,* or which make the guilty one endure the consequences of his deed; or again, those which consist in a purely reciprocal treatment. Indeed, apart from such non-expiatory penalties, punishment, as such, is regarded as useless, reproach and explanation being deemed more profitable than chastizement. On the average, this second mode of reaction is found more frequently among the older children, while the first is oftener to be found among the little ones. But the first, favoured as it is by certain types of family life and social relationships, survives at all ages and is even to be found in many adults.

Here are the questions we used concerning the various types of punishment. We begin by saying to the subject, "Are the punishments given to children always very fair, or are some fairer than others?" The child generally takes the latter view, but whatever he may answer, we proceed: "You know, it isn't at all easy to know how to punish children so as to be quite fair. Lots of fathers and teachers don't know how to. So I thought I would ask the children themselves, you and your friends. I shall tell you all sorts of silly things that little children have done, and you'll tell me how you think they ought to be punished." Then we tell the first part of the story (the account of the misdeed committed). The child invents a punishment, which we take note of, and we go on to say, "Yes, that might do. But the father didn't think of that. He thought of three punishments, and he wondered which would be most fair. I'll tell you what they were, and you will choose which it is to be." Care must be taken, once the child has chosen the best punishment, to ask him why it is the fairest. Then we ask in the child's own terminology which is the most severe (or the "stiffest" or the most "boring," etc.) and determine whether the child evaluates the punishment in terms of its severity or in accordance with some other criterion of retribution.

Here are the stories:

Story I. A little boy is playing in his room. His mother asks him to go and fetch some bread for dinner because there is none left in the house. But instead of going immediately the boy says that he can't be bothered, that he'll go in a minute, etc. An hour later he still has not gone. Finally, dinner time comes, and there is no bread on the table. The father is not pleased and he wonders which would be the fairest way of punishing the boy. He thinks of three punishments. The first would be to forbid the boy to go on the roundabouts the next day. There happened to be a fair the next day, and the little boy was to go and have a good time on the roundabouts. Well, as he wouldn't go and fetch the bread, he shan't go to the fair. The second punishment the father thought of was not to let the boy have any bread to eat. There was a little of yesterday's bread left in the cupboard and the parents are going to eat that, but as the little boy didn't go and fetch a fresh loaf, there will not be enough to go round. So the boy gets hardly any dinner to eat. The third punishment the father thinks of is to do to the boy the same thing as he had done. The father would say to him, "You wouldn't help your mother. Well I am not going to punish you, but the next time you ask me to do anything for you, I shall not do it, and you will see how annoying it is when people do not help each other." The little boys thinks that will be all right, but a few days later he wants a toy that is right at the top of the cupboard. He tries to reach it, but he is too small; he gets a chair, but it is still too high. So he finds his father and asks for his help. Then the father says, "Now, you remember what I said to you, old man. You wouldn't help your mother, so I don't feel inclined to help you either. When you make yourself useful I shall too, but not before."—Which of these three punishments was the fairest?

Story II. A boy has not done his sums for school. The next day he tells the teacher that he couldn't do his sums because he was ill. But as he had fine rosy cheeks the teacher thought that he was making it up, so she went and told his father and mother. The father wants to punish the little boy, but he can't decide between three punishments. First punishment: to copy out a poem fifty times. Second punishment: the father will say to the boy, "You say you are ill. Very well then, we shall take care of you. You shall go to bed for a whole day and take a dose of medicine to make you better." Third punishment: "You have told a lie. Now I shall not be able to believe you any longer, and even if you tell the truth I shall not be sure." The next day the boy gets a good mark at school. Whenever he gets a good mark his father gives him a penny to put in his money box. But this time when the boy comes home and says he has had a good mark the father says, "That may be true, old man, but as you told a lie yesterday I can't believe you any longer. I won't give you a penny to-day because I don't know whether what you are telling me is the truth. If you go several days without telling any lies then I shall believe you again and everything will be all right." Which is the fairest of these three punishments?

Story III. One afternoon a little boy was playing in his room. His father had only asked him not to play ball for fear of breaking the windows. His father had hardly gone when the boy got his ball out of the cupboard and began to play with it. And bang goes the ball against a window pane and smashes it! When the father comes home and sees what has happened he thinks of three punishments: 1) To leave the window unmended for several days (and then, as it is winter, the boy will not be able to play in his room). 2) Make the boy pay for having broken the window. 3) Not to let him have his toys for a whole week.

Story IV. A boy has broken a toy belonging to his little brother. What should be done? Should he 1) give the little fellow one of his own toys? 2) pay for having it mended? 3) not be allowed to play with any of his own toys for a whole week?

Story V. Playing ball in a passage (it was forbidden) a boy knocked over a pot of flowers and broke it. What should be his punishment? 1) To go into the wood and get a new plant and plant it himself? 2) To be smacked? 3) To have all his toys broken on purpose?

Story VI. A child is looking at a picture book belonging to his father. Instead of being careful, he makes spots on several of the pages. What shall the father do? 1) The child will not go to the cinema that evening. 2) The father will not lend him the book any more. 3) The child often lends his stamp-album to his father, the father will not take care of it as he has always done up till then.

Story VII. The leader of a band of robbers has died. Two candidates, Charles and Leon, stand for election to the leadership. Charles is elected leader. Leon is furious and denounces Charles to the police by means of an anonymous letter in which he accuses him of a robbery in which the whole band were involved. He tells the police where and how Charles is to be found. Charles is arrested. The robbers decide to punish Leon. What should they do? 1) Not give him any money for a month? 2) Turn him out of the band? 3) Accuse him too of being an accomplice by means of an anonymous letter?

Obviously the child is not asked all these questions at once, but only those that interest him. Equally obvious is the fact that these stories are extremely naïve, and that in real life many of the punishments suggested here would be applied according to a very different measure. But the essential thing to aim at in these interrogatories is to get the stories schematized, even if at times this means rather forcing the note, and presenting to the child types of punishment based on principles that are clearly distinct from each other. For it is with the principle that the conversation with the subject must concern itself and not with the detailed mode of its application.

Now it appears to us that the punishments described in this chapter, as likewise punishments in general, can be classed according to two distinct principles. Every action that is judged to be guilty by a given social group consists in the violation of the rules of the group and therefore in a sort of breach of the social bond itself. Punishment, as Durkheim has shown, therefore consists in restitution, in "putting things right," in a reinstatement of the social bond and of the authority of rules. But just as we have recognized the existence of two types of rules corresponding with two fundamental types of social relationship, so we must expect to meet in the domain of retributive justice with two modes of reaction and two types of punishment.

There are, in the first place, what we shall call *expiatory punishments,* which seem to us to go hand in hand with constraint and the rules of authority. Take any given rule imposed upon the individual's mind from without, and suppose the individual to have transgressed this rule. Independently even of the indignation and anger that will occur in the group or among those in authority, and which will inevitably be visited upon the transgressor, the only way of putting things right is to bring the individual back to his duty by means of a sufficiently powerful method of coercion and to bring home his guilt to him by means of a painful punishment. Thus expiatory punishment has an arbitrary character, arbitrary in the sense that, in linguistics, the choice of a sign is arbitrary in relation to the thing signified, that is to say, there is no relation between the content of the guilty act and the nature of its punishment. It is all one when a lie has been told whether you inflict corporal punishment on the transgressor, or take his toys away from him or condemn him to some school task: all that matters is that a due proportion should be kept between the suffering inflicted and the gravity of the misdeed.

And there are, in the second place, what we shall call *punishments by reciprocity* in so far as they go hand in hand with cooperation and rules of equality. Take any rule that the child accepts from within, that is to say of which he knows that it binds him to his equals by the bond of reciprocity (*e.g.,* not to lie, because lying does away with mutual trust, etc.). If this rule is violated, there is no need, in order to put things right again, for a painful coercion which will impose respect for the law from without; it will be enough for the breach of the social bond incurred by the transgressor to make its effects felt, in other words, it will be enough if the principle of reciprocity be brought into play. Since the rule is no longer, as before, something imposed from without, something which the individual could dispense with, but on the contrary constitutes a necessary relation between the individual and those around him, it suffices to make plain the consequences following upon the violation of this law in order to make the individual feel isolated and to make him long for a return to normal relations. Censure no longer needs to be emphasized by means of painful punishment: it acts with full force in so far as the measures taken by way of reciprocity make the transgressor realize the significance of his misdeeds.[3] In contrast, then, to expiatory punishment, punishment by reciprocity is, to use the terminology of linguistics again, necessarily "motivated"; misdeed and punishment, that is to say, are related both in content and nature, not to speak of the proportion kept between the gravity of the one and the rigour of the other. And so it follows that, various kinds of misdeeds being possible, we can distinguish in punishment by reciprocity a number of different varieties which will be more or less suitable and just according to the nature of the reprehensible act.

In order to classify these varieties let us return to our stories. To begin with, it is easy to see which are the punishments we regard as expiatory: not being allowed to go to the fair or the cinema (I and VI), copying a poem out fifty times (II), having one's toys taken away (III and IV), being smacked (V) or fined (VII). But of course any punishment, even some of the others suggested in these examples, can take on an expiatory character according to the spirit in which it is applied. A child will often explain that he has selected a given punishment because it was the most severe, although actually his choice seemed to be based on quite different principles. In such cases the punishment in question is clearly

---

[3] It is clear that measures of reciprocity also contain an element of suffering. But the pain is not inflicted for its own sake nor is it destined to instil respect for the law in the subject's mind. Such suffering as does occur (accompanied at times by material disadvantages) is simply an inevitable result of the breach of the bond of solidarity.

still of the expiatory order. As to punishments by reciprocity, they can be classed as follows, going, roughly, from the more to the less severe.

First there is exclusion—momentary or permanent—from the social group itself (story VII). This is the punishment that is often resorted to by children amongst themselves, as when, for example, they refuse to go on playing with an impenitent cheat. It is the punishment which one uses in ordinary life when one refuses to play a game with a child or take him a walk when experience has shown that he cannot behave on such occasions. The social bond is temporarily broken.

A second group can be formed by all those punishments that appeal only to the immediate and material consequences of the act: having no bread for dinner when you have refused to go and fetch some when there wasn't enough in the house (story I), being put to bed when you have pretended to be ill (II), having a cold room when you have broken the window pane (III). It is of punishments like this that Rousseau, Spencer and many others were thinking when they claimed that the child should be educated by natural experience alone. It is true that, as Durkheim has shown, the "natural" consequence of a misdeed is necessarily a social consequence, viz. the censure it provokes. Only Durkheim seems to think that censure, in order to be efficacious, should be accompanied by an expiatory punishment, when actually the direct and material consequences of the deed are often amply sufficient to fulfil this office. All that matters is that the transgressor should realize that this consequence, however natural it may be, is approved by the social group. This is why we have classed this kind of punishment among the punishments by reciprocity. When the child in story I has no bread for dinner, and the one in story III is left with a room *minus* a window pane, since the first had neglected to get the bread and the second had broken the window, what really happens is that the parents themselves refuse to put things right; they respond to their children's negligence by refusing to come to their aid. The punishment is still, therefore, one of reciprocity. Similarly, when the father in story II pretends to believe his son when he is lying and sends him to bed since he says he is ill, or again refuses henceforth to believe him even when he is speaking the truth (punishment III), he is really acting on reciprocity. True, the punishment is a "natural consequence" of the act, since the consequence of lying is either that the liar is taken at his word, or that he is no longer believed at all, but added to this is the fact that the father deliberately simulates credulity or suspicion in order to show the child that the bond of mutual trust is broken. So here again, the principle of reciprocity is at work. It is our belief, therefore, that all cases of so-called natural punishments imply reciprocity, because in all of them the group or the educator wishes to make the transgressor feel that the bond of solidarity is broken.

In the third place, there is the kind of punishment that consists in depriving the transgressor of the thing he has misused. For example, not to lend a child a book that he has made spots on (story VI). We have here a mixture of elements analogous to those which characterized the last two varieties: a sort of termination of contract owing to the conditions of the contract not having been observed.

Fourthly, we can group under the name of simple reciprocity, or reciprocity proper, those punishments that consist in doing to the child exactly what he has done himself. For example, not to help him (story I), to break his toys (story V), not to take care of his stamp album (story VI), to tell on him, if he has told on you (story VII). It need hardly be pointed out that this kind of punishment, while it is perfectly legitimate when we want to make the child understand the results of his actions, becomes irritating and absurd when it only means giving back evil for evil, and capping one irreparable destruction with another (stories I and VI).

Fifthly, there is purely "restitutive" punishment—paying for or replacing a broken or stolen object, etc. Durkheim was right in contrasting restitutive and retributive punishments. But if we divide the latter themselves into two types according as they are expiatory or due merely to reciprocity, restitutive punishment may be taken as the limiting case of punishment by reciprocity. For here censure no longer plays any part and justice is satisfied with a simple putting right of the material damage. Restitutive punishments, it should however, be noted, are often impure, and may retain an element of retribution. This is why we have classed them in the present division.

Finally, a sixth category might be distinguished which would consist of censure only, without punishment, not imposed by authority, but concerned only to make the transgressor realize how he has broken the bond of solidarity. But we must not complicate matters unnecessarily, and the question will be reserved for discussion later on.

The conclusion of this analysis is therefore that there are two types of punishment or retributive justice: expiatory punishment inherent in the relations of constraint, and punishment by reciprocity. Let us turn to the experimental data and see whether the child tends towards one or other of these according to the level of his development.

Mlle Baechler undertook to question 65 children between 6 and 12 years of age on these points, and I interviewed some thirty myself. The following statistics therefore deal with about a hundred children. But as each child may give answers that differ according to the story and will thus oscillate between expiatory punishment and punishment by reciprocity, we calculated by stories and not by children, taking as our unit each separate answer given by each separate child. As children can hardly be questioned on more than four stories at a time, this gives us a total of about 400 units.

It is obvious that in such a field as this, evolution does not proceed in exact step with age: there are too many interfering factors at work. But taking things broadly, we were surprised at the clearness which marked the evolution. We divided the children into three groups, aged respectively 6-7, 8-10, and 11-12 years (the last group including two backward subjects of 13), and we found the percentage of punishments by reciprocity out of the totality of answers to be as follows:

	6-7 yrs.	8-10 yrs.	11-12 yrs.
Children interviewed by Mlle B.	30%	44%	78%
TOTAL	28%	49%	82%

These figures, it need hardly be pointed out, cannot be regarded as of great importance. To begin with, they relate only to the children belonging to a certain ethnical group and a certain social stratum (the poorer parts of Geneva and a few children from an elementary school at Neuchâtel). Again, it cannot be denied that, however careful one may be (see *C.W.*, Introduction), the manner of asking the questions plays a very important part. Indeed, it is rather disturbing to find that the children one interviews oneself answer more often in conformity with one's own theory than do the children interviewed by other people! The personal factor here cannot be disregarded, and it renders all such statistics more or less open to suspicion. All we shall take from these figures is the fact that, roughly speaking, judgments of retributive justice seem to undergo a certain evolution as the child grows older: the younger children favour expiatory punishment, while the older ones tend more towards punishment by reciprocity.

Two important reservations must, however, be made. The first is that alongside of the problem of stages, there is the problem of types. Some minds are irrevocably attached to the idea of expiation (Joseph de Maistre as compared to Guyau . . .). They are, of course, the product of a certain kind of upbringing, of a certain kind of social and religious education. But their deepest features subsist independently of age. We would therefore not be at all surprised if in other social *milieux* the results of the interrogatory turned out to be quite different.

In the second place, when the children have to think of a punishment themselves, instead of choosing from among the various punishments proposed, they nearly always turn to expiatory punishment, and their choice is often astonishingly severe.[4] But this does not really contradict our present results. Of course, if the child's attention is not drawn to the different possible types of punishment—without even defining them, simply by presenting them to him as we do here—the subject will do no more than think of the punishments to which he is accustomed, namely those that are "arbitrary" and expiatory.

Let us now turn to the analysis of the cases. Here, to

[4] See, in this connection, the enquiries made by Knapp in *L'Intermédiaire des Educateurs.*

begin with, are examples of children who think arbitrary
punishments are the most "fair."

ANG (6) repeats story I correctly: "How should he be
punished?—*Shut him up in a room.*—What will that do to
him?—*He'd cry.*—Would that be fair?—*Yes.*" He is then
told of the three possible punishments: "Which is the fairest?
—*I'd have not given him his toy.*—Why?—*He'd been
naughty.*—Is that the best of the three punishments?—*Yes.*—
Why?—*Because he was very fond of his toy.*—Is that the
fairest?—*Yes.*" Thus it is not the principle of reciprocity that
carries the day, it is the idea of the severest punishment.

FIL (6), Story I: "*My daddy is bad to us. He puts us in
a dark cupboard, he does. Well, if I had a dark cupboard
I'd put him in there till the evening and I'd give him a damn
good box on the ear. And if I had a strap, I'd do nothing but
beat him.*" He chooses the third of the three punishments
"*because he'd like to go to the fair, so it'll annoy him*" (Fr.
Ça l'énerve alors).

ZIM (6), Story I: Zim does not think much of the last two
punishments. The third "*is not hard.*—Why?—*On the little
boy.*—Why is it not hard on him?—*It isn't much.*" The
second is also "*not much.*" The fairest is therefore the first
"*because he's not on the Roundabouts.*"

MORD (7), Story VI: The fairest punishment is to stop
him going to the cinema. "Why?—*It suits him better than
the other two. It's worse. It's lovely going to the Pictures.
But it's not lovely not giving him the album back.*—Why?—
*Going to the Pictures is lovely. But when he's had his book
five or six times he'll say, 'I've had enough of looking at it,
I don't care if he doesn't lend it to me any more.'*"

SYL (7½), Story II: "The fairest?—*To make her do fifty
lines. That's the worst punishment, because she isn't allowed
out.*"

MAY (7½), Story I: The fairest punishment is "*not to
give him any bread. That'll punish him most. That'll make
him go and fetch some other time.*" Story VI: "*I wouldn't
take her to the Pictures, because that is what she would like
best, the Pictures.*—What is the second punishment?—*I
wouldn't take care of her album. She likes collecting stamps.*
—Would that do?—*It wouldn't punish her enough. It*

wouldn't make her [become] *good enough.—-*Which is the worst punishment?—*Not taking her to the Pictures."*

ALI (7½), Story II: *"I'd make him write out fifty lines in his copy book. That would be a punishment, then he wouldn't do it again because he'd have to write them out again.—*Is that the fairest?—*It serves the little boy right. He didn't need to tell lies.* [It is the fairest] *because it is a strict punishment.* —Which is the fairest?—*Writing out fifty lines because it's a bore. He can't have any fun."*

BLA (7½), Story I: *"I wouldn't have let him go on the Roundabouts.—*Why?—*Because it's lovely on the Roundabouts!"*

PEL (7½), G., Story I: "Which do you think the fairest? —*Not to go on the Roundabouts.—*Why?—*Because he didn't help his mother.—*Which is the 'stiffest' of the three?—*Not to go on the Roundabouts."* Story II: "Which is the fairest of the three punishments?—*Copying out the poem fifty times.* —Why is that the fairest?—*Because it is the strictest."*

JEAN (8), Story I: "Which of the three punishments was the fairest?—*Not to go on the Roundabouts.—*Why was that the fairest?—*Because the child wants to go* [on the Roundabouts] *and he's not allowed to.—*Which of the three punishments does he hate most?—*Not going on the Roundabouts."*

SUT (8), same reaction to the first story. Story II: "Which is the fairest of those three punishments?—*When he was made to copy out the poem fifty times.—*Why was that the fairest?—*Because he ought to have done his sums, and he didn't.—*Which is the worst bore of the three?—*Copying out the poem fifty times."* Story IV: "Which of these punishments do you think is the fairest?—*The third* [taking his toys away].—Why is that the fairest?—*Because he shouldn't have broken his little brother's toy.—*And are the other two fair too?—*Yes, M'sieu.—*Let us take the second and third. Which is fairest, to make him pay for the toy he broke or to take all his toys away from him?—*To take all his toys away.—*Why is that fairer?— . . . —What does he hate most?— *Having his toys taken away."* Story V: "Which is the fairest? —*Having a toy broken.—*Why is that the fairest?— . . . — Which would have made him most angry of these three punishments?—*To have one of his toys broken."* Thus what counts is not reciprocity, even in this last case; it is the idea that the severity of a punishment determines its justice.

KEC (8), Story I: "Which is the fairest?—*Not to go on the Roundabouts.*—Is that the fairest?—*Yes.*—Why?—*Because he likes going on the Roundabouts.*" As to the other two, the fairest would be not to let him have any bread. "*If he likes bread, then he mustn't be given any.*"

BAD (9), Story I: "*I like the one about the Cinema best. Because that is the fairest, because he will have been stopped doing something he likes.*"

BAU (10), Story I: "*The Roundabouts is the best.*—Why? —*Because he liked that. He ought to be stopped doing what he liked doing best.*"

The general meaning of these answers is not hard to perceive. In these children's eyes, punishment consists, as a matter of course, in inflicting upon the guilty a pain that will smart enough to make them realize the gravity of their misdeed. Naturally, the fairest punishment will be the most severe. Each of the subjects questioned marks in his own way this linkage of the idea of retributive justice to the severity of the punishment, but the most characteristic expressions are, "It is worse" (Mord, Syl, etc.), "That will punish him most" (May), "A strict punishment" (Ali).

It is quite clear that none of these children mean the punishment to mark a break in the bond of solidarity nor to drive home the need for reciprocity: there is a predominance of expiatory punishment. True, there exists a certain ambiguity on this point. Many educationalists look upon punishment, even when it consists in inflicting "arbitrary" suffering, only as a preventive measure, aimed at avoiding repetitions of the fault. Only a minority regard punishment as strictly expiatory, *i.e.*, as serving to wipe out either by compensation or by the efficacy of suffering the actual fault that had been committed. How does the matter stand with children? The remarks made on punishment in general by the subjects questioned in the preceding interrogatory seem to confirm us in believing that the two attitudes coexist in each child, but in a confused and undifferentiated manner. For the child will at one time emphasize the vindictive aspect of punishment as of sheer chastisement inflicted by a higher power (see Fil, for ex-

ample), at others he comes of himself to the theory of preventive punishment. Thus, according to May, a given punishment is not sufficient because "it wouldn't make her [become]
good enough." But even here there is in the child's mind the
idea of a necessary compensation, and it would be contrary
to justice in his view not to punish the transgressor at all.
And as the punishments in question are chosen as a function
of the painful element they contain, this necessary compensation is thus equivalent to the notion of expiation.

Let us now turn to the children who regard punishment by
reciprocity as more just:

GEO (7), Story I: "Which of the three punishments is the
fairest?—*Not to help him.*—Why?—*He hadn't helped at
home, so it is almost the same thing.*—And if his father
hadn't thought of that punishment, which would be the
fairest?—*Not to go on the Roundabouts . . . Oh, no! That he
should have no supper. Because he wouldn't help his mother,
so he mustn't have any supper.*—Which of the three punishments is the least fair?—*The one of the Roundabouts.*—
Why?—*Because he was looking forward to them.*" Story III:
"Which is the fairest?—*To pay for the window pane.*—Why
is it the fairest?—*Because it will be as if he had paid for it
once* [=because it would be putting things right].—And
otherwise, which would be the fairest?—*To leave him with
the broken pane. That will teach him not to break windows.*
—Which punishment is the least fair?—*To take his toys away
for several days.*—Which is the worst bore?—*Not to play.*"

DESAR (7½), Story I: "Which of these punishments is
the fairest?—*That they shouldn't give him any bread.*—Why
is that the fairest?—*Because he didn't go to fetch any.*—
Which is the 'stiffest' of these three punishments, the one he
would like to have least?—*Not to go to the Roundabouts.*—
Then, which is the fairest?—*Not to give him any bread.*—
Why do you think that the fairest?—*Because he didn't go
and fetch the bread.*" Desar is fully aware of the relation of
cause to effect that enters into this punishment, but he does
not succeed in making it explicit. Story II: The fairest would
be not to believe him any more. "Why?—*Because not to believe him any longer would be quite true, because he told his*

school teacher a lie." Story III: "Which do you think would have been fairest?—*To pay for the window pane.*—Why?—*Because it wouldn't be fair for the mother and father to pay.*—What was the punishment that the little boy hated most, to pay for the window pane, or to be in a cold room?—*To have a broken pane* [to be cold]." Story V: "Which is the fairest? *To break one of his toys.*—Why is that the fairest?—*To break one of his toys because he broke the pot.*—Which of the three would he have hated most?—*To go and get a plant in the forest.*—And which was the fairest?—*To have one of his toys broken.*" Desar, it will be seen, leans towards reciprocity throughout, even in the paradoxical case of story V.

BERG (8), Story I: "*He ought not to have been sent to the Roundabouts.*—Would that be the fairest punishment?—*No, that's not fair. It ought to have been the toy he was stopped from* [reaching in the cupboard that should not have been given to him], *because he didn't help he oughtn't to be helped either.*—Is that the best punishment?—*Yes. He didn't help so they oughtn't to give him any help either.*

BAUM (9), Story I: "*The last is the best. Since the boy won't help, well his mother won't help him either.*—And which is the fairest of the other two punishments?—*Not to give him any bread, then he'd have nothing to eat at supper, because he wouldn't help his mother.*—And the first?—*That was the one he deserved least. He wouldn't have minded. He'd still have been able to play with his toys* [=he would still have been helped by having his toy fetched for him] *and he would have had bread in the evening.*" Story VI: "*I would dirty his album for him, because that would be the fairest punishment. It would be doing the same to him as he did.*—And of the other two, which is the fairest?—*I wouldn't have lent him the book again because he would have made spots on it again.*—And how about the first punishment 'to stop him going to the Cinema'?—*That one is the least fair. It does nothing to the album. It doesn't change the album, the book. It has nothing to do with the book.*"

DEC (9½), Story I: The fairest is the one of the toy. "Why?—*He didn't help his mother, so why should his mother help him.*"

RID (10), Story I: The best is "*the one of the toy, because it is to show him how one likes it when people don't give help.*—Which is the fairest?—*The one of the toy, because his mother does the same thing to him as he had done to her."* Story II: "Which is the fairest?—*The one when he was ill* [=when he was put to bed], *because as he said so* [that he was ill] *you had to believe it.*—And of the two others, which is the fairest?—*The one about the twopence, because since he liked having his twopence and had told a lie, then you oughtn't to believe him any longer.*—And the first (copying fifty times)?—*That's a bit thick. . . .* —Which of the three is the fairest?—*There are two more or less fair. The one of pretending he is ill and the one of not believing him."* Story VI: "Which is the fairest?—*Not the one of the Cinema, because that's rather too strict for having made spots.*—And which of the other two?—*The one of making spots on his album . . . it was right to do to him what he had done."*

NUS (11), Story I: *"I'd have given him a smacking."* The father thought of three punishments. (I tell them to him.) "Which do you think is the fairest?—*Not to give him any help.*—Do you think that is fairer than smacking him?—*Fairer.*—Why?—(He hesitates) . . . *Because it's doing about the same thing to him as he had done.*—And of the other two, which is the fairest?—*Not to let him have any bread.*——Why?—*Because he didn't fetch any."*

ROY (11), Story I: "Which punishment do you think the fairest?—*Not to give him any help, because that's fairer.*—Why is it fairer?—*It's doing the same thing."* Story II: The fairest is *"not to believe the son, because he tells lies. He told a lie once, and you think he's always telling them."* Story VI: *"Not to take care of his album, since the boy hadn't taken care."* Story VIII: *"I'd have written a letter, since he wrote a letter too."*

BUH (12½), Story I: "Which punishment is the fairest? —*The one of not having any bread for his supper.*—Why?— *Because he wouldn't go and get any.*—Which is the punishment he will hate the most?—*Not going on the Roundabouts.* —And the fairest?—*Not having any bread.*—Is not to go to the Roundabouts as fair as the other punishment or less fair?—*Less fair.*—Why?—*You shouldn't give him any help.* [The Roundabouts punishment is less fair] *because there is no connection between the bread and Roundabouts."* Story II: "Which do you think is the fairest?—*To make him go to bed.*—Why?—*Because he tried to make them believe he was ill.*—And which of the other two is the fairest?—*Not to believe him any longer.*—Why?—*Because he told a lie.*—Which is the punishment that has no connection?—*Copying out a problem fifty times.*—And which has most connection?—*Putting him to bed.*—And what about a fourth which would be not to punish him at all, would that do?—*He ought to be punished all the same."* Story IV: The fairest punishment is *"that he should give one of his toys to the little boy.*—Did you choose that one just because it came into your head, or because it seems to you more just?—*He took a toy away from the little boy, so it is right that he should give one back to him."*

It will be seen how different these children's reactions are from those of the preceding group. The value of a punishment is no longer measured by its severity. The essential point is to do to the transgressor something analogous to what he has done himself, so that he should realize the results of his actions; or again to punish, where it is possible, by the direct material consequences of his misdeed. Sheer reciprocity stands so high in the eyes of the child that he will apply it even where to us it seems to border on crude vengeance, as in breaking a toy (Story V), etc. The reason for this is, as we shall see later on, that between 7 and 10 sheer equality in all its brutality still outweighs equity.

A problem of interpretation arises nevertheless: have the answers quoted above really any moral significance, or was the child's intelligence alone concerned? For the supposition might be made that the child regards the question put to him simply as a test of his intelligence and seeks among the suggested punishments those that have some connection with the act, precisely because he has been asked to make a choice. In other words, he thinks more or less as follows: "They're suggesting three punishments to me, so there's a catch in this somewhere. Now some of them are connected with the action and some are not. Let's choose the one that is most like the misdeed, and then see whether that is the answer they want." Thus the choice would be dictated by the intelligence alone and not by a sense of justice.

But though the intervention of this factor could not, of course, be excluded from the interrogatory, we believe the tone of the answers to be primarily moral. When Geo (Story I) compares punishments by reciprocity and expiatory punishment, he emphasizes very clearly that the first are just, whereas the last is cruel. Note also Dec's little argument founded on the principle of sufficient reason! For the rest, not only will the sequel convince us of the growing importance of the ideas of reciprocity and equality in children between 7 and 12, but educational experience is there to tell us how the child reacts in everyday life. Now, without wishing to impose one system of moral education rather than another—we are speaking as psychologists and not as educationalists—it does seem to us to have been demonstrated that those teachers whose ideal it is to set cooperation above constraint succeed in accomplishing their aim without the use of expiatory punishments, and thus prove that children fully grasp the meaning of punishment by reciprocity. Even if among the very little ones censure and preventive measures (taking away from the child an object that he is going to break, etc.) are almost necessarily interpreted as expiatory punishments, the more the child develops, the better able he becomes to grasp the value of measures of reciprocity. And we believe, without wishing to press the point, that the answers obtained in the course of our interrogatory correspond to sentiments that have been really experienced by the child, either through his having in the past proved for himself the soundness of certain punishments by reciprocity, or by his having felt the doubtful character of many expiatory punishments and thus being more inclined to approve of the punishments by reciprocity proposed in our stories.

This leads us back to the second point touched upon at the beginning of this section, we mean the efficacy of expiatory punishments. It is a striking fact that in the early part of the interrogatory the children are almost unanimous in defending severe punishments both as legitimate and as educationally useful. They are sincere and eager votaries of the current morality. But considering how clearly, later on, many of them choose reciprocal as opposed to "arbitrary" punishment, may we not go a step further and ask whether the child is really convinced of the utility of punishment? Does he not often feel that a timely appeal to his generosity would lead to better results?

Let us try to penetrate into his judgment on this point with the following experiment. Let us first tell him the story of some misdeed chosen from among the usual childish faults. Then let us describe the two alternatives: on the one hand, a severe expiatory punishment, on the other, simple explanation with an appeal made to the principle of reciprocity, but not accompanied by any punishment whatsoever. And let us then ask the subject in which of these two cases a relapse is most likely to occur.

Here are the stories used to this end:

Story I. A. "A boy was playing in his room, while his daddy was working in town. After a little while the boy thought he would like to draw. But he had no paper. Then he remembered that there were some lovely white sheets of paper in one of the drawers of his father's desk. So he went quite quietly to look for them. He found them and took them away. When the father came home he found that his desk was untidy and finally discovered that someone had stolen his paper. He went straight into the boy's room, and there he saw the floor covered with sheets of paper that were all scribbled over with coloured chalk. Then the father was very angry and gave his boy a good whipping."

B. "Now I shall tell you a story that is nearly the same, but not quite (the story is repeated shortly, except for the last sentence). Only it ends up differently. The father did not punish him. He just explained to him that it wasn't right of him. He said, 'When you're not at home, when you've gone to school, if I were to go and take your toys, you wouldn't like it. So when I'm not there, you mustn't go and take my paper either. It is not nice for me. It isn't right to do that.'

"Now a few days later these two boys were each of them playing in their garden. The boy who had been punished was in his garden, and the one who had not been punished was playing in his garden. And then each of them found a pencil. It was their fathers' pencil. Then each of them remembered that his father had said that he had lost his pencil in the street and that it was a pity because he wouldn't be able to find it again. So then they thought that if they were to steal the pencil, no one would ever know, and there would be no punishment.

"Well now, one of the boys kept the pencil for himself, and the other took it back to his father. Guess which one took it back—the one who had been well punished for having taken the paper or the one who was only talked to?"

Story II. A. "Once there was a little boy who was playing in the kitchen while his mother was out. He broke a cup. When his mother came home, he said, 'It wasn't me, it was the cat. It jumped up there.' The mother saw quite well that this was a lie. She was very angry and punished the boy. How did she punish him?" (You leave it to the child to decide upon the punishment.)

B. *Idem.* "But this time the mother didn't punish him. She just explained that it wasn't very nice to tell lies. 'You wouldn't like it if I were to tell you lies. Suppose you were to ask me for some of the cake that's in the cupboard, and I said there was none left when really there was some, you wouldn't think that nice, would you? Well, it's just the same when you tell *me* lies. It grieves me.'

"A few days later, the two little boys were both playing in their kitchen. And this time they are playing with the matches. When their mother comes in, one of them tells a lie again, and says he was not playing with the matches. The other one owns up at once. Which one was it who told the lie again, the one who had been punished for breaking the cup, or the one who had only been talked to?"

The stories are, of course, extremely naïve. But they suffice, in our opinion, to bring out the child's mental orientation. If he really believes in punishments, he will show it. If he simply wants to please us rather than give his own thoughts, he will also answer in support of punishments (since in his eyes there is every chance that a gentleman who questions schoolboys will believe in punishment!). If the child replies in favour of simple explanation, it is, so it seems to us, because there is something in him that makes him look upon reciprocal generosity as superior to any form of punishment.

Now, out of the thirty children who were questioned on this point alone (not counting the supplementary questions put to the hundred children spoken of before) those of 7 and under declared themselves almost unanimously in favour of punishment, whereas more than half the cases between 8 and 12 answered in the opposite sense.

Here are examples of the first type:

QUIN (6). Repeats Story I correctly: "Which one brought the pencil?—*The one who was punished.*—Then what happened, did he do it again or not?—*Not again.*—And the one his father didn't punish?—*He stole again.*—If you had been the daddy, when they stole the paper, would you have punished them or explained?—*Punished.*—Which is fairest?—*To punish.*—Which is the nicest daddy, the one who punishes or the one who explains?—*The one who explains.*—Which one is fairest, the one who etc.?—*The one who punishes.*—If you had been the boy, which would you have thought was fairest, to be punished or to have things explained to you?—*Explaining.*—Supposing it had been explained to you, would you have done it again?—*No.*—And if you had been punished?—*No, I wouldn't have either.*—Which of the two boys didn't do it again?—*The one who was punished.*—What is the good of punishing?—*Because you're a bad boy.*"

KAL (6), Story II: "Which one told the lie about the matches?—*The one the mother punished properly,* [Kal chooses the dark cupboard as a punishment!] *he told the truth.*—And the one who had not been punished?—*He told a lie again.*—Why?—*Because he hadn't been punished.*—Why did the other one not tell a lie?—*Because he had been properly punished.*"

SCHMEI (7), Story I: "Guess what the boy who had been punished by his father did.—*He gave it back, because he was afraid his father would scold him again.*—And the other one? *He kept it, he knew his father* [thought he] *had lost it out of doors.*—Which of the two fathers was the most fair?—

The one who punished him properly.—Which of the two fathers was the most of a sport?—*The one who didn't scold, the one who explained.*—Which of the two boys loved his father best?—*The one when the father was a sport.*—Which boy was nicest to his father?—*The one who gave the pencil back to his father.*—Was that the one who had been punished, or not punished?—*Punished.*"

BOL (8), Story I: "Which one gave it back, the one who was punished, or the one who was not?—*The one who was punished.*—What did he think?—*He thought, 'I don't want to be punished again.'*—And what did the other one think? —*He thought, 'As I wasn't punished before, I won't be punished this time.'*—Which of the two fathers was the most fair?—*The one who punished.*—If *you* had been the father would you have punished him?—*I would have.*—Would you have whipped him?—*I would have put him to bed.*—Which of the two fathers was the most of a sport?—*The one who didn't punish.*—Which of the two boys was the nicest?—*The one who was punished.*—Which one was the nicest, the one whose father was fair, or the one whose father was a sport? —*The one whose father was fair.*—Supposing you had stolen something, would you rather they punished you or explained things to you?—*Punish me.* Should one be punished?—*Yes.* —Then the more one is punished the better it is.—*It makes you better.*"

Here, finally, is an intermediate case which is interesting as showing a weakening of the preceding beliefs.

FAR (8), Story I: "Which one gave it back?—*The one who was punished.*—Why?—*Because he got beaten.*—And the other?—*He kept it, because he hadn't been punished.*— Which of the two fathers is the most fair?—*The one who punished.*—Which one was most of a sport?—*The one who didn't beat him.*—Why is he more of a sport?—*Because he explained.*—Which of the two boys was the nicest?—*The one who was punished.*—Which of the two fathers was right?—*The one who didn't beat him.*—Which of the two fathers would you have given the pencil back to?—*To the father who didn't punish.*—Why?—*Because he was the nicest.* —If you had been the father, what would you have done?— *I wouldn't have punished him, I would have explained.*—

Why?—*So that he shouldn't steal again.*—Which of the fathers was the most fair?—*The one who punished.*—I've told you a story, now you tell me one, one that really happened, when you were punished.—*Yes. I ran into the field.* —Where?—*Into our field, in the grass. They hit me.*—And then?—*I didn't do it again.*—And if they hadn't beaten you? *I would have done it again.*—Should people always be punished?—*Always when you've been a bad boy.*"

It will be seen how closely all these children cling to the traditional view of punishment as morally necessary *qua* expiation and educationally useful to prevent a relapse into evil. The last cases quoted, it is true, consider it more "sporting" only to explain without chastising, but this is neither just nor wise. Only Far hesitates for a moment towards the middle of the interrogatory, but the tradition of his fathers is too strong for him, and he reverts to the customary morality.

Here, on the contrary, is a different set of opinions, which may be considered characteristic of a second type of moral attitude, and, up to a certain point, of a second stage in the social development of the child.

BRIC (8), Story I: "What did they do?—*One of them gave it back, the other one kept it.*—Which one gave it back? —*The one who was not punished.*—What did he say to himself?—*That he ought to give it back, because he hadn't been punished.*—And the other one?—*That he ought to keep it.* —Why?—*Because he was punished.*" The bell rings. Bric goes out for a quarter of an hour's break. We begin again. "What were we doing before break?—*Telling a story.*—Do you remember what it was?—*Yes, about little boys who had stolen. Then afterwards they found a pencil, and one of them gave it back and not the other.*—Which one gave it back?—*The one who had not been punished.*—What did he say to himself?—*That he ought to give it back because his father would be pleased.*—And the other one?—*He kept it.*—Why?—*Because he didn't want to please his father.*—Which of the two fathers would you like to be?—*The one who explains.*—And which of the two children?—*The one who was not punished.* —Why?—*Because then he'll know that he mustn't steal* [since it is explained to him].—And if he is punished, what will he do?—*Perhaps he'll try again and then not be punished.*"

SCHÜ (8), Story I: The boy who gives back the pencil is the one who has not been punished. "Why did he give it back?—*Because they explained to him* [about the first theft]. —Why?—*Because it's a better way to make him good.*— Which of the two fathers is most of a sport?—*The one who explained.*—And which is fairest, explaining or punishing?— *Explaining.*—Why did the one who was punished begin again?— . . . —And if they had explained to him, would he have begun again?—*No.*—Why?—*Because he would have understood.*—And wouldn't he have understood that you mustn't steal if he had been punished?—*He wouldn't have understood so well.*—Now listen to me carefully. I am going to change the story round a little. Let us say that things have been properly explained to both the boys. But one of them was also punished, and the other one was only talked to without being punished. Which of the two gave back the pencil later on?—*The one who was not punished.*—Why?— *Because he had understood things better than the other one.* —Why did the other one do it again?—*Because he hadn't understood things quite so well.*—Why not?—*Because he was scolded and explained to at the same time.*—Does your father not punish you?—*He more often explains.*—Do you think it fair that you should be punished?—*No, not fair.*— Why?—*Because I can understand much better when people explain things to me.*—Tell me about once when you were punished.—*Once I was staying with my Granny. I'm never punished at home. But at Granny's I was punished.*—What had you done?—*I had broken a glass.*—How were you punished?—*They boxed my ears.*—And does your father not box your ears?—*Hardly ever.*" Story II: Same answers. "Which one didn't do it again?—*The one that the father explained to.*—And the other one, who did it again, what did he say to himself inside?—*Daddy will punish me but he won't do anything afterwards. I'll tell a lie.*—Which of the two fathers was a sport?—*The one who explained.*—And which was the most fair?—*The one who explained.*"

CLA (9), Story I: "Which one gave it back?—*The one*

that his father explained to.—And what did the other say to himself?—*I may as well take it. Daddy won't see.*" "Which of the two fathers was the fairest?—*The one who didn't punish.*—Which is fairest, to punish or not to punish?—*Not to punish.*" "If you had been the boy, what would you have done?—*I'd have given it back.*—And if you had been punished?—*I'd have given it back all the same*[!]." "Which boy was nicest to his father?—*The one who gave back the pencil.* —But ordinarily, everyday, which one is nicest to his father, the one who is punished often, or the one who is not?—*The one that you explain things to.*—Why?—*Because you don't do it again.*—Which is best, to explain and then punish, or to explain and then forgive?—*To explain and then forgive.*"

It will appear immediately how different is these children's attitude from that shown by the others. Nor is this new reaction merely verbal. Of course the wild generalizations to which the interrogatory leads are apt to give the impression that the subjects are indulging their imaginations in the sugary form of morality current in some paradise of good children. But side by side with these cases, what psychological penetration some of the remarks reveal! When Schü, for example, seeks to show that the child who is punished is more likely than the other to begin again, he is obviously thinking of those all too frequent cases where the accumulation of punishments makes the offender insensitive and coldly calculating. "Daddy will punish me, but he won't do anything afterwards!" How often, indeed, one sees children stoically bearing their punishment because they have decided beforehand to endure it rather than give in to the superior will! And again when the same Schü compares the punishment meted out to him at his grandmother's with the ordinary reactions of his own father, it is hard not to recall the comparisons we have all made in our own childhood between the understanding attitude of one relative and the unpsychological severity of another.

It is our belief, therefore, that the answers examined above correspond, up to a given point, with the experiences of real life; and this would mark the existence of a certain evolution with increase of age in the judgments made by children on the subject of punishments. On the other hand, the interrogatory dealing with the more general and abstract question as to the use of punishments (and whether they are just, etc.) did not yield anything of very great interest, for at all ages the answers reflect the ideas of the child's surroundings rather than his personal feeling on the subject. A difference of attitude should, however, be noted between the younger and the older children with regard to the justification of punishment. For the little ones, the idea of expiation is necessarily bound up with the idea of preventing a relapse.

TRAP (6): "Should children be punished?—*Yes, when they're naughty, you punish children.*—What does 'naughty' mean?—*It means naughty, when children are naughty, when you punish them.*—Is it fair to punish?—*Yes, because if you've done nothing then it isn't fair, but when you have done something* [it is fair].—Is it a useful thing to punish? What is it for?—*Yes, because they'd only got to not disobey, because they were naughty.*"

ZIM (6): "Is it fair to punish?—*Yes, it's all fair.*—Is it useful to punish? What is it for?—*Yes, it's a good thing to punish them when they're silly; it's always a good thing.*"

MAIL (6): "Is punishing fair?—*Yes, because it's always fair.*—Is it useful?—*Yes, because it's for when you are naughty.*—What does it do [Fr. *fait?*]?—*It makes* [Fr. *fait*] *a punishment* [=it chastises]."

The older ones, on the contrary, concentrate above all and almost exclusively on the preventive utility with very definite diminution of the idea of expiation.

RAI (11): "Is is fair?—*Yes, because you make him realize that he ought not to have done a thing.*—Is it useful?—*Yes, because if you punish him once, he won't do it again.*"

DUP (11): "Is it fair?—*Yes.*—Is it useful?—*Yes, because afterwards you want to be helpful. You know that if you aren't you'll be punished.*"

CUI (12): "Is it fair?—*Yes, if you've done something wrong; punishments are not always fair; they ought to be in proportion to the fault.—Is it useful?—Oh yes, so as not to begin again."*

Let us now try to formulate our conclusions. Difficult as is the interrogatory on such delicate points, and deeply tinged with the phraseology of adult morality as are the answers, taking things broadly, the results we have obtained do nevertheless seem to us to converge. They seem to point to the existence of a sort of law of evolution in the moral development of the child. It would seem that we have to distinguish in the domain of justice between two types of reaction, one founded on the notion of expiation, the other on that of reciprocity. And though representatives of both types are to be found at all ages, it would seem nevertheless that the second tended to predominate over the first.

The choice of punishments is the first thing that brings this out. The little ones prefer the most severe so as to emphasize the necessity of the punishment itself; the other children are more in favour of the measures of reciprocity which simply serve to make the transgressor feel that the bond of solidarity has been broken and that things must be put right again. It is also brought out by the reactions of the subjects whom we questioned on the subject of relapses. The little ones think that a well-punished child cannot repeat its offence because it has realized the external and coercive authority of the rule in question, whereas many of the older ones hold that a child to whom, even without punishment, the consequences of his actions have been thoroughly explained is less likely to begin again than if he had been punished and nothing more. The same thing, finally, would seem to be confirmed by the short interrogatory on the utility and soundness of punishments in general: the little ones introduce an expiatory element into all their answers, whereas the older children are content to justify punishments by their preventive value. On this point, indeed, these older children take up an attitude that definitely contradicts that which they had been observed to hold in the last interrogatory. This is because here they feel concerned to defend in their own way the views that are generally held by those around them, whereas in the stories about relapsing the answers are more personal and more spontaneous.

These two types of attitude, which we believe we have been able to dissociate from one another, are naturally, in so far as they correspond to real facts, connected with the two moralities which we have so far traced in the behaviour and judgment of the child. The notion of expiation corresponds, of course, to the morality of heteronomy and duty pure and simple. For one whose moral law consists solely of rules imposed by the superior will of adults and older children, it follows that the disobedience of small children will naturally entail the anger of their elders and this anger will take the concrete form of some kind of "arbitrary" suffering inflicted upon the offender. This reaction on the part of the adult is legitimate in the eyes of the child in so far as the relation of obedience has been broken and in so far as the suffering imposed is in proportion to the fault that has been committed. In the ethics of authority any other punishment is incomprehensible. And since there is no reciprocity between commander and commanded, what happens is that even if the former inflicts upon the latter only a "motivated" punishment (simple reciprocity, consequences of the act, etc.) the child will see nothing in it but an expiatory chastisement.[5] Punishment by reciprocity, on the other hand, corresponds with cooperation and an autonomous ethic. Indeed it is impossible to see how the relation of mutual respect, which is the foundation of all cooperation, could possibly give rise to the idea of expiation or render it legitimate. It is, on the contrary, easy to see how censure (which is at the origin of any punishment whatsoever) can, in the case of cooperation, be accompanied by definite measures which have been taken in order to mark the break in the bond of reciprocity or to make the offender understand the consequences of his acts.

If, then, we admit this kinship between the two types of attitude relating to retributive justice and the two moralities

[5] We have to thank the head mistress of the *Maison des Petits* for the following clear confirmation of our statements. They tell us that the youngest pupils (4-6) can see nothing but expiatory punishment in the measures of reciprocity. The latter are not understood until about 7-8 on the average.

which we have distinguished up to the present, what explanation are we to give of the genesis and destiny of each one of these attitudes?

With regard to the first type, we believe that though partly rooted in the child's instinctive reactions, it is fashioned primarily by adult constraint. We shall have to analyse very closely this super-position of social influences on the spontaneous attitude of the individual if we wish to gain a more exact understanding of the idea of expiation.

Among the instinctive tendencies must above all be mentioned the vindictive tendencies and compassion. For both develop independently of adult pressure. Defensive and aggressive reactions are sufficient to explain how the individual, from at first inflicting pain upon his adversary in self-defence comes to make him suffer in response to all offences. Vengeance is thus contemporary with the earliest defensive manifestations. It is very difficult to say, for example, whether the fit of rage of a baby of a few months old merely expresses the need to resist unwelcome treatment, or whether it already contains an element of revenge. At any rate, as soon as blows appear (and they do so at an extraordinarily early date, independently of any adult influence) it would be hard to say where fighting ended and revenge began. Now, as Mme Antipoff in a short study on compassion [6] has very well shown, vindictive tendencies admit of being "polarized" very soon, under the influence of sympathy. Owing to its astonishing faculty for introjection and affective identification the child suffers with him who suffers, he feels that he must avenge the unfortunate as well as himself, and experiences "vindictive joy" at seeing any sort of pain inflicted upon the author of other people's sufferings.

But it is going a little too far simply to base the sense of justice on such reactions and to speak, as does Mme Antipoff, of "an innate and instinctive moral manifestation which, in order to develop, really requires neither preliminary experience nor socialization amongst other children." In order to prove her thesis, Mme Antipoff lays stress upon the fact

[6] H. Antipoff, "Observations sur la compassion et le sens de la justice chez l'enfant," *Arch. de Psychol.*, t. XXI, p. 208 (1928).

that the vindictive tendencies become directly polarized upon the transgressor. "We have here," she concludes, "an inclusive affective perception, an elementary moral 'structure' which the child seems to possess very early and which enables him to grasp simultaneously evil and its cause, innocence and guilt. We may say that what we have here is an *affective perception of justice*." We may mention at once that nothing in the very interesting observations quoted by Mme Antipoff goes to show this innateness. She deals with observations on the behaviour of children between 3 and 9, and it is obvious that at the age of three, a child has already come under all sorts of adult influences such as can account for the fact that its polarization is now only in terms of good and evil. The proof of this is that the child speaks; it says "serves him right" and "naughty boy," etc. How could it have learned these words without coming under the moral influence of the person who taught them to it, and without accepting at the same time a whole set of explicit or implicit commandments? In a general way, the problem may be stated as follows. How can the vindictive tendencies, even if they are polarized under the influence of compassion, give birth to the need for rewards and punishments and to retributive justice, unless the relations between individuals intervene to "regulate" this polarization, diminishing what is arbitrary and individual in the name of a normative element of either authority or reciprocity?

To our mind, when a child merely avenges some unfortunate for whom he feels immediate compassion, neither the sense of justice nor the idea of punishment is yet at work. All we have is an extension of the vindictive tendency. But even if this sort of disinterested vengeance is a necessary, it is not a sufficient condition for the development of justice, disinterested vengeance will only become a "just" punishment when *rules* come in and make precise the distinction between what is right and what is wrong. So long as there are no rules, revenge, even disinterested revenge, will rest only upon individual sympathy or antipathy and will thus remain arbitrary: the child will not have the feeling of punishing the guilty and defending the innocent, but simply of fighting an enemy and defending a friend. But as soon, on the contrary, as there are rules (and they appear very early—the boy of 3 observed by Mme. Antipoff is already saturated with them), as soon as we have rules, we get judgments of guilt and innocence and we get the moral "structure" of retributive justice. Where, then, do these rules come from?

Even if adults never interfered, the social relations subsisting between children would perhaps be sufficient to create them. The play of sympathy and antipathy is a sufficient cause for practical reason to become conscious of reciprocity. And the fact that the law of reciprocity leads to a certain type of punishment has, we believe, been sufficiently established in the preceding analyses. But in that case, the idea of expiation would never arise: mere vengeance would remain a private affair until such time as it would be considered immoral, and punishment by reciprocity would alone be held to be just.

But the adult intervenes. He imposes commands which give rise to rules that are regarded as sacred. Disinterested vengeance, once it has been "polarized" by these rules, becomes expiatory punishment, and the first type of retributive justice is constituted in this way. When the adult is angry because the laws he has laid down are not observed, this anger is held to be just, because of the unilateral respect of which older people are the object and because of the sacred character of the law laid down. When adult anger finds vent in chastisement, this vengeance from above appears as a legitimate punishment, and the resultant suffering as a "just" expiation. The idea of expiatory punishment is thus, taken as a whole, due to the conjunction of two influences: the individual influence, which is the desire for vengeance, including derivative and disinterested vengeance, and the social factor, which is adult authority imposing respect for given orders and respect for vengeance in cases where these orders are disobeyed. In a word, expiatory punishment is, from the child's point of view, revenge that may be likened to disinterested revenge (because it avenges the law itself) and that emanates from the authors of the law.

How, then, are we to explain the passage from the first to the second type of retributive justice? If the above remarks are correct, this evolution is nothing but a special case of the general evolution from unilateral to mutual respect. Since in every domain we have studied up till now, respect for the adult—or at any rate a certain way of respecting the adult—diminishes in favour of the relations of equality and reciprocity between children (and so far as is possible, between children and adults), it is perfectly normal that in the domain of retribution the effects of unilateral respect should tend to diminish with age. That is why the idea of expiation loses more and more of its power, and it is why punishments tend more and more to be ruled by the law of reciprocity alone. So that what remains of the idea of retribution is the notion, not that one must compensate for the offence by a proportionate suffering, but that one must make the offender realize, by means of measures appropriate to the fault itself, in what way he has broken the bond of solidarity. The situation can be expressed by saying that distributive justice (the idea of equality) definitely takes precedence over retributive justice, whereas in the beginning the converse was the case. We shall come to the same conclusion in paragraph 4 of this chapter. Let us add, finally, that the idea of reciprocity, often taken at first as a sort of legalized vengeance or law of retaliation expressed in quasi-mathematical form, tends of itself towards a morality of forgiveness and understanding. As we shall see later on, the time comes when the child realizes that there can be reciprocity only in well-doing. We have here a sort of repercussion of the form of the moral law on its content. The law of reciprocity implies certain positive obligations in virtue of its very form. And this is why the child, once he has admitted the principle of punishment by reciprocity in the sphere of justice, often comes to feel that any material punitive element is unnecessary, even if it is "motivated," the essential thing being to make the offender realize that his action was wrong, in so far as it was contrary to the rules of cooperation.

§ 2. COLLECTIVE AND COMMUNICABLE RESPONSIBILITY

We have neglected, so as to deal with it separately, a question which it may be useful to discuss in connection with retributive justice. Do children consider it just, in general or in cases where the offender is unknown, to punish the whole group to which he belongs? The question has a double interest, educational and psycho-sociological.

Educational, because collective punishment has long been resorted to in the class-room, and, in spite of the many protests that have been raised against this practice, it is still more widely used than is generally thought. A certain importance therefore attaches to the way in which this custom reacts upon the child's mind. And the matter interests us psychologically as well. The history of penal codes teaches us that responsibility was long considered to be collective and communicable. The date is comparatively recent when responsibility became individualized, and the more primitive conception survives to this day in many religious beliefs. M. Fauconnet, in the excellent book of which we have spoken, and which will occupy us again, has shown how the notion of communicable responsibility is connected with that of objective responsibility. Now, as we claim to have shown above, the child believes in objective responsibility. Is there, then, a parallel and complementary tendency to conceive of responsibility as communicable?

In order to solve this problem, we gave the children a certain number of stories which lent themselves to conversation and which reproduced situations in which the question of collective responsibility usually arises. These situations seemed to us to be three in number: 1) The adult does not attempt to analyse individual guilt and punishes the whole group for the offence committed by one or two of its members. 2) The adult wants to discover the transgressor, but the latter does not own up and the group refuses to denounce him. 3) The adult wants to discover the transgressor but the latter does not own up and the group is ignorant of his identity.—In each of these three cases you ask the child whether it is fair to punish the whole group, and why. We examined about sixty subjects between 6 and 14, which was a sufficient number, considering the relative uniformity in the answers obtained. The children questioned are not the same as those with whom we were concerned in the last section.

It should be noticed straight away that of the three situations contemplated, only the first is comparable to the situations that generate collective responsibility in primitive societies. But of course it is important to analyse the other two by way of corroborative proof.

Here are the stories of which we made use:

Story I. A mother tells her three boys that they mustn't play with the scissors while she is out. But, as soon as she is gone the first one says, "Let's play with the scissors." Then the second boy goes to get some newspapers to cut out. The third one says, "No, Mother said we mustn't. I shan't touch the scissors." When the mother comes home, she sees all the bits of cut-up newspaper on the floor. So she sees that some-one has been touching her scissors, and she punishes all three boys. Was that fair?

Story II. A lot of boys, as they were coming out of school, went to play in the street, and started throwing snowballs at each other. One of the boys throws his ball too far and breaks a window-pane. A gentleman comes out of the house and asks who did it. As no one answers he goes and com-plains to the school master. Next day the master asks the class who broke the window. But again, no one speaks. The boy who had done it says it wasn't he, and the others won't tell on him. What should the master do? (If the child does not answer or misses the point, you can add details to make things clearer.) Ought he to punish no one, or the whole class?

Story III. Some boys are throwing snowballs against a wall. They were allowed to do this, but on condition they did not throw them too high, because right high up there was a window, and the window-panes might get broken. The boys had a lovely time, all except one who was rather clumsy and who was not very good at throwing snowballs. Then, when no one was looking he picked up a pebble and put snow all around it so as to make a good hard ball. Then he threw it, and it went so high that it struck the window, broke the window-pane, and fell into the room. When the father came home he saw what had happened. He even found the pebble with some melted snow on the floor. Then he was angry and asked who had done this. But the boy who had done it said it wasn't he, and so did the others. They did not know that he had put a pebble in his snowball. What should the father have done, punished everyone, or no one?

Story IV. During a school outing, the teacher allowed the children to play in a barn, on condition that they put everything back as they found it before going away. One of them took a rake, another a spade, and they all went off in different directions. One of the boys took a wheelbarrow and went and played by himself, until he went and broke it. Then he came back when no one was looking and hid the barrow in the barn. In the evening when the teacher looked to see if everything was tidy he found the broken barrow and asked who had done it. But the boy who had done it said nothing, and the others didn't know who it was. What should have been done? (Should the whole class be punished or no one?)

Guided by the requirements of the experiment, we invented other stories on the same themes, but there is no need to report them here as the results obtained were poor. It will be noticed that stories I and II correspond respectively to the first two situations we distinguished a moment ago, and stories III and IV to the third.

With regard to the first of these situations we were unable in spite of our desire to do so[7] to discover in our children the least trace of collective responsibility. Little and big alike consider the mother of Story I to be unjust. You should punish each individual according to what he has done and not the group according to the misdeeds of one of its members. Here are some examples.

RED (6): "What do you think of that?—*The one who hadn't touched them, he ought to have told.*—Was it fair or not fair to punish them all three?—*No.*—Why?—*Because*

[7] We have often been told that by questioning children with a little diplomacy you can make them say anything you like. Here is an example to the contrary. We hoped very much—because we had counted upon it theoretically—that the little ones at least would answer in conformity with the notion of collective responsibility. This hypothesis proved to be false and our desire was not sufficient to suggest it to the subjects who were questioned.

there was one who hadn't done anything.—How many should have been punished?—*Two.*"

STAN (6) repeats the story as follows: "*Once there was a lady who was going shopping, and one of the boys took the scissors. The other one cut the paper, and the other one, he didn't do anything. In the evening she came back and she punished them all three.*—Is that fair?—*She should have scolded two of them and not scolded the third.*"

BOL (7): "*Once there was a mother who had three children. Then she went out to do some shopping, and then she told them not to touch the scissors. And then they did touch them.*—Yes, who did?—*The first and the second, but not the third.*—Yes, and then?—*And then when the mother came home she saw that they had been touching the scissors, and then she punished them.*—Yes, how?—*She sent them to bed without any supper.*—That's right. Now, what do you think of this story?—*It's pretty.*—Was it fair or not to punish all three?—*No. Only the first two.*—Why not all three?—*Because the third one hadn't disobeyed.*—And the other two?—*Yes, they had disobeyed.*—And then?—*They went to bed without any supper.*—Was it fair?—*Yes.*—They were three brothers. So two of them were punished. The third one didn't need to be punished?—*No.*"

SCRIB (9): "*The children oughtn't to have touched the scissors. She was quite right to punish them.*—Did she try to find out which one it was?—*She punished all three of them. She ought to have asked who had taken the scissors. She says, 'Since no one will own up, I shall punish all the children.' If no one had owned up she ought to have punished them all three, but otherwise it wouldn't have been fair, and she ought to have punished only two of them since they'd have owned up.*"

All the answers obtained are of this type. They show how utterly foreign to these judgments is the idea of the solidarity of the group as regards responsibility. This result is all the more remarkable when we consider that most children under 7, as we shall see later on, look upon everything that the adult does as "fair." It is therefore in opposition to this tendency to justify the adult in all things that these children, in the particular case of our interrogatory, reject the idea of collective responsibility. It is true that the child is quicker to discover adult mistakes in the sphere of retributive than in that of distributive justice: a wrongly applied punishment seems to them more unjust than inequality of treatment.

Scrib's spontaneous reflections on the expediency of punishing all the three children together if the first two had not owned up introduce us to situation II. Should the whole group be punished when the offender does not own up and when the innocent refuse to denounce him?

We are here in the presence of a problem which differs very widely from the classical question of collective responsibility in the evolution of social groups, but yet throws a certain light upon it. For the mere fact of the offender refusing to own up and his comrades refusing to give him away establishes within the group a solidarity greatly superior to that which existed in it before. To the naturally given solidarity is added a solidarity that is willed and accepted by all. Are these conditions in which the child will admit the principle of collective responsibility?

If we base our statistics upon age we get only a very indeterminate result. At every age there are children who in Story II and similar tales consider that the whole group should be punished, and there are children who think that it would be more just to punish no one. Thus both types of answer were found to be characterized by the same average age (about 9, as we questioned subjects between 6 and 12). But under this apparent homogeneity it is in fact possible to discern types of reaction that are quite distinct. According to children of one type—generally the youngest—everyone should be punished; not because the solidarity of the group renders the responsibility collective, but because each is individually guilty, seeing that no one will show up the author of the offence and that it would be a duty towards the master to do so. According to children of a second type—generally the elder ones—everyone should be punished, not because it is wrong not to "tell," but because by the mere fact of having decided not to denounce the offender the class recognizes its solidarity. This is collective responsibility of a kind, but is willed by the individuals and not in itself compulsory.

And finally there is a third type—roughly speaking of an intermediate age—according to whom no one should be punished; partly because it is right not to "tell," and partly because the guilty one is not known. It should be added that children of the first type, in addition to the argument reported above, think that everyone should be punished because a misdeed necessarily involves a punishment. By punishing everyone, justice is satisfied. Whereas children of the other two types regard the punishment of the innocent as more unjust than the impunity of the guilty. But these considerations appear far more clearly in connection with situation III, and we shall therefore not dwell upon them for the moment.

Here are examples of the first type.

RED (6), Story II: "And what did the master do?—*He punished them all.*—Why all of them?—*Because he didn't know who it was had broken the window-pane.*"—"What did the one who broke the pane do?—*He said they weren't to tell.*—And what did the others think about it?—*That they oughtn't to tell.*—And did the others think that was fair?—*Yes.*—What was?—*Not to tell.* [This in Red's opinion is where the fault lies, that no one should have denounced the offender. Hence the collective punishment.]—But was it fair that they should all be punished, or not fair?—*It was fair.*—Why?—*It wasn't known who did it.*—Have you ever been punished all together at home or at school?—*No. We are asked* [who is the offender] *and then we say.*"

BOL (7), story analogous to Story II: "What was he going to do?—*Punish them.*—Who?—*All four of them.*—Why?—*The mother didn't know who had done it, so they all four had to be punished.*—Why? Only one of them had thrown the snowball. Did the other three have to be punished too?—*Yes.*—Why?—*Because they wouldn't tell.*—And did the others think it was fair?—*No.*—Why not?—*Well, perhaps they did.*—Why?—*Because they wouldn't tell. So they all four had to be punished.*"

SCRIB (9), Story II: "What ought the master to have done? —*He ought to find out.*—He did ask the others but they wouldn't tell him anything.—*They ought to have told.*—What would you have done?—*I'd have told . . . because it's something wrong* [to break a window-pane] *that you musn't do. . . . It would be better to tell, because anyone who breaks a window ought to be punished.*—But these children didn't tell. What ought the master to do?—*He must punish the whole class because no one has told.*—Which is fairest, to punish everyone or to punish no one?—*Which is fairest? To punish the whole class because no one would tell. They ought to be punished.*—Listen. That day one of the boys was absent because he was at home, ill. It was the day he wasn't there that the master said he would punish the whole class and keep everyone back for an hour on Thursday.[8] Now when Thursday came, the boy was well again. Should he have been punished like the others, or not?—*He ought to be kept back; everyone must go together.* [It is true that] *the whole class was not there when the window was broken* [but] *he must be punished too, as the whole class is being punished."* This is about the most definite of the statements made by the children whom we questioned on the subject of collective responsibility.

HER (9), Story II: "What should be done?—*Punish the whole lot of them.*—Would that be fair?—*No, because the one who had done it said nothing, and he was the only one who ought to be punished.*—And should the others have told, or not?—*Yes, they ought to have told.*—If you had been one of the others, would you have told or not?—*I should have told the master.*—Would the others have thought that very nice of you?—*No.*—And if the master had punished everyone, would that have been fair?—*No.*—And what about punishing nobody?—*Not that either.*—What should have been done?—*Keep the whole class in for an hour.*—And would you have thought that fair?—*I'd rather be punished even if they hadn't found the one who was guilty.*—Even if it wasn't you?—*Yes."*

The two dominating ideas in these answers stand out clearly. On the one hand, there must be punishment, even if the innocent suffer; on the other hand, no one is com-

---

[8] Thursday is the weekly whole holiday in French and Swiss schools. [Trans.]

pletely innocent since the whole class refuses to denounce the offender. Worth noting is Scrib's idea of the solidarity of the class which is such that even an absent pupil should be punished along with the others when he comes back. This is the dawn of collective responsibility properly so called.

Here are examples of the second type: everyone should be punished because the class decides to stand together.

SCHU (13): *"The whole class should be punished.—Why? —Because if no one owned up, someone would have to be punished.*—Why must someone be punished?—*So that the one who broke the window should not have the whole punishment.* [Note the freely accepted solidarity.]—Why? Would you have thought it right to punish the whole class?—*Because they ought not to have left only one to be punished; it would have been mean to let him be punished.* [Note this forceful formula.]—And was it right of him not to own up?—*No, it wasn't right of him.*—What would you have done?—*I would have owned up.*—And the others?—*They might have told on him.*—Why didn't they?—*Because they get a thin time of it afterwards.* [Their friends take them to task.]—Why?— *Because there are fellows who are pals. They don't say anything.*—Why?—*So that he shouldn't be punished.*—Then what should be done?—*The master should make the whole class pay for the broken window.*—And supposing the gentleman says, 'I don't mind about having the window paid for; all I want is that the boy who broke it should be punished'? —*Then they must try and find him or else punish the whole class.*—And if one of the boys was absent on that day, should he be punished along with the others when he comes back?— *No, he mustn't.*—Why?—*Because he was not one of the gang."*

SCHMO (11) thinks that "decent chaps" do not tell on a friend if he is likely to be punished. But it is up to the master to punish the whole class, since the guilty one does not reveal himself. "If you had been at that school would you have thought it fair?—*No, not quite, but if I had been the master it is what I would have done."*

This type clearly differs from the first. It is right not to tell (and it is not the refusal to denounce the offender which should be aimed at in punishing the whole class), but since the class by keeping silence joins forces with the offender, by doing so it declares war on the master who henceforth has the right to act with severity. From the master's point of view, then, the collective punishment is admissible though in itself it is neither obligatory nor even just.

Here are examples of the third type of answer: the whole class should not be punished.

HOT (7½): "Which is the most fair, to punish everyone or no one?—*To punish the one who did it.*—But they don't know who it was.—*Then it is most fair not to punish anyone, since they don't know who did it.*" "And supposing the master simply says that everyone must stay on after school until the one who did it owns up, would that be fair?—*Yes, he is quite right then. That is different from before.*—And if everyone was kept on for two hours, would that be fair?— *No.*"

NIK (10): "Some people have told me that the whole class ought to be punished, some that no one should be. What do you think?—*Punish no one.*—Why?—*Because you don't know who it is.*—Is that quite fair or not?—*I don't know.*— Is it the fairest thing that could be done or not?—*Yes, it is.* —Why?—*Because it would mean punishing all the other children.*—To punish the whole class would be altogether unfair, would it?—*No.*—Why not?—*Because then the one who did it would be punished too.*"

For these childlren, clearly, individual responsibility alone comes into play: the essential thing is that the innocent should not be hit. It is more just, therefore, to punish no one. As for collective punishment, it is legitimate only in so far as it succeeds in reaching the offender himself.

Of these few facts noted in connection with situation II we can therefore say that only those of the second type resemble collective responsibility. For the children of the first type do not think of the fault as in any way com-

municable: if everyone is to be punished, it is because everyone is guilty, since the spectators of the misdeed refuse to
denounce its author. The responsibility is therefore general
and not collective. Only Scrib, in his desire to punish the
absent pupil, marks a momentary exception to this rule, and
anticipates the second type of answer. As to children of the
third type, they are definitely hostile to ideas of communicable
responsibility. So that only the second type remains, consisting curiously enough of the oldest children. But if in their
view the group is responsible, it is because it wishes to be
so and decides through solidarity to share the offender's
punishment. Is this attitude comparable in any way to that
of "primitive peoples" who consider the group to be con-
taminated by the misdeed of one of its members? Before
deciding this point let us turn to situation III.

The stories III and IV are those which enabled us to
analyse the children's reactions in regard to these situations.
An individual misdeed has been committed, but the group
does not know who is guilty: should it be punished as a
whole or should no one be punished? On this point the
children's reactions were perfectly definite. According to
the little ones, everyone should be punished, not because the
group is responsible but because there must be a punishment
at all costs, even if it strikes the innocent as well as the
guilty. According to the older ones, on the contrary, no one
should be punished because the penalty inflicted upon the
innocent is more unjust than the impunity of the guilty. The
older children are unanimous, at any rate from the age of
8-9, in saying that collective punishment is less just in the
present situation than in the case of situation II.

Here are examples of the reactions shown by the youngest
children.

MAR (6), Story IV: "What should have been done?—
Punish the little boy.—Did they know who it was?—*No.*—
Well then?—*Take a boy and punish him.*—Any boy?—*No,
you would change* [taking them in turn]."

FRIC (6), Story IV: "What should be done?—*Punish.*—
Punish how?—*In a dark room.*—Who?—*The one who broke
the cart.*—Did they know who it was?—*No.*—Then what

could they do?—*Put them all in a dark room.*—What did the others say?—*That it wasn't me who did it.*—What did they think then?—*That they shouldn't be put* [in the dark room].—If you were the teacher what would you do?—*Put them all in a dark room.*"

VEL (6), Story IV: Everyone is to be punished. "Is it fair to punish everyone?—*Yes, because he broke the little cart.*—Who do you mean by 'he'?—*The boy.*—Then is it fair to punish everyone?—*Yes. They should all be kept in after school.*"

STO (7), Story IV: "Then, should everyone be punished, or no one?—*I would punish half the class.*—And supposing you were in that half of the class, what would you say at being punished with the others?—*I would think that it was fair.*"

GRIB (9), Story III: "*Everyone should give a little towards paying for the window-pane.*—Which would be fairest, that everyone should pay or that no one should pay anything?—*Since it is someone in the class, everyone should give a penny.*" Story IV: "*Since no one can say who it was, the whole class must be punished. The one who had broken it wouldn't say, so he* [the master] *said that everyone should be punished.*"

HER (9), Story IV: "*If he* [the master] *couldn't find the one who broke it, he'd be better to punish the whole lot.*—But had the others seen him?—*No.*—Do you think it is fairer here in this story or in the first [Story II]?—*It is fairer in the second story because no one saw who it was.*—Why did they not tell in the first story?—*Because they didn't want to tell on him. There ought to be more punishing in the second one because no one knew who it was.*—Then why must you punish more if no one knows who it is?—*Because* [in Story IV] *the others couldn't tell on him since they didn't know.*—Were they right not to tell in the first story, or not?—*They were right not to tell.* [Her has therefore changed his mind since the first interrogatory.]—Shouldn't they have told?—*No.*"

The children's reaction is unmistakable. They accept collective punishment, but they do so, not because the group is responsible as a whole for the faults of one of its members, but simply because the guilty one is unknown, and that there must be a punishment at all costs. The fundamental fact in these cases is not the feeling of solidarity in the group, but of the necessity of punishment. Hence the curious answer given by Her, who deems it more just to punish everybody in this case than in situation II. For in the last case the children act quite rightly in not denouncing the offender, and it would not be very fair to punish them, whereas if the offender remains unknown, there is nothing left to do but to chastise the whole group.

We shall now give examples of the older children who regard collective punishment as unjust.

DELLEN (9), Story IV: "What should be done?—*Ask them who did it.*—Punish them?—*Yes.*—How?—*Ask who took the cart.*—But he won't own up. Must one be taken at random and punished?—*No. They don't know which one it is who broke the cart.*—Should no one be punished?—*Yes. . . . No, that still would not be fair because the one who broke it would not be punished.*—Punish everyone?—*No. Only the boy who broke the cart. It would not be fair to punish everyone because the others didn't break it.*—Punish two or three of them?—*No.*—No one at all?—*Yes, that would be fairest.*—But you told me that the one who broke the cart would not be punished then.— . . . —Should everyone be punished?—*No, because the others did nothing.*"

NIK (10), Story III: "Some say that the whole class should be punished, some that no one should. Tell me what you think.—*No one should be punished.*—Why?—*Because you don't know who it was.*—Do you think that is what would be fairest?—*Yes.*—Why?—*Because otherwise it would mean all the other children being punished.*" Story IV: "If you were the master what would you think was the fairest thing to do?—*Not to punish anyone.*—When would you think it fairest to punish them all, in the story where they all saw the boy break the window-pane, or in this one?—*In the first story.*—Why?—*Because they know and they won't say.*"

Even those among the older children who are attracted by the idea of collective punishment answer like Nik on the last point—namely that collective punishment is less just where the offender is unknown to the group. For where everybody knows the author of the misdeed and refuses to denounce him, there is voluntary solidarity, as we saw in the case of situation II. But here there is complete independence between the individuals. The great majority of the older children therefore consider general punishment as a greater injustice than the impunity of the guilty.

It should be noted, however, that in some cases the child comes somewhat nearer to the notion of collective responsibility. This happens when the punishment chosen lends itself to this extension of the idea and seems to strike, not only at the offender, but at the child in general in its carelessness and its inferiority. For after all it seems hardly fair to keep everyone in for an hour when this might be done to the offender alone. But if the whole class is punished by being forbidden to borrow tools in the future, this seems more reasonable. Such a measure strikes no longer at the innocent individual but at the child as such, the *genus* child like the *genus humanum* of the theologians. For since one member of the group has proved himself too clumsy to be allowed the use of a wheel-barrow, it is only normal that the group as a whole should be suspected of carelessness and that the responsibility should thus be extended to others.

Nuss (7), Story IV: "What should be done to them?— *They should have been told not to break the wheel-barrow.* —And did the master punish them or not?—*Yes.*—How?— *He told them not to touch things.*—Yes, but did he punish them?—*Yes. He said they must never touch tools again.*— Did the children think it was fair?—*Yes.*—Even those who hadn't done anything wrong?—*Yes.*"

These cases, along with that of Scrib (who wanted to have even the absent pupil punished), are those which come nearest to the classical idea of collective responsibility. And, as a matter of fact, even adults allow that a group may be penalized as when, for example, motorists or pedestrians are forbidden to go along a road where unscrupulous individuals have been guilty of reckless behaviour. But in this case, as in that of Nuss, the punishment is not expiatory; it is a precautionary measure directed against individuals in general rather than against the whole group as such.

On this point Mlle A. M. Feldweg has been kind enough to supply us with a valuable complement to our enquiry. She questioned some forty children between 5 and 13 by means of stories relating to situation I but which introduced into collective punishment the feature of being a general precautionary measure rather than an expiation properly so called. Here are two of these stories.

Story V. There was a school with only two classes—a class of big ones and a class of little ones. On Saturday afternoon, when no one was working very hard, the little ones asked the big ones to lend them one of their lovely animal books. The big ones lent it, telling them to take great care of it. But once, two of the little ones both wanted to turn over the pages at the same time. They quarrelled and some of the pages of the book got torn. When the older ones saw that the book was torn they declared that they would never lend it to the little ones again. Were they right or not?

Story VI. A mother gave her three little boys a lovely box of coloured crayons and told them to be very careful not to drop them in case the leads got broken. But one of them who drew badly saw that his brothers drew better than he did, and out of spite (or "because this made him angry") he threw all the crayons on the floor. When the mother saw this, she took the crayons away and never gave them back to the children again. Was she right to do this or not?

In contrast to Stories I and IV, these stories produced reactions that were apparently far more favourable to collective responsibility. For about half the children approved of the punishment in Story V and about one-fifth of that in Story VI. But if we try to find out the why of these judgments, we shall see immediately how totally foreign they are to truly collective responsibility.

It is significant, to begin with, that the general punishment should receive a far greater measure of approval (about half) in the case of Story V than in that of Story VI (about one-fifth). For the punishment described in Story V consists far more of a preventive or protective measure than of a genuine punishment. The punishment in Story VI, on the contrary, contains an element of repression which renders it quasi-expiatory; for the chalks in question were meant for the children from whom they were afterwards taken away, whereas in the first case we have to do with a book that had been lent and will now simply no longer be lent.

On the other hand, the hesitation and even change of opinion shown by the subjects favourable to collective punishment are sufficient to show that their minds are not made up, and, above all, that the problem is new to them and does not correspond to an acquired or already accepted idea. Finally, those answers that are definite hardly invoke anything more than the very idea of a preventive measure which we were emphasizing a moment ago. Here is an example of this type of answer.

RoL (7; 6), Story V: "Were the older ones right or not?— *They are right.*—Why?—*They* [the little ones] *will tear it again.*—It was only one or two of them who tore it.—*Yes, but the others may tear it too.*—Could the book be given to the ones who had done nothing, or not?—*Yes.*—Which would be fairest, to give it to them or not to?—*Not to give it them, because they don't listen to what the big ones say to them.*—Suppose you were in the little ones' class, and had done nothing, would you think that fair, or not?—*Yes.*— Why?—*Because it was quite right. There's no need to go and tear a book that cost a lot.*"

It is true that in certain rare cases an additional appeal seems to be made to the solidarity of the group as such. Here again, as in the case of Scrib (p. 238-9), one gets the impression that the child comes very near to collective responsibility. Here is one of these cases.

HOCH (9), Story VI: "Was the mother right?—*Yes.*— Why?—*Because she's afraid they will throw them on the ground.*—Who do you mean by 'they'?—*Perhaps the others too.*—Suppose you have two brothers, and one of them throws the crayons on the floor; is it fair or not that you and your other brother should not be able to draw any more?—*Yes. But they have got no colours left because of the brother. The other two ought to be allowed to draw.*—Will the third brother think that fair, or not?—*No, because in the family they always lend each other the pencils.*—Then what should be done?—*Take the pencils away from all of them.*

Here, it will be seen, it is the unity of the group, felt as such, that impels towards collective punishment. But Hoch is obviously very undecided in his opinion. Besides, as we have said before, such views only appear in about one subject out of ten at the most.

As to the other children, they are opposed to the idea of collective punishment even in regard to Stories V and VI. Here is the most interesting of the results obtained.

HUF (13; 6), Story V: *"It isn't right of them.*—Why?—*They should take the book away* [only] *from those who tore it.*—If it was you who had torn it, would you think it fair that it should be given back to the others and not to you?—*Yes, fair.*—Why not take it away from everyone?—*The others might say it was not fair."*

Story VI: "Was the mother right?—*No.*—What would you have done?—*I'd have taken them away from the one who got angry.*—For always, or not?—*For a certain time.*—And if it was you who had broken them, and no one was allowed to use the box, would you think that fair or not?—*I should think it was unfair. I should know that it was just to afflict* [inflict] *a punishment upon me.*—You wouldn't have thought it fairer that no one should be allowed to use the chalks?—*Yes, while I was still in a temper, but not afterwards. I should know that I was the* [only] *one who deserved to have the box of chalks taken away from me."*

In short, Stories V and VI, like the others, are insufficient to prove the existence of a spontaneous feeling for collective responsibility in the child. At the best, only in cases of very closely united groups, such as the family, does the child's judgment (as with Hoch) bear the fleeting impress of this collectivity. Broadly speaking, however, only such collective punishments are held to be just as can be regarded as preventive measures.

Such, then, are the results of our enquiry. The sum total shows that in none of the three situations imagined is any judgment to be found comparable to the classical notion of collective responsibility. There are, at the most, little indications here and there, to which we shall return in a moment. In situations II and III, on the other hand, we can observe two consistent reactions, each of which, taken by itself, may be regarded as bearing upon communicable responsibility.

The first of these reactions is the belief in the absolute necessity for punishment. This belief can be observed in the younger children, and even leads them to demand the punishment of all rather than let the guilty one escape. Such an attitude is obviously necessary for the development of judgments of collective responsibility: before a whole group can be regarded as sharing the offender's guilt, the necessity of expiatory punishments must first be allowed. Fauconnet's contention seems to us irrefutable on this point. The emotion aroused by the crime is, he says, the source both of the collective reaction in which the punishment consists, and of the transference by contiguity and resemblance of the responsibility itself. In a sense, then, we may say with Fauconnet that responsibility is born of punishment. But in the child this belief in the absolute necessity for expiatory punishment is not sufficient to liberate the judgment of collective responsibility. This is shown by our analysis of situation III—it is the unknown offender and not the group as such that is aimed at by the collective punishment contemplated by the child.

In the second place, we observed in situation II a sort of collective responsibility, but one that was voluntary and freely accepted: rather than denounce the offender, his comrades will declare their solidarity with him. Here again we come very near collective responsibility, but what this attitude lacks in order to be identified with the classical attitude is that the children should regard this solidarity as simply given and unavoidable.

The problem may be stated as follows. Is the classical idea of collective responsibility, *i.e.*, the necessity for whole group to expiate the faults of one of its members more akin to the first or to the second of these reactions, to the absolute necessity for punishment or to the voluntary solidarity of the group? The question is an important one. As the first of these two attitudes is that of the younger children, whose morality is one of constraint (objective responsibility, expiatory punishment, etc.), and as the second is that of the older children, whose morality is one of cooperation (subjective responsibility, punishment by reciprocity, etc.), it is essential that we should determine whether a moral belief, which in the eyes of many passes as "primitive," has taken its rise from one or other of these two ethics. Now, the results which we are trying to analyse here are doubly paradoxical. On the one hand, the only collective responsibility in which our children believe (the responsibility accepted by the group which wants to declare its solidarity) occurs among the older and not among the younger ones. On the other hand, the belief in obligatory expiation is strongest among the little ones and disappears precisely at the moment when this voluntary solidarity begins to develop.

But everything becomes clear when we grasp the fact that collective responsibility in primitive societies presupposes the union of two conditions which in the child are always dissociated—viz., a mystical belief in the necessity for punishment and the feeling of unity and solidarity within the group. The "primitive" is an adult living in organized societies. He may, under the influence of a gerontocracy, retain the essentials of a morality of constraint including the strictest ideas on the subject of retributive justice; but in spite of this and simply owing to the fact of the powerful structure of the group to which he belongs, his feeling of the individual's participation in the collectivity is extremely strong. Responsibility is therefore collective at the same time as it is objective and as punishment is expiatory. In the child, on the contrary, we have to consider two phases. During the first, adult constraint develops the notions of objective responsibility, expiatory punishment, etc. The first condition for the existence of collective responsibility is therefore present. But the second condition is still lacking. For during this stage the child is essentially egocentric, and if he does have a feeling of close communion with the group (egocentrism being by definition the confusion of the self with the not-self) it is primarily in connection with the adult or with the older child that this participation comes into play. There can therefore be no question of collective responsibility. During the second stage, on the contrary, the child enters more and more into the society of his equals, groups of which become organized in and out of school.

Here, therefore, there is some possibility of collective responsibility, and the group does in point of fact declare its solidarity with the offender in cases where the latter enters into conflict with adult authority. But at the same stroke the first condition has ceased to be fulfilled; the morality of co-operation has succeeded that of constraint and neither objective responsibility nor the belief in the necessity for expiatory punishment is any longer present. Hence we cannot speak of collective responsibility in the true sense. In our societies the child, as he grows up, frees himself more and more from adult authority; whereas in the lower grades of civilization puberty marks the beginning of an increasingly marked subjection of the individual to the elders and to the traditions of his tribe. And this is why collective responsibility seems to us to be missing from the moral make-up of the child, whereas it is a notion that is fundamental in the code of primitive ethics.

§ 3. "IMMANENT JUSTICE"

A problem connected with that of punishment and one which we shall have to examine before passing on to the study of distributive justice is that of so-called immanent justice. If our hypotheses are correct, then the younger the child (not counting the first two years, of course) the stronger will be its belief in the soundness and universality of expiatory punishment, and this belief will give way before other values in so far as the morality of cooperation predominates over that of constraint. During the early years of his life, the child must therefore affirm the existence of automatic punishments which emanate from things themselves, while later, under the influence of circumstances which affect his moral growth, he probably abandons this belief. This is what we shall now endeavour to show.

We told the children three stories in this connection.

Story I. Once there were two children who were stealing apples in an orchard. Suddenly a policeman comes along and the two children run away. One of them is caught. The other one, going home by a roundabout way, crosses a river on a rotten bridge and falls into the water. Now what do you think? If he had not stolen the apples and had crossed the river on that rotten bridge all the same, would he also have fallen into the water?

Story II. In a class of very little children the teacher had forbidden them to sharpen their pencils themselves. Once, when the teacher had her back turned, a little boy took the knife and was going to sharpen his pencil. But he cut his finger. If the teacher had allowed him to sharpen his pencil, would he have cut himself just the same?

Story III. There was a little boy who disobeyed his mother. He took the scissors one day when he had been told not to. But he put them back in their place before his mother came home, and she never noticed anything. The next day he went for a walk and crossed a steam on a little bridge. But the plank was rotten. It gave way, and in he falls with a splash. Why did he fall into the water? (And if he had not disobeyed would he have fallen in just the same?)

The first two questions were put by Mlle Rambert to 167 children from Geneva and the Vaudois Jura. (The same children with whom we shall concern ourselves in the sequel on the subject of distributive justice; these subjects have therefore not been questioned about punishments or communicable responsibility). We ourselves put question II and other analogous questions to children from Neuchâtel. With regard to the first two, Mlle Rambert was able to obtain statistics showing very clearly the influence of the child's mental age. Leaving aside the uncertain reactions which constitute about ⅙th of the total, the answers affirming the existence of immanent justice, those, that is to say, where the subject maintained that if the child had not stolen or disobeyed he would not have fallen into the water or would not have cut himself, revealed the following percentages:

AGE 6	AGE 7–8	AGE 9–10	AGE 11–12
86%	73%	54%	34%

In addition to this it should be noted that in a class of backward children of 13-14 the proportion of answers of the same type was found to be 57%, which shows again that these answers are in inverse proportion to the mental age. Here are examples of this belief in the immanent justice of things.

DEP (6), Story I: "What do you think of this story?—*It serves him right. He shouldn't have stolen. It serves him right.* —If he had not stolen the apples, would he have fallen into the water?—*No.*"

CHR (6), Story III: "Why did he fall in?—*God made him, because he had touched the scissors.*—And if he hadn't done what was wrong?—*Then the board would have held out.*— Why?— *Because he didn't touch* [would not have touched] *the scissors.*"

SA (6), Story I: "What do you think of that?—*The one who got caught was sent to prison, the other was drowned.* —Was that fair?—*Yes.*—Why?—*Because he had been disobedient.*—If he hadn't been disobedient would he have fallen into the water?—*No, because he hadn't* [= would not have] *been disobedient.*"

JEAN (6), Story II: He cut himself *"because it was forbidden to touch the knife.*—And if it had not been forbidden, would he also have cut himself?—*No, because the mistress would have allowed it.*"

GRA (6): Same answers for Story I. "What happened?— *The bridge cracked.*—Why?—*Because he had eaten the apples.*—If he had not eaten the apples, would he have fallen into the water?—*No.*—Why?—*Because the bridge would not have cracked.*"

PAIL (7), Story I: "What do you think of that?—*It's fair. It serves him right.*—Why?—*Because he should not have stolen.*—If he had not stolen, would he have fallen into the water?—*No.*—Why?—*Because he would not have done wrong.*—Why did he fall in?—*To punish him."*

SCA (7): "What do you think about it?—*Oh yes, I know. If we do anything, God punishes us.*—Who told you that?—*Some children. I don't know if it's true."* Story II: *"It serves him right. You ought to obey teacher.*—And if the teacher had allowed it, would he have cut himself sharpening a pencil?—*No. He wouldn't have cut himself if the teacher had allowed it."*

BOE (8), Story III: "What do you think?—*It serves him right. You shouldn't disobey.*—And if . . . etc.?—*No, he wouldn't have fallen in, because he wouldn't have done anything."*

PRES (9), Story I: "What do you think?—*He was punished as much as the other one, and even more.*—And if he had not stolen the apples, would he have fallen into the water as he was crossing the river?—*No, because he would not have needed to be punished."*

THÉ (10), Story I: *"He was punished. Neither of them ought to have stolen. If he hadn't fallen into the water he would have been caught.*—And if he hadn't been caught?—*He'd have fallen into the water. Otherwise he'd have gone on stealing."*

DIS (11), Story I: *"He had his punishment too.*—Was it fair?—*Yes.*—And if he hadn't stolen the apples would he have fallen into the water?—*No, because* [in that case] *he didn't have to be punished."*

Here are some examples of children who no longer believe in immanent justice, at least not in the stories we told them. But this does not prevent this belief from attaching itself to other objects, by becoming displaced and gradually spiritualized.

GROS (9), Story III: "Why did he fall in?—*Because the plank was worn out.*—Was it because he had disobeyed?—*No.*—If he had not disobeyed would he also have fallen in?—*Yes. He'd have fallen in just the same. The plank was worn out."*

FLEU (12), Story I: "And if he hadn't stolen the apples,

would he have fallen in too?—(He laughs.) *The bridge isn't supposed to know whether he has stolen the apples."*

BAR (13): *"It was perhaps a coincidence. But the punishment was what he deserved."*

FRAN (13), Story I: "And if he had not stolen the apples, would he have fallen into the water?—*Yes. If the bridge was going to give way, it would have given way just the same, since it was in bad repair."*

But between two groups of clear cases, we find a series of intermediate examples, which are very interesting from the point of view of child logic, and whose original feature consists in saying that the event mentioned in our stories is certainly a punishment, but that it would have happened in any case, even if there had been no previous offence.

SCHMA (6½), Story III: "Why did he fall into the water? —*Because he told a lie.*—And if he hadn't done that, would he have fallen in?—*Yes, because the bridge was old.*—Then why did he fall in?—*Because he disobeyed his mother.*—And if he had not disobeyed would he have fallen in just the same?—*Yes. The bridge was old, after all.*—Then why would the boy have fallen in who had not disobeyed?—*Not because of that.*—Why?— . . ."

MERM (9), Story II: "What do you think about it?— *It served the boy right who fell into the water.*—Why?—*It was his punishment.*—And if he had not stolen any apples, would he have fallen in?—*Yes, because the bridge was not firm. But then it wouldn't have been fair. He would not have done anything wrong."*

VAT (10): *"He was punished for his wicked deed.*—And if . . . etc.?—*May be he might have fallen in."*

CAMP (11), Story I: "And if he had not stolen would he have fallen in?—*Perhaps he would have if the bridge had been rotten. But perhaps it was that God punished him."*

The little ones obviously do not feel the contradiction. The case of Schma is typical of children under 7; it is agreed that the child falls into the water because he has disobeyed, but he would have fallen in even if he had not disobeyed. The older ones, on the contrary, feel the difficulty well enough, but they try to reconcile the two themes of immanent justice and mechanical chance.

Before taking up the question once again from the point of view of moral psychology, it will be well to ask whether and in what manner the child tries to picture the mechanism of this justice immanent in things which he seems to believe in. Does he establish an immediate bond between the offence and the physical punishment, or does he seek to find intermediate links in the form, for example, of miracles or of some sort of artificialist causality?

We have sometimes asked this very question. The subjects who answer "God did it" should immediately be put aside. This is sure to be a learnt formula. Many parents take advantage of the least coincidence that may occur between the minor accidents of which the child is a victim and his acts of disobedience, and declare with conviction, "You see, God has punished you," etc. But apart from this adult intervention we do not think that the question of the "how" really exists for the child. Whatever may be the manner in which belief in immanent justice first takes root, it seems quite natural to the child that a fault should automatically bring about its own punishment. For nature, in the child's eyes, is not a system of blind forces regulated by mechanical laws operating on the principle of chance. Nature is a harmonious whole, obeying laws that are as much moral as physical and that are above all penetrated down to the least detail with an anthropomorphic or even egocentric finalism. It therefore seems quite natural to little children that night should come in order to put us to sleep, and that the act of going to bed is sufficient to set in motion that great black cloud that produces darkness. It seems quite natural to them that their movements should command those of the heavenly bodies (the moon follows us in order to take care of us). In short, there is life and purpose in everything. Why then should not things be the accomplices of grown-ups in making sure that a punishment is inflicted where the parents' vigilance may have been evaded? What difficulty should there be in a bridge giving way under a little thief, when everything in nature conspires to safeguard that Order, both moral and physical, of which the grown-up is both the author and the *raison d'être?*

With the older children, from the age of about 8, this mentality tends to disappear little by little. Belief in the justice immanent in things also diminishes, the two processes being no doubt correlative. But where this belief does survive in our children, it is only among the little ones that it entails any sort of enquiry as to the "how" of its execution. What happens here is something analogous to the adult's use of finalism. A semi-educated man may very well dismiss as "contrary to science" a theological explanation of the universe, and yet find no difficulty in accepting the notion that the sun is there to give us light. Thus finalism, although at first united to a more of less systematic artificialism, comes to outlive it in the end and even—as does every habitual conception—to give the illusion of intelligibility. The idea of a justice immanent in things could not appear unaided in the mind of a child of twelve, but it may survive in such a mind, as indeed in that of many an adult, without for that matter creating problems or giving rise to difficulties.

We have not, therefore, observed any spontaneous reflections concerning the causal mechanism of immanent justice. Such preoccupations only appear in those who no longer believe that the physical universe functions like a policeman. Thus Fleu (age 12) could remark to us jokingly that "the bridge was not supposed to know whether the boy had stolen apples." The little ones do not ask themselves whether or not the bridge "knows" what happens: they act as though the bridge did know, or as though the *mana* which guides all things knew in place of the bridge; but they do not formulate this belief. All the same, we may ask ourselves what they will answer if they are pressed for a more exact statement. On this point, as in the case of our questions on child artificialism and animism, the child does not hesitate to invent myths, which have, of course, no value as beliefs, but which are the indices of an immediate and inexpressible connection established by himself.

SE (6½): *"It wouldn't have happened if he hadn't picked apples.*—Did the bridge know what the boy had done?

—*No.*—Then why did it break?—*Perhaps the thunder made the bridge break.*—And did the thunder know?—*Perhaps God saw, and then he made thunder by scolding. That broke the bridge and he fell into the water.*"

CUS (6): "Did the bridge know he had stolen?—*No, but it had seen.*"

EUR (6): "*The bridge must have known, since it gave way and he was punished.*" And in Story II: "Did the knife know?—*Yes. It heard what the teacher said since it was on the desk. And it said, 'since the boy is going to sharpen it, he'll cut himself.'*"

AR (6): "Did the bridge know?—*Yes.*—How did it know? —*It had seen.*"

GEO (7; 10): "And if he had not stolen any apples, would he have fallen into the water?—*No. It was his punishment, because he had stolen apples.*—Did the bridge know?—*No, but it broke because there was a wind, and the wind knew.*"

These answers must not, of course, be regarded as corresponding to beliefs. Only the last may perhaps be said to contain an element of spontaneous belief. For we have often had occasion to see (*C.W.* and *C.C.*) the intelligent rôle which the child seems to assign to the wind. Most of these answers therefore simply indicate that the child finds quite natural the connection between the fault that has been committed and the physical phenomenon which serves as punishment. When the child is forced to make this connection explicit, he invents a story—artificialistic in one case, animistic in the other. But this way of reacting proves nothing more than that nature, in the child's eyes, is the adult's accomplice, no matter what methods she may employ in the process.

Yet the intermediate answers quoted above raise a problem. Some children maintain that the bridge has given way as a punishment and that it would have given way even if the boy had not stolen the apples. This can be very simply explained if we remember that a form of causality to which the mind has attached itself during a given period (such as the physical and moral precausality of the child of 2 to 7) never disappears all at once but coexists for a time with the later

types of explanation. The adult is familiar with these contradictions and justifies them with a cloak of words. It is only
to be expected that they should appear all the more frequently in children.

Let us now come to the main point and ask what, from the
point of view of moral psychology, is meant by the facts we
have put on record. For this purpose it will be necessary to
state more precisely how the belief in the immanent justice in
things is born and how it passes away. The intellectual element of this belief is, moreover, such as to facilitate the
question of its origin.

Three solutions as to the problem of origin offer themselves for choice. The belief in immanent justice may be
inborn, or it may be the direct result of parental teaching,
or, again, it may be an indirect product of adult constraint—
a product, therefore, to which the child mind will itself have
contributed under the double aspect, intellectual and moral,
of its nature.

The first solution is highly improbable. It has, however,
been claimed that onanism gives rise to spontaneous feelings
of remorse and to auto-punishment in thought or in act,
whence it would be possible to infer in individuals the general
presence of a predisposition to see in the events of life the
mark of immanent justice. And as a matter of fact it cannot
be denied that we can observe in masturbators a systematic
fear of the retribution residing in things—not only the fear
of the result their habits may have upon their health, the fear
of making themselves stupid, etc., but also a tendency to
interpret all the chance misfortunes of life as punishments
intended by fate. But would all these attitudes develop in a
child who had not acquired the experience of punishment
from the world outside him? We are ready to believe that
such ideas arise independently of any direct adult instruction,
and in children whose habits are hidden from those around
them. But it is those persons around them who are, after all,
the indirect cause of this belief in punishments emanating
automatically from things, and facts of this kind seem to us
to speak far more strongly in favour of the third solution
than of the first. Too many taboos relating to sex are imposed
from the first years of life for the child's most secret reactions

in this domain to be regarded as really inborn. At any rate, in order to prove the absolutely spontaneous character of auto-punishment and of the beliefs connected with it, one would have to bring up a child in very special circumstances, if not outside social contact of any kind.

As to the second solution, it contains, as we have already seen, a large proportion of truth. A great many children think that a fall or a cut constitute a punishment because their parents have said to them, "It serves you right," or, "That will be a punishment for you," or, "God made it happen," etc. And yet, even if these propositions explain the majority of cases, we do not think that they cover the whole ground. In other words, we believe that situations frequently occur in which the child quite spontaneously considers an accident of which he is the victim as a punishment, and we believe that this happens without anything analogous having been suggested by the parents in other situations. According to this hypothesis, the child, having acquired, thanks to adult constraint, the habit of punishment, attributes spontaneously to nature the power of applying the same punishments. The third solution therefore seems to us to contain a part of the truth.

Apart from the facts relating to onanism, we may mention here several examples which show how easily such attitudes are adopted by the child.

I. A well-known German-Swiss psychiatrist has told us that one of the most vivid of his childish memories is that of having been prevented from taking apples out of a basket by the cover of the basket unexpectedly closing over it. The basket was open and the child had put his hand inside it, without, as a matter of fact, regarding himself as a thief, when the cover suddenly fell on to his arm. He immediately felt that he was doing wrong, and simultaneously that he was being punished. No one else was present at the scene.

II. Another memory. A child would often look for animals to add to his natural history collection. On days when he had anything to reproach himself with, he had the feeling that his bag was a bad one and that it was so because of his misdeeds.

III. We have cited elsewhere (*C.W.*, p. 149) the case of

the deaf-mute d'Estrella studied by W. James, who associated the moon with the punishments to which he was subjected.

IV. We have also described (*C.W.*, p. 101) the singular reactions of those children who looked upon nightmares as punishments for the faults they had committed during the day.

In these four observations, which could be added to indefinitely, it seems to us that the child's attitude takes shape without any direct influence on the part of the adult. The subject is the only person who knows what happens to him, and he takes good care not to talk about it to those around him. Of course one cannot prove that children have never heard their parents invoking immanent justice; it may be that all parents do so. But the ease with which the child interprets everything in terms of immanent justice seems to indicate that we have here a tendency corresponding to his own mentality; and this is all we wished to establish.

Belief in immanent justice originates therefore in a transference to things of feelings acquired under the influence of adult constraint. But this does not fully clear up yet the moral significance of the phenomenon. In order to understand it, we have still to ask how such beliefs disappear, or at any rate diminish in importance with the mental age of the child. For the progressive decrease of answers pointing to the existence of these beliefs as the child grows older is a result worthy of our attention. What are the factors that account for this diminution?

One might point simply to the child's growing experience and to his intellectual advance. Experience shows that wickedness may go unpunished and virtue remain unrewarded. The greater the child's intellectual development, the more clearly will he see this. Such an explanation, though true up to a point, would be too simple if it were brought forward to the exclusion of all others. For it is not such an easy matter to be guided by experience. The more we analyse the conduct which consists in consulting facts the more delicate and complex an operation does it appear. Not only does experience presuppose the active participation of intelligence, but in order to eliminate the affective factors which run the risk of falsifying our interpretations we also require a veritable ethic of thought, an ethic which can only come into being in certain individual or social situations. M. Lévy-Bruhl has shown very well how impervious to experience are primitive societies where the vital beliefs of the whole community are involved. And when we see how "primitives" contrive to justify a magical or mystical attitude after repeated failures, we cannot help being reminded of those of our contemporaries who can never learn from facts. To take only the case of immanent justice, how many simple souls still think that even in this life people's actions are the object of equitable rewards and punishments, and would rather assume some hidden fault to explain a neighbour's misfortune than admit the fortuitous character in the trials that befall mankind. Or how often do not the more charitably minded invoke the mystery of destiny to defend universal justice at all costs rather than interpret events independently of any presupposition whatsoever. It is obvious, then, that even for adults to accept or reject the hypothesis of immanent justice is a matter not of pure experience, of scientific observation, but of moral evaluation and of a general attitude.

It is therefore not mere experience, but moral experiences of a certain sort that will guide the child in one direction or another. What experiences do we mean? In the first place, we may assume that it is the discovery of the imperfection of adult justice. When, as is almost bound to happen, a child is submitted to unjust treatment by his parents or his teachers, he will be less inclined to believe in a universal and automatic justice. We may recall in this connection the crisis which M. Bovet has described in the sphere of filial piety and which is so important from the point of view of the evolution of beliefs. But this discovery of the inadequate character of adult justice is only one episode in the general movement which takes the child away from the morality of constraint and towards that of cooperation.

It would seem to be to this general process and to its consequences in regard to the idea of retribution that we must, in the last resort, look for an explanation of the progressive disappearance of "immanent justice."

§ 4. RETRIBUTIVE JUSTICE AND DISTRIBUTIVE JUSTICE

In the last three sections of this chapter we have been led to the conclusion that the importance of expiatory punishment seems to decrease as the child grows older and to the extent that adult constraint is replaced by cooperation. The time has now come for us to approach the study of the positive effects of cooperation in the domain of justice, and to do this we shall first have to analyse the conflicts that may take place between distributive or equalitarian justice and retributive justice. For it is easy, as we shall try to show, to assume that equalitarian ideas acquire their force from cooperation and thus constitute a form of justice which, while it does not contradict the more evolved forms of retributive justice (punishment by reciprocity is due to the progress of just such ideas), is yet opposed to the primitive forms of punishment, and even ends by giving the preference to equality whenever the latter is in conflict with retribution.

And such conflicts are very frequent in the life of the child. It often happens that parents or teachers favour the obedient child at the expense of the others. Such inequality of treatment, which is fair from the retributive point of view, is unjust distributively. How, then, will the child judge it at the different ages he traverses? To this end, we told our subjects three stories, asking each time whether or not it was fair to favour the well-behaved child. The difficulty of the interrogatory lies in the fact that two questions necessarily interfere with each other in such cases—that of the severity of the adult (a question of degree) and that of the conflict between retribution and equality (a question of principle). The second alone is of any interest, but it is difficult to eliminate the first. We limited ourselves to varying the stories in the following manner. The first mentions no special fault and establishes the conflict between retributive and distributive justice in the abstract; the second introduces only negligible faults and minor punishments; the third, finally, brings in a punishment which may strike the child as very severe. In spite of variations (which are marked of course by deviations in the average ages of the corresponding types of answer), the children's reactions evolve according to a relatively constant law. With the little ones punishment outweighs equality, whereas with the older ones the opposite is the case.

Here is the first story. "A mother had two little girls, one obedient, the other disobedient. The mother liked the obedient one best and gave her the biggest piece of cake. What do you think of that?" According to Mlle Rambert's statistics 70% of the children of 6 to 9 approve of the mother, and only 40% of those from 10 to 13. These figures are of value, of course, only as a general indication.

Here are some examples of children who put retributive justice above equality.

BAR (6): *"It was fair. The other one was disobedient.—* But was it fair to give more to one than to the other?—*Yes. She* [the disobedient one] *must always do what she is told."*

WAL (7): *"They both ought to have been given the same* [if they were good]. *And the naughty ought to have been given nothing. She just ought to have been good."*

GIS (7½): "The mother was quite right?—*Yes, because you must always obey your mother.*—Was it fair to give one of them more than the other?—*Yes, otherwise she would be more and more disobedient, and the mother doesn't love us very much. She likes better those who do what she tells them."*

BE (7; 9): *"It was right.*—Was it fair?—*Yes, so as to show the other one how she would love her if she obeyed so that she should become obedient."*

VER (8): *"She was right to reward the one who does what she is told.*—Was it fair?—*Yes. If they had both been obedient she would have given them both the big piece."*

GRA (9; 4): *"It was fair.*—Why?—*Because she did what she was told. The other one ought to be punished.*—Was it fair that the mother should love one better than the other?—*Yes, because the other was disobedient."*

HERB (9; 10): *"It was fair because the most obedient ought to have the best things. When we are obedient, people give us the best things."*

PIT (9): *"It was fair, because those who are obedient deserve more things than those who are disobedient.*—Was it fair that she should not love them both the same?—*Yes."*

BA (10; 5), a girl who is first in her class and whose character is inclined to be what children call "goody-good" (Fr. *"petit saint"*). "Was what the mother did fair?—*She was quite fair!* [Shrugs her shoulders.]—Why?—*Because she rewarded the one who obeyed her.*"

DEA (11): *"The mother was quite right.—Why?—Because she was obedient. The other hadn't the right to have as much as the one who obeyed her."*

Here, now, are examples of children who set equality above retributive justice.

MON (6), G.: "Is it fair?—*No.*—Why not?—*She ought to have given them both the same.*—Why?— . . . —Was what the mother did fair?—*No.*"

RI (7; 6): *"They ought both to be given some cake.*— Why?—*Because if they aren't, it isn't fair."*

SCA (7;6) repeats the story correctly and realizes that the measure involved is a repressive one. But he affirms: *"It isn't fair. They should always have the pieces that are the same. It's like at home, when there is a piece of cake that's bigger than the others I take it, and then my brother snatches it away from me."*

PA (8): *"They should be given the same amount."* Pa realizes that one of the girls has been given less than the other *"because she ought to have been good,"* but he insists there should be equality of treatment.

MER (9; 6), G.: *"The one who was disobedient ought to obey, but the mother ought still to give her the same as the other.—Why?—Because you can't have people being jealous."*

PRES (10; 0): *"The mother ought to have loved the other one too and been kind to her, then perhaps she would have become more obedient.*—Is it fair to give more to the obedient one?—*No.*"

THE (10; 7), G.: *"She ought to have given them both the same amount.—Why?—Because they were her daughters, she ought to have loved them both the same."*

SON (10; 7): *"If she gives more to the nicest one, it will make the other one worse.*—But wasn't it fair to give more to the most obedient one?—*No.*—Why?—*She shouldn't have been giving her everything just because she was nice.*"

JAX (11): "*The mother was wrong.*—Why?—*She ought to have given them each a piece of cake of the same size. Perhaps it was not her fault if she was disobedient. Perhaps it was her parents' fault.*—No. It was her fault.—*Still, she ought to have had the same piece of cake.*"

DIS (11), G.: "*She ought to have given them both the same.*—Why?—*Because she will only get naughtier and naughtier. She'll be revenged against her sister.*—Why will she be revenged?—*Because she'll only get a small piece of cake.*—Was it fair, what the mother did?—*No, it wasn't fair.*"

ERI (12; 5): "*She ought to love them both the same, without any difference between them. She may love the obedient one best, but without showing it, so as not to make anyone jealous.*"

HOL (12; 5), G.: "*Even though the other one was not obedient, she shouldn't have made any difference between the two. She should have punished her in another way.*—Why should there be no difference?—*Children should be loved the same. Sometimes the other one is jealous.*"

MAG (12; 11), G.: "*It wasn't fair. Perhaps it wasn't altogether the fault of the disobedient one. She ought to have been taught, and not only loved less. Otherwise, she'll grow more and more naughty.*"

DEJ (13; 2): "*It wasn't fair. On the contrary, the mother ought to have been just the same with the other one. Then perhaps she would have behaved better. Perhaps* [in this way] *she was jealous and sillier than ever. Whatever your children are like, you must love them all the same.*"

PORT (13; 10), G.: "*It wasn't fair. The other one saw that she wasn't loved. She didn't take any trouble to improve.*"

The two types of answer stand out in clear contrast to one another. For the little ones, the necessity for punishment is so strong, that the question of equality does not even arise. For the older children, distributive justice outweighs retribution, even after consideration of all the relevant data. It is true that both types of answer are to be found at every age, though in varying proportions; but it is only natural, given the multitude of possible influences, that on so delicate a point as this the moral judgment should evolve with less regularity than it does when occupied with simpler and more objective orders of ethical fact. In homes where punishment is meted out in large quantities and where rules are rigid and weigh heavily on the children, these, if they are not secretly rebellious, will continue for a long time to believe in the superiority of punishment over equality of treatment. In a large family where moral education depends more upon the contagion of example than upon constant parental supervision, the idea of equality will be able to develop much earlier. Thus there can be no question of clear-cut stages in moral psychology. All the more significant, therefore, is the evolution which we noted as taking place between the ages of 6 and 13, and of which the age of 9 would seem to be the turning-point. For the difference between 70% and 40% is a remarkable one, especially if it be borne in mind that after 12-13 preference is given to punishment in only 25% of the cases examined.

Before turning to the examination of the other two stories and trying to draw a lesson from them, let us pause once more to see how different is the attitude of children who set a premium on retribution from that of children who demand complete equality. The first do not attempt to understand the psychological context; deeds and punishments are for them simply so much material to be brought into some sort of balance, and this kind of moral mechanics, this materialism of retributive justice, so closely akin to the moral realism we studied before, makes them insensible to the human side of the problem. Whereas most of the answers we have quoted as examples of the predominance of equalitarian tendencies show signs of a singularly delicate moral sense—the mother's preference for the obedient child will discourage the other, will make it jealous, lead it to revolt, and so on. All the very sound remarks made by Pres, by Son, and by Eri are sufficient to show that the child is no longer preaching a little sermon, as do the upholders of punishment, but is simply trying to understand the situation, though naturally under the influence of what he has experienced or observed in his own life. It is in this sense, once again, that we can mark the contrast between cooperation, the source of mutual understanding, and constraint, the source of moral verbalism. Jax even goes so far as to think that children are not always disobedient through their own fault, but sometimes through that of their parents. The psychologist can only admire this expression of a point of view which the average adult still seems so little capable of adopting. In short, then, we may take it that children who put retributive justice above distributive are those who adopt the point of view of adult constraint, while those who put equality of treatment above punishment are those who, in their relations with other children, or more rarely, in the relations of mutual respect between themselves and adults, have learnt better to understand psychological situations and to judge according to norms of a new moral type.

It may be noted in passing how completely the results of this interrogatory confirm our findings in Section 1 concerning children's views on the utility of punishment. According to many of the older subjects questioned, it was the child to whom the results of his actions had been explained who was least exposed to a moral relapse, and not the child who had been severely punished. Similarly, in the present question, systematic punishment appears harmful to all those of the subjects whose psychological insight has become sharpened in the course of family and social life.

We now come to the second story. Its object is to facilitate the analysis of the same problem, but in connection with trivial deeds devoid of any moral importance. "One afternoon, on a holiday, a mother had taken her children for a walk along the Rhône. At four o'clock she gave each of them a roll. They all began to eat their rolls except the youngest, who was careless and let his fall into the water. What will the mother do? Will she give him another one? What will the older ones say?" The answers may be of three types. Not to give him another roll (punishment); to give him another, so that everyone should have one (equality), or to give him another because he is small (equity, *i.e.*, equality allowing for the circumstances of each, in this particular case the differences of age). Mlle Rambert obtained the following figures from the 167 children she questioned:

	PUNISHMENT	EQUALITY	EQUITY
Age 6-9 . . .	48%	35%	17%
Age 10-12 . .	3%	55%	42%
Age 13-14 . .	0%	5%	95%

We ourselves presented some other children with a variant of the same story framed so as to eliminate the factor of equity introduced by the difference of age. "A mother is on the lake in a little boat with her children. At four o'clock she gives them each a roll. One of the boys starts playing the fool at the end of the boat. He leans right over the boat and lets his roll fall in. What should be done to him? Should he have nothing to eat, or should they each have given him a little piece of theirs?" The figures here are from 6-8 years old, 57% for the punishment and 43% for equality; and 25% for punishment as against 75% for equality between the years of 9 and 12.

Here are example of answers favouring punishment.

VA (6½): *"He mustn't be given any more, because he let it fall in.—What* does the older brother say?—*He wasn't pleased, because the little one had let his roll fall into the water. He said it was naughty.*—Would it have been fair to give him any more?—*No. He shouldn't have let his drop."*

MON (6½), G.: *"He mustn't be given any more.—*Why not?—*Because the mother isn't pleased.—*And what would his elder sister have said?—*That he should be given another roll."* (Cf. the opposition between solidarity and retribution!)

PAIL (7): *"He shouldn't be given another. He didn't need to let it drop.—*And what would the older ones have said if the little boy had been given another roll?—*That it wasn't fair: 'He's let it drop into the water and you go and give him another one.'*—Was it right to give him another one?—*No. He hadn't been good."*

DED (8): *"She mustn't be given another one because she*

let it drop.—What did the mother do?—She was going to scold her.—What did her elder sisters think?—That it was quite fair because she had not been careful."

WY (9): *"Mustn't give her any more.—Why?—As a punishment."*

The answers favouring punishment in connection with the story of the boat are naturally of the same type. Here, however, are two other examples, which will show to what extent, in the case of those who put retribution before equality, the criterion remains heteronomous and dependent upon the will of the parents.

SCHMA (7): *"He didn't need to go and play the fool at the end of the boat. It would teach him for another time.—Then what should have been done?—Not to go shares.—And if the mother said they were to go shares?—Then they must do as she tells them.—But was it fair, or not?—Fair, because you have to do what your mother says."*

JUN (9): *"They shouldn't go shares because it was his fault.—His brothers decided to go shares. Was that fair?—I don't know.—Was it nice of them?—Yes, nice.—Fair and nice?—More nice than fair.—The mother tells them to go shares. Is it fair?—Yes, then it is fair."*

And here are cases of children for whom equality outweighs the necessity for punishment. As a matter of fact, there are already to be found in the preceding group subjects who appealed to equality. The careless child must be punished, otherwise he will get two rolls, which is contrary to equality. But the preoccupation here is only derivative and attaches itself only to the punishment, whereas the following children are actuated primarily by a search for equality which they set above any sort of punishment.

SCA (7): *"The little boy should be given another one because he is hungry.—And what do the others say?—He must be given some bread because the big ones have some, so he ought to have some [too]."*

ZI (8): *"He ought to be given some more, because little*

children are not very clever; they don't know what they are doing.—Was it fair to the older one or not?—*It isn't fair that the older one should have his roll, and not the little one. The older one ought to have gone shares."*

PER (11): *"He ought to be given some more, because it wasn't his fault that he let it drop, and it isn't fair that he should have less than the others."*

XA (12): *"He ought to have been given a little back by taking away from the roll what the child had already eaten.*— And what did the others say?—*If they were nice, they said, 'He is getting as much more as we have.' If they were horrid, 'Serve him right!'"* (Fr. *"Tant pis pour lui!"*).

MEL (13), G.: *"They should have divided up what the other children had left and given some to the little chap.*— Was it fair to give him any more?—*Yes, but the child ought to have been more careful.*—What does 'fair' mean?—*It means equality among everyone."*

Here are a few more answers obtained from the story about the boat. This story differs from the preceding one in that the fault is more clearly marked in the child who loses his roll, and in that the child is not represented as the youngest. There should therefore be all the more chance of punishment winning as against equality. Yet the reactions are the same as in the previous case, and the need for equality is even, after the age of 7-8, set up in opposition to the punishment demanded by the adult.

WAL (7): *"They ought to have gone shares.*—But the mother said, 'No. It serves him right. He played the fool. You mustn't go shares with him.' Was that fair?—*It wasn't fair because he would have less than the others.*—And when people play the fool, isn't it fair that they should have less than the others?— . . . —If you were the father what would you say?—*That he should be given some more."*

ZEA (8): *"They ought to have gone shares with him.*— Was it more fair or only nice of them to share?—*More fair.* —But the mother said, 'No, it's his own fault.'—*Well, I would have gone shares.*—Even if the mother said no?—*Yes, you ought to share."*

ROB (9): *"He ought to be given some more.—But he* played the fool.*—They ought to share.*—What had he done? *—He was playing. Sometimes you lose pennies that way. That's a lot worse!*—But the mother had said they were not to lean over the edge. What ought she to have said, that he should have some more, or not?*—That they ought not to go shares.*—And what would the other boys have said?*—That they ought to share, because it wasn't fair."*

SCHMO (10): *"They ought each to have given him a little piece.*—Would that have been fairer or only nicer?*—It was nicer, and fairer too.*—And if the mother says they mustn't share?*—They should obey but it wasn't fair."*

And now here are cases of children, who, though not possessing the requisite vocabulary, make the legal distinction between equity and justice. According to these children, from the point of view of pure justice, the boy who drops his roll should be given nothing more, because he has had his share along with the others, and if he loses what is his, that concerns himself alone. But in addition to considerations of pure justice, the circumstances of the individual must be taken into account. The child is small, clumsy, and so on; thus a kind of superior equality requires that he should be given some more. This more subtle attitude is naturally only to be met in the children of 9 to 12. Before this, the child already has these feelings, but does not succeed in distinguishing them from those of justice pure and simple. Here are examples.

DEP (9), G.: *"He must be given some more.*—What did the older ones say?*—It's not fair. You've given two to the kid and only one to us.*—And what would the mother have answered?*—She's the youngest. You've got to be sensible."*

BRA (9): *"He shouldn't have let it drop. He mustn't have another one. But it would be more fair all the same that he should have some more, that they should give him another.—* Would it be more fair, or only just more kind?*—More kind, because he didn't need to go and let it drop into the water."*

CAMP (11), G.: *"The little boy ought to have taken care. But then he was a little boy, so they might give him a little piece more.*—What did the others say?*—They were jealous*

and said that they ought to be given a little piece more too.
But the little one deserved to be given a little piece more. The
older ones ought to have understood.—Do you think it was
fair to give him some more?— . . . *Of course! It was a*
shame for the little one. When you are little you don't under-
stand what you are doing."

Now for our third story. We can put the matter briefly.
The answers obtained entirely confirm those given up to now.
But as the punishment in this case is particularly severe, the
feeling of equality is sooner in gaining the ascendant over
the need for retribution. "There was once a family with a lot
of boys. They all had holes in their shoes, so one day their
father told them to take their shoes to the shoemaker to be
mended. Only, as one of the brothers had been disobedient
several days before, the father said, 'You won't go to the
shoemaker. You can keep your holes since you have been
disobedient.'" The children of 6 to 7 were divided into 50%
for equality, 50% for punishment. But after the age of 8,
nearly nine-tenths are in favour of equality of treatment.

Here are two examples of children who approve of such a
punishment.

NEU (7): "What do you think about it?—*It is fair.*—Why?
—*Because he had disobeyed."*

FAL (7): *"It is fair.*—Why?—*Because he was naughty.*—
Is it fair or not that he should not have fresh soles to his
shoes?—*It is fair.*—If you were the father, would you take
his shoes to be mended or not?—*I wouldn't take them."*

And a few examples of subjects who prize equality.

ROB (9): *"It wasn't fair. The father had told them that*
they were all to be done."

WALT (10): *"It wasn't fair.*—Why?—*Because one boy*
would have a good pair of shoes and the other would have
wet feet.—But he had been disobedient. . . . What do you
think about it?—*That it was not fair."*

NUS (10): *"It isn't fair.*—What should the father have
done?—*Punish him in some other way."*

Thus, whatever may be the variations in our stories, the answers are always the same. In case of conflict between retributive and distributive justice, the little ones always favour punishment, and the older ones equality of treatment. The result is the same whether we are dealing with definitely expiatory punishments, as in Stories I and III, or with a punishment that is the consequence of the act, as in Story II. We may note, moreover, without as yet trying to interpret it, the fact that here, as in the case of moral realism, the child's reactions to the interrogatory—i.e., his theoretical reflections —are always a year or two behind his life reactions, that is to say, his effective moral feelings. A child of 7, say, who regards as just the punishments dealt with in our stories, would certainly feel their injustice if they were inflicted on him or on his friends. The interrogatory therefore inevitably distorts the moral judgment. But here, as before, the question is to know whether the products of the interrogatory simply lag behind those of life or whether they do not correspond to anything that has ever been really experienced. As in the case of moral realism, we believe that it is chiefly a matter of lagging behind, and that our results do correspond to what can be observed in real life, though separated from this by a time-lag. Broadly speaking, then, we may say that if punishment holds the day during the early years, it gradually makes way for equality during the course of mental development.

What is at the back of such an evolution? It is obvious that equality will prevail over punishment by reciprocity, since the latter is derived from it. As to expiatory punishment we have nothing new to say on the subject. It is impossible to see how such a notion could have come into being except under the influence of adult constraint. There is nothing in the idea of right and wrong that implies reward or punishment. In other words, it is only because of external associations that the altruistic or egoistic sentiments are bound up with expectation of rewards or punishments. And if this is so, whence can these associations arise if not from the fact that from its tenderest years the child's behaviour is submitted to the sanctions of adults?

But, this being so, how are we to account for the fact that retributive justice, which in all cases of conflict with distributive justice carries the day during the early years, should diminish in importance with the increase of years? It can hardly be maintained that the fear of punishments is less strong at ten than it is at six. On the contrary, from the age of seven to eight onwards school punishments are added to those already incurred in the family, and even if punishments are less frequent at this age than at four or five, they have, on the other hand, a certain gravity which renders them the more apt to impress the youthful mind. So that the feeling of retributive justice ought really to increase with the years, and should be sufficiently strong to hold in check the desire for equality wherever this shows itself. Why is this not so?

Evidently because of the intervention of a new factor. The desire for equality, far from assuming an identical form at every age, seems, on the contrary, to grow more acute as the child's moral development proceeds. Two solutions are conceivable. It may be that equalitarianism, like retributive justice, is the fruit of the child's respect for the adult. Some parents are extremely scrupulous in matters of justice and instil in their children a keen sense of equality. Thus distributive justice may perhaps be merely a second aspect of adult constraint. But it may also be the case that, far from being the direct result of parental or scholastic pressure, the idea of equality develops essentially through children's reactions to each other and sometimes even at the adult's expense. It is very often the injustice one has had to endure that makes one take cognizance of the laws of equality. In any case it is hard to see how such a notion could take on any reality for a child before he had come in contact with his equals either in the home or at school. The relation between child and adult as such does not allow for equality. And since equalitarianism is born of the contact of children with one another, its development must at least keep pace with the progress of cooperation between them.

We cannot as yet make our choice between these two hypotheses, for the analyses that will follow are essentially designed to facilitate this decision. But the facts we have presented already speak in favour of the second solution. For we have noticed that the champions of retributive justice are not generally those endowed with most psychological penetration. They are apologists rather than moralists or psychologists. The votaries of equality, on the contrary, have given proof of a delicate sense of moral distinctions. And this feeling of theirs seems very often to be the product of reflections made on the moral clumsiness of the adult. In any case it is remarkable with what force these children contrast the cause of justice with the decrees of authority. But all this is only an impression, and we must now pursue our analysis of distributive justice and equality among children.

§ 5. EQUALITY AND AUTHORITY

The first point to be settled in an enquiry of this kind is the form in which the possible conflicts between the sense of justice and adult authority present themselves and the relation in which they stand to the subject's age. If we appeal to our memories of childhood, we very often find as examples of injustices (apart, naturally, from cases of unmotivated punishments) inequalities of treatment on the part of our parents. For it is very difficult, when one is dividing a piece of work among a few children, or expressing one's affection or one's interest to each, to maintain a strict impartiality and to avoid hurting the feelings of the more sensitive. It happens particularly often that children experience, either continuously or in bouts, those "feelings of inferiority" on which Adler has laid so much stress, and which make the best of them jealous, in spite of themselves, of their brothers and sisters. The least mistake in the treatment of such sensitive children will keep alive in them a vague impression of injustice, with or without foundation. What, then, is going to happen when children are told in the crude schematic form that is indispensable to an interrogatory addressed to all, stories which pit the desire for equality against the fact of authority? Will the subjects who are examined put the adult in the right, out of respect for authority (justice being in this case confused with the Law, even if the latter is unjust), or will they defend equality out of respect for an inner ideal, even if the latter is in opposition with obedience? As might have been expected from the preceding results we found a predominance of the first solution among the little ones, and as the age of the subjects increased, a definite progression in the direction of the second.

We made use of the four following stories:

Story I. Once there was a camp of Boy Scouts (or Girl Guides). Each one had to do his bit to help with the work and leave things tidy. One had to do the shopping, another washed up, another brought in wood or swept the floor. One day there was no bread and the one who did the shopping had already gone. So the Scoutmaster asked one of the Scouts who had already done his job to go and fetch the bread. What did he do?

Story II. One Thursday afternoon, a mother asked her little girl and boy to help her about the house, because she was tired. The girl was to dry the plates and the boy was to fetch in some wood. But the little boy (or girl) went and played in the street. So the mother asked the other one to do all the work. What did he say?

Story III. Once there was a family with three brothers, one older one and two who were twins.[9] They all used to black their boots every morning. One day the big one was ill. So the mother asked one of the others to black his boots as well as his own. What do you think of that?

Story IV. A father had two boys. One of them always grumbled when he was sent messages. The other one didn't like being sent either, but he always went without saying a word. So the father used to send the boy who didn't grumble on messages oftener than the other one. What do you think of that?

Although we attach no magical value to figures, it may be of interest to mention here those obtained by Mlle Rambert on some 150 children of 6 to 12 from Geneva and the Canton of Vaud by means of Stories I and II. The regularity of these results shows that we have at any rate to do with a form of evolution that proceeds as a function of age. The

[9] This detail is added so as to eliminate the question of age which several subjects spontaneously introduced.

little ones incline to authority and even think the command given to the child quite just (not only should one obey, but the action commanded is just in itself, in so far as it conforms with the order given), whereas the older children incline to equality and think the order described in the story unjust.

Age	STORY I		STORY II	
	Obedience %	Equality %	Obedience %	Equality %
6 . .	95	5	89	11
7 . .	55	45	41.2	58.8
8 . .	33.3	66.6	22.2	77.8
9 . .	16.6	83.4	0	100
10 . .	10	90	5.9	94.1
11 . .	5	95	0	100
12 . .	0	100	0	100

For our part, we found at Neuchâtel, by means of Stories III and IV, that about 75% of the children of 5 to 7 defend obedience, and that about 80% of the subjects between 8 and 12 defend equality. But let us leave these figures and turn to the qualitative analysis which is alone of a nature to tell us what the child is trying to say and whether he knows what he is thinking about.

Four types of answers can be observed. First of all there are the children who regard the adult's order as "fair," and who thus do not distinguish what is just from what is simply in conformity with the order received or with the rule of obedience. Then there are the children who think the order unjust, but who deem that the rule of obedience comes before justice, so that it behoves us to carry out the order without comment. Children of this type can therefore distinguish justice from obedience, but think it evident that the latter must prevail over the former. In our statistics we have classed these two groups as one, seeing that they are linked together by all the intermediate cases. In the third place, there are the children who think the order unjust, and put justice above obedience. In the fourth place, finally, there are the children who also deem the order unfair, and do not necessarily regard blind obedience as incumbent upon the child in the story, but who think it better to be obliging and submit rather than argue and rebel. In the statistics we treated these two groups as one, owing to the autonomy given to the sense of justice in both cases.

Here are examples of the first type, which naturally finds no representatives except among the very little ones.

BAR (6½), G., Story I: *"She ought to have gone to get the bread.—Why?—Because she had been told to.—*Was it fair or not fair to have told her to go?*—Yes, it was fair, because she had been told to."*

ZUR (6½), Story I: *"He ought to have gone.—Why?— To obey.—*Was it fair, what he had been asked to do?*—Yes. It was his boss, his chief."* Story II: *"He should have gone.— Why?—Because his sister was disobedient. He ought to be kind."*

HEP (7), G., Story I: "Was it fair what she was asked to do?*—It was fair because she had to go.—*Even though it was not her job?*—Yes, she had been told to go."* Story II: *"It was fair because her mother had told her to."*

ZIG (8), Story II: *"He ought to have done both things because his brother wouldn't.—Is it fair?—It is very fair. He is doing a good deed."* Zig seems not to know the meaning of the word "fair." But he has given us elsewhere an unequal division as an example of unfairness. In this Story II, therefore, what is just is identified with what is in conformity with obedience.

JUN (9), Story III: "Was it fair?*—Yes, I think so.—*What did the second boy say?*—You ought to give three [boots] to one and three to the other.—*Very well then?*—But you must do as the mother said.—*But was it fair, or was it because the mother said so?*—It was fair!"*

The character of these cases is obvious. It would be an exaggeration to say that the child of 6-7 has no idea of justice. Several of the above subjects hesitate to say outright that the orders given in the story were fair. Only, what is just is not differentiated in their minds from what is in conformity with authority, and it is only in so far as there is no conflict with authority that the idea of equality intervenes. So that with the little ones it goes without saying that an order received, even if it is contrary to equality, is still just, since it emanates from the adult. Justice is what is law. With the older of the children quoted above, this no longer goes without saying, but they decide that it must be so.

Facts such as these lend confirmation to M. Bovet's[10] extremely interesting theory, according to which the child begins by attributing moral perfection to his parents and does not till the age of about 5-7 discover or face the fact of their possible imperfections. We shall return to this point. For the moment, the only question is whether such a systematic respect for the adult on the part of the child is of a nature to develop or to thwart the formation of equalitarian justice. With regard to the last set of answers examined, the hypothesis may be advanced that unilateral respect, which is of neutral content in relation to distributive justice—parents can use the respect conferred upon them equally to uphold the example of justice and to impose a rule that is contrary to justice, such as the right of primogeniture—that unilateral respect, then, does, *by the very nature of its mechanism,* constitute an obstacle to the free development of the sense of equality. Not only is there no possible equality between adults and children, but further, reciprocity between children cannot be produced to order. If it is imposed from without it leads only to a calculation of interests or remains subordinated to ideas of authority and external rules which are its very negation. According to the subjects whose answers we quoted above, what has been imposed is what seems just. It will be agreed that this is the very opposite of that autonomy required by the development of justice: justice has no meaning except as something that is above authority.

We shall now give examples from the second group of answers. The child always extols perfect obedience, but without complete inner acquiescence: authority still prevails over justice, but the two are no longer confused with one another.

CHRI (6), Story I: "Is it fair?—*No, the girl does more. She'll be jealous.*—Did she go or not?—*She went.*—Did she think it fair?—*No, she'll say, 'It wasn't me was to go and*

10 Bovet, *op. cit., The Child's Religion.*

fetch the bread.'—Why did she go?—*Because the chief wanted her to."*

DED (7), G., Story II: *"She ought to have gone because her mother told her to.—Was it fair?—No, because the other one ought to have gone."*

TRU (8; 7), Story II: *"She ought only to have done one [one job].—Why?—It isn't fair if the boy didn't go [to fetch the wood].—But he didn't go, and so?—She ought to have done it all the same.—Why?—To be obedient."*

HERB (9), G., Story II: *"She ought to have gone at once. —Why?—Because when you're asked to, you must go at once.—Was it fair?—No, it wasn't her turn.—Why did she go?—To do as she was told."*

NUSS (10), Story III: *"He ought to have done it, but it wasn't fair."*

WAL (10), Story III: *"They should have blacked three shoes each.—But the mother said one boy was to black two and the other four. Is that fair?—Not fair.—The mother went out. What did the boys do—as she had told them, or three boots each?—Three each.—Was that right?—It would have been better to have done as the mother said.—Was it fair?—As [= what] the mother said, it wasn't fair."*

REN (11), Story II: *"He did it.—Why?—You must obey. —Was it fair?—No, not very."*

Thus these children, while they uphold the supremacy of obedience, distinguish between what is just and what is imposed by authority. Here are examples of the third group, of those, that is to say, who set justice above submission.

WAL (7½), Story II: *"She shouldn't have gone because it wasn't her job.—Why should she not have gone?—Because it was not her job.—Was what the mother asked her to do fair?—Oh no. She shouldn't have gone. She should have done her work and the boy his.—And if the mother asked her to? — . . . She would go.—Why?—Because . . . she would have to."* Thus Wal gives material constraint its due, but does not recognize any inner obligation.

LAN (7; 6), Story I: *"He shouldn't have done it because it wasn't his job.—Was it fair or not to ask him to do it?—*

Not fair." Story II: *"He ought not to have done it because the girl had gone away and it wasn't fair."*

PAI (8), Story I: *"He said no, because it wasn't his job."*

DOL (8), Story III: *"It wasn't fair. They should each have been given one boot.*—But the mother had said they must.— *The other one should have been given a boot.*—Ought they to do as they were told, or divide things equally?—*They should have asked their mother."* Story IV: *"It's not fair. The father should have asked the other one too.*—But that is what the father had said.—*It's not fair.*—What should the boy have done? Gone the messages, or not gone, or told the father to send the other boy?—*He should have done nothing. Not gone."*

CLA (9; 8), G., Story II: *"She ought to have done her own work and not the other one's.*—Why not?—*It wasn't fair."* Story I: *"She oughtn't to have done it. It was not her job to do it.*—Was it fair to do it?—*No, it was not fair."*

PER (10): *"He wouldn't go. He said the other one ought to go."*

FRI (11), Story III: *"He shouldn't do it.*—But the mother said he must.—*The mother was wrong. It's not fair."*

SCHN (12), G., Story II: *"She shouldn't have done it. It's not fair that she should work twice as hard and not the other.* —What was to be done?—*She should have said to her mother, 'It's not fair. I ought not to do double the work.' "*

For these children, unlike those of the second group, equality outweighs everything—not only obedience, but even friendliness. The answers of the fourth type, on the contrary, present the special feature, that while he declares the order received to be unjust, the child thinks it should be carried out for the sake of being agreeable and helpful. Children of this group must not be confused with those of the second. For subjects of the second type consider that obedience comes before justice, whereas those whose reactions we are now going to examine recommend a voluntary mutual help which is superior both to bare justice and to forced obedience. The difference is therefore considerable. On the one hand, justice is subordinated to obedience, thus to a heteronomous principle, on the other hand, justice itself is extended along a purely autonomous line of development into the higher form of reciprocity which we call "equity," a relation based not on mere quality but on the real situation in which each individual may find himself. In this particular case, if strict justice is opposed to obedience, equity requires that the special relations of affection existing between parent and child should be taken into account. Thus a tedious job, even if it is unjust from the point of view of equality, becomes legitimate as a free manifestation of friendliness. Here are a few examples:

PER (11; 9), Story I: *"He went to fetch some.*—Was it fair?—*It wasn't fair, but it was obliging."*

BALT (11; 9), Story II: *"She did it.*—What did she think? —*That her brother was not very nice.*—Was it fair that she should do this?—*It wasn't fair, but she did it to help her mother."*

CHAP (12; 8) answers with regard to Story I that *"he thought his chief was a nuisance,"* but in connection with Story II he says: *"It depends on whether he's a good boy. If he is fond of his mother, he will do it; otherwise he'll do the same as his sister so as not to have to work any harder than her."*

PED (12; 5) himself makes the distinction which seems to us to characterize the present type most clearly, and this in connection with Story I: *"He must go and fetch the bread.*— What did he think?—*My master orders me to; I must help him.*—Was it fair?—*Yes, it was fair because it was from obedience. It wasn't quite fair if he was made to go, but if he accepted to, it was fair."* One could not formulate better the principle of autonomy which characterizes the attitude we are speaking of: if you are forced to do something against equality, it is unjust, but if you accept to do a service, you are doing something superior to strict justice, and you are behaving with equity towards your chief.

GIL (12), Story II: *"He wasn't pleased.*—Did he do it?— *Oh, yes.*—Was it fair?—*No.*—Why did he do it?—*To please his mother."*

FRI (12), G., Story II: *"She might have refused. She thought that her brother would go and have a good time and*

that she would have to work.—Was it fair or not to do it?—
Not fair.—Would you have done it or not?—*I would have
done it to please my mother.*"

A law of evolution emerges sufficiently clearly from all
these answers. True, we cannot speak of stages properly so
called, because it is extremely doubtful whether every child
passes successively through the four attitudes we have just
described. It is greatly a question of the kind of education
the child has received. Thus the fourth kind of reaction
might appear very early if one were willing to replace the
absurd principle of blind obedience ("You've got to do it,
and there's an end of it!") by an appeal to cooperation. A
little girl of three of our acquaintance used to accept every
suggestion from her mother, saying "I'll help you," where
her pride would have resisted any sort of constraint. In addition to which, and in order to anticipate the inevitable objection, we repeat what we have said before that results of
an interrogatory obviously come later in time than do those
of real experience.

With these reservations, however, it seems to us possible
to distinguish three broad stages in the development of distributive justice in relation to adult authority. (And we shall
see later on that the same holds good of the relations between
children.)

During the first stage, justice is not distinguished from the
authority of law: "just" is what is commanded by the adult.
It is naturally during this first stage that retributive justice,
as we saw in the last section, proves stronger than equality.
This first stage might therefore be characterized by the absence of the idea of distributive justice, since this notion implies a certain autonomy and a certain degree of liberation
from adult authority. But there may well be something rather
primitive in the relation of reciprocity, and the germs of
equalitarianism may be present from the first in the relations
that children have to each other. Only, so long as the respect
for the adult predominates, that is to say, throughout the
whole of this first stage, these germs could not give rise to
any genuine manifestations except in so far as they created
no conflict with authority. Thus a child of two or three years

will think it quite right that a cake should be equally divided between him and another child, or that he and a playmate should lend each other their toys. But if he is told that he must give more to the other child, or keep more for himself, he will promptly turn this into a duty or a right. It is unlikely, on the contrary, that such an attitude should survive for long in a normal child of ten or twelve; the sense of justice here is founded on an autonomous feeling that is superior to any commands that may be received.

During a second stage, equalitarianism grows in strength and comes to outweigh any other consideration. In cases of conflict, therefore, distributive justice is opposed to obedience, to punishment, and very often even to those more subtle reasons that come to the fore in the third period.

Finally, during a third stage, mere equalitarianism makes way for a more subtle conception of justice which we may call "equity," and which consists in never defining equality without taking account of the way in which each individual is situated. In the domain of retributive justice, equity consists in determining what are the attenuating circumstances, and we have seen that this consideration enters very late into children's judgments. In the domain of distributive justice, equity consists in taking account of age, of previous services rendered, etc.; in short, in establishing shades of equality. We shall come across fresh examples of this process in the course of the next section.

Let us now turn to the analysis of more cases in which respect for authority enters into conflict with the sense of justice. It may happen not only that the child desires equality with his own kind, but that in some circumstances he claims to be on a level with the adult himself. Mlle Rambert conceived in this connection the happy idea of studying the situation to which the child is so often submitted, namely that of being made to wait at the counter of a shop while the grown-up customers are being served. She asked her subjects: "Is it fair to keep children waiting in shops and to serve the grown-ups first?" The reaction was very definite. Only the very youngest of the subjects hesitated to say so, but the majority even of the six-year-olds maintained with astonishing precocity that each should be served in turn.

Here are two examples showing respect for adult priority.

SAN (6½): *"Little children are not in such a hurry as grown-ups."*

PAI (7½): *"Whoever comes first is served first.*—Have children as much right to be served as grown-ups?—*No, because they are smaller and don't quite know how to give an order. Grown-up people have a lot to do and have to hurry."* Pai adds that he is looking forward to growing up so as to *"be able to give orders."*

And a few examples of those who demand exact equality.

MART (9): *"They* [the salesmen] *ought not to keep children waiting.*—Why not?—*Because it's not fair to keep them waiting. Grown-ups should always be served last* [=in turn]. —Why?—*Because sometimes little children are just as much in a hurry and it isn't fair* [to keep them waiting].—Should they be served when their turn comes or before the grown-up people?—*When their turn comes."*

DEP (9): *"It isn't fair. Everyone should be served in turn."*

BA (10): *"They ought to have served him* [the child] *when his turn came.*—Why?—*Because it isn't fair to serve those who came afterwards."*

PRE (10): *"Even if he was little he shouldn't have been made to wait. He was shopping just as much as the grown-up people."*

It will be seen how definite is the desire for equality in these answers and how vividly they reflect the experiences of real life.

To conclude our examination of the various contacts between authority and equality, let us try to analyze two school situations where the same factors may come into play: Why should one not cheat at school?—and: Should one "tell" if it is in the adult's interest or if the adult has commanded it?

Cheating is a defensive reaction which our educational systems seem to have wantonly called forth in the pupil. Instead of taking into account the child's deeper psychological tendencies which urge him to work with others—emulation being in no way opposed to cooperation—our schools condemn the pupil to work in isolation and only make use of emulation to set one individual against another. This purely individualistic system of work, excellent no doubt if the aim of education be to give good marks and prepare the young for examinations, is nothing but a handicap to the formation of reasonable beings and good citizens. Taking the moral point of view only, one of two things is bound to happen. Either competition proves strongest, and each boy will try and curry favour with the master, regardless of his toiling neighbour who then, if he is defeated, resorts to cheating. Or else comradeship will win the day and the pupils will combine in organized cheating so as to offer a common resistance to scholastic constraint. The second of these two defence mechanisms appears chiefly in the older classes and, according to our personal memories, between the ages of 12 and 17. We hardly found a trace of it among the Elementary School children whom we examined.[11] In the first system the problem which arises is to know why cheating is reproved. Is it because the master forbids it, or because it is contrary to the equality between children?

Here again, the result of our enquiry is very definite. It shows a gradual diminution in the preoccupation with authority and a correlative increase in the desire for equality. This result is all the more remarkable, because in this particular case authority and equality are not the only possible solutions. For the answers to the question, "Why must you not copy from your friend's book?" can be classed under three heads: 1) "It is forbidden," "it is naughty," "it is deceit,"

---

[11] This may be because such confessions are neither easy to make nor to elicit. But as far as our personal recollections go, this cheating in common, though unconfessed, never seemed to us a sin. For years, as boys, we calmly did our home-work together and arranged to help each other in class within the limits of possibility. Nor was this clandestine work in common altogether useless, and we can recall many things that were learned by discussing them with our comrades. But of course this sort of thing diminishes individual effort to a great extent, a disadvantage from which precisely the work in common that is done in "Activity Schools" is free.

"a lie," "you get punished," etc. We group all these answers under one head because, if the child's argumentation be analysed, the ultimate reason always proves to be the adult's prohibition. It is naughty to cheat because it is deceiving, etc., and it is naughty to deceive because it is forbidden. 2) It is contrary to equality (it does harm to the friend, it is stealing from him, etc.). 3) It is useless (one learns nothing, one always gets caught, etc.). This third sort of answer is probably of adult origin: the child is merely repeating the sermon that has been preached to him when he has been caught stealing. It only appears after the age of 10. The percentages are: 5% at 10, 4% at 11, and 25% at 12. Reasons in favour of authority are invoked in the following proportions: 100% at 6 and 7, 80% at 8, 88% at 9, 68% at 10, 32% at 11, and 15% at 12. The decrease is therefore unmistakable. The great majority of the children simply say that cheating is forbidden. Only a small minority assimilates it to lying. Finally, equality is the reason defended by 16% of the children of 8 and 9 years old, 26% of those of 10, and 62% of those of 11 and 12. In the main, therefore, equality grows stronger with age, whereas the importance of adult prohibition decreases in proportion.

Here are examples of answers that appeal to authority.

MON (6½): "Why must you not copy from your neighbour?—*The master rows us.*"
DEP (6½): *"Teacher punishes us."*
THÉ (6½): *"Because it is naughty."*
MIR (6½): *"It's bad. You get punished."*

The definition "It is deceit" is given only by 5% of the children of 8 and 9 and by 10% of those of 10 to 12.

MART (9): *"He shouldn't have copied from his neighbour. He was being deceitful.*—Why must you not copy?—*Because it is deceit."*

Here are examples of children who appeal to equality.

THÉ (9; 7): *"You ought to try and find out yourself. It*

isn't fair they should both have the same marks. You ought to find out by yourself."

WILD (9; 4), G.: *"It's stealing her work from her.*—And if the master doesn't know?—*It's naughty because of the girl beside her.*—Why?—*The girl beside her might have got it right* [got a good mark] *and her place is taken away."*

Finally, let us quote a child to whom cheating is something perfectly natural and in whose case the solidarity between children is clearly stronger than the desire for competition.

CAMP (11; 10): "What do you think about cheating?—*For those who can't learn they ought to be allowed to have just a little look, but for those who can learn it isn't fair.*—A child copied his friend's sum. Was it fair?—*He ought not to have copied. But if he was not clever it was more or less all right for him to do it."*

This last attitude seems to be rather the exception among the children we examined. But no doubt many others thought the same without having the courage to say so.

If the letter only be considered in the answers appealing to equality, it might seem that competition was stronger in children than solidarity. But this is so only in appearance. In reality, equality grows with solidarity. This will appear from the study of one more question which we shall now analyse in order to obtain additional information on the conflicts between adult authority and equality or solidarity between children. We mean the question of "telling tales."

The contempt which every school child feels for tell-tales or sneaks (Fr. *"mouchards," "cafards"*)—the child's language is significant in itself—and the spontaneous judgment which is pronounced upon them are sufficient to show that this is a fundamental point in the ethics of childhood. Is it right to break the solidarity that holds between children in favour of adult authority? Any adult with a spark of generosity in him will answer that it is not. But there are exceptions. There are masters and parents so utterly devoid of pedagogic sense as to encourage the child to tell tales. In such cases, should one obey the adult or respect the law of solidarity? We put the question by laying the following story to the charge of a father whom we removed to a great distance both in time and space.

"Once, long ago, and in a place very far away from here, there was a father who had two sons. One was very good and obedient. The other was a good sort, but he often did silly things. One day the father goes off on a journey and says to the first son: 'You must watch carefully to see what your brother does, and when I come back you shall tell me.' The father goes away and the brother goes and does something silly. When the father comes back he asks the first boy to tell him everything. What ought the boy to do?"

Here, again, the result was perfectly clear. The great majority of the little ones (nearly nine-tenths of those between 6 and 7) are of opinion that the father should be told everything. The majority of the older ones (over 8) think that nothing should be told, and some even go so far as to prefer a lie to the betrayal of a brother.

Here are examples of the different attitudes adopted, beginning with that of complete submission to authority.

WAL (6): "What should he have said?—*That he* [the other] *had been naughty.*—Was it fair to say that, or not?— *Fair.*—I know a little boy in the same story who said to his father: 'Look here, it's not my business what my brother has done, ask him yourself.' Was he right to say this to his father?—*Wasn't right.*—Why?—*He ought to have told.*— Have you got a brother?—*Yes.*—Then we'll pretend that you have made a blot in your copy-book at school. Your brother comes home and says: 'I say, Eric made a blot.' Was it right of him to say this?—*He was right.*—Do you know what a tell-tale is?—*It's telling what he* [the other] *has done.*—Is it telling tales if your brother says that you made a blot?—*Yes.* —And in my story?—*It's not telling tales.*—Why?—*Because the father had asked him.*"

SCHMO (6): "*He ought to say that he* [the other one] *was naughty. He ought to say what the other one had done. The father had told him to.*—The child answered his father: 'Ask my brother yourself, daddy, I don't want to say.' Was it nice of him to say that, or not?—*Not nice, because the father had asked him.*"

DESA (6): "*He ought to have told. His father had asked him to.*—Should he have told, or not told?—*He ought to have told.*—If he answers, 'It's not my business what my brother does,' will that be all right?—*He might have said that.*—Is it best to say that or to tell what the brother did?—*Yes, it was better to tell what his brother did.*—Do you know what a tell-tale is?—*No.*"

SCHU (6): "Should he have told, or not?—*Yes, because his father told him to tell what his brother had done.*—Should he tell everything?—*When they are very silly and naughty* (Fr. '*des grandes vilaines manières*') *you must tell everything.*—And when they are a little silly and naughty (Fr. '*des petites vilaines manières*')?—*No, because it's not very naughty.* [This distinction anticipates the next stage!]—Is that telling tales?—*No, if you're asked to tell, it isn't telling tales.*—Might he have said, 'Jean will tell you himself'?—*No.*—Or else, 'You ask Jean. It is not my business'?—*No.*—Is it nice to tell tales about what your brother has done?—*Yes.*"

CONST (7), G.: "*He ought to have told. The father had asked him to.*—Do you know what telling tales is?—*It's telling things.*—Was it telling tales, or not?—*It was telling tales.*—Have you any sisters?—*Yes, one. She is eleven.*—Does she tell tales about what you do?—*Yes.*—Tell me about once when she did. Who did she tell tales to?—*To mother.*—Tell me about it?—*I didn't dare to go out. And I did go all the same.*—Was it nice to tell tales about that, or not?—*Nice.*—Was she right to tell about it or not?—*She was right.*"

SCHMA (8): "*He ought to have told.*—Was it fair, or not?—*Fair.*—Once he said that it wasn't his business.—*That was not fair, because his father had said he was to tell.*—Was he telling tales?—*Just then he ought to tell because his father had asked him, but other times he ought not to tell because he hadn't been asked.*"

IN (9): "*He ought to have told.*—I am going to tell you three stories: In the first, the boy did tell; in the second, he told the father to ask his brother himself; and in the third, he said that his brother hadn't done anything. Which was best?—*The first.*—Why?—*Because he told what he* [the brother] *had done, as his father had asked him to.*—Which way was the nicest?—*The first.*—And the fairest?—*The first one too.*—Do you know what telling tales is?—*Telling what someone else has done.*—And here?—*He didn't tell tales, he did what he was told.*"

Here are cases of children who are opposed to telling tales.

Tehu (10; 6): "*I wouldn't have told the father because it was telling tales. I would have said, 'He's been good.'*— But if it isn't true?—*I would have said, 'He's been good.'*— One child said, 'It's not my business. Ask him yourself.' Was that right?—*I can't say that, it's not my business. I would have said he had been good.*"

La (7½): "What do you think about it?—*I wouldn't have told because the father would have spanked him.*—You would have said nothing?—*No. I'd have said he hadn't done anything silly.*—And if the father asked you?—*I should say that he hadn't done anything silly.*"

Fal (8): "Should he have told?—*No, because that's telling tales.*—But the father had asked him to.—*He should have said nothing. Have said he'd been nice and good.*—Was it better to say nothing, not to answer, or to say that he'd been nice and good?—*Say he'd been nice and good.*"

Bra (9): "*It was rotten of him the one who went and told tales.*—But the father had asked him to. What should he have done?—*Not told tales.*"

Mcha (10): "*He should have said that he hadn't done anything.*—But the brother had played with his father's bicycle and burst one of the tyres. The father wouldn't be able to bicycle to his office the next day and would be late. —*All the same he shouldn't have told.* [Then after some hesitation] *He ought to tell so that he could put things right at once.*"

Here, finally, are two examples of subjects who hesitate. They are, as usual, the most illuminating, because they reveal the nature of the contradictory motives at the back of each of the two views of the matter.

ROB (9): *"I don't know.*—Should the boy have told?—*In a way it was fair, because the father had said so* [asked for it].—Then what should be done?—*He might have told the father a lie because* [otherwise] *it would have been telling tales. But he was bound to tell.*—Which was most of a sport, the one who told what the brother had done, or the one who told a lie?—*The one who didn't tell tales.*—And which would have been nicest?—*The one who hadn't told tales.*—Which would have been most fair?—*The one who told, because his father had said he must."*

WA (10; 3): *"He was quite right, because his father had told him to tell him* [a pause, during which he hesitates).—Are you sure, or were you hesitating?—*I was hesitating.*—Why?—*Because I was thinking that he might also say nothing, so that his brother shouldn't be punished.*—It's hard, isn't it?—*Yes.*—Then, which one do you think is the most of a sport?—*The one who said nothing.*—What would be the best thing to do?—*It would be best for him to say nothing.*—What would he have said?—*That he had been good."*

The mechanism of these judgments is clear. On the one hand there is law and authority: since you are asked to tell tales, it is fair to tell tales. On the other, there is the solidarity between children: it is wrong to betray an equal for the benefit of an adult, or at any rate it is illegitimate to interfere in your neighbour's business. The first attitude predominates among the younger children and is related to all the manifestations of respect for the adult which we studied before. The second prevails among the older children for reasons which have also been elucidated by all that has gone before. This second attitude is sometimes so strong that it leads the subject to justify lying as a means of defending a friend.[12] This interrogatory shows, even better than our

[12] It should be noted in passing that this is a clear case of a lie being evaluated as a function of the motive that inspires it. The children who think it "sporting" (Fr. *chic type*) to tell a lie to protect a brother told us very definitely that the same lie would be "naughty" (Fr. *vilain*) if told in self-protection.

previous results, the contrast of the two moralities—that of authority and that of equalitarian solidarity. The style of speech used by children in this connection is highly significant, and one may say that the terms used by children to describe behaviour in school are sufficient to differentiate the two types of reaction. The expression that symbolizes the first type most clearly is that of the *"petit saint."* [13] The "petit saint" (lit. little saint) is the boy who ignores his playmates and only cultivates the master, who always sides with the grown-ups against the children. It is the well-behaved submissive pupil. This is how he is described by some children of 10 to 12 years old: "It's a chap who is always hanging on to his mother's skirts." "It's a *lèche-cul* (a groveller)," "it's a *lèche-cuteur* (*idem*)," "a boy who tells tales," etc. The opposite of the "petit saint" is the *"chic type"* or sport, one who on occasions is up against the established order, but who is the incarnation of solidarity and equity between children: "It's a fellow who will give all he has to the others," "One who does not tell tales," "A boy who plays again with the others when he has won everything at marbles," "One who is fair," etc.

This is a psychological work, and it is not for us to take up a moral standpoint. And yet when it comes to foretelling character, it is perhaps worth while raising the question as to which of these two—the "petit saint" or the "chic type"—will develop into what is generally felt to be the best type of man and of the citizen? Given our existing system of education, one may safely say that there is every chance of the "chic type" remaining one all his life and of the "petit saint" becoming a narrow-minded moralist whose principles will always predominate over his common humanity.

The conclusion to be drawn from the above facts would therefore seem to be the following. Equalitarian justice develops with age at the expense of submission to adult authority, and in correlation with solidarity between children. Equalitarianism would therefore seem to come from the habits of reciprocity peculiar to mutual respect rather than

[13] English equivalents for these expressions will occur to the reader—"goddy-good," "pi," etc. [Trans.]

from the mechanism of duties that is founded upon unilateral respect.

§ 6. JUSTICE BETWEEN CHILDREN

If the result of our previous analyses is correct, the most favourable setting for the development of the idea of distributive justice and of the more advanced forms of retributive justice would seem to be the social relations between contemporaries. Expiatory punishment and the earlier forms of retributive punishment would seem to be created by the relations between children and adults. The time has now come for us to undertake a direct verification of these hypotheses by trying to see what is the child's conception of justice between comrades. Two points have to be considered —punishment between children and equalitarianism.

It cannot be denied that there are elements of retributive justice in social life among children. The cheat is sent to Coventry, the fighter gets back the blows that he deals, etc. But the problem is to know whether these punishments are of the same kind as those to which the child is generally submitted by the adult. It seems to us that they are not. Adult punishment gives rise in the child's mind to ideas of expiation. A lie, or an act of insubordination, for example, will mean being shut up, or being deprived of a pleasure. To the child this punishment is a sort of putting things right, which will remove the fault by placating authority. At any rate, the punishment is regarded as "fair" only in so far as the feeling for authority is present, together with remorse at having offended this authority. This is why, as the years go on and unilateral respect diminishes in strength, the number of punishments approved of by the child also grows sensibly less. As we saw at the beginning of this chapter, punishment by reciprocity gradually supplants expiatory punishment and in many cases even ends by being considered useless and harmful. Punishments between children, on the contrary (except in the relations of older to younger children as in games with rules), could hardly rest on authority and consequently could not appeal to the idea of expiation. And we shall see, as a matter of fact, that they nearly all fall under what we have called punishment "by reciprocity" and are considered "fair" in the measure that solidarity and the desire for equality among children is on the increase.

It is possible to distinguish two (more or less arbitrary) classes of punishments among children. The first belongs essentially to games, and is applied when a player infringes upon one of the rules or customs. The other appears as chance determines, wherever the bad behaviour of some calls forth the vengeance of others, and where this vengeance is submitted to certain rules which render it legitimate. Now we shall find that not one of this last variety of punishment can be classified among expiatory punishments. When a boy gives blow for blow, etc., he is not seeking to chastise, but simply to show an exact reciprocity. We shall see, moreover, that the ideal aimed at is not to give more than one has received, but to mete out its mathematical equivalent. As for collective punishments, they are nearly all of the type "by reciprocity," with one or two exceptions which we must now examine more closely.

In the sphere of play, for example, we found only non-expiatory punishments. The boy who cheats is excluded from the game for a period of time proportionate to the gravity of his offence. Marbles unlawfully won are restored to their owner or distributed among the honest players. Similarly, where things are exchanged, if the strong takes advantage of the weak, he is brought to order by others stronger than himself, made to restore goods acquired by illicit bargains, and so on. In none of all this is there expiatory punishment properly so called, but only restitutive penalties, acts of exclusion marking a breach in the bond of solidarity, and so on. Only in cases of exceptional gravity, on the occasion of those crimes which Durkheim characterizes as directed against the "strong and definite feelings of the collective consciousness," have we noted the appearance of expiatory punishment. For example, there is a certain boarding school in Neuchâtel where the "cafards" (sneaks) are ritually conducted "au jus" (to stew); which means that after school the whole body waits for them and leads them forcibly down to the edge of the lake, where they are ducked in the cold water with all their clothes on. But how is it that everyone regards this punishment as legitimate? There is obviously in each child the feeling of a moral authority presiding over executions of this kind. But is the authority that of the particular group taken at the moment when the event is happening? Do the children who at a given moment constitute a class and are united by relations of reciprocity, do these children, by the mere fact of being so grouped, succeed in creating a collective consciousness, which will impose upon each and sundry its sacred character and thus become the equivalent of adult authority? If this were the case the distinction between co-operation and constraint would become illusory: the union of a certain number of individuals living in reciprocity with each other would be sufficient to produce the most rigid of constraints. But things are not so simple as this, and in the facts we are discussing there is a factor of age and tradition which makes the example in question comparable to those in which pressure is brought to bear upon the child by the adult. For putting an offender "to stew" is an ancient and venerable custom, and the class which for the time being is invested with the divine right of chastising the criminal is fully conscious of carrying on a time-honoured tradition. And it is our belief that because of this constraint exercised by tradition the punishment seems just and becomes an expiation. I remember very definitely having been filled with two contradictory feelings when, as a school-boy, I was a witness for the first time of one of these sacred immersions. On the one hand, there was the feeling of the barbarity of the punishment (it was mid-winter), but on the other hand, there was the feeling of admiration and almost of respect for the "elders" of the class who could thus incarnate a part which we all knew to have been played by leaders of the older classes in similar circumstances. In short, the ducking of the sneaks, which was at first simply an act of vengeance and felt perhaps to be cruel by those who were not directly interested, had become for me, by being ritualized and transmitted from generation to generation, the expression of a just expiation. This shows that in the rare cases where punishments between children are truly expiatory, a factor of authority, of unilateral respect, of the constraint of one generation upon the other has been introduced. Wherever this factor plays no part, punishments between children are and remain merely punishments "by reciprocity."

We now come to "private" punishments. Private punishment is, at its origin, revenge—rendering evil for evil as one renders good for good. But can this vengeance be submitted to rules and to this extent appear legitimate?

We shall see that this is the case, and that this progressive legitimacy is in direct ratio to the growth of equality and reciprocity among children.

Mlle Rambert put the two following questions to the 167 children whom she interviewed: (I) "There was a big boy in a school once who was beating a smaller boy. The little one couldn't hit back because he wasn't strong enough. So one day during the recreation he hid the big boy's apple and roll in an old cupboard. What do you think of that?"—(II) "If anyone punches you, what do you do?"

The statistics show very clearly that reciprocity grows with age, and that in the same measure the punishment seems just. With regard to the first story, two answers are possible. "It was naughty," or "The little one was quite right to pay him back." The second answer was given in the following proportions:

Age 6	Age 7	Age 8	Age 9	Age 10	Age 11	Age 12
19%	33%	65%	72%	87%	91%	95%

Here are examples of children who do not approve of the little boy. Curiously enough, they are thus mostly the little ones themselves.

SAV (6): *"He oughtn't to have done it because it is naughty* (Fr. *méchant* [14]).—Why?—*Because you get hungry, and then you look and you can't find it again.*—Why did the little chap take his roll?—*Because the big one was naughty* (*méchant*).—Should he have taken it or not?—*No, because it's naughty* (*méchant*)."

PRA (6): *"He shouldn't have done it because it was the big boy's roll.*—Why did he do it?—*Because the big boy was*

[14] *"Méchant"* which, for the sake of naturalness in the dialogue, we have rendered as "naughty," conveys a sense of wickedness or violence which is not necessarily present in *"vilain."* [Trans.]

always beating the little one.—Should he have let him beat him?—*No. He ought to have defended himself. Not given in. Gone away.*—Why shouldn't he have taken the roll?—*It's not fair to take things. You mustn't take things."*

MOR (6): *"He shouldn't have taken it.*—Why?—*It's naughty (méchant).*—Why did he do it?—*The other one beat him.*—Was it fair to take it?—*Not fair. He ought to have told the teacher."*

BLI (6): *"He shouldn't have, because he was a thief.*— What should he have done?—*Tell his mother.*—Should he have hit back?—*No. His mother will scold him* [the big boy]."

DÉD (7): *"He shouldn't have done it because it wasn't nice of him.*—Why did he do it?—*Because his brother was always hitting him.*—What should he have done?—*Let the boy beat him and tell his mother. Not hit back."*

RIC (7; 6): *"He shouldn't have, because it's disobeying."*

TEA (8): *"He shouldn't have done it.*—Why?—*Afterwards the other boy looked for it everywhere and had nothing to eat.*—Why did he hide the roll?—*Because the big one had beaten him.*—Was it fair, then?—*No.*—Why?—*He should have told the master."*

MAR (9; 8): *"He shouldn't have done it.*—Why?—*Because it was stealing.*—But the other chap had beaten him.—*He should have told the master.*—Is it fair to take a revenge?—*Yes . . .* [hesitates] *no."*

PRES (10): *"Shouldn't have.*—Why?—*Because he was stealing.*—What should he have done?—*He should have complained."*

JAC (11): *"He shouldn't have done it because the big boy would have nothing to eat.*—Should he have let himself be beaten?—*No. He should have taken his revenge. Told someone to help him to take his revenge, but not take his roll."*

TRIP (12), G.: *"He wanted to take a revenge, but he shouldn't have. When people are unkind to us, we mustn't pay them back, we must tell our parents."*

It is easy to see what the attitude of these children is. Most of the little ones and a few of the older ones think that one should not take one's revenge, because there is a more legitimate as well as a more efficacious way of obtaining redress—to call in the grown-up. With these children it is a question of a petty calculation or of the predominance of the morality of authority over the morality of the relations between children. Telling tales (which constitutes an offence according to the latter code of morality) does not matter in the least, the great thing is to get fair treatment. For these children vengeance is wrong, but it is so at bottom because it has been forbidden. You must not render evil for evil, but you can have the fellow who wronged you punished. In addition to this, the little ones condemn the hero of the story because stealing is wrong, whatever may be the motive of the theft (moral realism). But with the older of the children quoted just now what predominates is not this complete submission or appeal made to adult justice—it is the idea that there is not sufficient correspondence between the theft of the roll and the blows that have been received. Thus Jac, who is typical of this attitude, tells us quite clearly that the little boy ought to have returned the blows or got an older boy to return them, but not to have taken the roll. Justice, therefore, resides in reciprocity and not in mere brutal revenge. One should give back exactly what one has received, but not invent a sort of arbitrary punishment whose content bears no relation to the punishable act. These subjects are therefore not very far from approving of the hero of the story. At any rate they argue from the same reasons.

Here are examples of those who approve of the little boy.

Mon (6½): *"He was quite right to have done it.*—Why? —*Because the big boy was always beating him.*—Was it fair to hide his roll?—*Yes.*—Was it right?—*Yes."*

Aud (7½): *"He was quite right.*—Why—*Because his brother shouldn't have beat him.*—Was it fair to take his revenge?— . . . [Does not understand the word.]—Was it naughty to do what the little boy did?—*Not naughty."*

Hel (7½): *"He ought to have done it.*—Why?—*Because the big boy was always teasing him.*—Was it fair to do it? —*Yes, it was fair.*—And was it right?— . . . [Thinks it over] *Yes, it is right."*

Jaq (7½), G.: *"He was quite right.*—Why?—*Because the*

*big boy was always beating him.—*Was it fair?—*Yes."* But elsewhere Jaq answers: "Is it fair to be avenged?—*Oh, no."* In her eyes, therefore, the little boy's behaviour is not an act of vengeance but a punishment by reciprocity.

WID (8; 9): *"He should have done it because the big boy was always beating him.—*Was it fair?—*Yes.—*Is it fair to take your revenge?—*You mustn't take your revenge."*

CANT (9; 3): *"He should have done it.—*Why?—*Because he had been beaten.—*Was it fair to do it?—*Yes.—*Was it right?—*He shouldn't have hidden it.—*Why?—*He need only have taken his revenge.—*How?—*He ought to have kicked him."*

AG (10): *"He was quite right because the big boy was mean.—*Was it fair?—*Yes, because the big boys mustn't beat the little ones."*

BACIN (11; 1), G.: *"He was right to do it because he couldn't defend himself.—*Was it fair to do what he did?— *Not very fair, because the big boy had been given the roll and the apple and then couldn't eat them.—*What would make it quite fair?—*Hit him back."* Thus the little boy's theft is tolerated failing the correct punishment which would consist in giving back exactly what one had received.

COLL (12; 8): *"In a way it is fair because there is nothing else he can do. In another way it is not fair to take his brother's roll."*

Thus we get one of two things. Either revenge is giving back exactly what you have received, and then it is fair (case of Cant), or else it is inventing in cold blood something unpleasant that will hurt the person who has hurt you—and then it is unfair (case of Jaq, Wid, etc.). But all the children are agreed upon one point in the story: the little boy would have done best simply to give back the blows he received; but given the impossibility of such a procedure, he may be allowed to restore the balance of things by hiding the big boy's lunch.

The second question—should one hit back?—raises no difficulties, and the answers it calls forth are extremely simple. While they affirm in perfect good faith that one must not take one's revenge (in the special sense of being revenged in cold blood) nor render evil for evil, the children maintain with a conviction that grows with their years that it is strictly fair to give back the blows one has received. Mlle Rambert obtained the following statistics, taking girls and boys separately.

		"It is naughty."	Give back the same. %	Give back more. %	Give back less. %
Age 6	Girls	82	18	—	—
	Boys	50	37.5	12.5	—
7	G.	45	45	10	—
	B.	27	27	46	—
8	G.	25	42	8	25
	B.	45	22	33	—
9	G.	14	29	—	57
	B.	29	57	14	—
10	G.	—	20	—	80
	B.	8	54	31	7
11	G.	—	33	—	67
	B.	—	31	31	38
12	G.	—	22	—	78
	B.	—	67	10	23

This will show that in spite of inevitable irregularities of detail there exists, in girls as well as in boys, a tendency that increases with age to consider it legitimate to give back the blows one has received. Whereas more than half of the six-year-olds and a large proportion of those between 7 and 8 still think that "It is naughty," this answer almost completely disappears after the age of 9. But while this evolution is common to boys and girls, the former differ from the latter on the question of whether one should give back more, or less, or exactly the same as one has received. Boys, especially towards the age of 7-8, are inclined to give more, the desire for equality gaining the ascendent later towards 11-12. Girls, on the contrary, as soon as they have ceased in the majority of cases to think it "naughty" to hit back, are of opinion that one should give back less than one has received.

Here, to begin with, are examples of those who think it "naughty" to hit back.

JEA (6), G.: "If anyone hits you what do you do?—*I tell teacher.*—Why do you not hit back?—*Because it is naughty.*"

SAV (6): "What do you do?—*I tell my mother.*—Do you hit back?—*No, I'm afraid of being hurt. I go and tell teacher, so she'll punish him.*—Why must the teacher punish him?—*Because he's naughty (méchant).*—If he has been naughty (*méchant*), is it fair to punch him back again?—*No, because that you would be* [=we would be] *naughty (méchant).*"

BRA (6), G.: "What do you do?—*I call my mother.*—Do you hit back?—*No.*—Why do you call your mother?—*Because he ought not to have given me a punch.*—Is it fair to hit back?—*It's not fair, it's naughty (méchant).*"

AU (7; 9): "*I go and tell my daddy.*—And if he's not there?—*I tell teacher.*—And if she is not there, do you hit back?—*No.*—Why?—*You get punished afterwards.*—Is it fair not to hit back?—*Yes. People love us afterwards, and mummy and daddy are pleased.*"

CHA (8): "*I tell teacher. I don't hit back. It's naughty (méchant).*"

NEN (9; 7), G.: "*I don't hit back at all. I want to show her a good example. I am not horrid (méchant) to her.*"

Here are examples of those who give back as many hits as they receive.

PRA (6½): "*I don't let them hit me.*—How many punches do you give?—*One for one. If he only gives me one, then I only give him one back. If he gives me two, I give him two. If he gives me three, I give him three.*—And ten?—*I give him that back too.*—Is it fair to hit back?—*Yes, it is fair.*—Why?—*Because he had hit me too.*"

SCA (7½): "*I hit him back. I don't want it* [the punch he gives me]. *I give it to the other boy.*—Is that fair?—*Yes. Oh, no. I was wrong. You must never hit back. That's what my daddy said. But I'm like that. I won't let people punch me and kick me.*" Thus Sca knows his lesson, but he hits back all the same, and thinks it fair to do so.

HEL (7½): "*I give him back two if he has given me two, six if he has given me six, four if he has given me four.*—Is it fair to hit back?—*Yes, it is quite right.*"

DIC (8½), G.: *"I defend myself. I hit back once for each hit.*—Why not oftener?—*Because the other one would give me twice as much* [and if I gave him back two for one, he would give me four].—Is it fair?—*Yes. Three for three. You mustn't give in. You must defend yourself.*—Is that right?—*Not very."* [Dic knows that it is not allowed.]

LUC (9; 7), G.: *"I hit her back again.*—How many hits do you give her?—*As many as she has given me.*—Why not more?—*So that they should add up the same.*—Is that right? —*Yes."*

PI (10): *"I give back one, and according how hard it is* [the blow received], *two.*—If you get five?—*Then I give five back.*—Why not more?—*It would have hurt him more."*

ER (10; 2) had answered to question I that the little boy ought not to have stolen the big boy's roll and apple: "Why? —*You mustn't take a revenge on people.*—Why?—*Because it isn't nice."* But when we ask him what he does when any-one gives him a punch, he answers, *"I give him one back. *—And if you get two punches?—*I give back two. You must never give more, otherwise the other boy gives you another again.*—Is it fair to hit back?—*Yes.*—And to take a revenge? —*Oh, no. To take a revenge is not the same as punching back."*

HEN (11; 2): *"I give him back a punch.*—If you are given two punches?—*I give back two.*—If you are given three?—*I give back three.*—Why not more?—*Because I don't want to be worse than he is. I give him back his own hits.*— Is that fair?—*No, because I ought to show myself better than he.*—Is taking your revenge the same thing as giving a punch?—*It's not the same. To hit back is to give a punch. To take your revenge is mean."*

ELIS (11), G.: *"I hit back.*—Is it fair to do that?—[She hesitates.] *Yes, it's fair.*—If anyone hits you once?—*I hit back once. If I hit back twice, it isn't fair."*

Here are examples of boys who hit back oftener than they have been hit.

JE (7): "What do you do when anyone gives you a punch? —*I give 'em back two.*—And if they give you three?—*I give them back four.*—Is it fair to do that?—*Yes."*

ET (10): *"If they give me one I give back two. If they give me two, I give back three."*

And of girls who give back less.

BOE (8; 5), G.: *"You ought to hit back.—If they hit you three times?—I hit back once.—Why not three times?—That would be naughty (méchant).—Is it fair to hit back?—No, you oughtn't to hit back."*

BER (10), G.: *"I hit him back less, because if I hit him back the same or more, he begins again.—Is it right to hit back?—No, it's not right."*

It will be seen by these examples that the children who do not hit back (most of them are from among the younger ones), are primarily submissive children who rely upon the adult to protect them, and who are more anxious to respect or make others respect the orders that have been received than to establish justice and equality by methods appropriate to child society. As for the children who hit back, they are far more concerned with justice and equality than with revenge properly so called. The cases of Er and Hen are particularly clear. These children disapprove of cold-blooded revenge and petty scheming, but they uphold exact reciprocity from a sense of justice. Among those who give back more blows than they receive there is, of course, a combative attitude, which goes beyond mere equality; but it is precisely this attitude which diminishes with age.

Let us now turn to a question which will serve as a transition between retributive and distributive judgment between children—why should one not cheat at games? You ask the child what is his favourite game, and you tell him the story of a little boy who cheated (*e.g.*, to change one's place more than necessary during a game of marbles). When the subject has stated that this is cheating, you ask him why one should not cheat at games. The answers fall under four heads: 1) It is naughty (forbidden, etc.). 2) It is contrary to the rules of the game. 3) It makes cooperation impossible ("You can't play any more"). 4) It is contrary to equality.

If we divide the children into two groups according to

age, the first from 6-9 (it will be remembered that it was round about 9 that rules began to be stabilized), and the second from 10-12, we shall note the following changes as we pass from one group to another. Answers appealing to the authority of rules (whether of morality or games) *i.e.*, answers of types I and II, drop from 70% to 32%, whereas answers of types III and IV, appealing, that is, to cooperation or to equality, rise from 30% to 68%. These data can, moreover, be given in greater detail. First type answers (simply it is naughty, forbidden, etc.) fall from 64% to 8%; while those of the second type are 6% before, and 24% after 9. Third type answers (cooperation) rise from 0% to 20%, and those of the fourth type (equality) from 30% to 48%.

Such a result as this is easy to understand if our analysis of game rules be brought to mind. According to the little ones, in whom unilateral respect predominates and who identify a game rule with a moral rule, to cheat is "naughty," like lying or using a rude word: it is forbidden by order and suppressed by punishment. Hence the abundance of type I answers before 8-9. This frequency might, of course, be explained by the difficulties which little children experience in analysing their thoughts, but there is, we believe, in addition to this, the moral element, to which we have just drawn attention. The older children, for whom rules have become a direct emanation of the autonomous group, condemn cheating for reasons which appeal to this very solidarity and to the resulting equalitarianism.

Here are examples of the first type.

DEM (6; 2): *"It's naughty* (Fr. *vilain.)*—Why?—*You must never cheat* (Fr. *frouiller).*—Why?—*My* [eldest] *brother told me."*

BRAIL (6): *"It's not fair. The others don't let us cheat* (Fr. *frouiller). They say, 'Go away!' "*

VAN (6½): *"Because you mustn't. It's naughty.*—Why?— *Because it's very naughty.*—Why is it naughty?—*Because you ought never to do it.*—Why not do it?—*Because it's very bad. You never must.*—Why must you never?—*Just because."*

GREM (7; 2): *"You mustn't.*—Why?—*Because it's naughty.*—Why?—*Because it's a bad thing to do."*

Gis (8), G.: *"Because it isn't nice (Fr. joli).—Why?—Must never cheat.—Why?—It's ugly.—Why?—You must never cheat. It's very naughty."*

These arguments simply amount to this, that the thing is forbidden. The answers of the second type are not very different.

Zur (6; 6): *"It's not the game.—Why?—Because he ought not to have done it.—Why?—Because the one who cheated (Fr. frouillé) has spoilt the game. You can't have fun any more.—Why?—It's naughty."*

Chri (6; 10): *"You mustn't cheat.—Why?—Because it isn't fair.—Why?—Because it wouldn't finish the game. The game would be wrong."*

Wal (7½): *"It's not allowed because it's not the game."*

Marg (9): *"It's not doing it right.—Why* must people not cheat?—*Because it's not the game.—Why?—You mustn't.—Why not?—It's not the game."*

And here are examples of the third type (cooperation).

Scha (7): *"People mustn't cheat. Otherwise you don't have them again* [=You don't play with the cheaters again]. *You don't like them.—Why?—Because you aren't good friends any longer.—Why?—They get naughty (Fr. méchants)."*

Go (7; 2): *"It upsets the game and makes the others angry. It mixes the game all up because he has made us angry. You can't play any more."*

Bru (9; 2): *"It spoils the game."*

Tis (10; 1): *"You don't want to play any more.—Why? —It isn't fair.—Why?—If everyone did that no one'll play any more."*

Wi (10): *"It's not doing it right. It's deceiving the others. —Why* must you do things right in a game?—*So as to be honest when we grow up."* [There is a boy who has understood how ·much more useful is a well-regulated game than a lesson in morals.]

Thev (10), G.: *"It's a bad action.—Why?—She acted*

wrongly. She shouldn't have done that.—And supposing she
had lost?—*It would have been better to lose than to deceive.*
—And supposing she had cheated and lost all the same?—
*She would have been punished [ipso facto]. It wasn't fair
that she should have won.*—Why must we not cheat?—*Because it's committing a lie."*

PERO (10): "*You say to them, 'If you are going to cheat
we won't have you any more.'*—Why?—*Because people who
cheat are rotters* (Fr. *des sales types*)."

ZAC (11): "*It isn't nice.*—Why?—*You can't have any nice
fun. You call him liar."*

BOIL (12): "*If people cheat, it's not worth while playing."*

And finally some cases of the fourth type (equality).

MER (9; 6): "*It's not fair.*—Why?—*The others don't do
it, so you mustn't do it either."*

THER (9; 7): "*It's not fair on the others."*

PER (11; 9): "*It's not fair. You win what you haven't the
right to [win]."*

GUS (11): "*It's not fair.*—Why?—*The others don't cheat,
so it isn't fair."*

GAC (12; 0): "*It would be unjust to the others."*

It is easy enough to see that between the answers appealing to cooperation and those that lay more stress on equality,
there are innumerable intermediate stages. In the child as
everywhere else solidarity and equalitarianism are interdependent. In short, there would seem to be two fundamental
types of answer—the one appealing to authority (types I and
II), the other to cooperation (types III and IV). Between
them, naturally, there are intermediate cases. Thus there is
not complete heterogeneity between the answers given by
Thev and those of type I. But broadly speaking, the two types
are distinct, and the second gradually gains preponderance
over the first.

It may be worth while, in this connection, to recall the
results of an enquiry made on lying (Chap. II,. § 4), and
which also has a certain bearing upon the problem of equal-

ity between children. Is it as bad (*vilain*)[15] to lie to one's companions as to grown-ups, or is it different? According to Mlle Rambert's results, 81% of the subjects between 6 and 9 think it worse to lie to adults, while 51% of those between 10 and 13 that it is equally bad to lie to children, and of these, 17% are even of opinion that it is worse to lie to a companion than to an adult.

Let us now turn to the questions of distributive justice properly so-called, in the relations between children. We studied in this connection the two points that seemed to us most important—equality between contemporaries, and the problem of differences in age. Here are two stories that were used for the analysis of the first of these two questions.

STORY I. Some children are playing ball in a courtyard. When the ball goes out of bounds and rolls down the road one of the boys goes of his own free will to fetch it several times. After that he is the only one they ask to go and fetch it. What do you think of that?

STORY II. Some children are having their tea on the grass. They each have a roll that they have bought, and put it down beside them to eat after their brown bread. A dog comes up very softly behind one of the boys and snatches away his roll. What should be done?

We shall not require lengthy analysis to sort out the answers: the children were unanimous in demanding equality. In the first story, it is not fair that it should always be the same child who works for the group, and in the second, each should give the victim enough to supply him with a share that will be equal with that of the others. We lay stress on these answers, simply because in analogous stories, but where the desire for equality found itself pitted against adult authority, the younger children very often, it will be remembered, put authority in the right (§ 5).

Here are some examples.

[15] The word "*vilain,*" which we have throughout translated as "naughty," can also mean "horrid," and therefore has a slightly different shade of meaning when used between children. [Trans.]

WAL (6), Story I: *"It isn't fair.—Why?—Because another boy should go."* Story II: *"They must share.—Why?—So as all to have the same."*

SCHMA (7), Story I: *"It's not fair, because they should have asked the others, and each in turn."* Now, in the story about the father who sent one boy on more messages than the other, Schma had answered, "It is fair, because the father said. . . ."

As to Story II: *'The others must share with him so that he should have a piece."* Then we ask, just to see whether this desire for equality keeps authority at bay, "But if the mother doesn't want him to be given any more. She says he need only have stopped the dog taking the roll. Is it fair?— *Yes. He need only have been careful.*—And if the mother had said nothing, what would have been fairest?—*They ought to have shared."*

DELL (8), Story I: *"It's not fair. They ought to have gone themselves."* Story II: *"They ought to have shared."*

ROB (9), Story I: *"They should each have gone in turn."* Story II: *"They should have shared.*—The mother said they mustn't.—*That's not fair."*

FSCHA (10), Story I: *"Another one ought to have gone."* Story II: *"They ought each to have shared a half with the boy who had none."*

We have already met with so many examples of the progressive development of equalitarianism (§ 5), that we need press the point no further.

But there remains the question as to what children think about differences of age. Should precedence be given to the seniors, or should the younger ones be favoured, or should all be treated equally? We presented the two following stories to our subjects:

STORY I. Two boys, a little one and a big one, once went for a long walk in the mountains. When lunch-time came they were very hungry and took their food out of their bags. But they found that there was not enough for both of them. What should have been done? Give all the food to the big boy or to the little one, or the same to both?

STORY II. Two boys were running races (or playing marbles, etc.). One was big, the other little. Should they both have started from the same place, or should the little one have started nearer?

The second question is complicated by the fact that the game is an organized one, and consequently regulated by tradition. The first, on the other hand, gave rise to a very interesting reaction. The younger children are in favour of equality or else, and chiefly, of precedence begin given to the big boys out of respect for their age; whereas the older children are in favour either of equality or else, and chiefly, of precedence being given to the little boys out of equity.

Here are examples of the little ones' answers.

JAN (7½): *"They should both have been given the same. —They gave most to the little boy. Was it fair?—No. They should all have had the same. All half.*—Aren't little children more hungry?—*Yes.*—If you had been the little boy what would you have done?—*I'd have given less to myself and more to the big boys."*

NEV (7½): *"The big boys should have had most.*—Why? —*Because they're bigger."*

FAL (7½): *"The big boy should have had most.*—Why? —*Because he's the eldest.*—If you had been the little one, would you have given most to the big one?—*Yes.*—Ought they to have more, or is it that they want more?—*They ought to have more."*

ROB (9): *"A little more to the big one.*—Why?—*Because he is the eldest.*—Who gets most hungry during walks, little boys or big ones?—*Both the same.*—If you were out on a walk with a boy of twelve and there was only one piece of bread between you, what would you do?—*I'd give him most.* —Would you think that was all right?—*Yes, I'd want to give him most."*

Here are children in favour of equality.

WAL (7): *"Each must be given the same.*—Why? Another time they had five bars of chocolate. The little boy asked for three. Was it fair?—*They ought to have had two and a half each.*—Supposing you are going for a walk with a boy, and you are the biggest, and keep most for yourself. Is it fair?—*Not fair.*"

Nuss (10): "*They ought to have gone shares.*—The little boy said, 'I'm the smallest so I ought to have most.' Is it fair? —*Not fair.*—The big boy said he had right to most because he was the biggest. Is that fair?—*They ought each to have taken the same amount.*—You are ten. Suppose you are going for a walk with a boy of fifteen who gives you most of what there is, what would you think of it?—*It would be nice of him.*—And fair?—*It would be still more fair both to be given the same.*"

And examples of equity.

Schmo (10): "*They should have given more to the little boy because he was smaller.*—They both ate the same. Was it fair?—*Not quite so fair.*"

Bra (10): "*The same for everyone.*—They gave the little one most; was it fair or not?—*It was fair.*—Oh, no. The big boy kept most for himself, because he was the biggest. Was it fair?—*It wasn't fair.*"

As to the games, the answers differ according as the game is a race or marbles. Running races is relatively uncodified, and this freedom from rules allows for the little ones being favoured. In the game of marbles, the authority of the rules complicates the reactions. The little ones demand equality because it is the inviolable rule of the game, whereas the older boys are inclined to make exceptions in favour of the little ones. Here are two examples of the younger children's reactions.

Bri (6). In running races: "*The little boy must have a start because the big boy can run faster than the little one.*" But in marbles it must be "*the same for both.*"—Why?— *Because* [if both do not start from the same point and the little one is helped] *God will make it happen that the big boy hits the marbles, and the little one can't.*" To make an exception is thus identified with cheating, which will be punished by divine justice.

WAL (7): In running races one must put *"the smallest boy a little farther forward,"* but at marbles *"all at the coche* [the starting-line].—Why?—*You always start at the line."*

And one example of the reaction in older children.

BRA (10): In races the little ones must have a start. At marbles the same applies, *"Because it is always done when they are two or three years younger."*

In conclusion, we find that the notions of justice and solidarity develop correlatively and as a function of the mental age of the child. In the course of this section, three sets of facts have appeared to us to be connected together. In the first place, reciprocity asserts itself with age. To hit back seems wrong to the little ones because it is forbidden by adult law, but it seems just to the older children, precisely this mode of retributive justice functions independently of the adult and sets "punishment by reciprocity" above "expiatory punishment." In the second place, the desire for equality increases with age. Finally, certain features of solidarity, such as not cheating or not lying between children, develop concurrently with the above tendencies.

§ 7. CONCLUSION: THE IDEA OF JUSTICE

To bring our enquiry to a close let us examine the answers given to a question which sums up all that we have been talking about. We asked the children, either at the end or at the beginning of our interrogatories, to give us themselves examples of what they regarded as unfair.[16]

The answers we obtained were of four kinds: 1) Behaviour that goes against commands received from the adult—lying, stealing, breakages, etc.; in a word, everything that is forbidden. 2) Behaviour that goes against the rules of a game. 3) Behaviour that goes against equality (inequality in punishment as in treatment). 4) Acts of injustice connected with

[16] As a matter of fact this term is not understood by all, but it can always be replaced by "not fair" (Fr. *pas juste*).

adult society (economic or political injustice). Now, statistically, the results show very clearly as functions of age:

	Forbidden	Games	Inequality	Social Injustice
6-8 . .	64%	9%	27%	—
9-12 . .	7%	9%	73%	11%

Here are examples of the identification of what is unfair with what is forbidden:

AGE 6: *"A little girl who has a broken plate," "to burst a balloon," "children who make a noise with their feet during prayers," "telling lies," "something not true," "it's not fair to steal,"* etc.

AGE 7: *"Fighting," "disobeying," "fighting about nothing," "crying for nothing," "playing pranks,"* etc.

AGE 8: *"Fighting each other," "telling lies," "stealing,"* etc.

Here are examples of inequalities:

AGE 6: *"Giving a big cake to one and a little one to another." "One piece of chocolate to one and two to another."*

AGE 7: *"A mother who gives more to a little girl who isn't nice." "Beating a friend who has done nothing to you."*

AGE 8: *"Someone who gave two tubes* [to two brothers] *and one was bigger than the other"* [taken from experience, this!] *"Two twin sisters who were not given the same number of cherries"* [also experienced].

AGE 9: *"The mother gives a* [bigger] *piece of bread to someone else." "The mother gives a lovely dog to one sister and not to the other." "A worse punishment for one than for the other."*

AGE 10: *"When you both do the same work and don't get the same reward." "Two children both do what they are told, and one gets more than the other." "To scold one child and not the other if they have both disobeyed."*

AGE 11: *"Two children who steal cherries: only one is punished because his teeth are black." "A strong man beating*

a weak one." "A master who likes one boy better than another, and gives him better marks."
AGE 12: *"A referee who takes sides."*

And some examples of social injustice.

AGE 12: *"A mistress preferring a pupil because he is stronger, or cleverer, or better dressed."*
"Often people like to choose rich friends rather than poor friends who would be nicer."
"A mother who won't allow her children to play with children who are less well dressed."
"Children who leave a little girl out of their games, who is not so well dressed as they are."

These obviously spontaneous remarks, taken together with the rest of our enquiry, allow us to conclude, in so far as one can talk of stages in the moral life, the existence of three great periods in the development of the sense of justice in the child. One period, lasting up to the age of 7-8, during which justice is subordinated to adult authority; a period contained approximately between 8-11, and which is that of progressive equalitarianism; and finally a period which sets in towards 11-12, and during which purely equalitarian justice is tempered by considerations of equity.

The first is characterized by the non-differentiation of the notions of just and unjust from those of duty and disobedience: whatever conforms to the dictates of the adult authority is just. As a matter of fact even at this stage the child already looks upon some kinds of treatment as unjust, those, namely, in which the adult does not carry out the rules he has himself laid down for children (*e.g.*, punishing for a fault that has not been committed, forbidding what has previously been allowed, etc.). But if the adult sticks to his own rules, everything he prescribes is just. In the domain of retributive justice, every punishment is accepted as perfectly legitimate, as necessary, and even as constituting the essence of morality: if lying were not punished, one would be allowed to tell lies, etc. In the stories where we have brought retributive justice into conflict with equality, the child belonging to this stage sets the necessity for punishment above equality of any sort. In the choice of punishments, expiation takes precedence over punishment by reciprocity, the very principle of the latter type of punishment not being exactly understood by the child. In the domain of immanent justice, more than three-quarters of the subjects under 8 believe in an automatic justice which emanates from physical nature and inanimate objects. If obedience and equality are brought into conflict, the child is always in favour of obedience: authority takes precedence over justice. Finally, in the domain of justice between children, the need for equality is already felt, but is yielded to only where it cannot possibly come into conflict with authority. For instance, the act of hitting back, which is regarded by the child of 10 as one of elementary justice, is considered "naughty" by the children of 6 and 7, though, of course, they are always doing it in practice. (It will be remembered that the heteronomous rule, whatever may be the respect in which it is held mentally, is not necessarily observed in real life.) On the other hand, even in the relations between children, the authority of older ones will outweigh equality. In short, we may say that throughout this period, during which unilateral respect is stronger than mutual respect, the conception of justice can only develop on certain points, those, namely, where cooperation begins to make itself felt independently of constraint. On all other points, what is just is confused with what is imposed by law, and law is completely heteronomous and imposed by the adult.

The second period does not appear on the plane of reflection and moral judgment until about the age of 7 or 8. But it is obvious that this comes slightly later than what happens with regard to practice. This period may be defined by the progressive development of autonomy and the priority of equality over authority. In the domain of retributive justice, the idea of expiatory punishment is no longer accepted with the same docility as before, and the only punishments accepted as really legitimate are those based upon reciprocity. Belief in immanent justice is perceptibly on the decrease and moral action is sought for its own sake, independently of reward or punishment. In matters of distributive justice, equality rules supreme. In conflicts between punishment and equality, equality outweighs every other consideration. The same holds good *a fortiori* of conflicts with authority. Finally, in the relations between children, equalitarianism obtains progressively with increasing age.

Towards 11-12 we see a new attitude emerge, which may be said to be characterized by the feeling of equity, and which is nothing but a development of equalitarianism in the direction of relativity. Instead of looking for equality in identity, the child no longer thinks of the equal rights of individuals except in relation to the particular situation of each. In the domain of retributive justice this comes to the same thing as not applying the same punishment to all, but taking into account the attenuating circumstances of some. In the domain of distributive justice it means no longer thinking of a law as identical for all but taking account of the personal circumstances of each (favouring the younger ones, etc.). Far from leading to privileges, such an attitude tends to make equality more effectual than it was before.

Even if this evolution does not consist of general stages, but simply of phases characterizing certain limited processes, we have said enough to try to elucidate now the psychological origins of the idea of justice and the conditions of its development. With this in view, let us distinguish retributive from distributive justice, for the two go together only when reduced to their fundamental elements, and let us begin with distributive judgment, whose fate in the course of mental development seems to indicate that it is the most fundamental form of justice itself.

Distributive justice can be reduced to the ideas of equality or equity. From the point of view of epistemology such notions cannot but be regarded as *a priori*, if by *a priori* we mean, not of course an innate idea, but a norm, towards which reason cannot help but tend as it is gradually refined and purified. For reciprocity imposes itself on practical reason as logical principles impose themselves morally on theoretical reason. But from the psychological point of view, which is that of what is, not of what should be, an *a priori* norm has no existence except as a form of equilibrium. It constitutes the ideal equilibrium towards which the phenomena tend, and the whole question is still to know why, the facts being what they are, their form of equilibrium is such and no other. This last problem, which is of a causal order, must not be confused with the first, which can be solved only by abstract reflection. The two will coincide only when mind and reality become coextensive. In the meantime let us confine ourselves to psychological analysis, it being understood that the experimental explanation of the notion of reciprocity can in no way contradict its *a priori* aspect.

From this point of view it cannot be denied that the idea of equality or of distributive justice possesses individual or biological roots which are necessary but not sufficient conditions for its development. One can observe in the child at a very early stage two reactions which will play a very important part in this particular elaboration. Jealousy, to begin with, appears extremely early in babies: infants of 8 to 12 months often give signs of violent rage when they see another child seated on their mother's knees, or when a toy is taken from them and given to another child. On the other hand, one can observe in conjunction with imitation and the ensuing sympathy, altruistic reactions and a tendency to share, which are of equally early date. An infant of 12 months will hand his toys over to another child, and so on. But it goes without saying that equalitarianism can never be regarded as a sort of instinct or spontaneous product of the individual mind. The reactions we have just alluded to lead to a capricious alternation of egoism and sympathy. It is true, of course, that jealousy prevents other people from taking advantage of us, and the need to communicate prevents the self from taking advantage of others. But for true equality and a genuine desire for reciprocity there must be a collective rule which is the *sui generis* product of life lived in common. There must be born of the actions and reactions of individuals upon each other the consciousness of a necessary equilibrium binding upon and limiting both "alter" and "ego." And this ideal equilibrium, dimly felt on the occasion of every quarrel and every peace-making, naturally presupposes a long reciprocal education of the children by each other.

But between the primitive individual reactions, which give the need for justice a chance of showing itself, and the full possession of the idea of equality, our enquiry shows the existence of a long interval in time. For it is not until about 10-12, at the age where, as we saw elsewhere, children's societies attain to the maximum of organization and codification of rules, that justice really frees herself from all her adventitious trappings. Here, as before, we must therefore distinguish constraint from cooperation, and our problem will then be to determine whether it is unilateral respect, the source of constraint, or mutual respect, the source of cooperation, that is the preponderating factor in the evolution of equalitarian justice.

Now on this point the results of our analysis seem to leave no room for doubt. Authority as such cannot be the source of justice, because the development of justice presupposes autonomy. This does not mean, of course, that the adult plays no part in the development of justice, even of the distributive kind. In so far as he practises reciprocity with the child and preaches by example rather than by precept, he exercises here, as always, an enormous influence. But the most direct effect of adult ascendancy is, as M. Bovet has shown, the feeling of duty, and there is a sort of contradiction between the submission demanded by duty and the complete autonomy required by the development of justice. For, resting as it does on equality and reciprocity, justice can only come into being by free consent. Adult authority even if it acts in conformity with justice, has therefore the effect of weakening what constitutes the essence of justice. Hence those reactions which we observed among the smaller children, who confused what was just with what was law, law being whatever is prescribed by adult authority. Justice is identified with formulated rules—as indeed it is in the opinion of a great many adults, of all, namely, who have not succeeded in setting autonomy of conscience above social prejudice and the written law.

Thus adult authority, although perhaps it constitutes a necessary moment in the moral evolution of the child, is not in itself sufficient to create a sense of justice. This can develop only through the progress made by cooperation and mutual respect—cooperation between children to begin with, and then between child and adult as the child approaches adolescence and comes, secretly at least, to consider himself as the adult's equal.

In support of these hypotheses, one is struck by the extent to which, in child as well as in adult society, the progress of equalitarianism goes hand in hand with that of "organic" solidarity, *i.e.*, with the results of cooperation. For if we compare the societies formed by children of 5-7 with those formed at the age of 10-12, we can observe four interdependent transformations. In the first place, while the little ones' society constitutes an amorphous and unorganized whole, in which all the individuals are alike, that of the older children achieves an organic unity, with laws and regulations, and often even a division of social work (leaders, referees, etc.). In the second place, there exists between the older children a far stronger moral solidarity than among the younger ones. The little ones are simultaneously egocentric and impersonal, yielding to every suggestion that comes along and to every current of imitation. In their case the group feeling is a sort of communion of submission to seniors and to the dictates of adults. Older children, on the contrary, ban lies among themselves, cheating, and everything that compromises solidarity. The group feeling is therefore more direct and more consciously cultivated. In the third place, personality develops in the measure that discussion and the interchange of ideas replace the simple mutual imitation of the younger children. In the fourth place, the sense of equality is, as we have just seen, far stronger in the older than in the younger children, the latter being primarily under the domination of authority. Thus the bond between equalitarianism and solidarity is a universal psychological phenomenon, and not, as might appear to be the case in adult society, dependent only upon political factors. With children as with adults, there exist two psychological types of social equilibrium—a type based on the constraint of age, which excludes both equality and "organic" solidarity, but which canalizes individual egocentrism without excluding it, and a type based on cooperation and resting on equality and solidarity.

Let us pass on to retributive justice. In contrast to the principles of distributive justice, there does not seem to be in the ideas of retribution or punishment any properly rational or *a priori* element. For while the idea of equality gains in value as intellectual development proceeds, the idea of punishment seems actually to lose ground. To put things more precisely, we must, as we have already done, distinguish two separate elements in the idea of retribution. On the one hand there are the notions of expiation and reward, which seems to constitute what is most specific about the idea of punishment, and on the other, there are the ideas of "putting things right" or making reparation, as well as the measures which aim at restoring the bond of solidarity broken by the offending act. These last ideas, which we have grouped under the title of "punishment by reciprocity," seem to draw only on the conceptions of equality and reciprocity. It is the former set of ideas that tends to be eliminated when the morality of heteronomy and authority is superseded by the morality of autonomy. The second set are of far more enduring stuff, precisely because they are based upon something more than the idea of punishment.

Whatever may be said of this evolution of values, it is possible here, as in connection with distributive justice, to assign three sources to the three chief aspects of retribution. As we saw above (§ 1) certain individual reactions condition the appearance of retribution; adult constraint explains the formation of the idea of expiation, and cooperation accounts for the eventual fate of the idea of punishment.

It cannot be denied that the idea of punishment has psycho-biological roots. Blow calls for blow and gentleness moves us to gentleness. The instinctive reactions of defence and sympathy thus bring about a sort of elementary reciprocity which is the soil that retribution demands for its growth. But this soil is naturally not enough in itself, and the individual factors cannot of themselves transcend the stage of impulsive vengeance without finding themselves subject—at least implicitly—to the system of regulated and codified sanctions implied in retributive justice.

Things change with the intervention of the adult. Very early in life, even before the infant can speak, its conduct is constantly being subjected to approval or censure. According to circumstances people are pleased with baby and smile at it, or else frown and leave it to cry, and the very inflections in the voices of those that surround it are alone sufficient to constitute an incessant retribution. During the years that follow, the child is watched over continuously, everything he does and says is controlled, gives rise to encouragement or reproof, and the vast majority of adults still look upon punishment, corporal or otherwise, as perfectly legitimate. It is obviously these reactions on the part of the adult, due generally to fatigue or impatience, but often, too, coldly thought out on his part, it is obviously these adult reactions, we repeat, that are the psychological starting-point of the idea of expiatory punishment. If the child felt nothing but fear or mistrust, as may happen in extreme cases, this would simply lead to open war. But as the child loves his parents and feels for their actions that respect which M. Bovet has so ably analysed, punishment appears to him as morally obligatory and necessarily connected with the act that provoked it. Disobedience—the principle of all "sin"—is a breach of the normal relations between parent and child; some reparation is therefore necessary, and since parents display their "righteous anger" by the various reactions that take the form of punishments, to accept these punishments constitutes the most natural form of reparation. The pain inflicted thus seems to re-establish the relations that had momentarily been interrupted, and in this way the idea of expiation becomes incorporated in the values of the morality of authority. In our view, therefore, this "primitive" and materialistic conception of expiatory punishment is not imposed as such by the adult upon the child, and it was perhaps never invented by a psychologically adult mind; but it is the inevitable product of punishment as refracted in the mystically realistic mentality of the child.

If, then, there is such close solidarity between the idea of punishment and unilateral respect *plus* the morality of authority, it follows that all progress in cooperation and mutual respect will be such as to gradually eliminate the idea of expiation from the idea of punishment, and to reduce the latter to a simple act of reparation, or a simple measure of reciprocity. And this is actually what we believe we have observed in the child. As respect for adult punishment gradually grows less, certain types of conduct develop which one cannot but class under the heading of retributive justice. We saw an example of this in the judgments made by our subjects on the topic of "hitting back"; the child feels more and more that it is fair that he should defend himself and to give back the blows he receives. This is retribution without doubt, but the idea of expiation seems not to play the slightest part in these judgments. It is entirely a matter of reciprocity. So-and-so takes upon himself the right to give me a punch, he therefore gives me the right to do the same to him. Similarly, the cheat gains a certain advantage by the fact of cheating; it is therefore legitimate to restore equality by turning him out of the game or by taking back the marbles he has won.

It may be objected that such a morality will not take one very far, since the best adult consciences ask for something more than the practice of mere reciprocity. Charity and the forgiving of injuries done to one are, in the eyes of many, far greater things than sheer equality. In this connection, moralists have often laid stress on the conflict between justice and love, since justice often prescribes what is reproved by love and *vice versa*. But in our view, it is precisely this concern with reciprocity which leads one beyond the rather short-sighted justice of those children who give back the mathematical equivalent of the blows they have received. Like all spiritual realities which are the result, not of external constraint but of autonomous development, reciprocity has two aspects: reciprocity as a fact, and reciprocity as an ideal, as something which ought to be. The child begins by simply practising reciprocity, in itself not so easy a thing as one might think. Then, once he has grown accustomed to this form of equilibrium in his actions, his behaviour is altered from within, its form reacting, as it were, upon its content. What is regarded as just is no longer merely reciprocal action, but primarily behaviour that admits of indefinitely sustained reciprocity. The motto "Do as you would be done by," thus comes to replace the conception of crude equality. The child sets forgiveness above revenge, not out of weakness, but because "there is no end" to revenge (a boy of 10). Just as in logic, we can see a sort of reaction of the form of the proposition upon its content when the principle of contradiction leads to a simplification and purification of the initial definitions, so in ethics, reciprocity implies a purification of the deeper trend of conduct, guiding it by gradual stages to universality itself. Without leaving the sphere of reciprocity, generosity—the characteristic of our third stage—allies itself to justice pure and simple, and between the more refined forms of justice, such as equity and love properly so called, there is no longer any real conflict.

In conclusion, then, we find in the domain of justice, as in the other two domains already dealt with, that opposition of two moralities to which we have so often drawn the reader's attention. The ethics of authority, which is that of duty and obedience, leads, in the domain of justice, to the confusion of what is just with the content of established law and to the acceptance of expiatory punishment. The ethics of mutual respect, which is that of good (as opposed to duty), and of autonomy, leads, in the domain of justice, to the development of equality, which is the idea at the bottom of distributive justice and of reciprocity. Solidarity between equals appears once more as the source of a whole set of complementary and coherent moral ideas which characterize the rational mentality. The question may, of course, be raised whether such realities could ever develop without a preliminary stage, during which the child's conscience is moulded by his unilateral respect for the adult. As this cannot be put to the test by experiment, it is idle to argue the point. But what is certain is that the moral equilibrium achieved by the complementary conceptions of heteronomous duty and of punishment properly so called, is an unstable equilibrium, owing to the fact that it does not allow the personality to grow and expand to its full extent. As the child grows up, the subjection of his conscience to the mind of the adult seems to him less legitimate, and except in cases of arrested moral development, caused either by decisive inner submission (those adults who remain children all their lives), or by sustained revolt, unilateral respect tends of itself to grow into mutual respect and to the state of cooperation which constitutes the normal equilibrium. It is obvious that since in our modern societies the common morality which regulates the relations of adults to each other is that of cooperation, the development of child morality will be accelerated by the examples that surround it. Actually, however, this is more probably a phenomenon of convergence than one simply of social pressure. For if human societies have evolved from heteronomy to autonomy, and from gerontocratic theocracy in all its forms to equalitarian democracy, it may very well be that the phenomena of social condensation so well described by Durkheim have been favourable primarily to the emancipation of one generation from another, and have thus rendered possible in children and adolescents the development we have outlined above.

But having reached the point where the problems of sociology meet those of genetic psychology, we are faced with a question of too great moment to allow us to rest content with these indications, and we must now compare our results with the fundamental theses of sociology and psychology concerning the empirical nature of the moral life.

Chapter 4

The Two Moralities of the Child and Types of Social Relations

WHETHER we wish it or not, the questions we have had to discuss in connection with child morality take us to the very heart of the problems studied by contemporary sociology and social psychology. Society, according to Durkheim's followers, is the only source of morality. If this is so, then there is no discipline in a better position to discover it than child psychology. Every form of sociology will in fact inevitably lead to a system of pedagogy, as readers of Durkheim's excellent book on *L'Education Morale* will have had occasion to note. It is for this reason that we intend, in spite of the difficulties attending an attempt of this kind, to examine some of the more significant of the sociological and ethico-psychological theories of the day, and to compare them with our own findings. We shall abstain from any discussion that would be too general in character, and shall confine ourselves to those spheres in which the theories of social psychology in vogue have a direct bearing upon the child. With this aim in view, the following points seem to us to deserve examination. The ideas of Durkheim and Fauconnet on responsibility, which gave rise to Durkheim's writings on punishment in schools, Durkheim's theory of authority as the source of the moral life of the child, the theories of M. Baldwin, and above all those of M. Bovet on the genesis of the moral sentiment, and finally certain educational ideas concerning autonomy of conscience in the child.

But in order to prevent any misunderstanding, we must point out from the first that in these discussions on educational matters proper, it is as psychologists and not as educationalists that we approach the subject. Educational facts are facts of social psychology, perhaps, indeed, the most important of their number, and while we do not wish to establish a system of education on the results of our enquiry, we cannot abstain from asking, for example, whether a given authoritarian procedure is, as Durkheim maintains, really necessary to the constitution of the moral life. This question is one of pure, as well as of applied, psychology. Whether a cure recommended by some doctors will kill the patient or cure him is a matter that interests the physiologist as well as the doctor, and it is as an experimenter, not as a practitioner, that we wish to speak of the subject of education.

§ 1. The Theories of Durkheim and Fauconnet on Responsibility[1]

M. Paul Fauconnet in his excellent book on *La Responsabilité* has developed Durkheim's ideas on retributive justice and penal law in a striking and original manner. He ends by showing that the earliest and, in his view, the purest form of responsibility is no other than the objective responsibility of which we found so many examples in connection with children. No better theme could be better found, therefore, to assist us in the critical examination of what probably constitutes the quintessence of Durkheim's teaching, the idea, namely, that society is always one and the same, and that its permanent features are such as to ensure the existence and invariability of moral values.

Responsibility is, according to M. Fauconnet, the "quality belonging to those who must . . . in virtue of a rule be chosen as the passive subjects of a punishment" (p. 7); to be responsible is to be "justly punishable" (p. 11). Now the comparative study of different societies about which we have sufficient information allows us to establish a sort of evolu-

[1] P. Fauconnet, *La Responsabilité, Etude de Sociologie*, Alcan, 1920.

tionary law which dominates the whole history of responsibility. Starting with far richer and more comprehensive forms, responsibility has only gradually shrunk to its present dimensions. To begin with, in contemporary civilized communities, responsible subjects consist exclusively of adults who are alive and in their right minds. In older or noncivilized societies, as in the Middle Ages, and frequently in more recent times, responsible subjects included children, insane persons (even recognized as such), the dead, animals and above all collective groups as such. The study of situations generative of responsibility leads to the same conclusion. In our communities, intention (or other psychological features, such as negligence, forgetfulness, etc.) is a necessary condition of responsibility. Ethically, the intention is everything. Legally, there must be a *corpus delicti,* but there is no offence without intent, imprudence or negligence. Now, "as we trace our way back through the history of penal law, we gradually come to purely objective responsibility" (p. 105). In other words, in primitive ethics or in archaic law, responsibility is ascribed even to involuntary acts, accidents, acts committed without either negligence or imprudence. In short, primitive responsibility is above all objective and communicable, ours is subjective and strictly individual.

What, then, is responsibility? In order to solve this problem, M. Fauconnet, true to the spirit of Durkheim, seeks to explain the phenomena, not by establishing the laws governing their making or growth but by emphasizing the elements that are invariable and common to every stage. Note should be taken of this fundamental point of method. Thus philosophical explanations of responsibility are to be put aside as ignoring the early forms of the phenomenon in question. Evolutionary doctrines, like Westermark's and others, have this disadvantage that they reduce the early forms to moral or intellectual aberrations, as though our present conceptions constituted the supreme norm or necessary outcome of all that preceded them. If, on the contrary, we ascribe the same value to all cases brought to light by the comparative method, we shall see that even if the punishment does not maintain an unequivocal and well-defined relation to the victim, it is always clearly determined in relation to the crime. In other words, crime has been punished in all times and in all places, and if the punishment does not fall directly upon the head of the culprit, it will always reach someone or other. A crime taken as a material act independent of the motives involved is a sort of centre of infection which must be destroyed, together with everything around it, both far and near. "The penalty is directed against the crime. It is only because it cannot reach the crime that it is deflected on to a substitute for the crime" (p. 234).

This is where the theory of crime elaborated by Durkheim comes in. Every society consists primarily in a collection of beliefs and feelings forming a whole which must be defended. The kernel of these beliefs is the feeling of the sacred, the source of all morality and religion. Whatever offends against these powerful and well-defined feelings is crime, and all crime is sacrilege. A crime that breaks down the social bond takes on, by the mere fact of doing so, a mystical significance. It is a source of impurity and contamination, and its repercussions, visible and invisible, are incalculable. It must therefore be suppressed, and things must be put right. Punishment is the mystical procedure that will effect this restitution.

Consequently it matters very little on whom the punishments fall. The great thing is that they should be inflicted and that they should be proportionate to the crime. Thus there is an "institution of responsibility." Moreover, it is easy to understand how the choice of the responsible subject comes to be made. The process takes place in virtue of a mechanism of transference which obeys the usual laws of psychological transference. First, there is an affective transference: the emotions aroused by the crime are carried over to everything that touches it from near or far. Then there is a judgment: the community decides that a given individual is responsible, and this judgment is dominated by relations of contiguity and resemblance. It follows, naturally, that the culprit himself, when he can be found, is held to represent the *maximum* of relationship with the crime. But failing this, anything that touches the crime must be punished. Thus responsibility descends from outside upon the culprit or any of his substitutes, and transforms them into scapegoats or instruments of social purification. Thus responsibility has a very definite function: "to make the realization of the penalty possible by letting it play its useful part" (p. 297). Now this rôle is essentially moral: "It is only on the condition that punishments exist that the existence of morality itself is ensured: punishment, and consequently responsibility have therefore a share in the value of morality" (p. 300).

But there remains a problem. How is it, if this is the essence of responsibility, that this "institution" should have evolved to such a point that we are no longer able, at first sight, to make head or tail of its primitive forms? How has responsibility come to shrink in this way and to be directed on none but the one intentional, adult, and normal culprit? Why has responsibility individualized and spiritualized itself in this fashion?

Far from constituting the necessary culmination in an inner transformation of responsibility, its contemporary form results, on the contrary, according to Fauconnet, from a gradual weakening of primitive values due to the action of antagonistic factors. The general cause of this evolutionary process would therefore seem to be external to responsibility itself—it is pity and humanitarianism. For though the community may be outraged by crime, antagonistic feelings will appear at the moment of punishment, and, as Ihering has said, the story of penalties is the story of constant abolition. This is why responsibility shows a constant tendency to shrink.

In the beginning, the community will punish anyone, and the individual is only a means to an end. In our day, we punish almost against our wills, and the culprit is given every chance of defending himself and of escaping punishment.

This gives rise to two fundamental consequences. In the first place, "we may say that in the course of its evolution, responsibility becomes individualized. Collective and communicable in elementary communities, it is, in principle, strictly personal in the most civilized societies." Only in Theology, that is to say, in the most conservative of our institutions, does the idea of Original Sin keep alive the idea of collective responsibility; Adam's fall leaves upon the whole of humanity a stain that calls for expiation. In law and in ethics such ideas would revolt us. But our purely individual responsibility is nothing but a bastard form of the real thing. "We are generally taught that responsibility is individual by nature, communicable by accident. The history of responsibility, strictly personal in character, is supposed to have been achieved in the course of evolution. We are led, however, to present the facts under a totally different light. The expanding and contagious character of responsibility has seemed to us to be its fundamental feature. The individualization of responsibility is the result, on the contrary, of a limiting and attenuating process. Far from purifying it and perfecting it, the forces that individualize responsibility are antagonistic to its nature. Strictly personal responsibility is like the last positive value of a responsibility that is tending towards zero-point. From this point of view, the evolution of responsibility appears as a regression. What one takes to be perfect responsibility is responsibility whittled down to vanishing point" (pp. 343-4).

Hence a second aspect of the evolution of responsibility—its spiritualization. Primitive responsibility is above all objective. A crime is "first and foremost a material event. And the bond uniting the crime to whoever is responsible for it is nearly always, to begin with, a material bond" (p. 345). But, "in the eyes of our contemporaries, responsibility arises in the conscience of the man who is responsible, on the occasion of a spiritual act, by reason of a psychological relation between the conscience and the act. These features contrast line for line with the objectivity described above" (pp. 345-6). The cause of this phenomenon of spiritualization is that society, which begins by being external to men's minds, "becomes more and more immanent to the individual. More and more of him becomes socialized with time, and the contribution of social life is added to and modifies what is of psycho-organic origin. The spiritualization of moral or religious ideas expresses this veritable penetration of the social into the individual" (p. 367). In short, if responsibility takes account of intentions only, it does so in virtue of the same process as that by which it has become individualized. "As social life becomes individualized it becomes more interiorized" (p. 351). So that our moral consciousness is nothing but the interiorized residuum of the collective consciousness. But this is not a gain. "Like the individualization of responsibility, its spiritualization in the course of history appears therefore as an immense impoverishment, a perpetual abolition. Subjective responsibility, far from being, as is generally thought, responsibility *par excellence,* is only an atrophied form of responsibility" (p. 350).

But one must not be too absolute. There are still in our societies traces of collective and objective responsibility, and M. Fauconnet claims to find examples of it in the present trend of criminal law in Italy. The primitive form has therefore not been completely killed by the existing form. "So true is it that the former is still a living branch on the common stock from which the latter has gradually become detached" (p. 377). From the educational point of view, it will therefore be natural to come with Durkheim to the conclusion of the necessity for a systematic method of school punishments as the only means of reviving in men's minds the permanent source of all responsibility.

For ourselves we know of no thesis so well suited as this doctrine of Durkheim's and Fauconnet's to throw light on the problems raised by the affirmation of the moral unity of society. For M. Fauconnet has accomplished a *tour de force.* He has tried to explain by the permanence belonging to the conditions of the collective consciousness a phenomenon of which he, more successfully than anyone else, has traced the evolution down history. Nor do we wish to dispute M. Fauconnet's subtle analysis and masterly classification of the facts he has collected. The kinship between the phenomena of objective responsibility that can be observed in the child and the phenomena that characterize primitive social constraint furnishes, on the contrary, an excellent confirmation of the hypothesis that the initial externality of social relations is bound to bring with it a certain moral realism. What seems to us more questionable is the general interpretation he gives of responsibility, of punishment, and of the relations holding between moral facts and society regarded as a fixed and unchanging whole.

The great lesson of comparative sociology is that there exist at least two types of responsibility—one objective and communicable, the other subjective and individual, and that social evolution has gradually caused the second to predominate. Having established this, two solutions were equally conceivable: to define responsibility by the direction it took in history, by its *vector*, or to define it by its constant structural elements.

On the strength of Durkheim's methodological postulates, M. Fauconnet has chosen the second solution. He tells us at once that what interests him in the history of responsibility is not so much the transformations as the invariables. And what leads him to this choice is the deep and fundamental unity of social facts. "However diverse civilizations may be, there is such a thing as civilization" (p. 20). But it may be questioned whether such a method is satisfactory beyond a given point. What would we think of a psychologist who, in his explanation of causality and number, put magical and mystical views of causality on the same level as Einstein's treatment of causality or as the theory of complex numbers? If you look only for the elements that are common to all stages and eliminate all considerations of direction, you will achieve nothing but a flimsy and static residue (what, after all, do the elements common to all the different stages of causality amount to?), or else you will lay all the stress—as we fear M. Fauconnet has done—on the primitive forms. Now it is, no doubt, indispensable to be acquainted with the primitive forms of the facts one wishes to analyse, but their subsequent evolution furnishes data of at least equal importance upon the conditions of their genesis. To put the matter more clearly, we should try both to determine the direction of the successive stages, and to establish the invariables common to all these stages. But what is invariable is not a given structural feature—otherwise the primitive form could always be erected into the "true" form—but only the function. As for the structure, it varies indefinitely in so far as its variations are subjected to its function, and the laws of evolution controlling such variations are more instructive than the features peculiar to any particular stage.

It is neither with the laws of the evolution of responsibility that M. Fauconnet deals, nor with the function that is common to its different stages. He tells us clearly why it is not the laws of its evolution. And neither is it the common

function, taken independently of the structure of the phenomenon, since nowadays our responsibility is no longer
either communicable or objective, and since M. Fauconnet
considers these two features as constitutive of "true" responsibility.

Now the psychological data of child morality suggests to
us an interpretation of responsibility which, while it takes
full account of the valuable results obtained by M. Fauconnet,
seems to us to fulfil the double claim of invariability or
functional continuity and of directed structural evolution.
For we have recognized the existence of two moralities in the
child, that of constraint and that of cooperation. The morality
of constraint is that of duty pure and simple and of heteronomy. The child accepts from the adult a certain number
of commands to which it must submit whatever the circumstances may be. Right is what conforms with these commands; wrong is what fails to do so; the intention plays a
very small part in this conception, and the responsibility is
entirely objective. But, first parallel with this morality, and
then in contrast to it, there is gradually developed a morality
of cooperation, whose guiding principle is solidarity and
which puts the primary emphasis on autonomy of conscience,
on intentionality, and consequently on subjective responsibility. Now it should be noted that while the ethics of mutual
respect is, from the point of view of values, opposed to that
of unilateral respect, the former is nevertheless the natural
outcome of the latter from the point of view of what causes
this evolution. In so far as the child tends towards manhood,
his relations with the adult tend towards equality. The unilateral respect belonging to constraint is not a stable system,
and the equilibrium towards which it tends is no other than
mutual respect. It cannot, therefore, be maintained with
regard to the child that the final predominance of subjective
over objective responsibility is the outcome of antagonistic
forces in relation to responsibility in general. Rather is it in
virtue of a sort of inner logic that the more evolved follow
upon the more primitive forms, though in structure the
former differ qualitatively from the latter.

Why, then, in an extremely schematic way, should the
same thing not hold good of society? It is no mere metaphor

to say that a relation can be established between the individual's obedience to collective imperatives and the child's obedience to adults in general. In both cases the human being submits to certain commands because he respects his elders. Society is nothing but a series (or rather many intersecting series) of generations, each exercising pressure upon the one which follows it, and Auguste Comte was right in pointing to this action of one generation upon the other as the most important phenomenon of sociology. Now when we think of the part played by gerontocracy in primitive communities, when we think of the decreasing power of the family in the course of social evolution, and of all the social features that characterize modern civilizations, we cannot help seeing in the history of societies a sort of gradual emancipation of individuals; in other words, a levelling up of the different generations in relation to each other. As Durkheim himself has pointed out, one cannot explain the passage from the forced conformity of "segmented" societies to the organic solidarity of differentiated societies without invoking the diminished supervision of the group over the individual as a fundamental psychological factor. The "denser" the community, the sooner will the adolescent escape from the direct constraint of his relations and, coming under a number of fresh influences, acquire his spiritual independence by comparing them with one another. The more complex the society, the more autonomous is the personality and the more important are the relations of cooperation between equal individuals. Now, if cooperation follows as naturally as this upon constraint, and consequently the morality of mutual respect upon that of authority, there seems no reason why subjective responsibility should be looked upon as a bastard form of "primitive" responsibility. The most one could say would be that rational mentality was a bastard form of prescientific or "prelogical" mentality, and that independent morality was an attenuated form of elementary religions. It seems to us, on the contrary, that if the phenomena of education may legitimately be regarded as exhibiting in embryo the principles of social phenomena, then subjective responsibility is the normal outcome of objective responsibility, in so far, at least, as the constraint of conformity gives place to a cooperation based upon social differentiation and upon individualism. So that it is not only because pity and humanitarianism exercise a check upon penalties that objective and communicable responsibility is weakened. It is because the ideas of involuntary crime and even of expiatory punishment lose all meaning in the morality of autonomy. Conceptions of offence and punishment evolve at the same time as those of duty, of right and wrong, and of distributive justice. The two types of morality distinguished by M. Fauconnet seem to us, therefore, to be connected with two general attitudes, with the two moralities we have grown accustomed to, and the evolution from one to the other is not contingent but goes of a piece with the psycho-sociological transformation that characterizes the passage from the theocratic conformity of so-called "primitive" societies to the equalitarian solidarity of modern times. The heteronomy that goes with constraint begets objective responsibility, just as the autonomy that goes with mutual respect and cooperation begets subjective responsibility. For the morality of cooperation, the germs of which are present in any society, is stifled by the constraint prevalent in conformist societies. But the social differentiation and "organic" solidarity peculiar to civilized communities allow it to expand, and thus explain the transformation of responsibility.

Let us examine M. Fauconnet's arguments more closely and make our choice between the two interpretations. Although he brings out very clearly the difference between our conceptions and those of primitive times, M. Fauconnet tries to soften the contrast by looking for signs of objective responsibility and even for promising revivals of archaic notions in our own times. Thus in speaking of the Italian school of jurisprudence, which regards the criminal as an irresponsible degenerate, society itself being responsible for his condition, M. Fauconnet declares: "Only by returning to its own source can responsibility be renewed and sustained" (p. 344). Thus the responsibility of the community in the case of the delinquent drunkard is compared to that of the clan in the case of an individual violation of the taboo. But at this point, we fear that a confusion has crept in. If elementary communities look upon responsibility as collective, they do so in order to extend, as it were, the surface of application of the penalty, and in order the better to chastise and thus increase the mystical efficacy of the expiation. But in declaring society responsible for the crime of one of its members, what the modern mind seeks to do is, on the contrary, to diminish the latter's responsibility and to soften his punishment. In regarding a drunkard as the victim of society we seek to remove all intentionality and precisely all element of guilt from his misdeeds. Of course, traces of collective responsibility are still to be found among us, as when in war a whole nation is made responsible for the faults of its rulers, or in religion where the whole of humanity is condemned to perdition because of the sins of its first progenitors. These certainly are instances of collective responsibility. But such judgments are not generally made by the normal collective consciousness and should be regarded as residua, or regressions, rather than as a "renovation" of responsibility.

Another argument used by M. Fauconnet is that in penal law there must be a *corpus delicti*. But this is a circumstance of a practical nature rather than an ideal principle to be adhered to by the collective consciousness. If judges could really "try the reins and the heart," if, without risk of error, with the same or even greater certainty than they use in establishing the proof of simple matters of fact, they could lay bare the intention behind the act, then it is undoubtedly the guilty intention itself that would incur punishment. It is therefore for lack of infallibility and not because of any positive principles of objective responsibility that justice confines its activities to material acts, in which restricted domain it already encounters difficulties enough.

In short, modern responsibility tends to be entirely individual and entirely subjective. But one must go further than this. Between the primitive conception of responsibility and certain existing ideas on the subject there is a difference, not only of degree, but of kind. In the case of the first, punishment is the moral conception *par excellence*. And as the primitive notions are all realistic, the idea of punishment, for lack of differentiation between the psychical and the physical, has, to begin with, a meaning that is as much magical as mystical. The crime being a centre of physical and psychical infection, its punishment will have effects that are both material and spiritual. Except in regard to certain theological conceptions, these ideas have become completely foreign to our way of thinking. At the same time, the idea that a good action deserves its reward and an evil one its punishment, is one that is still very widespread. This conception, which combines very easily with that of subjective responsibility, we willingly allow to be a product of primitive, objective, and quasi-materialistic notions of responsibility. But it will be admitted that a great many of our contemporaries have freed themselves of this idea. To the minds of many, not only, needless to say, should good be sought for its own sake, but punishment of any kind is immoral. If, with M. Fauconnet, we identify responsibility with punishment, it will be only in reference to those chosen few that we shall talk of an "attenuation of responsibility." But the whole point about these people is that they dissociate responsibility from punishment, and reject punishment as energetically as they cultivate the idea of responsibility. Of course we must distinguish here between the legal and the moral point of view. From a purely legal point of view, punishment is perhaps necessary for the defence of society, though modern writers on the subject also tend to place the idea of social re-education and re-adaptation above that of expiation. But from the moral point of view, there is always something ambiguous about the idea of punishment, and the least we can say of it is that it renders autonomy of conscience impossible. M. Guyau's brilliant defence of this theory will be remembered, and if it lacked a certain depth, the same charge can hardly be laid to one of the most substantial reactions ever made against the Kantian Ethics, which, like so many, only went half the way to true autonomy—we mean the ethical system of F. Rauh.

In a word, inner responsibility, which goes with autonomy of conscience and arises from the relations of cooperation, is not simply derived from the form of responsibility that is bound up with the idea of expiatory punishment, and consequently with constraint and heteronomy: a new type of moral attitude has replaced a superannuated attitude, and the continuity of the two events in time must not be allowed to hide the difference of their nature.

In conclusion—and this is what we want to establish, for

it will be invaluable to us in what follows—social constraint
and cooperation lead to results that do not admit of comparison. Social constraint—and by this we mean any social
relation into which there enters an element of authority and
which is not, like cooperation, the result of an interchange
between equal individuals—has on the individual results that
are analogous to those exercised by adult constraint on the
mind of the child. The two phenomena, moreover, are really
one and the same thing, and the adult who is under the
dominion of unilateral respect for the "Elders" and for tradition is really behaving like a child. It may even be maintained
that the realism of primitive conceptions of crime and punishment is, in certain respects, an infantile reaction. To primitive
man, the moral and the physical universe are one and the
same thing, and a rule is both a law of nature and a principle
of conduct. For this reason, crime threatens the very existence of the universe and must be mystically set at naught by
a suitable expiation. But this idea of a law that is both physical
and moral is the very core of the child's conception of the
world; for under the effect of adult constraint the child cannot conceive the laws of the physical universe except in the
guise of a certain obedience rendered by things to rules. As
to ideas of punishment and expiation, how could they have
become so widespread in the adult community if men had
not all first been children, and if the child had not been from
the very beginning of his mental development respectful
towards the decisions of the adult who reprimands him and
punishes him? Under the effects of social differentiation and
cooperation, on the contrary, the individual is less and less
dominated by the cult of the past and by the forced conformity which accompanies it. He then becomes really adult,
and the infantile traits that mark the conformist spirit make
place for the features that are the outcome of cooperation.
Thus autonomy of conscience takes the place of heteronomy,
whence we have the transformations studied by M. Fauconnet
in the domain of responsibility, and the criticisms which come
to be raised against the very idea of expiatory punishment;
thus the purely interior responsibility which blames itself for
not reaching a certain ideal follows upon the responsibility
born of the reactions of the group. It is true that this inner

responsibility remains a social phenomenon; unless individuals cooperated, conscience would be ignorant of right and of the sense of guilt. But this is a phenomenon of different order from that of the facts of constraint, though it constitutes in a fashion the form of equilibrium towards which the whole history of responsibility tends.

§ 2. DURKHEIM'S DOCTRINE OF MORAL AUTHORITY: I. INTRODUCTION

Durkheim's ethical teaching, which strikes so sincere a note and is imbued with such a deeply scientific spirit, certainly raises the gravest question we have to face in our interpretation of the facts of child psychology. Where we see a struggle between two moralities, and between two types of social relations, Durkheim affirms the unity of all moral and social facts. True, no one has realized better than he the deep sociological foundation for the struggle between independent and transcendent morality, but while we believe the first to have been prepared for by the solidarity amongst children themselves and the second to have proceeded from the constraint of the adult over the child, Durkheim regards all morality as imposed by the group upon the individual and by the adult upon the child. Consequently, from the pedagogic point of view, whereas we would be inclined to see in the "Activity" School, in "self-government," and in the autonomy of the child the only form of education likely to produce a rational morality, Durkheim upholds a system of education which is based on the traditional model and relies on methods that are fundamentally those of authority, in spite of all the tempering features he introduced into it in order to allow for inner liberty of conscience.

Before examining *L'Education Morale* let us devote a little thought to the problem of Durkheim's moral sociology in general. For Durkheim's ideas on the child can only be understood in terms of his general sociology, and as his ideas on children resemble so closely those of common sense and current pedagogy we shall have to examine them very closely if we wish to uphold the soundness of our own theories on the subject.

In his book on the division of labour, *La Division du*

Travail Social, the least dogmatic and, theoretically, the most suggestive of his works, Durkheim has shown greater caution than he did later on with regard to the unity of social facts and consequently the identity of moral facts with each other. There are two great types of society: on the one hand, there are the conformist communities whose solidarity is segmented or mechanical; and on the other, there are the communities differentiated from within by division of labour and possessing organic solidarity. The first are exclusive of inner freedom and of personality, the second mark the growth and expansion of individual dignity. Now, social differentiation is a recent phenomenon, as yet hardly defined and apt to overthrow our social habits and moral rules. By causing a break-down in traditional conformity, differentiation applies a check to the theological symbols connected with conformity, and since in communities of the first type morality depends upon religion and the external forms of religion, our first duty will be actually to create a new morality for ourselves. Our equilibrium is threatened. We need an inner equivalent of the outer solidarity that belongs to conformity. What we lose in the material constraint of traditional institutions we must gain in inner morality, in a personal cultivation of solidarity.

It seemed, then, according to this presentation of the subject, that social pressure appeared under two different manifestations: constraint properly so called in conformist societies, and inner obligation in cooperation. It seemed, at any rate, as though moral feelings would have to present themselves under almost opposite forms according as they belonged to the heteronomy of an obligatory conformity or to the autonomy belonging to personality in differentiated and organic societies. The tendency of Durkheim's later works, however, was to reduce constraint and cooperation to unity, and above all to fuse into a single explanation the analyses he gave of the different aspects of morality.

In the case of constraint, Durkheim has stretched his definition of the word to cover all social phenomena whatsoever. Whether he is talking of the inward attraction felt by the individual for universal human ideals, or of the coercion exercised by public opinion or police, it is all constraint. The "externality" of the social phenomenon gives rise to the same generalizations. Logical and moral principles are external to the individual in the sense that the individual mind would not have been able to work them out unaided. But so are verbal signs, mystical symbols or economic values, in the sense that it is not in the individual's power to alter them at will. In a word, society is always one and the same, and the differences between cooperation and obligatory conformity are more a matter of degree than of quality.

Morality is treated in the same way. Morality is born of religion, since obligatory acts were first sanctioned in so far as they proceeded from the idea of the sacred. Just as the sacred is what inspires both a respectful fear and a feeling of attraction, so do moral conceptions present two irreducible, but inseparable aspects—obligation and duty on the one hand, and on the other, the sense of the good or of a desirable ideal.

Again, just as the sacred gives rise to ritual prohibitions and positive commands, so does morality forbid and compel without giving reasons. The Categorical Imperative is thus a direct emanation from social constraint. The object of morality and the source of respect can be only society itself, as distinct from individuals and superior to them.

On the main thesis of Durkheim's doctrine, *i.e.*, the explanation of morality by social life, and the interpretation of its changes in terms of the varying structure of society, we can naturally only agree with his sociological school, because of the results of our enquiry. We found that the purely individual elements of morality could be traced either to the feeling of respect felt by the younger for the older children, which explained the genesis of conscience and duty, or to the feelings of sympathy felt by the child for those around him, which made cooperation possible. Instinctive tendencies, together with others more or less directly connected with them, are thus a necessary but not a sufficient condition for the formation of morality. Morality presupposes the existence of rules which transcend the individual, and these rules could only develop through contact with other people. Thus the fundamental conceptions of childish morality consist of those imposed by the adult and of those born of collaboration between children themselves. In both cases, that is to say, whether the child's moral judgments are heteronomous or autonomous, accepted under pressure or worked out in freedom, this morality is social, and on this point Durkheim is unquestionably right.

But the matter does not end here, and it remains to be seen whether the unity of all social facts postulated by Durkheim is not such as to rob morality of its most fundamental and most specific characteristic—its normative autonomy. The danger of the sociological explanation—and Durkheim was the first to notice it—is that it may compromise morality by identifying it with reasons of state, with accepted opinions, or with collective conservatism; in a word, with everything that the greatest reformers have attacked in the name of conscience. And we do not think that the solution given by Durkheim to this crucial problem is likely to remove our doubts. We ask the reader's forbearance in laying so much stress on this much discussed problem. But it is one that in spite of any contrary appearance is so important in child psychology—Durkheim's pedagogy proves this if nothing else —that we must not be afraid of appearing to utter truisms in our effort to remove all possible misunderstanding.

Durkheim seems to have remained undecided on this essential point. In some passages he seems to attribute moral value to prevalent opinion by the mere fact that it is prevalent. "The affinity between habit and moral practice is even such that any collective habit almost inevitably presents a certain moral character. Once a form of behaviour has become habitual in a group, any departure from it provokes an impulse of disapproval very closely akin to that called forth by moral faults properly so called. Such habits command, in a measure, the special respect that is paid to moral practices. While all collective habits are not moral, all moral practices are undoubtedly collective habits. Consequently, whoever is refractory to all that is habit may very easily prove so to morality" (*Education Morale*, p. 31). But in other places— and the passages we shall now quote seem to us to express Durkheim's own ideal far better than those in which he defends "collective habit"—Durkheim seems to say the exact opposite. "It has been objected to this view that it subjects the mind to the prevailing moral opinion. But this is not so, for the society which morality tells us to desire is not society as it appears to itself but society as it really is or tends to be. And it may happen that society's own consciousness of itself, acquired in and through opinion, may be an inadequate reflection of the underlying reality. Public opinion may be full of anachronisms which make it lag behind the actual state of society" (*Sociologie et Philosophie*, p. 51). And most important of all, in answer to a criticism by M. Parodi, Durkheim did not hesitate to declare before the "Société française de Philosophie" that according to his system of Ethics it was the consciences of great individuals that were in the right when they came into conflict with public opinion. It may be granted, for instance, that public opinion in Athens condemned Socrates, but it was he who was in the right and not the Athenians, because "Socrates expressed more faithfully than his judges the morality that suited the society of his time" (*ibid.*, p. 93).

Clearly, one must make one's choice between these two solutions. But this is just what Durkheim could not admit, for the choice would at the same time settle the problem of constraint and cooperation. For, either society is one, and all social processes, including cooperation, are to be assimilated to pure constraint alone, in which case right is bound to be determined by public opinion and traditional use; or else, a distinction must be made between actual and ideal society, that is to say, between "opinion" and society such as it is "really tending to be," in which case one is inevitably led to distinguish between constraint and cooperation more fundamentally than Durkheim wished to do, so as to place moral values above reasons of state.

For how, we would ask, is it possibe to distinguish between society as it is and society as it is tending to become? Under a *régime* of compulsory conformity, *i.e.*, of more or less unadulterated social constraint, such a distinction is unthinkable. A given set of beliefs and practices are handed to the individual, and morality consists in preserving them as such. Involuntary alterations may, of course, occur in the established usage, and the breach may become appreciable between the new and the traditional usage. But the ideal is at one's back, not before one's eyes. For what constraint imposes is an already organized system of rules and opinions; you can take this system or leave it, but any form of argument or personal interpretation is irreconcilable with conformity. In differentiated communities like ours, on the contrary, new relations between individuals become conceivable, germs of which, indeed, were already to be found in primitive communities, particularly in matters of technical labour. In the midst of the network of groupings which constitute our present society, individuals agree, not so much to preserve a set of dogmas and rites, as to apply a "method" or set of methods. What one affirms is verified by the others; what one has done is tried out and tested by the others. The essence of experimental behaviour—whether scientific, technical, or moral—consists, not in a common belief, but in rules of mutual control. Everyone is free to bring in innovations, but only in so far as he succeeds in making himself understood by others and in understanding them. This cooperation, which, it must be admitted, is in many spheres still far from prevailing over social constraint, though it constitutes the ideal of democratic communities, is the only thing that allows for the distinction between what is and what ought to be. For the word "method" implies that certain provisional truths have been established, but above all that there is more to discover and that progress depends on compliance with certain norms. In this way the characteristics of the ideal are safeguarded. The essence of social constraint and of external authority, on the contrary, is to identify what is with what ought to be, the ideal state of things being thus conceived as already realized.

Durkheim's refusal to admit any other difference than one of degree between constraint and cooperation must be due to the fact that the two processes are connected by an endless series of intermediate links. As he showed in his first work, it is to the extent that a community grows in volume and in density that division of labour, individualism and cooperation triumph over compulsory conformity. The hypothesis may therefore be advanced that in all communities the social totality exercises constraint upon the individuals, and that this constraint takes the form of cooperative solidarity in our civilization, whereas it remains limited to a compulsory conformity in primitive communities. Only this factual continuity, which we in no way wish to deny, does not exclude a qualitative contrast in the results. One may conceive of cooperation as constituting the ideal form of equilibrium towards which society tends when compulsory conformity comes to break down. As this ideal is approached, the character of social life comes to differ qualitatively from its primitive state, although the movement between the two forms is continuous.

Let us approach the matter as psychologists in order to see more clearly its relationship to the two moralities of the child. Durkheim, except on rare occasions, has in mind only society as made up of adults. Everything happens, in his books, as though the group as a total synthesis simply exerted its pressure upon all individuals independently of their age. Now let us imagine a community of which the members had always been each other's contemporaries, and had lived their lives without experiencing either the constraint of the generations preceding them, or the education of the generations following them. However many centuries we allow these individuals to have lived, and however collective we picture their psychology, the chances are a thousand to one against their ever reproducing the sociology to which we have been accustomed in the communities described as "primitive." These people would gradually discover a language, a logic, a science, an ethic, and a metaphysic of their own, but allowing for groping experiments, for errors, and for momentary collective deviations, one cannot imagine anything that would lead them to accept a social constraint as firmly crystallized as those of the communities in which compulsory conformity holds its sway. For it seems to us obvious that all the elementary social phenomena would be radically different from what they are if communities had never been formed except by individuals of the same age and ignorant of the pressure of one generation upon the other. The younger child feels respect for the older, and for its parents —and the more simply constituted the society in which he lives, the more durable a part does this unilateral respect pay in the life of an individual, as the respect for age and elders in the more primitive communities seems to show. Without this unilateral respect one simply does not see how the ethics and the logic peculiar to social constraint and conformity could ever have come into being. In the moral sphere, it may very well be that such facts as ritual obligations and prohibitions, moral realism and objective responsibility would not exist without the respect which the child feels for the adult. But one can go a step farther and surmise that the outstanding features of "primitive mentality" can be explained by a conjunction of the childish mentality with the effects of the constraint exercised by one generation upon the other. Primitive mentality would therefore be due to social constraint being refracted through the childish mind.[2] In our civilization, on the contrary, with its foundation of cooperation and individual differentiation, the egocentric mentality of the child hardly enters into fundamental social phenomena except in the case of those which constitute "survivals," as Durkheim has called them, or which are "behind-hand in relation to the existing state of society." The development of the sciences, of industry, the economic division of labour, rational morality, and democratic ideas, all seem to be so many conquests standing in no relation to the constraint of the generations upon one another and arising directly from a cooperation that is independent of age.

In short, social constraint may be regarded from the psychological point of view as arising partly from the constraint exercised by the adult upon the child, and as exercising in consequence of this a "consolidating" effect upon child mentality. This assumption gains force if, as we showed in the course of our enquiries, social constraint does not really suffice to "socialize" the child but accentuates its egocentrism. Cooperation, on the other hand, seems to be essentially the social relation which tends to eliminate infantile phenomena. And this is enough to show that cooperation,

[2] In saying this, we do not, of course, wish to return to the pre-sociological phase of psychology, but simply to show that within the framework established by sociology there is everything to be said for reinstating psychological analysis. There is at the present day far more parallelism than antagonism between sociological studies and psychological research.

while constituting the ideal form of equilibrium towards which constraint approaches in so far as social condensation liberates the younger generations, leads eventually to results that are qualitatively the opposite of constraint. It shows finally that if, with Durkheim, we wish to distinguish between opinion and reason, between the observance of custom and that of moral norms, we must at the same time make a vigorous distinction between a social process such as constraint, which simply consecrates the existing order of things, and a social process such as cooperation, which essentially imposes a method and thus allows for the emancipation of what ought to be from what is.

We can now turn to the examination of the really ethical part of Durkheim's sociology. Two parts should be distinguished here: the theory of duty or of moral obligation, and the theory of good or autonomy of conscience. With regard to duty we cannot but subscribe to Durkheim's theory, at any rate from the point of view of static sociology. It seems to us incontestable not only that the totality of duties in a given society is bound up with the structure of this society, but also that the very form of duty (the feeling of obligation) is connected with the constraint exercised by the society on the individuals. From the genetic point of view, on the other hand, it can be maintained that the pressure of an adult upon a child is sufficient to give rise to the sense of duty in the latter's mind and to do so independently of the pressure to which the adult is subjected on the part of the whole society. But we do not regard these facts as contradictory of Durkheim's teaching, whatever Durkheim himself might have thought about it. It is therefore unnecessary to press the point any further, the more so as we shall deal with it again in connection with M. Bovet's theory.

The theory of the morally good, on the other hand, seems to us to present difficulties which arise from those very relations between constraint and cooperation of which we have just spoken. Very rightly, Durkheim begins by contrasting good and duty, and pronounces these two aspects of the moral life so different as to be irreducible. And yet soon after this, Durkheim almost identifies them in so far as they seem to him inseparable, and for him every moral act partakes both of the obligation belonging to duty and of the desirability which characterizes what is good. And these two notions are given to us as having a common origin: good and duty both come from the feeling of the "sacred," the sacred being at once imperative and desirable, just as is society itself, of which the sacred is only the reflection.

Now this common origin is just what seems to us questionable. True, there is no feeling of duty without desirability, and therefore without a certain feeling of the good. But the reason for this is clear. Unilateral respect, which is at the back of all consciousness of duty, consists of a *sui generis* mixture of fear and love, which implies in consequence an element of desirability. But the converse is not true. Actions can be good, yet devoid of any element of obligation.[3] There are even individuals, as Durkheim himself remarked, to whom goodness matters far more than duty, and the converse is also true.

Durkheim, it is true, explains these individual differences in such a way as to fit them into his theory. "Each individual," he says, "expresses the common morality in his own way; each understands it, envisages it from a different angle; perhaps no one mind is completely adequate to the morality of its own time" (*Sociol. et Phil.*, p. 56). In consequence, then, there would seem to be a "common morality" existing as such in society and regarded by the various individuals each from his own point of view. This would explain why in reality the good and duty are indissociable, each individual being free to stress one or other of these two aspects of the moral life, which would thus be rendered mutually irreducible.

But we shall have to examine more closely those relations between common morality and individuals; for the whole of the part played by society in the genesis of moral ideas is here the point at issue. When a number of travellers are climbing a mountain or exploring a tract of country, one can say that their individual points of view are always inadequate, because they cannot see everything that there is to be seen, or because they cannot see it simultanously. If

[3] According to Durkheim (*Sociologie et Philosophie*, p. 65) no moral acts are "purely desirable, for they always require effort." But effort is not necessarily the same thing as obligation.

"common morality" constitutes an object that is thus external to the individuals, it goes without saying that the separate minds will always be inadequate, and that their respective viewpoints will be reconcilable only in the absolute of such a realism. But another solution is possible, and one which Durkheim does not seem to have envisaged, namely that "common morality" does not consist in a "thing" given to individuals from without, but in a sum of relations between individuals. Common morality would thus be defined by the system of laws of perspective enabling one to pass from one point of view to the other, and allowing in consequence the making of a map or objective representation of the mountain or country. In this case each individual perspective could be different from the others and yet at the same time adequate and in no danger of jeopardizing the coherence of the whole. It is true that this whole is extremely complex and that the individual consciences are also perhaps inadequate in the first sense of the term. But the point is that the second sense should also have its share of truth, as we believe to be really the case. For while duty constitutes a collection of commands more or less identical in each case, the good demands in addition a certain margin of personal elaboration and autonomy. Which surely means that far from being the result of constraint, it can be explained only by cooperation.

In this way we are led to examine the curious argumentation by means of which Durkheim defines the object of what is morally good. This object cannot be the individual, since egoism is rejected by every kind of ethics. Therefore, "if each individual taken separately is incapable of giving any moral value to conduct, *i.e.,* has *in himself* no moral value, neither does the numerical sum of such individuals possess any value" (*Sociol. et Philos.*, p. 73). Thus, "now that we have eliminated the individual subject, there remains no possible objective for moral activity than the *sui generis* entity formed by a plurality of individual subjects associated in such a way as to form a group; there remains only the collective subject" (p. 74). Society must therefore "be regarded as a personality qualitatively different from the individual personalities of which it is composed" (p. 54), and altruism becomes legitimate in so far as the other person incarnates society. For "though society is something different from the individual, and though it can be found in its entirety in none of us, yet there is not one of us in whom it is not in a manner reflected" (*Education Morale,* p. 93).

It should be noted, in the first place, that such an explanation of altruism could equally well be made to justify egoism. For, after all, I am as much a reflection of society as anyone else, and this inner reflection seems to me far more direct than those that are refracted through other people's personalities. Apart from this interpretation, these passages from Durkheim's writings can have only one meaning: what we love in others is not so much the individual as the possibility of a bond of affection, not so much the friend as friendship. An inhuman formula if the moral fact remains external to the individual, and is imposed upon him from without, but one of singular profundity if the good constitutes the law of perspective and the rule of reciprocity which aim at bringing about mutual understanding. Then what we seek in the other person is the very thing that enables the other person to come out of himself while yet remaining most profoundly himself.

The good, in short, is not, like duty, the result of a constraint exercised by society upon the individual. The aspiration to the good is of different stuff from the obedience given to an imperative rule. Mutual respect, which constitutes the good, does not lead to the same conformity as unilateral respect, which characterizes duty. In our modern societies, no doubt, the difference between the two has become dulled, for the content of duty can be more and more identified with the good. This is why Kantian Ethics, in its form a morality of duty, is in its content a morality of autonomous will, and defines the good by a universality which rests on reciprocity itself (though in Kant's personal mentality there are many traces of heteronomy and legalism). But in primitive communities the opposition is almost complete between the whole set of legal prohibitions or taboos laid down by the morality of duty and the rules of justice and reciprocity which grow up between individuals without always being codified. It is only in differentiated societies that, as ritual obligations diminish along with conformity, the morality of good wins against the morality of duty, and becomes transmitted from one generation to another until it comes to constitute the actual content of the duties themselves.

In conclusion, the fundamental difficulty of Durkheimism seems to us to be the illegitimate identification of constraint and cooperation. In the moral sphere, this means that the identification of good and duty is pushed too far and, what is worse, that morality is made subservient to social conformity. There can be no complete moral autonomy except by cooperation. From this point of view, morality is still a social thing, but society cannot be regarded as a completed whole nor as a system of fully realized values. The morality of good develops progressively and constitutes, in relation to society, a form of ideal equilibrium, as it were, which rises above the false and unstable existing equilibria which are based on constraint.

§ 3. THE THEORY OF AUTHORITY ACCORDING TO DURKHEIM: II. MORAL EDUCATION

We now reach what is to us the fundamental point of the controversy, that is to say, Durkheim's ideas on child psychology in relation to sociology. For the course of lectures embodied in his *Education Morale* is the most powerful effort made on scientific lines to justify the conceptions on which traditional education rests. Whereas nearly all child psychologists, Stanley Hall, Dewey, Claparède, etc.—speaking, it is true, more from the child's point of view than from that of society—have denounced the delusions of the scholastic method, Durkheim, taking his stand on society and approaching the child from that standpoint is, on the contrary, extremely conservative. We must therefore test the soundness of his arguments in the light of the actual facts of child morality.

Let us start with a discussion of the principle involved, not only because this work of Durkheim's forms a wonderfully coherent whole, but because in many ways he reaffirms here what was stated in his earlier writings.

There are, according to Durkheim, three elements in morality: the spirit of discipline, the attachment to social groups, and the autonomy of the will. The spirit of discipline (*l'esprit de discipline*) is in itself fundamental, since morality consists in a body of rules sanctioned by society. "To regularize conduct is a fundamental function of morality" (p. 30). But there is more in the idea of rule than merely the notion of regularity: there is *authority*. "By authority must be understood the ascendency exercised over us by any moral power that we recognize as superior to ourselves" (p. 33). Morality is thus a system of commands, and individual conscience nothing but the product of the interiorization of these collective imperatives. It is also true that discipline, far from thwarting the growth and expansion of the individual, is the sole condition for the development of personality (p. 52).

The *attachment to social groups* is no less important. Individuals possessing no moral value in themselves, the group is the only legitimate end. But here again, far from checking individual initiative, this end enriches personality: we are all social beings, and there is no real antagonism between the individual and society (p. 80). Moreover, "What shows that morality is the work of the community is that it varies as do communities" (p. 98). It is true that beneath all the variations of morality there remains a basis that is permanent and unchanging, but this is because society, though it evolves, retains certain constant features: "A society remains, up to a point, identical with itself, throughout the course of its existence. Under the changes it undergoes its fundamental constitution is always the same. The ethical system which it practises therefore presents the same degree of identity and constancy" (p. 121). Finally, it should be noted that the spirit of discipline and the attachment to a group constitute, in the last analysis, one and the same phenomenon. No individual possesses authority or prestige in himself. "Society alone stands above individuals. From it therefore emanates all authority. It is society that bestows upon such and such human qualities that *sui generis* character, that prestige which raises the individuals who possess it above themselves" (p. 103).

This unity of discipline and attachment to groups also explains the profound identity of duty and good. "Duty is morality in so far as it commands; it is morality conceived as an authority which we obey because it is authority, and for no other reason. Good is morality conceived as something desirable, which entices the will to its service, and provokes a spontaneous longing. Now it is easy to see that duty is society, in so far as it lays down rules and sets limitations to our nature; whereas the good is also society, but in so far as it is a reality richer than our own, and one to which we cannot become attached without a resulting enrichment of our being" (p. 110). These two elements of morality are therefore only "two different aspects of the same reality" (p. 112), and if it be true that our societies lay more stress on good than on duty, and that we are losing the sense of collective discipline (p. 116), then it becomes the urgent task of education to restore the unity of our moral consciousness by reconciling the good and duty once again.

The third element of morality is the *autonomy of the will.* It is contrary to rational morality to impose anything whatsoever on science itself. "It is a rule, not only of logic, but of morality, that our reason must only accept as true what it has spontaneously recognized as such" (p. 123). But the Kantian solution which explains autonomy by the rational will reduces obligation to "an accidental character, as it were, of the moral law" (p. 125). But it is necessary, on the contrary, to justify autonomy without disparaging the principle of obligation and authority. "Kant has shown better than anyone else that there was something religious in the feeling with which the moral law filled even the highest reason. Now we can have religious feeling only for some being, real or ideal, who seems to us superior to the faculty by which we conceive it. For the truth is that obligation is an essential element of moral precept" (p. 126). Durkheim claims to find this reconciliation of autonomy and social authority in a comparison with natural science. It is only by learning the laws of nature, by using them without trying to infringe them, that we become free of nature. Now "in the moral order there is room for the same autonomy, and there is room for no other. Just as morality expresses the nature of society, and that society cannot be known directly any more than can physical nature, so individual reason can no more legislate for the world of morals than it does for the material universe. . . . But this order which the individual, as an individual, has not created, has not deliberately willed, can become his by science" (p. 133). In short, autonomy consists in understanding the why and wherefore of the laws which society lays upon us and which we cannot choose but accept.

After this analysis, Durkheim asks how we can instil the elements of morality in the child. Durkheim's principle is very elastic when he comes to deal with educational matters, far more so, indeed, than the sociological doctrine would have led one to suppose. On the one hand, the child does not of itself possess the elements of morality, and we must therefore "inform its nature." But on the other hand, "educational action . . . does not work upon a blank sheet of paper. The child has a nature of its own, and since it is this nature that must be informed, we must, if we are to work upon it effectually, begin by trying to know it" (p. 147). It is these introductory remarks, so wise and so much in tune with the contemporary educational movement, that have led us to submit Durkheim's ideas to a searching critical examination.

Unfortunately, under the influence of a "pre-notion," hard to account for in a sociologist, and especially in one so methodical, Durkheim thinks of children as knowing no other society than adult society or the societies created by adults (schools), so that he entirely ignores the existence of spontaneously formed children's societies, and of the facts relating to mutual respect. Consequently, elastic though Durkheim's pedagogy may be in principle, it simply leads, for lack of being sufficiently informed on the subject of child sociology, to a defence of the methods of authority.

First question: How to form the spirit of discipline in the child? It should be noted from the first "that the mental states which education must produce in the child are only virtually present, and exist only in a general form that is very far removed from that which they are destined to take." This is particularly true "of the spirit of discipline. We may say indeed that not one of the elements that compose it is present in its entirety in the mind of the child" (p. 148). One of these elements is the taste for a regular life. Now the child

is all fantasy, all restlessness. "The outstanding feature of infantile curiosity is that it is unstable and fleeting" (p. 149).
The spirit of discipline, on the other hand, means moderation
and self-control. Now the child knows no limit to its desires,
sets no curb to its emotions and instinctive tendencies. It is
true that in spite of this there are "two characteristics constitutive of the infantile mental makeup which respond to
our influence; these are 1) childish traditionalism; 2) the
child's openness to suggestion, especially to imperative suggestion" (p. 153). At this point, Durkheim makes the very
penetrating observation that in spite of his restlessness the
child is a "lover of routine" (p. 153). The rituals attached
to eating, going to bed, etc., show the hold which habit has
over his nature. "Thus the child is at the same time unstable and misoneistic" (p. 154). Like primitive man, the
child is a traditionalist (p. 155). At the same time, everyone has noticed its suggestibility as well as the enormous
ascendency which the example of those around it exercise
upon its nature.

It is these features of child psychology which render futile
all those "oft-repeated arguments as to whether the child is
born moral or immoral, or whether it possesses in itself the
positive elements of morality and immorality. Put in this way,
the problem admits of no definite solution. To act morally
is to conform to the rules of morality. But the rules of
morality are external to the child's conscience; they are
worked out apart from him; he only comes in contact with
them at a definite point in his life" (p. 167). This decisive
moment in the making of the spirit of discipline arrives when
the child goes to school. In the family altruistic leanings and
feeling of solidarity are stronger than duty. At school, on the
contrary, there must be rules. These rules must be cultivated
for their own sake. They constitute "an instrument of moral
education which it would be hard to replace" (p. 171). It is
therefore the master's business to impose them. "Since it is
by the master that rules are revealed to the child, everything
rests with him. Rules can have no other authority than that
which he confers upon them: that is to say, than that of
which he suggests the idea to the children" (p. 176). The
lay teacher must be a kind of priest of society. "Just as the

priest is the interpreter of God, so he is the interpreter of the great moral ideas of his time and his country" (p. 177). But, on the other hand, the teacher's authority must give way before that of the rule, "for the rule ceases to be itself if it is not impersonal, and if it is not represented as such to people's minds" (p. 178).

Durkheim is therefore opposed to the form of education based on individual interests and free initiative which is advanced by the "Activity School" under all its forms. He answers Montaigne with the classic argument: "Life is not all play; the child must prepare himself for pain and effort, and it would therefore be a disaster if he were allowed to think that everything can be done as a game" (p. 183). There must therefore be not only a firm discipline in schools, but also penalties that will enforce this discipline.

But what exactly do we mean by a penalty? Some people look upon it as preventive measure. But the superficiality of such a justification has been recognized, since it attributes to the child or delinquent a capacity for prevision which is utterly foreign to their natural impulsiveness. Others, again, take a penalty to be an expiation. Durkheim, while he rejects the materialistic form of the doctrine of expiatory suffering, thinks, nevertheless, that "something of this theory should be retained. The part of it to be retained is the principle that the penalty wipes out the fault, or at any rate makes up for it as much as is possible. But the penalty does not possess the power of reparation because of the suffering it implies: for suffering is an evil, and it would be absurd to suppose that one evil can compensate for another and nullify it" (p. 188). If suffering wipes out the fault, this is because "the fundamental function of a penalty" is "to reassure those spirits whose faith may—indeed must—have been shaken by the violation of the law, even though they were not aware of it, to show them that this faith is as justified as it was before, and, especially in the case of schools, that it is still held by the person who first gave it to the children" (p. 191). Thus a punishment wipes out a fault in so far as the pain inflicted proves to the child that the teacher has taken this misdeed seriously. So that the essence of a penalty is to symbolize blame: "The punishment is only the material sign of an inner state; it is a system of notation, a language, by means of which either public opinion or the schoolmaster's conscience expresses the feeling aroused in them by the censured act" (p. 201).

As for Herbert Spencer's theory of natural punishment, it rests on the illusion that education comes from nature, whereas in reality it is a social process. Punishment should undoubtedly be regarded as the natural consequence of the fault committed, but the consequence in this case is not the physical result of the guilty actions themselves. Punishment is the result of the fault only in so far as the latter sets afoot a movement of disapproval symbolized by the former. "The true punishment, like the true natural consequence, is censure" (p. 205).

It should be noted here that coercive in character as is this type of pedagogy, Durkheim protests vigorously against corporal punishment, and shows himself a very subtle psychologist in doing so. Corporal punishment, which is unknown to most primitive communities, developed with the school and reacted on the family. How did it take its rise in the school? This is "a special case of a law which could be formulated as follows. Whenever two peoples, two groups of individuals belonging to different levels of culture, are brought into continuous contact with each other, certain feelings will develop which will make the group which has or believes itself to have the higher culture tend to do violence to the other group" (p. 219). Thus, faced with his pupils, the master can easily be led to violence, or even megalomania: since the school "has by nature a monarchical form, it easily degenerates into despotism" (p. 224).

These considerations on discipline apply equally to the second element of morality: how to form in the child a normal attachment to the social groups that surround him. The psychological origin of this part of our moral life is to be sought for in our faculty for sympathy and in our altruistic and disinterested tendencies. Now the child is "neither purely altruistic nor purely egoistic, but both at the same time, though to a far lesser extent than we are" (p. 260). It will therefore be enough to extend his social circle progressively in order to educate him. Before going to school he has known family life and the society of friends, in which altruism is strengthened by ties of blood and comradeship. And in order to prepare him for political society which does not possess these characteristics, school is the obvious intermediary. Civic and historical teaching are sufficient to initiate the child to the values attaching to adult society.

Such, then, in broad outline is Durkheim's moral pedagogy. We cannot enter upon a discussion of a work so sincere, so lofty in inspiration as that which we have just summarized without a feeling of profound respect for the memory of its author. But such is the seriousness of the questions at stake, that we must not hesitate to examine these theories of Durkheim's in detail and in a spirit of complete freedom. The greatest tribute we can pay to his vigorous scientific spirit is to forget for a moment his immense authority.

Now, the doctrinal foundation for Durkheim's pedagogy is so contrary not only to the apparent achievements of present-day child psychology, but also to all that seems to have been established by the new pedagogy (and this is more serious, for the experiments of pedagogy will always be more conclusive than those of the laboratory), that we find it impossible to accept Durkheim's conclusions as they stand. In spite of the force and fertility of its methods and principles, Durkheim's sociology carries with it a fundamental difficulty—that, namely, which we pointed out a little while ago, and of which the effects are now apparent in child psychology. Not content with showing that the main key to human psychology is to be found in social life, Durkheim tries to make of society a whole, a "being," and this realism, like all realism, has given rise to those antinomies which a methodical relativism alone can avoid. There are no more such things as societies *qua* beings than there are isolated individuals. There are only relations; these relations must be studied simultaneously from outside and from inside (there being no possible conflict between psychology and sociology), and the combinations formed by them, always incomplete, cannot be taken as permanent substances. It is therefore impossible to subsume under one concept the many and diverse effects which social life exercises upon the development of the individual. The unwarranted identification of constraint and cooperation is therefore what we shall once again have to discuss, for this identification vitiates the whole of Durkheim's pedagogy, as it vitiates his ethics. Let us then examine from this point of view the three elements which Durkheim recognizes in morality.

The spirit of discipline, it must be agreed, constitutes the starting-point of all moral life. There must be, not only a certain regularity of behaviour, but rules, and rules clothed with sufficient authority. No one will seriously deny that this is the price to be paid for the development of personality. We can also agree with Durkheim when he sees in the individual as such nothing but a creature of habit and routine. Thus it is social life that elaborates rules properly so called, and this point of view receives full confirmation from our enquiries: all the rules followed by children in all the domains we examined are due to social relations.

Only—and herein resides the whole problem of education as of morality, and even of logic—is there only one type of authority and one type of rules? Durkheim settles the question almost without discussing it, and without seeming to suspect that alongside of the social relations between children and adults there exist social relations that apply distinctly to the groups which children form among themselves. The passages in which Durkheim commits this most disastrous *petitio principii* are probably among the most dogmatic in the whole of his works. All authority comes from Society with a big S ("la" societé, p. 103); the schoolmaster is the priest who acts as an intermediary between society and the child (p 177); everything therefore rests with the master (p. 176), and rules are a sort of revelation (p. 176) which the adult dispenses to the child.

Now, if psychological observation gives one indubitable result, it is that, far from limiting himself to the rules laid down by his parents and teachers (those which he very often observes least closely), the child ties himself down to all sorts of rules in every sphere of his activity, and especially in that of play. These rules are no less social, but they rest on different types of authority. Now the question that educationalists asked themselves was whether these rules distinctive of children's societies could not be utilized in class, and their experiments few in number and little known though they were towards 1902-3 and 1906-7 (the dates of Durkheim's lectures), have given birth to a system of moral pedagogy, called *self-government,* which is at the opposite pole from the Durkheimian pedagogy.[4] A fundamental problem of psychology thus comes to be formulated as follows: Do these different kinds of rules obey the same psychosociological laws, or do they not? This is the question which has occupied us throughout this book, and our answer has been in the negative.

For it seemed to us that there existed at least two extreme types of rules and of authority—rules due to unilateral respect, and rules due to mutual respect. Durkheim tells us that the individual as such has no authority. But even if this statement is well founded (which we shall consider in connection with M. Bovet's theory), the fact remains that the playmate, or older child, constitutes, like the schoolmaster or the parent, a reflection, not of Society (with a big S), but of this or that society thought of by the child, and that the respect felt for a fair-minded companion in a match of marbles is different from that called forth by an adult. And these two types of rules lead to opposite results. The rule of constraint, which is bound up with unilateral respect, is regarded as sacred and produces in the child's mind feelings that are analogous to those which characterize the compulsory conformity of primitive communities. But this rule of constraint remains external to the child's spirit and does not lead to as effective an obedience as the adult would wish. Rules due to mutual agreement and cooperation, on the contrary, take root inside the child's mind and result in an effective observance in the measure in which they are incorporated in an autonomous will.

If this distinction is based on fact we may in the very name of sociology ask the following question. Contemporary civilized society, that, namely, to which we are seeking to adapt the child, is tending more and more to substitute the rule of cooperation for the rule of constraint. The essence

[4] See, in particular, Ad. Ferrière's fine book, *L'Autonomie des Ecoliers,* Collection des Actualités Pédagogiques, Neuchâtel et Paris.

of democracy resides in its attitude towards law as a product of the collective will, and not as something emanating from a transcendent will or from the authority established by divine right. It is therefore the essence of democracy to replace the unilateral respect of authority by the mutual respect of autonomous wills. So that the problem is to know what will best prepare the child for its future task of citizenship. Is it the habit of external discipline gained under the influence of unilateral respect and of adult constraint, or is it the habit of internal discipline, of mutual respect and of "self-government?" It may be, of course, that only those who have gone through the external discipline imposed by a master will be capable later on of any inner discipline. This is the commonly accepted view, but it requires to be verified. The proof, however, would not be an easy one to establish, for considering the large number of people who reject all discipline as soon as they have escaped from school and home ties, or who for the rest of their lives are capable only of external discipline and legal morality, it may very well be that it is in spite of adult authority, or in spite of certain kinds of adult authority, that the best of our young people sooner or later adopt a disciplined way of living.

For ourselves, we regard as of the utmost importance the experiments that have been made to introduce democratic methods into schools. As Foerster[5] has so ably said, it is unbelievable that at a time when democratic ideas enter into every sphere of life, they should have been so little utilized as instruments of education. If one thinks of the systematic resistance offered by pupils to the authoritarian method, and the admirable ingenuity employed by children the world over to evade disciplinarian constraint, one cannot help regarding as defective a system which allows so much effort to be wasted instead of using it in cooperation.

One should study, for example, the evolution of a born educator like Sanderson to see how this headmaster, who was at first a partisan of strict authority and even of corporal punishment, ended by introducing democracy and the system

[5] F. W. Foerster, *L'Ecole et le Caractère*. Fr. translation by Bovet.

of collaboration into his boarding-school.[6] We therefore do not at all agree with Durkheim in thinking that it is the master's business to impose or even to "reveal" rules to the child. A "priest" is the last thing a schoolmaster should be: he should be an elder collaborator, and, if he has it in him, a simple comrade to the children. Then only will true discipline come into being—discipline that the children themselves have willed and consented to. Every educationalist who has really made the experiment has found that this is what actually happens. The sense of a common law which, as we have shown in connection with the rules of a game, is possessed by children of 9-12, shows clearly enough how capable is the child of discipline and democratic life, when he is not, as at school, condemned to wage war against authority.

It is true that the problem of discipline is bound up with that of functional education as a whole. Autonomous and inner discipline can exist in a class only to the extent that the work enlists the major part of the child's spontaneous initiative and activity. Interest being, according to Dewey, the participation of the "Ego" in the work done, it is obvious that it is necessary to the elaboration of a discipline proper to a system of autonomy.

Only the Activity School, *i.e.*, that in which the child is not made to work by means of external constraint, but where he works of his own free will (from the psychological point of view the work done in these two cases is completely different)—only the Activity school is able to realize co-operation and democracy in the class-room. Now it is precisely the principle of the Activity School that Durkheim is disputing in his refutation of Montaigne and Tolstoi, and in doing so he makes use of the traditional objection that life is not a game, and that it is not by playing that the child will learn to make efforts.

Nowadays, after the many Activity Schools that have been established in Europe and America, it would no longer be possible to use such an argument. Every practising teacher

[6] H. G. Wells, *A Great Headmaster.*

who has made the experiment in favourable conditions, has observed—and anyone who watches a child outside school hours will have noted the same thing—that if a child is interested in what he does he is capable of making efforts to the limits of his physical endurance. The problem can therefore be stated in the same terms as above, but under the following general formula: Who is the man who will be capable of the greatest energy in precisely those circumstances where life is not a game? Is it the man who has best learnt as a child to make this voluntary and spontaneous effort, or the man who has never worked except in obedience to a command? The present writer has in this connection some very definite recollections. In his class—a little class in a little town in Switzerland—there were, as there are in all classes, a few thoroughly lazy boys, a few sound and conscientious boys, and a few who were only moderately good pupils in school, but who went in for "interesting things" at home—chemistry, the history of aviation, zoology, Hebrew, anything you like except what was on the curriculum. The conscientious boys, who did not take school life as a game have, some of them, become civil servants, while others have filled minor academic posts, and so on; they cannot really be regarded to-day as models of active energy. The same thing happened to the lazy ones, when they did not disappear altogether. As to the moderately good, after being told throughout their school life that "If only you spent on your homework a quarter of the time you spend on your personal pursuits, you would do exceedingly well," they ended by giving up all their time to these personal pursuits, and are now very sorry they were not able to extend this method to many branches of learning in which they have remained ignorant. It should be added, however, that among our masters were some who not only understood but encouraged and utilized this turn of mind and who, like elder comrades, as it were, really enriched our fund of knowledge because they had the tact to guess everything and impose nothing.

In short, effort, like every other form of behaviour, requires to ripen, and its primitive forms, though very different from the final product which alone receives the sanction of adult morality,[7] may well be indispensable to the normal development of the individual. It is therefore not wasting a child's time to let him acquire by himself the habit of work and of inner discipline. In the moral as in the intellectual domain we really possess only what we have conquered by ourselves. And if a child is to achieve a desire for work and the habit of making efforts, we must take his interests and the special laws of his activity into account, and we must not impose upon him from the first a system of methods and ways too much like our own. Besides, do we ever in our own lives carry out an effort that is comparable to that which we require of children? The tedious obligations laid upon us by ordinary life, or the painful tasks called forth by exceptional circumstances never set our effort going unless we accept them, and we can only accept them by really understanding them. And this is something very different from that often meaningless obedience which we claim to be a right preparation for life and which as often lays the foundations of revolt or passivity. This does not mean that the best method of education is to let children do exactly as they like, or that the individual's own instincts will lead him to effort, work, and discipline. For work and discipline to come into being there must be—and on this point Durkheim is perfectly right—an organized social life. But the foundations of this social life can be laid without despotism or constraint. The school, according to Durkheim, is a monarchy founded on divine right. We have seen that children are capable of democracy. These youthful tendencies should be utilized and not lost or set up against adult authority, as is so often the case in school life or in the dreams of adolescence.

Thus the whole question of punishment requires revision. According to Durkheim expiatory punishment is necessary, because it is a symbol of censure. But we have here at least two points that require closer investigation: who should impute the blame, the master or the community, and is it really necessary that blame should be symbolized by expiatory suffering?

[7] Claparède (*Educational Experiment and Child Psychology*) has written conclusively on this point.

As to the first point, educationalists who have applied self-government have been gradually led to give up adult punishment and to allow free play to retributive justice as exercised by the tribunals constituted by the children themselves. One need only read the reports of these children's debates and judgments to form an opinion on the immense progress represented by this innovation.

As to the psychological character of punishments, must we admit without argument that expiatory suffering is necessary in order to symbolize blame and reassure people's consciences? Even if the symbol is necessary for those who are incapable of understanding the reasons for which blame is imputed, it loses all significance for those who understand these reasons. Moreover, if the punishment has no other relation with the act it punishes than this relation of being a simple sign, it will always be "arbitrary" in its content. Now this is just what the rational mind cannot allow, and what those people try to avoid, who want to make the punishment the natural result of the action. Durkheim, it is true, objects to such a view on the ground that the natural consequence of the action is the disapproval and consequently the punishment which it provokes. But this is to give a very wide meaning to the term "natural." One might as well say that the natural consequences of disobedience are the master's anger and the resulting blows he delivers, which is the last thing Durkheim would approve of. By "natural" Durkheim means a well-defined social reaction, and one that has been defined, by means of judgments of moral value. In that case would it not be more natural to be content to impute blame without symbolizing it by arbitrary suffering, or to content oneself with punishments having the approval of the morality of mutual respect, such as punishment by reciprocity? In short, on this point as on so many others, Durkheim strikes us as trying artificially to maintain the unity of the morality of authority with rational morality. Hence his efforts to safeguard the idea of expiation which the morality of cooperation can only denounce as materialistic and immoral.

If we consult the children themselves—and this is the only possible course for a psychologist who wishes to observe the laws governing the evolution of moral consciousness and not merely to lay down an *a priori* ethic—we find that the punishment that seems most fair at the stage of cooperation is that which is based on the idea of reciprocity. Now, to return to Durkheim's argumentation, is not this type of punishment sufficient to "reassure people's consciences," and to "symbolize" blame? Punishment by reciprocity, instead of being an arbitrary symbol, is "motivated" by its own content. As for the childish conscience, it will be all the more "reassured" with regard to the authority of rules, owing to the fact that in the case of punishment by reciprocity this authority emanates, not from adult revelation but simply and solely from mutual and autonomous respect.

We come now to the attachment to social groups. Durkheim very reasonably remarks in this connection that the child is neither fundamentally selfish, as has so often been held, nor purely altruistic, as has also been maintained, but both egoistic and altruistic, though to a lesser degree than the adult. This state of things is, in our opinion, bound up with the phenomenon of childish egocentrism in which we have tried to find the key to the psychological phenomena characteristic of the child mind. For in childhood, society and the individual are as yet undissociated, so that while the child is in the highest degree suggestible to his adult surroundings, whether through imitation of example or through constraint, he yet contrives in a purely unconscious manner to reduce everything to his own point of view. This state of things combines very easily with the psychological attitude that characterizes conformist societies, and we saw, in connection with the game of marbles, how easy is the synthesis of egocentricity and constraint; but it is strongly opposed to cooperation, in so far as the latter implies personalities that are both conscious of themselves and able to submit their point of view to the laws of reciprocity and universality. The whole problem is therefore how to take the child out of his egocentricity and lead him to cooperation.

Durkheim remarks, in this connection, that the only societies known to the child are the family and his friends, whereas the aim of social education is to prepare him for his country and for the more specifically human feelings. The school is therefore the necessary link. All this is perfectly true, but here again we are faced more irrevocably than ever with the problem of constraint and cooperation. The modern ideal is cooperation—dignity of the individual and respect for general opinion as elaborated in free discussion. How are we to bring children to this spirit of citizenship and humanity which is postulated by democratic societies? By the actual practice of cooperation, as soon as this is psychologically possible, by what Foerster has so happily called "democracy at school," or by a verbal initiation into the mechanism of adult society? Will the lessons in history and sociology, will training in citizenship and instruction in the elements of law, have the least effect on the youthful mind if the school still remains the system of monarchical authority favoured by Durkheim? For who will turn out to be the best citizen, the "sport," the "chic type" of youthful communities, or the pupil who can give the best answers in his history and civic instruction examinations? The question is worth considering.

One last point remains; its educational application is not dealt with in the MSS. which Durkheim has left of his course of lectures, but their author has studied it in connection with the elements of morality, we mean the autonomy of the will. The position which Durkheim adopts with regard to Kantian Ethics is extremely suggestive, and his penetrating remarks on the subject reveal more than all the rest of his work, the strength and the weakness of his own doctrine. According to Kant, the autonomy of the moral will is due to its rational character, the feeling of obligation belonging to duty as such being the result of sensibility. Durkheim points out, quite rightly in our opinion, that in this case the obligation belonging to pure duty becomes "in a way an accidental feature of the moral law" (p. 125). Now, according to Durkheim, everything proves "that the moral law is invested with an authority that claims respect even from reason" (p. 125), "and that it is therefore the work of an entity, real or ideal, which is superior to the faculty that has conceived it" (p. 126). And as this higher being is no other than society itself, the only possible autonomy is free submission on the part of individual reason to the laws of society.

The enormity of such a solution is obvious. Because Durkheim seeks to assimilate to one another constraint and co-operation, duty and good, he actually comes to identify the two most antithetical conceptions of obligation—the heteronomous submission of reason to the "higher entity" and the necessity residing within reason herself. That obligation in the first sense of the term, *i.e.*, duty in so far as it implies unilateral respect and the feeling of authority as such, that obligation in this sense should be external to morality, is the logical outcome of the Kantian critique, but it is also the natural consequence of the morality of cooperation. This will shock only those who are incapable of experiencing for themselves the higher and purely immanent feeling of obligation, which is the product of rational necessity. "Duty," says Durkheim, "is morality in so far as morality commands; it is morality conceived as an authority which we must obey, *because it is authority and for this reason alone*" (p. 110. The italics are ours). Well, if this is duty, all one can say is that it is quite incompatible with the morality of cooperation. Besides, even if Durkheim the sociologist would have found himself embarrassed by such a conclusion, Durkheim the man, Durkheim the free and generous spirit, showed by the whole of his career that the latter was his real faith.

Cooperation, mutual respect, therefore imply something more than the illusory autonomy described by Durkheim; they postulate the complete autonomy of reason.[8] When Durkheim reminds us that the individual is unable of himself to create morality, this by no means implies that the person (*i.e.*, the individual in so far as he submits to the norms of reciprocity) is not free to judge of everything by his reason alone. Nothing could be truer than to say that autonomy presupposes a scientific knowledge of social as of natural laws and the ability to recognize these laws at work. But social laws are unfinished and their progressive formation presupposes the unfettered cooperation of personal reason. The autonomy of reason has therefore nothing to do with individual fancy, but it stands in direct contradiction to the idea of external authority recognized as such. As Rauh has

[8] On this point, see amongst other works M. D. Parodi's excellent book, *Le Problème moral et la Pensée contemporaine*, 3rd ed., 1930.

so penetratingly shown, to be personal is to "situate oneself," which does not mean that one must not first "inform oneself." In order to foster autonomy in the child it is therefore very useful to "inform" him scientifically, but to do this it is not sufficient to make him submit to the dictates of adult society and to explain from outside the reasons for this submission. Autonomy is a power that can only be conquered from within and that can find scope only inside a scheme of cooperation.

In conclusion, then, we find that on every point of moral sociology and pedagogy Durkheim's teaching presents both an *optimum et pessimum*. Profoundly true in its conception of moral facts as social and bound up with the structural and functional development of collective groups, it overlooks the essential difference existing between cooperation and constraint. Hence Durkheim's illusion that an education which makes use only of unilateral respect can lead to the results that are peculiar to the morality of mutual respect. Hence, in moral psychology, his confusion between the heteronomous character peculiar to pure duty and the quality of fundamental autonomy which belongs to the good as such. Hence, finally, in his general sociology the unwarranted identification of the equilibrium of fact constituted by constraint and that other, ideal equilibrium—still social though in another sense of the term—which is constituted by cooperation, the limit and norm of every human group that has ever come into being.

§ 4. M. Pierre Bovet's Theory

The premises on which M. Bovet bases his theory are at once very near to and very far removed from those of Durkheim. Like Durkheim, M. Bovet refuses to account for the moral feelings by means of the psychological phenomena belonging to the individual as such. At any rate, in speaking only of individuals, M. Bovet is of opinion that an isolated being would never develop in himself a sense of moral obligation, a feeling which does not admit of being reduced to those facts of adaptation, of habit, or of instinctive affectivity to which it has been compared. Like Durkheim again, M. Bovet rejects the Kantian attempt to interpret respect as an effect of rational law, and endeavours, on the contrary, to explain rational rules by respect, and respect by the empirical conditions of social relations themselves. Finally, like Durkheim, M. Bovet carefully distinguishes between the feeling of the good and the sense of duty. Only, where Durkheim speaks of society as of a thing which exercises pressure upon the individuals, M. Bovet is thinking only of the relations existing between individuals. Moreover, it is sufficient in his view that there should be contact between two individuals for one to respect the other, and for those moral values to appear which are born of this respect. The analysis of the facts of conscience seems to him, therefore, to fulfil all the demands of moral psychology, without involving the necessity for an initial sociological enquiry. It is this difference of method rather than any divergence of doctrine which seems to us best to define the contrast between Durkheim's theory and that of M. Bovet.

But if, in view of recent work done on the subject, a sort of parallelism be allowed between the sociological method, which describes facts from outside, and the psychological method, which still regards social facts as fundamental, even if they are interpreted in terms of consciousness, the opposition between Durkheim and M. Bovet reduces itself to very little. It is with those theories that try to explain the moral law as something inborn, or as due to the individual's own experience alone, that the sociological point of view is incompatible. Once you admit, with M. Bovet, the necessity for contact between at least two individuals in order to constitute an obligatory rule, questions of detail lose their importance. Psychologists and sociologists can labour together in the erection of a science of the facts of morality.

It is in this spirit of cooperation that we should like to discuss the ideas of M. Bovet after those of Durkheim. If the former seem to require the acceptance of the latter—or of as much as we have retained of the latter—the converse also seems to be true, and M. Bovet's method seems to us to be indispensable to anyone who wishes to formulate a problem of moral psychology in experimental terms. The success that has attended sociological research has no doubt very nearly stifled the interest that was taken about twenty years ago in attempts made at establishing a systematic analysis of the facts of will and consciousness of rules, and this probably explains why the new departure made by M. Bovet did not create more of a sensation. But if one compares the conclusions of a remarkable and too little quoted article of his[9] with the poor and unreliable results of the deliberate introspection then current in the study of will, one cannot help thinking that here was a point of view which, except that it was not worked out on a large scale, deserved to be placed on the same level as Durkheim's. For our part, if the observations contained in the present work survive independently of the provisional interpretations which have served as a framework for them, we do not hesitate to declare that this article of M. Bovet's was the true begetter of our results.

What are the conditions of the feeling of obligation in the mind? Limiting the question to the psychology of duty which he opposes to that of the feeling of good, M. Bovet answers that two conditions are necessary and their union sufficient for the fact of obligation to take place: that on the one hand the individual should receive commands, and on the other, that he should respect the person who gives him these commands. No commands, no rules, and consequently no duties; but without respect, the rules would not be accepted, and the rules would have no power to compel the mind.

We can deal briefly with the first point, since it is common to Durkheim and Bovet. Its significance comes to this, that in a given individual there exist no duties that emanate from himself. For in the first place, moral rules or duties cannot be reduced to factors of purely individual psychology. Habit, for example, does not suffice to explain duty, since it is not accompanied by a feeling of obligation; there are even habits against which we feel it is our duty to struggle. But in that case could not spontaneous duties and even feelings of remorse arise that were free from all external influence? The psychology of sexual phenomena has given occasion for such hypotheses. But when one examines matters more closely one realizes that without the commands coming from those

[9] P. Bovet, "Les conditions de l'obligation de la conscience," Année psychol., 1912.

around him—and in this domain no one can escape from innumerable explicit and implicit commands—the individual's mind would never add any moral judgment to the purely physiological impressions of pleasure or of depression. In the second place, and resulting from this, we cannot regard as primitive any lines of conduct which the individual imposes on himself, and which in reality take their rise in inter-individual behaviour. Thus a command or a suggestion which one gives oneself inwardly may be the starting-point of a feeling of obligation. But these are either mere replicas or based by more or less remote analogy on directions and suggestions connected with commands that have been received. For instance, I decide to start work at such and such a time; but where would the feeling of obligation, or, in case of default, the feeling of dissatisfaction which accompany my actions come from if I had not learnt in my childhood to work at fixed hours and to keep my engagements?

As to the second point, this is where M. Bovet's originality comes in. Commands given by those in the child's immediate surroundings do not seem to him to bring about of themselves any sense of obligation in the child mind. The child as well as the adult sometimes hears rules formulated at which he is content to smile, or which even cause his moral judgment to revolt. How is such a phenomenon, in which sociologists will claim to see the clash of heterogeneous constraints, psychologically possible? Because, says M. Bovet, the command does not compel of itself. If it is to arouse in the mind the feeling of duty, the command must come from an individual who is respected by the subject. It matters not whether this individual has himself created the contents of the command or whether he simply conveys a command as he has received it. The main thing is that he should be respected by the subject. Then, and then only, will the command produce a sense of duty in the latter's mind.

Thus the conception which M. Bovet has formed of respect is equally removed from that urged by Kant and that expounded by Durkheim. In Kant's view respect is not an ordinary feeling arising like any other under the influence of a person or a thing. Its appearance is occasioned by the moral law in a manner which is inexplicable, and if we feel respect for certain individuals, we do so, in so far as they incarnate, as it were, this very law. According to M. Bovet, on the contrary, the law is not the source of respect. It is respect for persons which causes the commands coming from these persons to acquire the force of law in the spirit that feels respect. Thus respect is the source of law. In Durkheim's view as in Kant's there is no respect for individuals; it is in so far as the individual obeys the rule that he is respected. But this rule, far from simply emanating from reason, results as does respect itself, from the authority of the group. In a sense, then, law is the daughter of respect, but of the respect of the individual for the group. To this M. Bovet answers that if in adult society respect for the man and respect for the rule are in fact indissoluble, in the child the former can be seen to precede the latter. It is a fact that the child in the presence of his parents has the spontaneous feeling of something greater than and superior to himself. Thus respect has its roots deep down in certain inborn feelings and is due to a *sui generis* mixture of fear and affection which develops as a function of the child's relation to his adult environment.

It should be noted, in this connection, that this attitude of the child towards his parents does not only in M. Bovet's opinion, explain the genesis of the sense of duty. In filial piety we have the psychological source of the religious sense.[10] For in virtue of his very respect, the young child attributes to his parents the moral and intellectual qualities which define his idea of perfection. The adult is omniscient, omnipresent, just and good, the source both of the uniformities of nature and of the laws of morality. Naturally, the child does not give spontaneous expression to such a belief, for it is unnecessary for him to formulate and impossible for him to codify the "pre-notions" which are a matter of course to him and which condition in all their detail his moral judgment and his conception of the world. But, as M. Bovet has rightly remarked, the intensity of certain crises in a child's life is sufficient to show how firmly rooted were the implicit attitudes which circumstances have thus undermined.

[10] P. Bovet, *op cit., The Child's Religion.*

The discovery of a fault in the behaviour of his parents will completely upset the child's confidence. The discovery of an intellectual failing or of some unforeseen limitation of the powers of the adult will jeopardize his faith in a world order. It is then that the primitive filial sentiments, and in particular the demand for intellectual and moral perfection, may be transferred to the ideal beings which the collective conceptions of the day suggest to the religious consciousness of the individual.

But this is not the whole matter. If at first the adult is a god for the child, and if the commands coming from the parents suffice to establish that consciousness of duty which most religions have identified with the divine will, the fact remains that reason plays a part in the constitution of the moral ideal. For how are we to explain the genesis of personal conscience if originally everything is heteronomous? M. Bovet suggests the following solution. On the one hand, reason works over moral rules, as she works over everything, generalizing them, making them coherent with each other, and above all extending them progressively to all individuals until universality is reached. Thus, whoever receives a command draws from it logical consequences which apply even to the person who issues the command. On the other hand, there is bound to be in the course of mental development a certain clash between the various influences received. Commands cut across and more or less contradict each other, and the more numerous the individuals respected the more divergent obligations will the respecter have to reconcile with each other. In this way reason cannot choose but introduce the necessary unity into the moral consciousness. It is through this work of unification that the sense of personal autonomy comes to be conquered.

It is by referring back to these same processes that M. Bovet disposes of the objection which has been made to his as to Durkheim's theory. If, it has been said, everything comes to the child from outside, and if moral rules are at the start nothing but commands coming from the surrounding authority, how does the "good" come to free itself from mere custom, and how does "good" respect come to be contrasted with "bad" respect? So long as the influences which the child is under are limited, admits M. Bovet, it goes without saying that the subject's ideal cannot go beyond that of those who inspire it. But as soon as the influences begin to cut across each other, reason establishes hierarchies and progress becomes possible in relation to the commands originally received.

Finally, it should be recalled that these developments apply only to the consciousness of duty. Side by side with the morality of duty M. Bovet upholds the claims of the feeling of the good, though he does not attempt to explain it. The existence of this inner ideal peculiar to the idea of good is what in the last analysis guarantees the endurance of the autonomy of conscience: "We shall compel ourselves to see clearly the grounds of our respect; criticizing it in order to establish in ourselves orders of value, and ranking our respects in accordance with these. When the question of respect presents itself to us, we will survey critically our sentiments, instinctive or habitual, in the name of our ideal; asking ourselves what it is that we respect in the object of our respect, and repudiating the lower forms of respect." (*The Child's Religion*, p. 155).

Such, in broad outline, is M. Bovet's theory. Before placing it alongside of the results of our enquiries, let us try to state more precisely wherein it completes and wherein it corrects the doctrine advanced by Durkheim.

It will be well, in this connection, to introduce into sociology the luminous distinction made by F. de Saussure in linguistics between the static or synchronistic point of view and the genetic or diachronistic point of view. For from the static point of view the Durkheimian theory of duty is unassailable, and to describe the facts in terms of inter-individual psychology would only complete the sociological description without altering it. More exactly, these two descriptions are parallel, or imply one another. As against this, however, Durkheim has drawn from his profound static analyses a genetic sociology that was bound to be hypothetical, and it is on this point that psychologists and sociologists risk having to part company.

Moral authority and respect, claims Durkheim, can exist only in so far as the whole of a group exercises pressure on the individual minds. Society, as such, is therefore the origin of respect and obligation, and the relation between two individuals is insufficient to explain the genesis of any of the facts of duty. When, therefore, one individual respects another he does so only in so far as the other is invested with social authority. Parents and teachers have power over the child because they embody the morality of the group. Against this rather hazardous genetic theory M. Bovet sets up the facts of child psychology: it is man as such that the child respects in his parents, and if the child accepts the morality of the group, he does so in so far as it becomes embodied in respected beings.

From the static point of view, the point of view of the permanence and functioning of social phenomena, this problem, which recalls that of the river and its banks, is of no importance whatsoever. The great majority of the commands prescribed by the adult for the child are the actual rules of the morality of the group, and as these rules have fashioned the personalities of the parents before being handed on to the children it is idle to ask whether the child respects the persons in so far as they are subject to the rules, or the rules in so far as they are incarnated in these persons.

But from the genetic point of view it is very important to determine whether one can speak of a social relation where only two are involved, or whether an organized group is necessary to the constitution of the elementary moral feelings. Now on this point M. Bovet's argument seems to us conclusive. In the first place, there seems to be no doubt that the feelings of authority and respect appear during the first two years, before language, as soon as the little creature has discovered in the big person someone like himself and yet infinitely greater than himself. The feelings compounded of sympathy and fear resulting from this situation explain why the child accepts the examples and, as soon as he has mastered language, the commands coming from his parents, and why, to the simple fact of imitation, there comes so early to be added the feeling of rules and obligation. Since all the writers on the subject have thought of respect as connected with rules, the early impressions we have just mentioned cannot be classed anywhere except among the facts of respect.

Now, as far as the earliest of all rules are concerned, those, namely, that relate to eating, to sleeping, to cleanliness, and other activities of the infant, there is no room for any doubt. It is not because they are current in the social group and in all civilized families that the baby accepts them, it is because they are imposed upon him by grown-ups who are both attractive and formidable. In the second place, during the years that follow, the most superficial observation will show that the child obeys particular as well as general commands. If Durkheim were right, only the rules observed by the parents themselves and thus emanating from the group before being transmitted to the children would be respected by the latter. Now, this is simply not the case. When I ask my children not to touch my work-table, this rule becomes one of the laws of their universe without my being subject to it myself or appearing before them as the priest of society. They respect this command simply because I am their daddy.

We have laid some stress upon these genetic considerations not, we repeat, because they have great importance for the mechanism of duty in a given society that is already completely organized, but because they justify the method we have adopted throughout this book. Society begins with two individuals, as soon as the relation between these two individuals modifies the nature of their behaviour, and all the resulting phenomena can be described just as well in terms of inter-individual consciousness as in the general terms of sociology proper. For, apart from the special question of the genesis of respect, the parallelism between the ideas of M. Bovet and those of Durkheim seems to us to be complete. Durkheim explains duty under its heteronomous form by means of the social constraint of conformist communities, whereas he accounts for the development of personal conscience by social condensation and differentiation and the resulting individualism. In the same way, Bovet explains elementary duties by the respect felt by the little for the big, and the progressive autonomy of conscience by the fact of the clash of the influences received. Thus the two authors use different languages to describe the same mechanisms.

But if the languages adopted are parallel and not contradictory to each other, it should be added that psychological explanation cannot account for all aspects of moral development without taking into consideration the general shape of different societies as a whole. It seems to us that two problems in particular must be dealt with in connection with M. Bovet's theory—the problem of filial respect and the problem of the liberation of individual minds.

We can certainly say, in spite of Durkheim's objections, that in a little child's respect for his parents and in filial piety in its simplest form we have psychological data that are independent of the structure of the surrounding society. But if the parents are really gods for the child, and the rules of primitive morality can all be reduced to the parents' commands, one may wonder how progress is possible, not so much in the individual in our society but in the actual history of moral ideas. In our modern communities an individual has only to discover other points of view than those to which he is accustomed and thus to become conscious of a moral ideal that is superior to persons, and he will soon be capable of judging his parents, he will cease to deify them and will thus liberate his mind and make it accessible to innovations. But in primitive gerontocratic communities (and if M. Bovet is right the more primitive a community, the more gerontocratic it must be), how will the mind ever come to conceive of a moral ideal that is superior to accepted custom? Even where the filial feelings are transferred to the collective religious symbols, the gods can hardly be better than men, and mystical rules than the dictates of common use. In point of fact, not till the advent of the most developed religions have men conferred upon the gods a moral purity that was without alloy. However desirous elementary religious may often appear of attaining this purity, the morals and wishes of primitive deities are singularly like the prevailing customs and rules of the community in question. How are we to explain the fact that humanity ever emerged from this state of affairs?

It is at this point that it seems to us all-important to consider the general form or shape of societies. In order to raise the moral level of the gods and to leave behind one the morality of obligatory commands for the sake of the morality of an autonomous conscience, a dual process is necessary:

there must be a spiritualization of filial respect and a liberation of individual minds. Such processes can be accounted
for, according to M. Bovet, by the fact that the influences
brought to bear cut across each other; and the first condition
for this to take place effectively is that the social environment should be sufficiently dense and sufficiently differentiated. As Durkheim has shown in a passage that has become
classical, social condensation alone and the resulting differentiation are capable of explaining the liberation of individual
minds. Thus, and thus only, will the individual be capable
of judging the commands he has received from earlier generations. Then only will filial respect submit to the control of
reason, and moral consciousness place above and beyond
persons an ideal of good that transcends all duties and all
commands.

But in thus completing M. Bovet's point of view with that
of Durkheim have we really disposed of all our difficulties?
The moment has come for us to return to the child and to
compare the theories we have been discussing with the result
of our previous enquiries. We can put the matter in a nut-
shell by saying that M. Bovet's doctrine seems to us completely to conform to the facts concerning the starting-point
of child morality, but when it comes to the evolution of
conscience in the child, the only way to be faithful to the
spirit of this doctrine is to extend it and to distinguish two
types of respect.

We are faced here with a difficulty that is exactly analogous
to that which was raised by Durkheim's point of view—a circumstance sufficient in itself to confirm the parallelism between
the two points of view. How, we may ask, if all his duties come
from personalities that are superior to him, will the child
ever acquire an autonomous conscience? Unless we assume
something more than the morality of pure duty, such a development seems to us quite inexplicable. Since the content of
these duties conforms by definition to the rules accepted by
the parents themselves, it is impossible to see how the morality
of duty would ever authorize the child to modify these rules
and to criticize his parents: the formation of an inner ideal,
that is to say, the morality of good, seems to be the only
thing that will account for this phenomenon. Now, does the

clash of influences received suffice, together with the intervention of reason, to explain the appearance of this ideal?
It would seem that it does not. It is easy to see how under
the influence of contradictions due to commands interfering
with each other reason will assume the right to define its
duties more clearly, to generalize their contents, in a word, to
polish and codify the material of morality. But according to
M. Bovet's hypotheses, reason can prescribe nothing. It speaks
in the indicative mood, not in the imperative. In short, there
is no way out of the heteronomy that belongs to the play of
commands, even if this play be indefinitely complicated; only
by attributing legislative power to reason can we account
for autonomy.

But M. Bovet, differing in this from Durkheim, who did
everything to make his system a self-contained whole, has
left the road open, and even invites us to extend his analyses.
Not only has he always drawn a distinction between the sense
of duty and the feeling for good, without subsequently trying
to identify these two irreducible realities, but in addition to
this, by representing respect to us as a relation between one
person and another that is capable of various possible combinations, he invites us to think of respect as itself becoming
differentiated in the context of concrete psychological states.

And this is why, alongside of the primitive respect felt by
the inferior for the superior, or, as we have called it, "unilateral respect," we have claimed to distinguish a "mutual"
respect towards which the individual tends when he enters
into relation with his equals, or when his superiors tend to
become his equals. The quasi physical element of fear which
plays a part in unilateral respect then gradually begins to
disappear in favour of the purely moral fear of falling in the
esteem of the respected person. The need to be respected thus
balances that of respecting, and the reciprocity resulting from
this new relation is sufficient to abolish all element of constraint. At the same time, the commands vanish and turn into
mutual agreement, and rules that have been freely consented
to lose their character of external obligation. Nor is this all.
For since the rule is now subjected to the laws of reciprocity,
it is these same rules, rational in their essence, that will become the true norms of morality. Henceforward reason will

be free to lay down its plan of action in so far as it remains rational, that is to say, in so far as its inner and outer coherence is safeguarded, *i.e.*, in so far as the individual can adopt a perspective such that other perspectives will accord with it. Thus out of anomy and heteronomy, autonomy emerges victorious.

But need we make things so complicated, and would not M. Bovet's language suffice to describe the same facts? Let us try to translate our observations into terms of simple (unilateral) respect and see whether our own dualistic terminology is an advantage or a disadvantage.

Let us imagine the case of two children of the same age and both belonging to that stage of codification of rules the characteristics of which we observed most clearly round about the age of 11. It is perfectly true that while respecting the personality of the other, each child may in turn outstrip his playmate if, indeed, his prestige does not eclipse the latter's once and for all. Thus there is never complete equality, except in theory and as an ideal. We might therefore describe the facts of mutual respect as follows: 1) A gives a command to B. 2) B accepts this command because he respects A (unilateral respect). 3) But A puts himself mentally in B's place (this would be the new fact marking a departure from the egocentrism of the initial stages). 4) A therefore feels bound himself by the command he has given B. Moreover, just as one's duties towards oneself are the result, thanks to a sort of transference, of one's duties towards others, so every kind of mutual respect could also be regarded as due to a series of transferences of unilateral respect. Respect, limited in the first instance to the parents only, would be transferred by the child to adults in general, then to older children, and finally to his contemporaries, so that the contents of duty would be progressively extended to include all individuals, including oneself. Thus all forms of respect would, in so far as they were sources of moral obligation, derive from unilateral respect, and their common character would find an explanation in the original object of this primitive respect.

This terminology would certainly have the advantage of emphasizing the functional unity of the phenomenon of respect. In addition, and for this very reason, it would tend to bring closer together, but without confusing them, the morality of good and that of duty. Duty would occur whenever and wherever there was respect, commands, and therefore rules. On the other hand, the sense of the "good" would be the result of the self-same tendency which urges individuals to respect each other and to place themselves inwardly in each other's minds. We distinguished, in connection with cooperation and mutual respect, "constituted" rules resulting from reciprocal agreements, and "constitutive" standards, or norms serving to define the actual laws of reciprocity. In M. Bovet's language constituted rules, at whatever level in the development of respect they found themselves, would be nothing but duties, and constitutive norms would define the good.

This translation of our results into the language of M. Bovet will be sufficient to show how largely our own researches have merely been an extension of his, and the apparent divergences between us simply a matter of language. But this translation, by the mere fact of being possible, brings out the conclusion we particularly wished to emphasize, namely, the relative heterogeneity of duty and good. For, as M. Bovet has himself constantly recognized, there is nothing in the actual form of duty that forces its contents to conform with good. Duties are not obligatory because of their contents but because of the fact that they emanate from respected individuals. There may therefore be duties that have nothing to do with morality (M. Bovet mentions the obligations of custom) and duties that are immoral (in so far as they are contrary to the morality of reciprocity). The individual who obeys such commands no doubt experiences a feeling of doing what is good in so far as he is respecting someone else and submitting to someone else out of respect, but this does not establish the value of the commands coming from the respected individual. Now, if we have thus to distinguish on the one hand a unilateral respect as the source of duties whose contents are in principle extraneous to the good (though in actual fact they may, of course, coincide), and on the other, an ideal of reciprocity which defines the good itself, such as it will sooner or later appear to the moral consciousness, would there not be a certain advantage in isolating under the name of mutual (respect) the special type of respect whose peculiar characteristic it is to constitute the feeling of good? If the good is taken, not as a Platonic ideal, which could be unintelligible from a psychological standpoint, but as a form of equilibrium immanent in the mind, it is desirable, so it seems to us, to establish a difference in kind between unilateral respect, which leads to the recognition of heteronomous norms, and mutual respect, which recognizes no law but its own mutualness and which thus leads to the formation of norms that function within itself. We can say, of course, that if A respects B, and *vice versa*, this is because A was first respected by B and then placed himself at the same point of view as B. But this is a completely new operation in relation to respect pure and simple; for if B simply respects A without the feeling being returned, he will regard as duties all the commands laid upon him by A, however arbitrary they may be and however foreign to the laws of reciprocity. But as soon as A identifies himself morally with B, and thus submits his own point of view to the laws of reciprocity, the product of this mutual respect is bound to be something new, because the norms admitted from now onwards will necessarily be contained within this very reciprocity.

We grant, of course, that in point of fact traces of unilateral respect and of inter-individual constraint are to be found everywhere. Equality exists in theory only.[11] It may therefore very well be the case that mutual respect is never to be found pure and unadulterated, but is only an ideal form of equilibrium towards which unilateral respect is guided as the inequalities of age and of social authority tend to disappear. From this point of view M. Bovet's language is no doubt more accurate than ours, but this seems to us to be at the cost of certain difficulties on other points. For what, after all, is a "transference"? Can we really say that a feeling remains identical with itself when its object is changed? Are we not the victims of a genetic illusion when we postulate the

[11] On this point we may refer the reader to the discussion which we entered upon with M. Blondel before the Société française de Philosophie (see *Bulletin Soc. franç. Phil.*, pp. 120-3, 1928).

permanence of a tendency throughout its history and transformations? Would it not be better to define psychic realities
in terms of the system in which they are involved at a given
moment of their development? To see the exact proportion
in which the synchronistic and the diachronistic factors are
distributed, fine shades must be distinguished and minute
differences taken into account. According to M. Bovet mutual
respect, having been derived from unilateral respect, remains
in a sense identical with it or, at any rate, is still based upon
it. In our view, mutual respect, being involved in a different
system of equilibria, deserves to be distinguished from the unilateral variety.

The only essential point in this whole debate is the following. It matters very little whether mutual respect and cooperation are real states or limiting forms of equilibrium. The
unique contribution of cooperation to the development of
the moral consciousness is precisely that it implies the distinction between what is and what ought to be, between
effective obedience and an ideal independent of any real
command. If unilateral respect and social constraint were
alone at work, moral good would be given once and for all
under the imperfect and often grotesque forms assigned to it
by the duties and regulations of existing society. But cooperation and mutual respect, in so far as they involve indwell-
ing norms that are never exhausted by "constituted" rules,
play an irreplaceable part as catalytic agents and give a definite direction to moral evolution. From this point of view,
it is unnecessary to try and determine up to what point these
new realities diverge from constraint and unilateral respect in
the world of fact. The one thing we have to remember is
that in the psychology of norms the successive stages are not
everything: the direction itself, the *vector*, as M. Lalande
would say, counts for more than anything else. And in this
matter the terminological differences which separate us from
M. Bovet in nowise bar the way to our fundamental agreement as to methods and results.

§ 5. THE POINT OF VIEW OF J. M. BALDWIN

If we had been treating the subject in chronological order,
we ought to have dealt with Baldwin before discussing M.

Bovet's theories. But though the theory he put forward is closely analogous to that of Bovet, Baldwin's manner of formulating the problems is far less precise, and it was therefore necessary to study M. Bovet's doctrine first in order to elucidate that of his predecessor. Moreover, as Baldwin stands almost exactly half-way between Durkheim and Bovet, we shall be able to deal with him more briefly than if we had had to follow step by step the actual development of the various theories relating to child morality.

Baldwin, it will be remembered, claimed that psychological and sociological research must work on parallel lines because the individual and the communal minds are interdependent. Collective consciousness is nothing more than "the generalization" of the contents of individual consciousness. But conversely (and this is where Baldwin seems to be on the side of the sociologists) there is nothing present in individual consciousness which is not the result of continuous collective elaboration.[12]

The most familiar, and from the point of view of Baldwin's moral psychology, the most fundamental example of this solidarity between the social and the individual is that of the consciousness of self. What could be more intimate and more strictly "individual" in appearance than the feeling of being oneself and different from others? Now, in a famous analysis, Baldwin has shown that this feeling is really the result of inter-individual actions and of imitation in particular. Far from starting from any consciousness of self, the baby is ignorant of himself as a subject and locates his subjective states on the same plane as physical images: this is the "projective" stage. How then does the child ever come to discover himself? As far as his own body is concerned it is easy enough to see that he does so thanks to a progressive comparison of it with other people's bodies, a process that is part and parcel of that of learning to imitate. It is because it has a visual perception of another person's mouth and imitates the movements of this mouth that the baby of 10 to 12 months learns to give its various buccal sensations an analogous form; and so on. In the same way, with regard to

---

[12] See especially J. M. Baldwin's *Psychology and Sociology.*

psychical qualities, it is by imitating other people's behaviour that the child will discover his own. In this way the individual passes to the "subjective" stage in which he is conscious of possessing an "I" that is identical with that of others. But once his attention has been directed upon himself in this way, the child becomes capable of the converse process. Having little by little come to assign to himself all the forms of conduct he has observed in others, he learns simultaneously to ascribe to others the feelings and motives of which he is conscious in himself. In this way there is constituted an "ejective" process which in its alternations with the other two constitutes the whole of personal life. For, as the shuttle flies backward and forward between ejection and imitation, equilibrium is maintained between consciousness of self and awareness of others, just as their mutual elaboration had been previously ensured by the same process.

After this it will be easy to understand what is Baldwin's idea of moral consciousness. Moral consciousness appears when the self is no longer in a state of harmony, when there is opposition between the various tendencies that constitute it (tendencies which, as we have just seen, are themselves of external origin). Whence comes this lack of harmony? From the fact that sooner or later the child is compelled to obey the adult, and that in obeying he experiences something quite new. For obedience is neither mere imitation nor ejection. Obedience creates a new self, a fraction of the self that dominates the rest. The truth is that in the very act of learning to obey the child builds up for himself what Baldwin calls an "ideal self," a self that is submissive to the dictates of adults, a self, that is to say, traced on the pattern of their superior self. Obedience is thus a sort of transcendent imitation accompanied by a *sui generis* subjectivity and ejection, which in fact constitute nothing more nor less than moral consciousness itself and the evaluation of acts in terms of this consciousness. This amounts, therefore, to practically the same thing as Bovet's idea, according to which commands received create a sense of inner obligation. Like Bovet, Baldwin lays stress upon the fact that there are no innate duties: every obligation is the result of the pressure exercised by the social environment. But, adds Baldwin, once the words of command have been received, they become so thoroughly incorporated that they create a new self. "And the sense of this my self of conformity to what he teaches and would have me do—*this is, once for all, my conscience.*" [13] This ideal self is thus simply the self of the father or of any other "copy for imitation." "It is not I, but I am to become it. Here is my ideal self, my final pattern, my 'ought' set before me." [14]

This explains the striking resemblance which exists between the contents of individual consciences and the exigencies of society. The moral sentiment "is in society because it is in all the individuals; but it is in each individual because it is already in society. It is one of these 'arguments in a circle' with which nature so often reasons out the development problem" (p. 299). Such a proposition seems either a truism or a superficial account of the matter. But if we remember Baldwin's profound treatment of the development of the self as bound up with life in common, we cannot but recognize the value of the above formula. For in the adult's own life the moral sentiments remain closely dependent upon the opinions of others. "Even the more subtle and intimate judgments which we pass upon ourselves are liable to the same influence: we judge ourselves in some degree by the meed of reproach or commendation which we receive from others" (p. 312).

Here, then, is the refutation of those theories which attempted to reduce the facts of inner obligation to the facts belonging to the psychology of the individual as such, as, for example, the facts of habit or sympathy. Duty cannot be reduced to our spontaneous habits, says Baldwin; it is a "habit of violating habit" (p. 55). As for sympathy, it has of itself nothing moral in the eyes of conscience. To be sensitive alone is not to be good; sympathy must be canalized and steadied. Thanks to imitation and to "ejection," sympathy is natural to the self. But before this sympathy can acquire a moral character there must be a common law, a system of rules.

[13] J. M. Baldwin, *Social and Ethical Interpretations in Mental Development,* p. 51, Macmillan, 1897.
[14] J. M. Baldwin, *loc. cit.* p. 36.

How does the individual attain to the consciousness of this rule or common norm which defines the good? The starting-point is that the child should become accustomed "to the presence of something in him that represents his father, mother, or in general *the law-giving personality.*" Moreover, "obligations instead of diminishing only increase" with age, because the examples to be followed grow more and more in number (p. 300).

During a second phase, the child applies to everyone else the moral laws elaborated in this way. For every characteristic acquired by imitation gives rise to an "ejection." "After the child has obeyed and learned by obedience he himself sets the law of the house for the other members of it. And the law then becomes 'common law' " (p. 54). This common law is absolute for two reasons. On the one hand, thanks to the commands received or, as Baldwin puts it, to the "words of command" coming from the environment, this law is imperative. On the other hand, in applying the law to everyone else the child discovers that in actual practice no one, not even "the persons who make the law," yield it strict obedience. And this discovery, instead of weakening the child's belief in the law, leads him on the contrary to place the moral law above particular individuals.

Thanks to this process the nature of the ideal changes. Up till now the moral "good" had been tied to concrete examples. "Law, in the child, is personal in all his transition period to a true ethical self; it is an embodiment, a self which is essentially 'projective,' which he cannot represent nor anticipate in detail" (p. 323). But in so far as the child realizes that no one in actual fact obeys the law, he learns to place the law above individual wills and to conceive of it as an absolute transcending the whims or the authority of the parents themselves.

Whence a third and final stage, during which the notion of an ideal good comes to give a content to the law itself. For up till now the law consisted only in a sort of generalization or rather sublimation of the orders received. But once detached from persons, the "words of command" are raised to the rank of something absolute. Henceforward, thanks to the work of practical intelligence, the actual content of the law is elaborated along autonomous lines. "When the child reflects on his social relationships and arrives at the beginning of a habit of intelligent submission, which he then in turn prescribes to others also, he shows a new sort of end not before found in him. None of the partial thoughts—none of his private schemes—is now his end; no person completely fulfils his new ideal, his ideal of personality, long or very well" (p. 326). In this way we can explain both the possibility of moral progress and the inner liberty of conscience. The individual "is now launched on a sea of intellectual turmoil and endeavour, which by its restlessness and change, its setting of ideals and its violation of them, make social life and progress possible" (p. 326).

Such are the main ideas of Baldwin's moral psychology. Is this interpretation of the relation between the consciousness of duty and the morality of good entirely satisfactory? That is what we have now to examine, and in doing so we shall try as far as possible to bring back the discussion to the ground covered by the concrete observations given in the present volume.

It should be noted in the first place that without the intervention of reason, which Baldwin particularly stresses, the social processes invoked by our author are not sufficient to explain the development of the autonomy of conscience. It is easy enough to see how the child, starting from imitation and ejection, will incorporate in his self the "words of command" issuing from his social environment and finally conceive of the law as superior to individuals. But without the intervention which Baldwin attributes to practical reason, this law will never be more than a simple generalization of the commands the child has received. How does Baldwin escape this conclusion? By bringing in as a sort of adventitious factor the child's actual intelligence, which is supposed to remould the contents of the commands and build up a personal ideal.

But presented in this way the reasons Baldwin invokes in his explanation of moral development run the risk of appearing heterogeneous to one another. On one side we should have the play of social relations, the source of conformity and duty, on the other individual intelligence, the source of autonomy and the morality of the good. As a matter of fact, every reader of *Genetic Logic* knows what pains Baldwin took to account for the evolution of childish reason by means of the social factors spoken of just now in connection with morality. Thus logic, like duty, he tells us, seems at first to be simply the reflection of the pressure exercised by those around the child: this is the "syndoxic" phase, corresponding to simple obedience in the moral sphere. Then through a play of "ejections" and of generalizations characterizing discussion, reflection, and discursive logic, the rules of logic end, like the rules of morality, by becoming superior to individuals: this is the "synnomic" phase, corresponding to the inner ideal of the morality of the good.

But thus in invoking, as Baldwin does, childish intelligence to explain the liberation of the mind from imperatives of external origin, one cannot escape the following contradiction—namely that rational logic is itself derived from social processes from which it is supposed to free itself in matters of moral psychology. In reality, logic and morality are entirely parallel, and if one agrees with Baldwin that both develop as a function of a collective elaboration, one has no right to appeal to the one in order to explain the transformations of the other. Both logic and morality begin with conformity and end in autonomy. If we wish to account for this evolution, we must do so by changes that are inherent in social behaviour itself. It is a question, therefore, whether Baldwin's social psychology really suffices to make us understand why constraint gives way to cooperation, or whether Baldwin, like so many others, does not in the last analysis tend to give priority to the relation of constraint over against the relation of cooperation.

The two chief difficulties of Baldwin's doctrine on this point seem to be the following. Baldwin explains the early stages of the child's mentality by imitation and pressure of the social environment, but he does not take sufficient account of the egocentrism inherent in the elementary level of consciousness. In dealing with the later stages he therefore fails to make the social factor sufficiently interior to consciousness, and to see in the laws of reciprocity the rational norm that will confer upon the common rules the autonomy necessary to this interiorization.

We shall deal quite shortly with the first point, as it touches more upon the psychology of intelligence than upon the theory of the facts of morality. In a famous passage Baldwin has admirably shown how "adualistic" consciousness is originally, placing as it does on one and the same plane what is internal and external, subjective and objective, even psychical and physical. But he has not noticed, at least so it seems to us, that to such an adualism there necessarily corresponds an illusion of viewpoint such that the individual places himself at the centre of everything and explains all things in terms of this egocentric perspective. In the psychology of the intellect it is this egocentrism that seems to us to explain the logic and the causality peculiar to the child: his difficulty in handling relations and in forming objective causal series, etc. From the social and moral point of view, it is this egocentrism that explains why, though he is so absorbed in others that he conforms to examples and commands received from without, the child yet introduces into every piece of collective behaviour an irreducible element of individual interpretation and unconscious deformation. Hence the *sui generis* attitude found among the smaller children with regard both to rules of games and to their parents' commands—an attitude of respect for the letter of the law and of waywardness in its application.

While, therefore, we are in agreement with Baldwin's very profound theory relating to the genesis of consciousness of self, we wish, nevertheless, to add a remark to what he says on the rôle of imitation. One can hardly deny, indeed, after reading our author's analyses, that the self can only know itself in reference to other selves. But imitation will never enable us to perceive in ourselves anything but what we have in common with others. In order to discover oneself as a particular individual, what is needed is a continuous comparison, the outcome of opposition, of discussion, and of mutual control; and indeed consciousness of the individual self appears far later than consciousness of the more general features in our psychological make-up. This is why a child can remain egocentric for a very long time (through lack of consciousness of self), while participating on all points in the minds of others. It is only by knowing our individual nature with its limitations as well as its resources that we grow capable of coming out of ourselves and collaborating with other individual natures. Consciousness of self is therefore both a product and a condition of cooperation.

This has brought us to the second question—that of the later stages and the autonomy of conscience. Are the logical "synnomic" rules and the corresponding moral rules as well fitted as Baldwin thinks them to secure the liberty of reason? If we accept the definitions he gives, they undoubtedly are. "At the logical stages of social culture the individual sooner or later comes to criticize in a measure the social formulæ and to reject them in such and such of their details by making use of his individual judgment. In this way the syndoxic becomes personal and synnomic" (*Thoughts and Things,*). But if we consider the way in which Baldwin explains the genesis and functioning of this social "synnomic" state we feel less certain that the processes he invokes are really sufficient to account for the contrast existing between the results of cooperation and those of constraint. For, suppose we take a command and impose it upon a few individuals who, in their turn, will impose it upon others, thanks to the mechanism of "ejection." Even if it irradiates the whole of the social group and is elevated to the dignity of absolute law superior to the individuals, such a rule can acquire no new value from the mere fact of its generality. There are in every social group usages accepted by all but which are none the less irrational or even immoral. How will individual criticism, by means of which Baldwin defines the "synnomic," succeed in really transforming the content of the "syndoxic" rules into a content that is rational and in conformity with the moral ideal? Only on condition that under the "constituted" rules there should be at work a system of "constitutive" norms. For a set up of customs to acquire a new value in the eyes of autonomous conscience, it is not enough that these customs should have been ratified after discussion by the majority or the sum total of the individuals; this ratification must result from a genuine agreement founded on the laws of reciprocity which constitute reason. Of course, when Baldwin speaks of individual criticism, of reflection, and of discussion, he certainly means reason itself. But it would be an illusion to suppose that the play of imitations and ejections which develop the self and ensure a balance between the individual and the social group is sufficient to explain the development of these rational norms. These mechanisms account for one fact alone (incidentally one of fundamental importance), namely, that the individual, in spite of his egocentrism, finds himself dominated in his earliest years by a system of rules that are external to him and imperative in nature. But to pass from this to the rational law internal to the mind something more is wanted than a mere ratification on the part of individual intelligence; there must be relations of a new type between individuals who meet as equals, relations founded on reciprocity, relations that will suppress egocentrism and suggest to the intellectual and moral consciousness norms capable of purifying the contents of the common laws themselves.

§ 6. CONCLUSIONS

The analysis of the child's moral judgments has led us perforce to the discussion of the great problem of the relations of social life to the rational consciousness. The conclusion we came to was that the morality prescribed for the individual by society is not homogeneous because society itself is not just one thing. Society is the sum of social relations, and among these relations we can distinguish two extreme types: relations of constraint, whose characteristic is to impose upon the individual from outside a system of rules with obligatory content, and relations of cooperation whose characteristic is to create within people's minds the consciousness of ideal norms at the back of all rules. Arising from the ties of authority and unilateral respect, the relations of constraint therefore characterize most of the features of society as it exists, and in particular the relations of the child to its adult surrounding. Defined by equality and mutual respect, the relations of cooperation, on the contrary, constitute an equilibrial limit rather than a static system. Constraint, the source of duty and heteronomy, cannot, therefore, be reduced to the good and to autonomous rationality, which are the fruits of reciprocity, although the actual evolution of the relations of constraint tends to bring these nearer to cooperation.

In spite of our wish to confine the discussion to the problems connected with child psychology, the reader will not have failed to recognize the affinity of these results with those of the historical or logico-sociological analyses carried out by M. Brunschvicg and M. Lalande. *Le Progrès de la Conscience dans la Philosophie occidentale* is the widest and the most subtle demonstration of the fact that there exists in European thought a law in the evolution of moral judgments which is analogous to the law of which psychology watches the effects throughout the development of the individual. Now to indulge in philosophic enquiry is simply to take increasing cognizance of the currents of thought which enter into and sustain the states of society itself. What the philosopher does is not so much to create something new as to reflect the elaborations of the human mind. It is therefore of the utmost significance that the critical analysis of history of which M. Brunschvicg has put to fresh use should have succeeded in bringing to light in the evolution of Western philosophic thought the gradual victory of the norms of reciprocity over those of social conformism.

As to M. Lalande, what he says on "la Dissolution" as also on the social character of logical norms, has shown more than any other work on the subject the duality that lies hidden in the word "social." There are, M. Lalande tells us, two societies: existing or organized society, whose constant feature is the constraint which it exercises upon individual minds, and there is the ideal or assimilative society, which is defined by the progressive identification of people's minds with one another. The reader will recognize here the same distinction as we have been led to observe between the relations of authority and the relations of equality.

Some of M. Lalande's minor contentions would, indeed, stand in the way of our complete agreement with his ideas taken as a whole. It does not seem to us at all certain, for example, that "evolution" in the sense of progressive organization is necessarily bound up with a society based on constraint. The passage from the homogeneous to the hetero-

geneous which M. Lalande agrees with Spencer in taking as
the mark of evolution leads no doubt to social differentiation.
But this differentiation is precisely, as the sociologists have
pointed out, the condition of a break with the conformity
due to constraint, and consequently the condition of personal
liberation. Moral equality is not the result of an advance
towards homogeneity, assuming that agreement can be
reached on the meaning of this word, but of a mobility
which is a function of differentiation. The more differentiated
the society, the better can its members alter their situation in
accordance with their aptitudes, the greater will be the opportunity for intellectual and moral cooperation. We cannot,
therefore, take the identification of minds, which, for M.
Lalande, is the supreme norm, to be the same thing as cooperation. Without attempting to evaluate this "vector," and
limiting ourselves to the mere description of psychological
facts, what the morality of the good seem to us to achieve
is reciprocity rather than identification. The morality of the
autonomous conscience does not tend to subject each personality to rules that have a common content: it simply obliges
individuals to "place" themselves in reciprocal relationship
with each other without letting the laws of perspective resultant upon this reciprocity destroy their individual points of
view.

But what do these minor discrepancies matter since it is
thanks to M. Lalande's teaching that we are able to dissociate
what the sociologists have so often tended to confuse? And
above all, what do the concepts that are used in the interpretation of the facts matter, so long as the method employed
is the same? For in the work of M. Lalande we have an
example of that rare thing—research on the evolution of
norms conducted well within the limits of the psycho-sociological method. Without in any way neglecting the demands
of rationality, this great logician has been able to discern in
intellectual and moral assimilation processes admitting of
analysis in terms of social psychology while implying by
their very "direction" the existence of ideal norms immanent
in the human spirit.

This concordance of our results with those of historico-
critical or logico-sociological analysis brings us to a second

point: the parallelism existing between moral and intellectual development. Everyone is aware of the kinship between logical and ethical norms. Logic is the morality of thought just as morality is the logic of action. Nearly all contemporary theories agree in recognizing the existence of this parallelism —from the *a priori* view which regards pure reason as the arbiter both of theoretical reflection and daily practice, to the sociological theories of knowledge and of ethical values. It is therefore in no way surprising that the analysis of child thought should bring to the fore certain particular aspects of this general phenomenon.[15]

One may say, to begin with, that in a certain sense neither logical nor moral norms are innate in the individual mind. We can find, no doubt, even before language, all the elements of rationality and morality. Thus sensori-motor intelligence gives rise to operations of assimilation and construction, in which it is hard to see the functional equivalent of the logic of classes and of relations. Similarly the child's behaviour towards persons shows signs from the first of those sympathetic tendencies and affective reactions in which one can easily see the raw material of all subsequent moral behaviour. But an intelligent act can only be called logical and a good-hearted impulse moral from the moment that certain norms impress a given structure and rules of equilibrium upon this material. Logic is not co-extensive with intelligence, but consists of the sum-total of rules of control which intelligence makes use of for its own direction. Morality plays a similar part with regard to the affective life. Now there is nothing that allows us to affirm the existence of such norms in the pre-social behaviour occurring before the appearance of language. The control characteristic of sensori-motor intelligence is of external origin: it is things themselves that constrain the organism to select which steps it will take; the initial intellectual activity does actively seek for truth. Similarly, it is persons external to him who canalize the child's elementary

---

[15] We have further developed this point at the Ninth International Congress of Psychology which met at New Haven (U.S.A.). See *Ninth International Congress of Psychology, Proceedings and Papers,* p. 339.

feelings, those feelings do not tend to regulate themselves from within.

This does not mean that everything in the *a priori* view is to be rejected. Of course the *a priori* never manifests itself in the form of ready-made innate mechanisms. The *a priori* is the obligatory element, and the necessary connections only impose themselves little by little, as evolution proceeds. It is at the end of knowledge and not in its beginnings that the mind becomes conscious of the laws immanent to it. Yet to speak of directed evolution and asymptotic advance towards a necessary ideal is to recognize the existence of a something which acts from the first in the direction of this evolution. But under what form does this "something" present itself? Under the form of a structure that straightway organizes the contents of consciousness, or under the form of a functional law of equilibrium, unconscious as yet because the mind has not yet achieved this equilibrium, and to be manifested only in and through the multitudinous structures that are to appear later? There seems to us to be no doubt about the answer. There is in the very functioning of sensori-motor operations a search for coherence and organization. Alongside, therefore, of the incoherence that characterizes the successive steps taken by elementary intelligence we must admit the existence of an ideal equilibrium, indefinable as structure but implied in the functioning that is at work. Such is the *a priori*: it is neither a principle from which concrete actions can be deduced nor a structure of which the mind can become conscious as such, but it is a sum-total of functional relations implying the distinction between the existing states of disequilibrium and an ideal equilibrium yet to be realized.

How then will the mind extract norms in the true sense from this functional equilibrium? It will form structures by means of an adequate conscious realization (*prise de conscience*). To ensure that the functional search for organization exhibited by the initial sensori-motor and affective activity give rise to rules of organization properly so called, it is sufficient that the mind should become conscious of this search and of the laws governing it, thus translating into structure what till then had been function and nothing more.

But this coming into consciousness or conscious realization is not a simple operation and is bound up with a whole set of psychological conditions. It is here that psycho-sociological research becomes indispensable to the theory of norms and that the genetic parallelism existing between the formation of the logical and of the moral consciousness can be observed.

In the first place it should be noticed that the individual is not capable of achieving this conscious realization by himself, and consequently does not straight away succeed in establishing norms properly so-called. It is in this sense that reason in its double aspect, both logical and moral, is a collective product. This does not mean that society has conjured up rationality out of the void, nor that there does not exist a spirit of humanity that is superior to society because dwelling both within the individual and the social group. It means that social life is necessary if the individual is to become conscious of the functioning of his own mind and thus to transform into norms properly so called the simple functional equilibria immanent to all mental and even all vital activity.

For the individual, left to himself, remains egocentric. By which we mean simply this—Just as at first the mind, before it can dissociate what belongs to objective laws from what is bound up with the sum of subjective conditions, confuses itself with the universe, so does the individual begin by understanding and feeling everything through the medium of himself before distinguishing what belongs to things and other people from what is the result of his own particular intellectual and affective perspective. At this stage, therefore, the individual cannot be conscious of his own thought, since consciousness of self implies a perpetual comparison of the self with other people. Thus from the logical point of view egocentrism would seem to involve a sort of alogicality, such that sometimes affectivity gains the ascendant over objectivity, and sometimes the relations arising from personal activity prove stronger than the relations that are independent of the self. And from the moral point of view, egocentrism involves a sort of anomy such that tenderness and disinterestedness can go hand in hand with a naïve selfishness, and yet the child not feel spontaneously himself to be better in one case than

the other. Just as the ideas which enter his mind appear from
the first in the form of beliefs and not of hypotheses requiring verification, so do the feelings that arise in the child's
consciousness appear to him from the first as having value
and not as having to be submitted to some ulterior evaluation. It is only through contact with the judgments and evaluations of others that this intellectual and affective anomy will
gradually yield to the pressure of collective logical and moral
laws.

In the second place, the relations of constraint and unilateral respect which are spontaneously established between
child and adult contribute to the formation of a first type of
logical and moral control. But this control is insufficient to
eliminate childish egocentrism. From the intellectual point of
view this respect of the child for the adult gives rise to an
"annunciatory" conception of truth: the mind stops affirming
what it likes to affirm and falls in with the opinion of those
around it. This gives birth to a distinction which is equivalent
to that of truth and falsehood: some affirmations are recognized as valid while others are not. But it goes without saying that although this distinction marks an important advance
as compared to the anomy of egocentric thought, it is none
the less irrational in principle. For if we are to speak of
truth as rational, it is not sufficient that the contents of one's
statements should conform with reality: reason must have
taken active steps to obtain these contents and reason must
be in a position to control the agreement or disagreement
of these statements with reality. Now, in the case under discussion, reason is still very far removed from this autonomy:
truth means whatever conforms with the spoken word of the
adult. Whether the child has himself discovered the propositions which he asks the adult to sanction with his authority,
or whether he merely repeats what the adult has said, in both
cases there is intellectual constraint put upon an inferior
by a superior, and therefore heteronomy. Thus, far from
checking childish egocentrism at its source, such a submission
tends on the contrary partly to consolidate the mental habits
characteristic of egocentrism. Just as, if left to himself, the
child believes every idea that enters his head instead of
regarding it as a hypothesis to be verified, so the child who

is submissive to the word of his parents believes without question everything he is told, instead of perceiving the element of uncertainty and search in adult thought. The self's good pleasure is simply replaced by the good pleasure of a supreme authority. There is progress here, no doubt, since such a transference accustoms the mind to look for a common truth, but this progress is big with danger if the supreme authority be not in its turn criticized in the name of reason. Now, criticism is born of discussion, and discussion is only possible among equals: cooperation alone will therefore accomplish what intellectual constraint failed to bring about. And indeed we constantly have occasion throughout our schools to notice the combined effects of this constraint and of intellectual egocentrism. What is "verbalism," for example, if not the joint result of oral authority and the syncretism peculiar to the egocentric language of the child? In short, in order to really socialize the child, cooperation is necessary, for it alone will succeed in delivering him from the mystical power of the world of the adult.

An exact counterpart of these findings about intellectual constraint is supplied by the observations on the effect of moral constraint contained in the present book. Just as the child believes in the adult's omniscience so also does he unquestioningly believe in the absolute value of the imperatives he receives. This result of unilateral respect is of great practical value, for it is in this way that there is formed an elementary sense of duty and the first normative control of which the child is capable. But it seemed to us clear that this acquisition was not sufficient to form true morality. For conduct to be characterized as moral there must be something more than an outward agreement between its content and that of the commonly accepted rules: it is also requisite that the mind should tend towards morality as to an autonomous good and should itself be capable of appreciating the value of the rules that are proposed to it. Now in the case under discussion, the good is simply what is in conformity with heteronomous commands. And as in the case of intellectual development, moral constraint has the effect of partly consolidating the habits characteristic of egocentrism. Even when the child's behaviour is not just a calculated attempt to reconcile his individual interest with the letter of the law, one can observe (as we had occasion to do in the game of marbles) a curious mixture of respect for the law and of caprice in its application. The law is still external to the mind, which cannot therefore be transformed by it. Besides, since he regards the adult as the source of the law, the child is only raising up the will of the adult to the rank of the supreme good after having previously accorded this rank to the various dictates of his own desires. An advance, no doubt, but again an advance charged with doubtful consequences if cooperation does not come and establish norms sufficiently independent to subject even the respect due to the adult to this inner ideal. And indeed so long as unilateral respect is alone at work, we see a "moral realism" developing which is the equivalent of "verbal realism." Resting in part on the externality of rules, such a realism is also kept going by all the other forms of realism peculiar to the egocentric mentality of the child. Only cooperation will correct this attitude, thus showing that in the moral sphere, as in matters of intelligence, it plays a liberating and a constructive rôle.

Hence a third analogy between moral and intellectual evolution: cooperation alone leads to autonomy. With regard to logic, cooperation is at first a source of criticism; thanks to the mutual control which it introduces, it suppresses both the spontaneous conviction that characterizes egocentrism and the blind faith in adult authority. Thus, discussion gives rise to reflection and objective verification. But through this very fact cooperation becomes the source of constructive values. It leads to the recognition of the principles of formal logic in so far as these normative laws are necessary to common search for truth. It leads, above all, to a conscious realization of the logic of relations, since reciprocity on the intellectual plane necessarily involves the elaboration of those laws of perspective which we find in the operations distinctive of systems of relations.

In the same way, with regard to moral realities, cooperation is at first the source of criticism and individualism. For by comparing his own private motives with the rules adopted by each and sundry, the individual is led to judge objectively the acts and commands of other people, including adults. Whence the decline of unilateral respect and the primacy of personal judgment. But in consequence of this, cooperation suppresses both egocentrism and moral realism, and thus achieves an interiorization of rules. A new morality follows upon that of pure duty. Heteronomy steps aside to make way for a consciousness of good, of which the autonomy results from the acceptance of the norms of reciprocity. Obedience withdraws in favour of the idea of justice and of mutual service, now the source of all the obligations which till then had been imposed as incomprehensible commands. In a word, cooperation on the moral plane brings about transformations exactly parallel to those of which we have just been recalling the existence in the intellectual domain.

Is there any need, by way of conclusion, to point to the educational consequences of such observations? If education claims to be the direct application of what we know about Child Psychology, it would not be necessary. It is obvious that our results are as unfavourable to the method of authority as to purely individualistic methods. It is, as we said in connection with Durkheim, absurd and even immoral to wish to impose upon the child a fully worked-out system of discipline when the social life of children amongst themselves is sufficiently developed to give rise to a discipline infinitely nearer to that inner submission which is the mark of adult morality. It is idle, again, to try and transform the child's mind from outside, when his own taste for active research and his desire for cooperation suffice to ensure a normal intellectual development. The adult must therefore be a collaborator and not a master, from this double point of view, moral and rational. But conversely, it would be unwise to rely upon biological "nature" alone to ensure the dual progress of conscience and intelligence, when we realize to what extent all moral as all logical norms are the result of cooperation. Let us therefore try to create in the school a place where individual experimentation and reflection carried out in common come to each other's aid and balance one another.

If, then, we had to choose from among the totality of existing educational systems those which would best correspond with our psychological results, we would turn our methods in the direction of what has been called "Group

Work" and "self-government." [16] Advocated by Dewey, Sanderson, Cousinet, and by most of the promoters of the "Activity School," the method of work by groups consists in allowing the children to follow their pursuits in common, either in organized "teams" or simply according to their spontaneous groupings. Traditional schools, whose ideal has gradually come to be the preparation of pupils for competitive examinations rather than for life, have found themselves obliged to shut the child up in work that is strictly individual: the class listens in common, but the pupils do their home work separately. This procedure, which helps more than all the family situations put together to reinforce the child's spontaneous egocentrism, seems to be contrary to the most obvious requirements of intellectual and moral development. This is the state of things which the method of work in groups is intended to correct. Cooperation is promoted to the rank of a factor essential to intellectual progress. It need hardly be said that this innovation assumes value only to the extent that the initiative is left to the children in the actual conduct of their work. Social life is here a complement of individual "activity" (in contrast to the passive repetition which characterizes the method of teaching by books), and it would have no meaning in the school except in relation to the renovation of the teaching itself.

As for self-government, the fine works of F. W. Foerster (*op. cit.*) and Ad. Ferrière[17] have rendered unnecessary the task of reminding our readers of its principles. M. Ferrière in particular, has described with great care and with that proselytizing fervour which characterizes all his educational works the various modes of government of children by themselves. It is hard to read his book without being filled both with the hope of seeing the experiments he analyses carried out more generally, and with the satisfaction at finding in the principles that characterize children's republics what

[16] We refer the reader, on this point, to our "Rapport sur les procédés de l'Education morale," read at the Fifth International Congress on Moral Education in Paris, 1930.

[17] Ad. Ferrière, *L'Autonomie des Écoliers,* Coll. des Actualités pédag. Delachaux et Niestlé.

we already know, thanks to the psycho-sociological study of the moral life.

As to F. W. Foerster, his moral pedagogy is still in our opinion too much tinged with the cult of authority or unilateral respect, and, above all, too much attached to the idea of expiatory punishment. But this makes the preoccupation with autonomy and self-government, which appears in the rest of his work, the more significant.

But pedagogy is very far from being a mere application of psychological knowledge. Apart from the question of the aims of education, it is obvious that even with regard to technical methods it is for experiment alone and not deduction to show us whether methods such as that of work in groups and of self-government are of any real value. For, after all, it is one thing to prove that cooperation in the play and spontaneous social life of children brings about certain moral effects, and another to establish the fact that this cooperation can be universally applied as a method of education. This last point is one which only experimental education can settle. Educational experiment, on condition that it be scientifically controlled, is certainly more instructive for psychology than any amount of laboratory experiments, and because of this experimental pedagogy might perhaps be incorporated into the body of the psycho-sociological disciplines. But the type of experiment which such research would require can only be conducted by teachers or by the combined efforts of practical workers and educational psychologists. And it is not in our power to deduce the results to which this would lead.

Index of Subjects

Activity Schools, 287, 358, 364, 405

Affection, desire for reciprocal, 176, the starting-point of the good, 195

Ambivalence, 192

Animism, 144, 145, 190, 257, 258

A priori, 317, 318, 321, 398, 399; as an ideal equilibrium, 399

Artificialism, 144, 145, 190, 256, 257, 258

Auto-punishment, 259

Categorical Imperative, 343

Cheating, at games, 296, 305 ff., 323; at lessons, 286 ff.

Compassion, 229, 230

Constraint, adult moral, as a socializing factor, 89; founded on unilateral respect, 86, 100, 107-08, 316, 335, 347-48, 362, 363, 395; cause of belief in expiatory punishment, 227-29, 231, 297, 399-40, and in immanent justice, 259, 260, 261; cause of lying, 139, of moral realism, 135, 163, 173, 176, 186, 190, and of revolt, 138, 192; consolidates egocentrism, 61, 70, 90-94, 110, 163, 186-87, 190, 194, 368, 401-03; inevitable in matters of food, sleep, cleanliness, etc., 53, 89, 178, 180, 182, 191, 379; parallelism with intellectual constraint, 110, 194, 402, 404; perhaps a secondary growth, 176; of groups, 101, 106, 189, 204, 205-06

Constraint, social, not identical with cooperation, 340; cause of primitive ways of thought, 340 ff.; consolidates egocentrism, 348, 395

Cooperation as a socializing factor, 46, 70, 92; founded on mutual respect, 86, 94-95, 107, 174, 228, 316, 335, 337, 395; necessary for autonomy, 70, 71, 76, 95, 96, 107, 335, 337, 339, 353, 362, 371, for truthfulness, 164, 167, 171, 174, and for personality, 95-96; as a rationalizing factor, 91, 107, 187, 370, 400; anti-mystical intendency, 62, 64, 83, 100; destroys egocentrism, 187, 368, 404 ff.; as a state of equilibrium, 36, 90, 96, 104, 341, 347, 348-49, 371, 385-86, 395; never pure, 86, 90; never completely realized, 96; the source of good, 195, 351; as a method of education, 287 (footnote), 404, 405; wrongly assimilated to constraint by Durkheim, 342-43

Democracy, and democratic ideal, 65, 71, 74, 76, 325, 346, 363; in schools, 363, 366, 369

Difficult children, 112, 192

Discipline, external and internal, 363, 364, 404

Education, 50, 87, 168, 194, 404-05; punishment in, 213, 218, 233; democracy in, 363, 364; experiment in, 218, 364, 404, 405, 406

Effort, not identical with obligation, 350, 366

Ego, consciousness of, 92, 93, 95, 96, 251, 387-90, 392-93, 394, 395

Egocentricism, definition of, 35-36, 251; dual character of in practice of rules, 27, 28, 29, 33-34, 35, 36-37, 40-41, 46, 54, 62, 93, 99, 102, 393, 402-03;

[1] This index does not claim to be exhaustive, either in its references or in its headings, these being supplementary to those in the Table of Contents. It is meant, primarily, to point to the way in which the author has connected some of the leading ideas in his book.—[Trans.].

Index of Names